W9-ALL-979

11/14

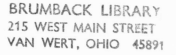

14
DAY
BOOK

THREE MINUTES IN POLAND

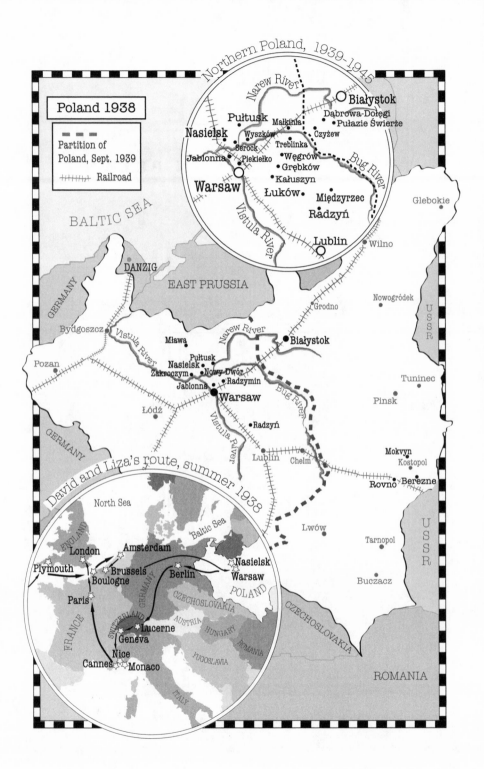

Poland 1938

- - - Partition of Poland, Sept. 1939
++++++ Railroad

Northern Poland, 1939–1945

BALTIC SEA

Narew River

Białystok
Pułtusk
Nasielsk
Wyszków
Małkinia
Dąbrowa-Dołęgi
Pułazie Świerże
Czyżew
Serock
Treblinka
Jabłonna
Piekiełko
Węgrów
Grębków
Kałuszyn
Warsaw
Łuków
Międzyrzec
Radzyń
Lublin
Glebokie
Wilno

Vistula River
Bug River

DANZIG
EAST PRUSSIA
GERMANY
Grodno
Nowogródek
U S S R

Bydgoszcz
Vistula River
Narew River
Białystok

Pozan
Mława
Pułtusk
Nasielsk
Zakroczym
Nowy Dwór
Jabłonna
Radzymin
Warsaw
Tuninec
Pinsk

Łódź
Radzyń
Vistula River
Bug River

GERMANY
Lublin
Chelm
Mokvyn
Kostopol
Rovno
Berezne

David and Liza's route, summer 1938

Lwów
Tarnopol
Buczacz
U S S R

North Sea
Baltic Sea

ENGLAND
London
Amsterdam
Nasielsk
Plymouth
Brussels
Boulogne
Berlin
Warsaw
POLAND
Paris
FRANCE
GERMANY
CZECHOSLOVAKIA
AUSTRIA
HUNGARY
Lucerne
SWITZERLAND
Geneva
ROMANIA
Nice
Cannes
Monaco
YUGOSLAVIA
ITALY

CZECHOSLOVAKIA

ROMANIA

THREE
MINUTES
IN
POLAND

DISCOVERING
A LOST WORLD
IN A 1938
FAMILY FILM

GLENN KURTZ

FARRAR, STRAUS AND GIROUX   NEW YORK

Farrar, Straus and Giroux
18 West 18th Street, New York 10011

Illustration credits appear on pages 413–415.

Library of Congress Cataloging-in-Publication Data
Kurtz, Glenn.
    Three minutes in Poland : discovering a lost world in a 1938 family film / Glenn Kurtz.
        pages   cm
    ISBN 978-0-374-27677-5 (hardback) — ISBN 978-0-374-71080-4 (e-book)
        1. Jews—Poland—Nasielsk—History—20th century.   2. Jews—Poland—Nasielsk—
Biography.   3. Community life—Poland—Nasielsk—History—20th century.
4. Holocaust, Jewish (1939–1945)—Poland—Nasielsk.   5. Nasielsk (Poland)—History—
20th century.   6. Nasielsk (Poland)—Biography.   7. Kurtz, Glenn—Family.
8. Amateur films—History—20th century.   9. Kurtz, Glenn—Travel.   10. Holocaust
survivors—Biography.   I. Title.

DS134.66.N28 K87 2014
947.7'9—dc23

                                                                    2014008516

Designed by Abby Kagan

Farrar, Straus and Giroux books may be purchased for educational, business, or
promotional use. For information on bulk purchases, please contact the Macmillan
Corporate and Premium Sales Department at 1-800-221-7945, extension 5442,
or write to specialmarkets@macmillan.com.

www.fsgbooks.com
www.twitter.com/fsgbooks • www.facebook.com/fsgbooks

1   3   5   7   9   10   8   6   4   2

For the people we have lost . . .

[The gale] swept the squares clean, leaving behind it a white emptiness in the streets; it denuded the whole area of the marketplace. Only here and there a lonely man, bent under the force of the wind, could be seen clinging to the corner of a house.

—BRUNO SCHULZ, "The Gale"

CONTENTS

PART THREE

PART ONE

Thanks for the
telegram

HOLLAND-AMERICA LINE
ROTTERDAM — NEW YORK

On the boat June
days. To-morrow
we land at Plymouth
England. then Boulogne
France - then Rotterdam
Holland. We get off
at Rotterdam. Regards
to the whole gang
and to the Misses Northrups

Printed in the Netherlands

Carte Postale
(Union Postale Universelle)

Shirley Kurtz
c/o Camp Oquaga
Andes N.y.
usa

1

ARTIFACTS

IN THE SUMMER of 1938, my grandparents David and Liza Kurtz sailed from New York to Europe for a six-week summer vacation. Together with three friends they visited England, France, Holland, Belgium, and Switzerland, and, passing through Germany, they made a side trip to Poland, where both my grandparents were born.

I'm holding a postcard from this trip that my grandfather sent to his daughter, my aunt. The card shows a painting of the Holland-America liner *Nieuw Amsterdam* crossing a green-black sea. Spray at the ship's waterline and whitecaps on the waves give the impression of motion. The black hull and white Art Deco superstructure gleam against clouds tinged with pink and blue. Smoke ribbons from twin yellow smokestacks. A bird trails off the stern.

On the reverse side, my grandfather writes, "On the boat five days. Tomorrow we land at Plymouth, England, then Boulonge, France [he misspells Boulogne]—then Rotterdam, Holland. We get off at Rotterdam."

My aunt Shirley Kurtz Mandel produced this postcard three years after I first asked what she knew about her parents' 1938 trip to Europe. The manila envelope containing this and about thirty other postcards and letters from David and Liza had been stuffed in a box of unrelated papers, forgotten for more than half a century. Shirley rediscovered it in late 2011 when, after sixty-three years, she moved out of her New York apartment.

One year after my grandparents' vacation, Europe would be at war. On September 1, 1939, the German army overran Poland, and within a few years, with terribly few exceptions, the Jewish inhabitants of the Polish towns my grandparents had visited would be murdered.

But David and Liza Kurtz could not foresee the future. My grandparents and their friends were tourists, relatively prosperous American tourists, blissfully unaware of the catastrophe that lay just ahead. They rode across Europe with trunks of clothing, stayed at five-star hotels, shopped, and admired the sights. They visited art galleries and cathedrals, they strolled in the Jardin Exotique overlooking the old city of Monaco, they rode a small-gauge railroad through the Swiss Alps to the highest train station in Europe, the Jungfrau. Like tens of thousands of other Americans in the summer of 1938, my grandparents toured Europe's grand attractions for their own pleasure.

The postcard my grandfather sent to his daughter has an English one-pence postage stamp with the cancellation *"Paquebot*—Posted at Sea." It is postmarked Plymouth, Devon, 29 July 1938, 6:30 p.m. From this, I learn the date of my grandparents' departure, July 23, 1938, and that slender fact opens onto a wealth of period detail, giving me for the first time a glimpse at the scene as my grandparents begin their voyage.

"Rains Delay Sailing of Nieuw Amsterdam," reported the *New York Times* the day after their embarkation. "The Holland-America liner Nieuw Amsterdam, under command of Captain Johannes Bijl, commodore of the line, sailed from her Hoboken pier forty minutes behind schedule after awaiting the arrival of four passengers from Philadelphia who had been delayed by a washout on the highway." The four Philadelphians, "all prominent socially," according to the *Times*, had called ahead from Plainfield, New Jersey, when the road north was "hidden by swirling water." The *Nieuw Amsterdam* was a stylish new ship. Its maiden voyage in May 1938, two months earlier, had been celebrated with lavish coverage in newspapers and magazines. This departure was less glamorous, the return leg of the ship's fourth round trip, but still worth a few column inches devoted to society gossip. A July 23 piece in the *Times* entitled "Ocean Travelers" noted that Mrs. Adam L. Gimbel, Mrs. Mary van Renssalaer Thayer, and Mr. and Mrs. John B. Ballantine would be among the 850 people on board when the ship finally sailed under cloudy skies that Saturday. The *Washington Post* considered it newsworthy to report "Mr. and Mrs. E. C. Rick will sail on the Nieuw Amsterdam this month for an extended tour in England, France, Switzerland and Italy. They will visit the Empire Exposition in Glasgow, Scotland, and later they will stop at Oxford to attend lectures at the university."

Mr. and Mrs. David Kurtz of Flatbush, Brooklyn, are not mentioned in the newspapers. They were comfortable but not prominent socially. Their travel plans concerned only the immediate family, and as a result, tracing their movements through Europe in the summer of 1938 has proved to be a challenge. I have been trying to determine their precise date of departure and the name of the ship for years. I know it now only because my aunt happened to save this postcard.

I would never have known about my grandparents' trip at all or felt compelled to spend years trying to unearth its details had David and Liza not brought home a unique memento of their travels, which also happened to survive. On this vacation, my grandfather carried a 16mm home movie camera. He shot fourteen minutes of black-and-white and Kodachrome color film. He captured scenes of the ocean crossing and of a ferry ride in Holland. He filmed my grandmother and their friends walking in the Grand Place in Brussels, sunning themselves on the Mediterranean coast near Cannes, feeding pigeons in a Parisian park. And he documented three minutes of their visit to Poland, footage of ordinary life in a small, predominantly Jewish town, one year before the outbreak of World War II.

More than seventy years later, these few minutes of my grandfather's home movie would transform their summer vacation into something of lasting, even of historical, significance. Through the brutal twists of history, my grandfather's travel souvenir became the only surviving film of this Polish town. Eventually, his home movie would become a memorial to its lost Jewish community and to the entire annihilated culture of Eastern European Judaism.

What moments are worth recording? Which stories and memories are passed down, and which are lost? How much detail is preserved in the few artifacts that happen to survive? And how close can these artifacts bring us to the people who left them behind? These questions have haunted and surprised me in the years since I discovered my grandfather's 1938 film.

The postcard my grandfather sent from the *Nieuw Amsterdam* at the start of this voyage is addressed to Shirley Kurtz at summer camp in Andes, New York. Above the ship, where the clouds are darkest gray and most roseate pink, David has written, "Thanks for the telegram." The telegram has not survived. My grandfather's message is only two sentences long. After briefing his daughter on their itinerary, he concludes, "Regards to the whole grand and to the Mirskys. Mother and Dad." My aunt Shirley, now ninety-two, was sixteen years old in July 1938. She has fond memories of Camp Oquago for girls, which had opened just a few years before and was in business until 1993. The Mirskys, she tells me, were the camp's owners. She remembers that Mr. Mirsky had a thick Yiddish accent. But she has no idea who or what "the whole grand" is. We puzzle over the word, trying to make it "gang" or "group" or "crowd." But it says "the whole grand." It might refer to a sports team or to her bunkmates at camp. It's possible my grandfather made a slip of the pen. We'll never know. Unlike the missing telegram, these words have been preserved. But their meaning is lost.

Taken by itself, it is a prosaic postcard, one of only a handful from my grandparents that has come down to me. Its value, like that of so many otherwise unimportant things, depends on context, on the scale of its information and the connections this enables us to forge, the snippet of a larger story it reveals. "On the boat five days." "We get off at Rotterdam." History is constructed from fragments like this, preserved by chance, puzzled over, connected. Because preservation alone is not enough. Every flea market and junk shop has shoe boxes full of postcards just like this one, with feathered edges and looping, half-legible script. All of them once carried messages woven into the fabric of individual lives. Now they're just atmospheric old postcards. With time, information and context tend to fray. Eventually they unravel completely.

* * *

I found the film of my grandparents' trip in the closet at my parents' house in Palm Beach Gardens, Florida, in 2009. As soon as I saw what was captured in its images, I knew it had to be restored. My grandfather had filmed just a few minutes of one day in Poland. But this footage preserves impressions of daily life in a way that memory, photographs, and documents cannot. Viewing the film, we see hundreds of faces with individual expressions. We see the patterns and colors of dresses, a sign over a doorway, flowers in a shop window. We see the intricacies of small-town society in the groups that form on the street. We see the way a hand gesture or the peculiar set of someone's mouth or brow defines a personality or a relationship. We see the extraordinary pride of a young woman fortunate enough to accompany the American visitors during their brief tour of the town. We see the prevalence of shoving as a means of communication. If only for the sake of these details, I felt, the film was an important piece of history. It was evidence of a world violently destroyed.

But the longer I spent with my grandfather's film, the richer and more fragmentary its images became. A film, by itself, preserves detail without necessarily conveying knowledge. When I first viewed the footage, I saw hundreds of people, their manners and movements, the way they responded to my grandfather's camera and to each other. Yet each moment stood in isolation. The camera had recorded only the surfaces. Everything meaningful, everything that explained *what* I was seeing, existed outside or was buried inside the frame. Who are these people? What brought them to be on the street, in view of my grandfather's lens, on that day, in that moment? What relation, if any, do they have to my grandparents? And what became of them, each one, individually? Every image, every face, was a mystery.

I began to search, to research, to find out what might still be learned from this film and what, so many years later, might still be discovered about this town and its people. It's a challenge to reconstruct the history of ordinary lives. Ultimately, my search would absorb four years and would fling me across the United States, to Canada, England, Poland, Israel; into archives, homes, basements, film preservation laboratories, a grove of trees in a former Jewish cemetery, and an irrigation ditch at an abandoned Luft-waffe airfield—all to make sense of a few hundred feet of film. Yet in the end, chance—luck, or fate—played the biggest role in shaping this history.

Through a series of coincidences that in retrospect seem obvious, I met a man who appears in this film as a thirteen-year-old boy. He appears for a split second as my grandfather sweeps the camera past a crowd of chil-dren. This man lost everything in the Holocaust: his home, his family, his identity. But somehow he survived, and my grandfather's home movie survived, and seventy-three years after that moment captured on film, this man was able to view the film and, in some sense, to relive the moment. His recollections give voice to the silent figures in the film. My grandfather's film, he told me the first time we spoke, gave him back his childhood.

By circuitous paths, this man's memories would lead me to other sur-vivors and to the families of some of those who did not survive. From among the hundreds of faces visible in my grandfather's film, the people I met would identify a few individuals they knew and remembered, some who lived through the war and many who did not, some who would have remained entirely unknown, and some who would have otherwise been faceless names on a document, nameless faces in an image. But more than this, the recollections that the survivors shared with me animated the im-ages in my grandfather's film, fleshing out with stories many of the faces we see. From these stories, often from stray remarks made years apart, an intricate web of connections would eventually grow. Fragments of mem-ory intersected with fragments of film, with fragments found in the few documents that still exist, in postcards, letters, photographs, and artifacts. And in the interconnections of these surviving fragments, I began to catch fleeting glimpses of the living town—a cruelly narrow sample of its relation-ships, contradictions, scandals. In this way, it became possible to save this small Jewish community, this shtetl, from the fate of so many others that were also destroyed and that have now succumbed to the one-dimensional tyranny of lists. Like my grandfather's film, the fragmentary history I as-sembled preserves a little of the town's vibrant complexity, the details that made its life and death distinct from others and made these people differ-ent from millions like them.

* * *

I smooth the fraying edges of my grandfather's postcard before placing it in an archival sleeve. Originally meant only for my aunt, this postcard is now a node in the intersecting stories that have grown out of my grandparents' 1938 vacation, stories defined in every part by improbable survival. My grandfather probably thought nothing of it when he posted this casual greeting. I'm certain he never imagined that a grandson, seventy-five years later, would read it with amazement, or that the information it contains, prosaic as it may be, would one day shed light on the life of a Polish town destroyed in the Holocaust.

So much about the story of my grandfather's film is untraceable. I'll never know how my grandparents felt as their ship pulled away from the pier and put out to sea. I'll never know what they experienced when they set foot in Poland again, forty-five years after emigrating to the United States. I'll never know what they thought once they returned to New York, or what they would have thought about the significance their trip and this film have since come to possess. But thanks to my aunt, I can now resolve one question that has long been a mystery to me. Although it turned up late in my search, this postcard allows me to document the start of my grandparents' journey, information recorded nowhere else. David and Liza Kurtz sailed from Hoboken on the Holland-America liner *Nieuw Amsterdam* on a rainy Saturday afternoon, July 23, 1938, at 12:40 p.m., bound for Rotterdam. Now I know how the story begins.

IIIIIIIIIIIIIIIII

I could also begin with my own journey, the moment I became interested in my grandparents' trip. It's a roundabout story that requires a brief detour into fiction.

In 2008, I was working on a novel set in Vienna, about two brothers, assimilated Jews, who escape from the city after the German invasion of Austria on March 12, 1938. I had lived in Vienna for several years in the 1980s, just after college, and I remained fascinated by the city and its history. On the seventieth anniversary of the Anschluss, I attended a lecture marking the occasion at the Austrian Cultural Forum in New York City.

The program that night featured a collection of amateur films documenting the German invasion, including a home movie by an anonymous cameraman that had been discovered recently in the Vienna flea market. By an extraordinary coincidence, this orphaned film contained unique footage of the harassment of Viennese Jews in the days following the Germans' triumphant arrival. The cameraman captured Hitler's motorcade driving down Vienna's famous Ringstrasse. In the film's final six seconds, a well-dressed man is forced to scrub the street on his hands and knees, a crowd of Viennese gleefully watching.

These so-called *Reibpartien*—"cleaning parties"—were a Viennese specialty. They were often instigated by neighbors and frequently noted in the press. A *Time* magazine article on March 28, 1938, entitled "Spring Cleaning," reported: "Hapless Jews were set to work scrubbing Fatherland Front posters off lampposts, Schuschnigg plebiscite slogans off sidewalks. Leering young Nazis jibed, 'Who has found work for Jews? Adolf Hitler!'" The insightful British journalist G.E.R. Gedye wrote, "From my window I could watch for many days how they would arrest Jewish passers-by— generally doctors, lawyers or merchants, for they preferred their victims to belong to the better educated classes—and force them to scrub, polish and beat carpets . . ." A few iconic photographs document this form of harassment, but there were no known moving images. Then these six seconds of film were discovered.

After the program, I spoke with the presenter, Michael Loebenstein, who was then a researcher at the Austrian Film Museum in Vienna and is now CEO at the National Film and Sound Archive in Canberra, Australia. We subsequently became friends, and he kept me informed of his quest to identify the origin of this film. Analyzing frame by frame, Michael identified locations, retraced the cameraman's steps. He even determined the man's height by measuring the angle of certain shots. In April 2010, when we met again at the Film Museum café in Vienna just opposite the opera house, he announced, "I have managed from the most fleeting clues to establish who the person was who shot the film." It was a masterpiece of detective work, though still incomplete. "I know a lot about this person," Michael told me, "but I haven't got a name." He had also been unable to identify the victim of the harassment, and this in particular bothered him. "Usually, I'm quite good at separating my private emotional life and my professional life. But the thing about film is, on the one hand, it is such a technical medium, and on the other hand, it is something that touches you on the most fundamental human level."

Intrigued by this story, I decided to adapt it as the frame for my novel. *A reel of old film lies forgotten in Vienna's flea market*, I wrote, setting the scene on a cold March Saturday in 2005. *The vendors have carted their wares back to wherever they store them during the week. Old coats, silver knives, vacuum cleaner parts, fake Gucci bags, the odd leather-bound copy of* Mein Kampf. *Now newspapers scrape the pavement and go airborne, folding and flapping as if they really knew how to fly.* Hurrying across the square, Mara Reshen, the main character, absently plucks the film from the trash. Over the following pages, she becomes increasingly obsessed with the people in the film. *Who are they? What became of them?* Researching the images, she eventually uncovers the story of the two brothers and their attempt to escape the terror of Nazi Vienna. *Are they still alive?* she wonders. *Could I return these moments to the people who lost them?*

In the course of writing the novel, I had to learn about the chemical composition of film and about the condition issues a film from the 1930s would suffer, assuming it had been stored negligently. Motion picture film is made up of three distinct elements: the base, the gelatin emulsion, and a layer of color dyes for color film or metallic silver for black-and-white. The base is made of a heavy plastic—in the case of 16mm home movie film from the thirties and forties, cellulose diacetate. This is a moderately stable substance that will last for years under the right conditions, unlike 35mm nitrate stock from the same era, which is prone to disintegration and spontaneous combustion. But cellulose diacetate is susceptible to something called "vinegar syndrome." Over time, the plastic loses certain chemical compounds—primarily acetic acid, also known as vinegar—which causes it to shrink. Depending on how the film is wound and stored, this shrinkage will warp the base in different ways, and each kind of warp puts stress on the emulsion. It will crack, it will scratch, it will wrinkle. In the worst cases, the emulsion will detach from the base entirely. The emulsion carries the image. It's composed of gelatin, the same gelatin you eat, made of horse hooves, bones, proteins, a very nineteenth-century recipe. Because it is organic, the photographic emulsion will attract fungus and bacteria. These feed on the image. The emulsion may dissolve in water, expand or contract with humidity. It will collect dust and dirt. Color dyes fade, metallic silver corrodes. All of this degrades the quality of the images.

While reading about film preservation one day in September 2008, I remembered my family's small collection of home movies. I hadn't thought of these films in twenty-five years.

In my childhood house in Roslyn, Long Island, I knew exactly where our family films had been stored—in the den, in the cabinet beneath the television, alongside old cameras, slide carousels, and the portable transistor radios that no longer functioned. The stack of brown, silver, and black film cans was in the back of the cabinet, in the dark recesses, and I must have reached past them every time I rummaged around there as a kid, fingering the ancient gadgets that had so many attractive knobs, dials, and meters.

All our old photographic equipment was sold off in 1990 during the great deaccessioning that occurred when my parents retired to Florida. My father was not a sentimental man when it came to possessions. He tore the photographs from my grandparents' passports and tossed away the pages of visas and stamps. He discarded almost everything in the basement, all the junk in the closets and cabinets.

In September 2008, suddenly curious, I called my parents to ask whether our family films still existed. My father thought they must have been thrown away. A month later, I flew down to Florida from New York and hunted in the recesses of new closets, these, too, by now overstuffed with things. It wasn't until my third attempt, in March 2009, that I succeeded in locating the old stack of film cans in an unlabeled cardboard box in my parents' closet, behind the Scrabble and Monopoly boxes, beneath unbuilt model airplane kits.

There was a film of my parents' wedding in 1952; film from their honeymoon in Mexico City; films of my brother Roger as a baby learning to crawl, pestering Duchess, the dog. There were home movies of my father's sister, my aunt Shirley, and her son. Film of my grandparents at a summer house in Long Beach. Film of my grandparents' 1938 trip to Europe. They all reeked of vinegar.

I was still working on my novel, describing Mara's growing obsession with the enigmatic silent images in the abandoned film she had discovered. I worked on that book of fiction for another two years, until the story I had imagined happened to me.

||||||||||||||||||||

The vinegary film I discovered in my parents' closet had deteriorated so severely it could not be projected. It had shrunk, curled on itself, and fused into a single, hockey puck–like mass. In any case, we no longer had a projector. In the early 1980s, however, some of the footage had been transferred to videotape, probably the last time anyone had viewed it. I found the cassette in a drawer at my parents' house and brought it home with me, along with the film in its dented aluminum can. In March 2009, I stood in the living room of my New York City apartment, the VCR remote control in my hand. I pressed the button, and my grandparents' voyage began again.

OUR TRIP TO HOLLAND BELGIUM POLAND SWITZERLAND FRANCE AND ENGLAND. 1938. The image wobbled and cracked, like a pane of glass breaking over and over. Then I saw Liza Kurtz, my grandmother, lounging on a deck chair on board what I now know is the *Nieuw Amsterdam*, sometime between July 23 and July 30, 1938. She's a dark-haired, regal woman in her late forties and wears oval sunglasses, a plaid blazer, and a matching hat. She has a thick book in her lap. The bookmark's tassel twirls in the wind.

Sitting next to her are my grandparents' friends and traveling companions, Louis and Lillian "Rosie" Malina, and Mr. Malina's sister, Essie, who had married my grandfather's uncle, David Diamond. Louis is sitting at the end of the row of chairs, reading. Between him and my grandmother, the other two women are asleep.

Liza looks up. Maybe David calls to her. *Smile for the camera.* My grandmother does not smile. A few seconds later, my grandfather shifts position. Louis keeps reading his book. The two sleeping women remain

Our Trip To
HOLLAND, BELGIUM
POLAND, SWITZERLAND
FRANCE and ENGLAND
1938

asleep. But in this shot my grandmother smiles for the camera, after first turning away to adjust her hat.

Suddenly they've arrived in Holland. There are people with wooden shoes and winged white hats. My grandmother coaxes a little girl in costume to wave for the camera. Essie and Louis stand beneath a hand-painted sign advertising a café-restaurant with a *"vue sur la mer."* Louis and the three women walk along a gravel path in a garden or park. They come down the steps of an imposing building. In the background stands a doorman or guard, the buttons on his uniform catching the light. They're no longer in Holland. Perhaps they're in Belgium. There are no obvious landmarks.

The film jumps around, a series of scenes in black-and-white, then a segment in brilliant color. They're on a boat crossing a tranquil blue lake. It must be Switzerland because soon they're in the mountains, my grandfather clearly impressed by the peaks and glaciers. He angles the camera down a thousand-foot waterfall beside the train. In the next shot, the waterfall is in a valley far below them. The Hotel Jungfrau stands in the foreground. My grandfather pans across the mountaintops.

Now Louis, a cigar in his mouth, gazes at a palace with a red roof, situated on a promontory overlooking the sea. It must be the Mediterranean, southern France. For fifty-one seconds they admire the coastline. My grandmother helps Essie tie her sunbonnet. For thirteen seconds they walk beside bright pink flowers planted beneath tall windows. Are they still in France? In England? Rosie Malina is laughing. My grandmother points past where my grandfather is standing and speaks to him. It seems she's telling him to film something else, to film over there.

The final minute of footage documents the journey home. Walking four abreast, Liza, Essie, Louis, and Rosie promenade along an enclosed deck. A sailor or steward follows them with his eyes. A square, numberless clock above their heads shows that it's just past seven. A few moments later, the three women stand behind a window, the ocean reflected in the glass, waves rippling across their faces.

The voyage is almost over. The ship enters New York Harbor. My grandfather's gaze lingers on the Statue of Liberty. As they steam up the Hudson, he pans south across the skyline on a bright late-summer day.

The Empire State Building, the Woolworth Building, the oddly sparse profile of lower Manhattan. Then, with the Palisades passing behind them, the five travelers step in front of the camera one by one. Essie, in a red coat with a fur collar, wears a beret with a pom-pom on top. For six seconds she points steadily at something ahead, looking serious, slightly ill at ease. Louis, round-faced and dapper in his dark gray double-breasted suit, a white handkerchief in his left breast pocket, raises his hand in a kind of salute, touching his fingers to his forehead, then waving at my grandfather. Rosie, in a black dress, black gloves, black hat, squints into the sunshine. She's a small woman, and the wind flutters her dress and seems about to knock her over. Like her sister-in-law, she points a finger insistently at something behind my grandfather for the five seconds she's on-screen. My grandmother is next. She's wearing a black sombrero-style hat and a belted tan overcoat with mounds of fur on the shoulders. A red rose is pinned to her lapel. She walks directly toward the camera and flashes a radiant smile. Finally, for the only time, my grandfather appears. He's wearing a gray suit and a short, red-accented tie that wants to free itself in the breeze. The front flap of his jacket is folded under, making him look slightly disheveled. He says something, sweeps his finger across the horizon, then singles out a spot to emphasize. Maybe he's comparing New York to the European cities they've just visited. Maybe he's indicating the direction to their home in Brooklyn. The final frames show the crowd on the pier in New York, white hats and gray suits, upraised arms greeting the ship's arrival.

My grandfather shot a tourist film intended solely for the family. Almost every scene features someone waving to the camera or waving the camera away. The image shakes; the lens moves too quickly. This is what you expect from a novice cameraman traveling with his wife and close friends. *See?* he seems to say. *We're here.*

But when I watched this film for the first time, standing in my living room in March 2009, my fingers tightened around the VCR remote. Mixed in with the tourist shots, after a park in Belgium and before the mountains of Switzerland, were three minutes of my grandparents' visit to Poland. Three minutes of a fourteen-minute film. Three minutes, mostly in color, showing a vibrant Jewish community in the summer of 1938, one year before the war, just three months before *Kristallnacht*. The instant these scenes appeared, everything else faded away.

This is what I saw: Perhaps a hundred people crowd the street in front of a black sedan. The children jump up and down, making faces. It's a silent film, but I can tell the kids are shouting. They run to remain in the frame as my grandfather pans across the building fronts. Adults linger in the background, clustered by open wooden doors. There are workers in torn shirts and religious men in long black overcoats. Some women wear kerchiefs; most are bareheaded. Many of the girls have fashionable bobs. In the background, my grandmother and Rosie Malina laugh at the commotion my grandfather and his home movie camera have created. My grandfather sweeps the lens across the crowd. He tries to film above the pulsing mob of children, but they push forward and jut their faces into the frame.

People rush into a building. The camera jumps. Now there's a long procession as people exit the building. It must be the synagogue. A lion is carved into an upper panel of the ten-foot-tall door. Louis Malina emerges, escorted by a man in a gray cap. A man in a black coat tries to free his arm from the grasp of another man, who shakes his fist. Twenty, fifty, perhaps seventy people exit, first men, then women. My grandmother wears a straw hat banded by what looks like fruit. Rosie Malina is next to her. A woman carrying a child follows. My grandmother says something to her over her shoulder.

Then they are indoors. The film is in color, but the lighting is very bad. People around a table are shadows, silhouettes. Red flowers stand in the window—lilies, I believe. The camera moves across the room. Curious onlookers gather outside and peer in the window. A man snatches the hat of the man in front of him and waves it in the air. Inside, an old woman, whose profile shows she's missing most of her teeth, laughs with the woman beside her.

On the street again. A boy leans in from the right side and grins excitedly. *Hey, look!* he must be saying. The images are suddenly crystalline, the colors sharp. My grandfather films the same façades as before, but now he focuses on the people, three rows of children with adults scattered around. A woman in a red, green, and black dress has her arm on the shoulder of a girl with blond braids. The girl's dress has diagonal stripes. Another woman wears a black-and-white dress, the colors meeting in a zigzag across her chest. Two young men stand in the background, in black coats and black caps with short brims. One of them has a little beard. The other has his hand on his hip. A woman in a gray smock peeks from a storefront, views the scene, and retreats. The sign above her head is almost legible.

For forty seconds, my grandfather pans across the faces of schoolchildren, teenagers, adults, old men and women. They stand patiently, a little self-consciously, or they jostle each other. The girl with blond braids scoots sideways, keeping pace with the camera. An old man with a long white beard leans against a doorway. A girl with a bright red ribbon in her hair turns her head. A boy grins, exposing a gap between his front teeth. All of them gaze into the lens of my grandfather's camera.

Then we're outside a home. My grandmother comes down the steps, her arm held by a stately black-haired woman. Rosie Malina descends. Then Louis, accompanying a distinguished elderly man. A young woman bustles onto the stoop. She wears a white kerchief and a green dress with red piping at the neck and waist and on the edge of a pocket. She wags a finger menacingly at the children swarming her doorstep. A universal gesture, *Go away! Scram!* She takes Essie Diamond by the elbow and helps her down the stairs.

Three minutes. The scene ends. My grandparents continue their trip. They visit Switzerland and the south of France. They travel to Paris and on to London. They board the ship that will carry them home.

My father and my aunt were unanimous about the Polish town seen in the film: *Berezne*, they said, my grandmother's birthplace. Berezne, on the Polish-Ukrainian border, a shtetl with a population of about four thousand people, three thousand of whom were Jews. My aunt identified the Malinas and Essie Diamond, my grandparents' lifelong friends. Beyond that, she had only fragmentary recollections, passed down from her mother. "There were wooden sidewalks," Shirley said when we discussed the film on the phone. "There was a button factory."

I consulted my sister, Dana, the genealogist in the family. Dana is a whiz with databases. She easily found the U.S. Customs declaration documenting my grandparents' return from Europe. They had sailed from Southampton on August 31 on the RMS *Queen Mary*, which had set the transatlantic speed record earlier that summer. They arrived in New York on Labor Day, Monday, September 5, 1938, at nine thirty in the morning.

With the date, historical details were relatively easy to learn. There were 1,993 passengers aboard the *Queen Mary* when it docked that morning, a seasonal record for a westbound passage, according to the *New York Times*. Among them were the movie star Douglas Fairbanks and the stage actor Raymond Massey, who was preparing to play the title role in *Abe Lincoln in Illinois* on Broadway. Sir Henry Chilton, the British ambassador to Spain, was also on board. "Asked what he thought about the threats of war in Europe, the diplomat replied that they would be cleared up without hostilities." The *Chicago Daily Tribune* reported on September 6 that the *Queen Mary* had ferried $24 million worth of gold, the largest amount ever transported to New York on a single ship. The *Christian Science Monitor* dubbed it "a flight of capital from war-scared Europe." The following week, the British prime minister, Neville Chamberlain, would visit Adolf Hitler in Berchtesgaden, seeking a political resolution to the crisis over the Sudetenland in Czechoslovakia. On September 30, Chamberlain, the master strategist of appeasement, returned triumphantly to London from the Munich Conference and waved a slip of paper above his head. "Peace for our time," he declared.

David and Liza Kurtz landed in New York as they had departed, unnoticed by the press. After a six-week tour of Europe, they filled out their customs declaration, then made their way home to their three children and to their comfortable, mostly anonymous life. The film of their summer vacation was sent to Rochester, New York, to be developed. I don't know when it returned, or whether my grandparents viewed it with their friends or their family. I don't know when it came to reside in a cabinet in my family's den in Roslyn. Indeed, when I first watched the film in March 2009, I didn't know anything about it at all.

In her genealogical files, however, Dana found a copy of a typewritten newsletter, the *Babette Gazette*, Volume 1, Number 1, dated May 21, 1939, Shirley Kurtz, Editor-in-Chief. The three-page paper records a meeting in Brooklyn of the descendants of Haskell Bab, or Babczuk, my grandmother's grandfather, a native of Berezne. The newsletter carried a feature by one of my grandmother's six sisters, Rose, "Childhood Days in Brezner." "On the West side of the house are two windows and on the north a door leading into the kitchen," Rose writes, describing the family home in Poland. "On the East side of the room is a door leading into a bedroom. This is the room that our Cousin Dave Kurtz mentioned in his speech. The room he tried to sleep in on his visit to Brezner. It is almost an historical room, at least to our family, for I and a few more in our family were born in this very room."

So Dana's family archive confirmed it: David and Liza Kurtz had visited Berezne—or Brezner, Berezno, Berëzno, Brezhna, Берёзно, בערעזנע—and had spent the night in the family home, sleeping in the room where my great-aunt Rose and my grandmother Liza were born. David gave a talk about the visit to a gathering of his wife's relatives in May 1939, almost a year after their trip.

That was what I learned from a few phone calls to my family. The formal history I gathered from the *Encyclopedia of Jewish Life Before and During the Holocaust* and a little online searching: In September 1939, Berezne, located thirty-four miles northeast of Rovno (now Rivne), fell into the Soviet zone of occupation following the invasion and partition of Poland. The town was partially destroyed on July 6, 1941, two weeks after the German army attacked the Soviet Union. The German occupiers established a ghetto and a *Judenrat*, a Jewish council. On August 25, 1942, Berezne's Jewish inhabitants, along with other Jews from the surrounding area—a total of 3,400 people—were marched to a pit by the town cemetery and murdered by German and Ukrainian policemen with machine guns. Of the three thousand Jews who lived there in 1938, 150 survived the war.

Standing in my living room, playing the home movie again on my VCR, I realized my grandfather's three minutes of film might be the only moving images in existence of the town and its inhabitants prior to their destruction.

2

PRESERVATION

"YOUR FAMILY FOOTAGE is unique," e-mailed Leslie Swift, a film archivist at the United States Holocaust Memorial Museum in Washington, D.C., a few days after I'd sent her a copy of the VHS recording on DVD. My family and I had agreed that David's film belonged in an archive. Despite the unplayable condition of the 16mm original and the very low quality of the second-generation copy, Swift responded immediately. "It fits right within our collecting parameters," she wrote.

At the end of March 2009, I drove from New York to Washington to hand-deliver the film. Leslie Swift met me in the museum's research library, a bright study space perched on the building's fifth floor. Eight months pregnant with twins, she eased herself into a chair at the long pine reading table. I pulled the canister from my briefcase. In the light of the green-shaded reading lamp, it looked almost moldy. "You never know what's going to turn up," Swift said, looking at the battered can. "We get these phone calls out of the blue, and it's like, 'Oh! Here's this great collection that we didn't know was there, and nobody knew was there.'"

Swift, who quickly asked me to call her Leslie, had interned at the museum's photography archives in the mid-1990s. Her internship turned into a job, and after a few years as the reference archivist in the photographic division, she transferred to the museum's Steven Spielberg Film and Video

Archive, where she acquires, catalogues, and researches moving images about all aspects of the Holocaust period.

"People think that everything we have is going to be corpses and this really depressing imagery, and it's not," she told me. "To us, prewar Jewish life is a very important part of the story. It wouldn't occur to us not to collect something like this."

We opened the can and inspected my grandfather's film, a smelly, black disc, half an inch thick and about six inches in diameter.

The Steven Spielberg Film and Video Archive contains more than a thousand hours of footage. But of this, only fifty-seven hours were shot by amateurs. The rest consists of propaganda and military films, newsreels, or other professionally produced material, often tainted with a political agenda.

"The emphasis in Holocaust documentation has usually been— necessarily, to some degree—on documentation produced by the perpetrator," Leslie said, explaining why she found David Kurtz's film so exciting. "Home movies were produced by members of the victim group or by bystanders or witnesses." She referred to the scenes where Liza and the Malinas walk or speak with the residents of the town. "Here are these people who have emigrated, who have gotten out, who look very different now from the people they're visiting, and yet still have this connection, still have this intimacy that we can see in the footage." The difference between the visitors' modern clothing and the everyday dress of the townspeople already tells a story, she said. But the scenes also provide insight into the town's social life, and they reveal individual personalities in unguarded moments, dimensions absent from newsreels or propaganda films. Moments like this endow home movies with such poignance, Leslie said, and they constitute an irreplaceable documentary resource.

Even within the museum's collection of home movies, however, David Kurtz's film is unusual, Leslie continued. Many of the home movies in the archive depict larger towns or cities. It is less common to see a small town. Interior scenes are also infrequent, like those in David's film showing people sitting around a table or the brief glimpse of a woman fixing her hair. Above all, color film is exceptionally rare, and therefore especially valuable. Black-and-white images create distance between the present and the Holocaust period. But color images cross that boundary. They have an immediacy that can be startling. In particular, color footage from the pre-war period helps make real a part of the history easily overshadowed by the events that followed.

Leslie showed me to one of the computer stations in the library, where we viewed a few collections already in the archive, family films from other Americans who had either lived in Europe before the war or who had gone back, like my grandparents, to visit. There were images of Kraków and Warsaw, of children preening for the camera and families walking in a park. Footage similar to what my grandparents had captured. Ordinary people doing mostly ordinary things. The very ordinariness makes these films so important. Strangely, ordinariness is one of the rarest things preserved on film.

"I try to resist being too romantic, because I think that it's not productive," Leslie said, again referring to David Kurtz's home movie. "But here are the people in the village, and they're living their lives, they're excited to see a camera. And everything is about to change in a horrible way."

Yet if we focus only on what is about to happen, she said, we lose something essential about the people in the film and the reality of their lives. These few minutes document a place and a period when the people we see were not yet victims. "You know what's going to happen to the vast majority of them. You don't ever forget that. But it's also just fun to watch people have a good time."

꙳꙳꙳꙳꙳꙳꙳꙳꙳꙳꙳

I donated my grandfather's home movie to the United States Holocaust Memorial Museum in memory of David and Liza Kurtz. But I have no memory of David Kurtz. He died in 1958, before I was born. A picture of him sat on the piano in our den during my childhood, showing a soft-featured man in a white open-neck shirt, holding a cigar. He looks off to the side with slightly hooded eyes and a firm, engaged expression. For my entire life, people have told me we would have liked each other, that we shared some ineffable trait of sensibility passed down in DNA. I know

David enjoyed reading, especially Shakespeare, and he could quote pas-
sages from the plays at length. I know he ate cold cereal for breakfast and
did not like to eat alone. According to my cousin Bernice, on Saturday
mornings, when his children would have preferred to sleep late, David
would call up the stairs, "Do I have to eat breakfast by myself?" Bernice is
two months older than my aunt Shirley, and they frequently had sleepovers
when they were kids.

Liza Kurtz lived to about ninety-five. I was twenty when she died in
1983, but I do not recall ever hearing her speak of her travels to Europe or
elsewhere, and she had traveled quite a lot. I think she loved to travel more
than anything, and if my grandfather did not wish to accompany her, she
went alone. In 1939, the year after the trip to Europe, Liza took off by train
across Canada and boarded a ship for Alaska. When the war broke out in
Europe, she sent a postcard: *I heard the terrible news. Should I come home?*
A postcard, not a telegram. She was in no rush to return. This is the story
Shirley tells. Is there more to it? Some suppressed subplot of marital strife?
These details have not come down to me. Those who remember agree that
Liza Kurtz was an adventurous and imperious woman who dominated the
family and demanded subservience from her daughter and daughters-in-
law. The worst of this was before my time, though my aunt and my mother
still chafe at the memories. When I knew her, my grandmother remained
elegant and commanding. She was reserved and proud, and she absolutely
hated getting old. Liza was not a grandmother to gather the grandchildren
at her knees and tell stories.

Sometimes I envy others their loquacious grandparents, the kind
Daniel Mendelsohn describes in his magnificent book about the fate of
his Polish relatives, *The Lost: A Search for Six of Six Million.* Recalling his
grandfather, Mendelsohn writes: "So he would come each summer to
Long Island and I would sit at his feet as he talked. He talked about that
older sister who'd died *a week before her wedding*, and talked about the
younger sister who was married off at nineteen to that older sister's fiancé,
the hunchbacked (my grandfather said), dwarflike first cousin whom first
one and finally the other of these lovely girls had had to marry because,
my grandfather told me, this ugly cousin's father had paid for the boat

tickets that had brought those two sisters and their brothers and mother, brought all of my grandfather's family, to the United States, and had demanded a beautiful daughter-in-law as the price."

How wonderful, I sometimes think, to have had a grandparent so overflowing with family history, this sweeping, run-on sentence of immigrant Jewish life. I recognize Mendelsohn's kindred Long Island childhood, the cheek-pinching, card-playing, lacquer-nailed old relatives, the lavish suburban bar mitzvah. But my family was not like that. Stories about where they were from and where they had gone were not part of my inheritance. Although we gathered every Friday night for dinner at Grandma Liza's apartment in New York City, the talk around the table was not of the exciting personalities and adventures of my ancestors. Perhaps I was not interested; perhaps I should have asked more questions. But as a kid, I begged instead to be excused after the meal and went into the bedroom to watch TV with my sister or with Shirley's husband, my uncle Jack—*Time Tunnel* and *Mission: Impossible*. Now, for information about my grandparents, about their lives and travels, I am left with fragments and anecdotes, a scattering of documents, photographs, and a cardboard box of films.

My sister, Dana, has amassed a trove of official papers establishing the names and dates and inconsistencies of our family history. According to a document in the Polish State Archive, David Kurtz was born in 1888. He never had access to this document, and consequently, he didn't know his own birthday. Perhaps jokingly, he chose to celebrate it on Christmas, December 24 or sometimes December 25. Thanks to Dana, we know it was December 2, 1888, at 10:00 p.m., "*nokh dem groysn shney*," after the big snow, as his mother, Leah Diamond Kurtz, recalled to Shirley, and Shirley in turn recalled to Dana. David's father, called Himan on his U.S. citizenship papers, Hermann in the 1900 census, and Hyman in 1920, was born on January 15, 1864, 1869, or 1870. He arrived in New York from the town of Nasielsk, Poland, just north of Warsaw, "on or about" June 5, 1885. But Dana has so far been unable to find evidence of his arrival in the United States. "I have no proof we're here," is how she puts it. We know that Hyman Kurtz was a tailor and became a naturalized U.S. citizen on Octo-

ber 14, 1892, by which time his wife and son were with him in New York. The math indicates that he traveled back to Poland at least once between 1885 and 1892, since David was born in Nasielsk in 1888. David Kurtz became a U.S. citizen when he was four years old, on the same day his father was naturalized. After this, we know he was admitted to DeWitt Clinton High School, then located on West Thirteenth Street in Manhattan, on February 2, 1903, and left school a month later, on March 3, 1903. He was fourteen years old. He set out to make a living.

Dana has a bankbook, issued to David Kurtz by the Manhattan Savings Institution at 644 Broadway, showing the first deposit on June 15, 1909, for $32. In 1909, at age twenty-one, David was in the neckwear business, meaning he manufactured collars. According to a piece of stationery that has survived, his office was on West Houston Street. By January 1910, the bankbook shows a balance of $88.06. But the account languishes until 1920 and is finally closed on September 12, 1938, with a balance of $56.86, just a week after David and Liza Kurtz returned from their trip to Europe. Almost no other documentation from these years has been preserved. And yet these were the years during which David Kurtz prospered.

By 1912, he had moved his office to 699 Broadway and was manufacturing boys' shirts, which remained the family business until my father sold it in 1990. The first mention of David's business activity I've uncovered is a help-wanted ad placed in the *New York Times* on January 13, 1919, when he was thirty-one years old. "Salesman for Pacific coast; resident Chicago; Middle West, also Canada; side line, well-known boys' blouses and boys' shirts; commission." By that time he was married and my grandmother was three months pregnant with their first child, my uncle Jerry.

Liza Kurtz was born Lena Saltzman in Berezne, Poland, on October 12 in 1888, 1890, 1891, or 1892—there are documents with each of these dates, though 1888 seems most reliable. Unlike the Ephrussi family in Edmund de Waal's beautiful memoir, *The Hare with Amber Eyes*, the Saltzman family was not part of the cultural aristocracy of nineteenth- and early-twentieth-century Europe, much to Liza's chagrin. There are no references to my great-grandparents, aunts, or uncles in the works of Proust, Rilke, or Isaac Babel. The Saltzmans left Poland unnoticed in the 1890s, part of the first great wave of Jewish emigration, and arrived in the United States without leaving so much as a ship's manifest for us to ponder. We still do not know the exact year. Chaim Saltzman, Liza's father, was not known as a skillful businessman. However, there is a family story that Chaim created a hundred-year calendar of Jewish holidays that came to the attention of the Zionist leader Theodor Herzl. Shirley says the two men corresponded, though no letters have survived. Liza, one of seven sisters, worked in a millinery shop as a young woman, and she retained a lifelong love of extravagant hats. There is a photograph of her around age twenty wearing a dark, tightly fitted suit and a hat easily three feet in diameter,

topped with a cascade of ostrich feathers. Remarkably, I think you don't notice the hat first. Instead, you notice her face, the expression of proud determination. She was a woman who could make a hat like that fade into the background.

Her friends and members of the extended family referred to her as Lena, and this is the name on her stationery and on most official papers. But for reasons I have never been able to learn, my family always called her Liza. Apparently, sometime in the 1950s, she decided she liked this name better. I always knew her as Grandma Liza. It feels strange to call her by any other name.

In the early 1910s, Liza was the treasurer of the Young Knickerbockers Club in Brooklyn. I have not been able to locate any information about this club. There was another Knickerbocker Club on Fifth Avenue and

Twenty-Eighth Street, organized in 1871. An article from 1915 praises that club's new Colonial-style home on Fifth Avenue at Sixty-Second Street as "expressive of the conservatism, if not the traditional exclusiveness, of the club." This doesn't sound like a place where David Kurtz and Liza Saltzman would have been welcome. But the story has it that my grandparents met at the Young Knickerbockers Club, where Liza was the treasurer and, according to Shirley, always wore gloves.

"My Dear Sweetheart," David writes on November 22, 1911, on stationery of the Emerson Hotel, Baltimore, Maryland. "I am writing this letter at 12 P.M. midnight and just thinking how I would much rather have spent the evening with you. The ride on the train took five hours, but it seemed like a month." How fortunate I am to have a love letter from my grandfather to my grandmother! But there are hints in the letter that Lena Saltzman was not an easy woman to court. "Dear Lena, I was very sorry to have to go away, and I miss you probably as much as you miss me. When I telephoned you, you did not even as much as wish me good luck. I have no doubt that you do wish me good luck. But I would have felt a whole lot better if I heard you say it." The feeling among my relatives is that, for the entirety of their married life, David continued to wait for Liza to utter these or any encouraging words.

Yet David was clearly smitten. He goes on to talk about business. "I got an order just before I left the shop for $100.00 to be shipped Dec. 28th." And he laments that all the $2.00 rooms at the Emerson Hotel were occupied and he has had to pay $5.00 for a room with a bath. "Where in the world so many people get the money to pay for such expensive places as this, is more than I can understand but I hope someday I will find it out and be able to live with you in such a place. I wish it were to-day." He signs the letter, "your loving boy, Dave."

No love letters from Liza have survived. Whatever her outward demeanor, however, my grandmother evidently found David's attention pleasing. David Kurtz and Liza Saltzman married on August 18, 1912, at Capital Hall, Brooklyn. Dana has a copy of the invitation, printed on cream paper in Gothic letters. "Mr. & Mrs. H. Saltzman and Mr. & Mrs. H. Kurtz request the pleasure of your presence at the marriage ceremony of their children Lena to David Kurtz." I could quibble with the grammar, but in the absence of family stories, this is all I have.

In my father's papers, I discovered another of David's letters, this one from 1937—a letter I wish I had discovered earlier. Apparently, my grandparents had traveled to Europe in the summer of 1937, too, making the 1938 trip their second European vacation in as many years. The letter, which David seems to have had fun writing, reveals a little more of his personality.

"Dear Children," my grandfather writes on July 9, 1937, describing the scene as they embarked on the Italian liner *Conte di Savoia*, bound for Naples. "When we arrived at the pier I spied Mr. Bernstein standing amongst a tumult of a crowd. The poor fellow had been waiting for hours— with a bouquet for Mother. Mighty nice of him—then we arrived at our stateroom—bedlam broke loose—people almost got killed in the rush— our friends had been drinking and having a wild time by the time we arrived. Here is a list of those at the boat—Well, never mind. George was our chauffeur, but on the boat he thought he was the Admiral of the Italian Navy and did he get soused. Jerry was afraid to ride home with him. Finally at 12 noon the boat pulled out and we were waving kisses as long as we could see anyone on the pier. They showed such joy at seeing us go, but to us it was a deep thrill of joy to see how many friends we have. Finally— when away from shore—we went into the stateroom—and there scattered all over the place was a roomful of flowers, books, boxes, and telegrams— a hundred of them—and every other package seemed to be from Toots Baker. I'll bet that kid spent a week's wages. It was all so thrilling."

I wish David had listed the names of those who showed such joy at seeing them leave. "Well, never mind." He makes a joke of it, but so casually is information lost. Excavating family history from documents and artifacts, I'm at the mercy of shifting moods, of what gets set down on paper or where the camera lens points. To reconstruct the context, I have to rely on what others recollect when I happen to ask.

Shirley doesn't recall Mr. Bernstein, who waited for hours with a bouquet for my grandmother. Another story gone. But she remembers George, also known as "Sunshine," who was a handyman, a black man who did odd jobs for my grandparents and several neighboring families in Flatbush. Jerry, my uncle, my aunt's older brother, was eighteen years old in July 1937. "Toots Baker," I was surprised to learn, refers to my cousin Lee, my grandmother's niece, daughter of her sister Rose, who described the family home in Berezne in the sole surviving issue of the *Babette Gazette*. I can hardly imagine a less likely "Toots," yet there she is. When I knew her, she was a plump, dowdy woman who had married an older man named Sig late in life. We, the grandchildren, the cousins, rather meanly called them "Sig and Fig." Why she would spend a week's wages on gifts for my grandparents is another juicy tidbit of family history lost.

I never knew my grandfather, and I knew my grandmother only in her increasingly embittered old age. My uncle Jerry never told me stories. He was killed in a plane crash in July 1963, an event that in part explains my grandmother's bitterness. I knew about this crash, growing up. But we never talked about it, and it is only recently that I've tried to learn some of the details. More research, more documents, which made me start in horror one night in 2011, since this crash plays a role in the TV series *Mad Men*. In its aftermath, the advertising agency of Sterling Cooper Draper Pryce has the job of helping Mohawk Airlines restore its reputation. A photo of my uncle Jerry stood next to my grandfather's portrait on our piano in Roslyn.

"I didn't want to throw away my mother's writing or my father's writing," Shirley told me when I asked why she had saved David and Liza's postcards. Because her parents had held these pieces of paper, the cards felt somehow alive with their touch. I feel this, too, when I hold the family photographs, letters, and postcards that have come down to me, a magical belief that I might reach through the paper to the people on the other side, and that they might reach out to me. As if, by possessing and preserving a postcard, a photo, or a film, we could cheat loss, cheat death.

A ship is leaving port. The white hull looms above the excited well-wishers, portholes almost obscured by a tangle of paper streamers. "Thousands of people today would almost as soon leave their suitcase behind when they travel, as their movie camera," says an advertisement for the

Kodak home movie camera my grandfather carried in 1938. "For no other power on earth can do what a movie camera does—give you a living, indelible record of your most glorious experiences. Days at sea with cloud and wind and ocean—your first glimpse of a tropical port . . . magical . . . seductive—the alien, fascinating street life of foreign cities—You think your memory will hold it all—but no. It slips away, grows dim. Only a movie camera can bring it back to you with all its freshness and thrill."

This is false advertising of a religious intensity. *What you film will never die*, it promises. *A living, indelible record.* As if filming your life were perfect preservation. As if film were heaven for memories.

iiiiiiiiiiiiiiiiiii

Vinegar syndrome is a kind of Alzheimer's of film. Once it starts, it cannot be halted, and the process is autocatalytic, meaning it feeds on itself, accelerating as the film is progressively destroyed. Since my grandfather's film had been transferred to VHS in the 1980s, the original footage had remained untouched in its can. Unfortunately, keeping commercial diacetate film stock in a sealed metal can in a cardboard box in Florida combines three of the worst storage methods. When the film began to lose its chemical stabilizers, the metal can had sealed in the acetic acid that leached from the plastic, providing more fuel for disintegration. What little acid had escaped was absorbed by the cardboard box and thus spread to all the neighboring films, infecting them. Florida's humid conditions had caused the plastic to swell, exacerbating the process. If David Kurtz's film had been left undisturbed in my parents' closet for just a few more months, it would have consumed itself completely, devouring every image on the reel.

As soon as Leslie Swift at the Holocaust Museum received the original 16mm reel, and as one of her last tasks before going on maternity leave, she sent it to Russ Suniewick, the president and cofounder of Colorlab Corporation, in Rockville, Maryland, one of the premier film preservation laboratories in the country. Colorlab works regularly with the Holocaust Museum, the National Archives, the Smithsonian Institution, and many other film repositories, and provides archival mastering for leading documentary filmmakers such as Ken Burns.

The first step in the long process of rescuing the images in my grand-father's film was "replast," replasticizing the film base by replacing the chemicals it had lost. For this, Suniewick turned it over to AJ Rohner, a staff technician who specializes in small-gauge and severely damaged film. Rohner sealed the reel of film in a canister with a cocktail of water, glycerin, and acetone. As the liquid evaporated, the film absorbed the vapor and slowly softened from a hockey puck to something wrinkled and ragged, with a profile like uncombed hair.

Once the plastic relaxed enough to be safely unwound, a superficial examination revealed the film to be a reversal print composed of four sections, two color Kodachrome and two black-and-white. Rohner separated the four sections, wound them onto new archival cores, and placed them in individual containers for additional treatment, since color and black-and-white film respond to the process differently. All four sections were still in replast two months later when I visited the lab in May 2009. "Don't breathe in too much," Rohner cautioned when he opened the containers to show me the disassembled film in its toxic sauna. It would remain in replast for four months.

Rohner's inspection of the individual segments yielded several pieces of important information. Codes marked on the edge of the film helped determine with certainty that it was manufactured in 1938. Another code imprinted on the film during exposure recorded the make and model of my grandfather's camera, a Magazine Ciné-Kodak with an Anastigmat 25mm f/1.9–f/16 lens.

Kodak had introduced the Magazine Ciné-Kodak in 1936, a year after the company pioneered Kodachrome 16mm color film. "One . . . Two . . . Three . . . It's loaded!" says an advertisement from January 1936. "Flip open the camera cover, insert a film magazine (loaded with one of Eastman's two films that are available for black-and-white, or with Kodachrome for full color movies), close the cover . . . that's all there is to it. No threading of film, no delay. Change from one type of film to another in five seconds, and shoot away."

David took Kodak's advice. He frequently changed from one type of film to another and shot away. Most likely, he ended the 1938 trip with four spent film magazines, two color and two black-and-white, which he sent back to the Eastman facility in Rochester to be developed and spliced into a single print. This explained why the scenes in the film were out of order. Since my grandfather had swapped film magazines on the go, the sequence of images in the print did not follow the sequence in which he shot them.

Rohner's condition report noted the following issues for the black-and-white sections: "Emulsion severely separating from base, severe crazing, edgeweave on non-drive side, severe cupping towards base, buckling, high shrinkage. Very brittle." For the color sections: "Emulsion beginning to separate from base, ferrotyping, crazing on base, cupping towards base, edgeweave on drive side, color dyefade." Like a hospital chart with every arrow pointing down, this report catalogued the aging film's rapid physical decline.

Ferrotyping occurs when film is stored tightly wound under humid conditions. The emulsion swells in the humidity and adopts the characteristics of what it is pressed against. Since in this case the emulsion of one loop was pressed against the base of the next, it took on a smooth, glossy surface. This new texture interferes with the transmission of light, leaving a splotch on the image that looks like a puddle of water.

Edgeweave, cupping, and buckling describe distortions to the film base, different ways it curls and warps. The effect this has on the emulsion, the chemical compound that carries the image, will depend on how the film is wound, with the base or the emulsion facing out. My grandfather's film cupped toward the base, which meant the film base was inside the cup, while the emulsion was outside. This caused the image to stretch, producing cracks, called crazing. "Crazing is what looks like little spiderwebs," said Rohner. "There's nothing you can do about that."

Shrinkage affects the film in other ways, as well. Because film adheres to physical standards of 8, 16, and 35 millimeters, any significant deviation in the size of the film will prevent it from feeding properly through the equipment. For film restoration, shrinkage of up to 0.5 percent is considered normal, while anything over 1.5 percent will present problems. An instrument called a shrink meter is used to determine the percentage. My grandfather's film was literally off the gauge, at over 3 percent.

To an extent, warping and shrinkage can be addressed in a second phase of replast. "Once it's as pliable as we think it's going to get," Rohner explained, "we wind it tight, and then we wrap it with this blue leader," a thick processing film that would normally be used to keep a printer threaded. When wrapped around the warped film, blue leader exerts an even pressure all around, forcing the shrunken edge to stretch. Tightly wrapped, the film is returned to the replast cans. "In the can it's going to be forming itself back into a flat state. And once that's done, we'll unwind it, hand-clean it, and send it to Tommy."

Because the original's deterioration cannot be halted, duplication is the only effective means of preserving the content of old film. But duplicating even mildly warped film is like trying to photocopy a book with a stiff binding: one side of the image will always be out of focus and appear to melt into the gutter. To compensate for this, Tommy Aschenbach, a duplication specialist, has retrofitted an old telecine machine, which the technicians call a Rank, after the manufacturer, Rank Cintel. Instead of the standard lens, Aschenbach's machine is equipped with a digital camera that enables him to change f-stop and so expand the possible depths of field. In this way, he can obtain clear shots of irregular and warped film. "His Rank has a lot more leeway, focus-wise," was how AJ Rohner described it. The digital camera sits above the film gate, looking down onto the image. Beneath the gate, Aschenbach has constructed a light box with LEDs that throw red, green, and blue light through the film, exposing it to the camera. Once each image is captured as digital data, color correction and other image manipulation can be performed in a software program such as Final Cut Pro.

No matter how the film is duplicated, the most perilous stage of the process is the physical transportation of the original film through the machine, with its fixed metal sprockets and rollers. "Plenty of things can go wrong," said Rohner, who assists Aschenbach with this stage of the process. "What I'll end up having to do is to loosen the tension on the Rank over here, the telecine, use all sorts of rubber bands on the rollers and everything. Otherwise, it's snapping left and right."

Like human memory, commercial home movie stock may last perhaps eighty, occasionally even a hundred years. This means that unless they are duplicated, the majority of home movies shot on film will disappear within a generation or two. According to Russ Suniewick, president of Colorlab, memories saved on video won't even last that long. "What are people going to look at eighty to ninety years from now?" he asked as he showed me around the lab's facilities. "The answer is, from our perspective, nothing. There's nothing on magnetic oxide tape that will last. And so we've stopped taking records. And when you talk about this, people roll their eyes and say, 'Well, hard drives this, and disks that,' you know, the whole fallacious thing. It's not gonna happen." Both magnetic and optical storage formats—videotape, digital discs, and drives—decay much faster than commercial film stock. Despite living in the cloud, there is no heaven for digital data. And in fifty years, even if our CDs, DVDs, flash drives, and YouTube accounts retain their contents, which is unlikely, there will be no devices or software with which to read them. Skip even one generation of technological change and the precious photos, videos, or letters on the floppy disks in the closet become inaccessible or illegible.

What moments are worth saving? My grandparents had no way to know their vacation movie would become the unique record of life in a Polish town before the war. The film itself sat for seventy years unused and uncared for. And yet, within a few months of the end of its life, the information on my grandfather's brittle and shrunken film was saved, in a transmigration of images. Duplication could not reverse the damage the images had already suffered, nor could it restore information lost during the process of transferring the old film to new stock. But with proper storage, the new polyester-base archival print should last more than five hundred years. It is not an indelible record, but it is one of the very few home movies that will be passed down to future generations.

In July 2009, Colorlab sent an archival print of David Kurtz's film to the United States Holocaust Memorial Museum, where it became the "Kurtz Collection," catalogue number 2870. The original footage, no longer viable, was also returned to the museum. There it was laid to rest in a cold, dark climate-controlled storage facility. It would survive perhaps another year.

〰〰〰〰〰

In July 2009, as Colorlab was finishing its work, I was back at my parents' home in Florida. In 1991, shortly after my parents retired, my father, Milton Kurtz, had suffered a massive stroke. He wasn't expected to survive, but he did. The stroke left him partly paralyzed and unable to speak. Over the next two years, with determination, hard work, and my mother's untiring support, he recovered much of his mobility. He learned to speak again, learned to write, to eat, to dress and groom himself with his left hand. By the stroke's third anniversary, he was driving a car, even playing a little golf. It was, the doctors said, a miracle.

For the next eighteen years, my father went to the gym every day. He exercised to keep up his strength and balance, and he worked diligently at home to improve his ability to form words. If you didn't know he'd had a stroke, it might take several minutes before you noticed the impediment in his speech. During all these years, which others thought of as a cruel fate, my father was unflaggingly cheerful. He was so happy to be alive, he told me. Managing his handicaps seemed a small price to pay. "You have to keep going," he said, an imperative that simplified over the years into "go, go, go."

In the first week of October 2008, he suffered another stroke. It was relatively minor, not even visible on the CAT scan. But it hit my father where he was weakest, where the other stroke had hit him. And now he was eighty-three instead of sixty-five. However minor, the second stroke was devastating.

My trips to Florida in October 2008 and March 2009, when I located my grandfather's film, were not simple family visits. I flew to Florida then not to dig through closets but to visit my father in the hospital and to help my mother. After this second stroke, my father could not swallow well enough to eat, so a feeding tube was inserted into his stomach. He could no longer talk or move himself. He was completely physically disabled.

But his mind was perfectly clear. He preserved all the memories and experiences, all the language and images of a lifetime. Yet everything was sealed inside, inaccessible, incommunicable. He could nod and shake his head. He could change his facial expression and gesture with his left hand.

One day, a week or so after the stroke, when my father had been transferred out of the ICU and my mother was making arrangements for him at an inpatient rehab facility, I was sitting with him at the hospital. I asked how he felt. He put his fingers to his temple, gunlike, and pulled the trigger.

It wasn't a melodramatic gesture—at least I didn't think so. It was a statement, articulated as clearly as he could with the limited means available to him. After eighteen years of fighting, he'd had enough. He didn't think he had the strength to start over again.

After many years of having a difficult, distant relationship, my father and I had become quite close after his first stroke. We didn't talk directly about many important things, how we felt or what we meant to each other. He wasn't a sentimental man about things like that, either, or if he was, he didn't know how to express it, even when he could. But in those years before the second stroke, we had a sort of intuitive understanding, an unspoken acknowledgment of deep emotion. He told me about his service in the navy in World War II, and about his early days in business with his father. And when he had difficulty communicating something, I was often the one who could translate for him, give his thoughts expression for the rest of the family.

So when he pulled the trigger at his temple with his left hand, I wasn't shocked.

"You're stuck," I said. "You're going to have to go back to rehab."

He shrugged his shoulder. *So be it.*

A week later, he was transferred from the hospital to a facility not far from our house, where for three months he'd receive daily physical, occupational, and speech therapy. He tried as hard as he could to recover some means, physical or verbal, to connect with the people around him. He made friends with the therapists, as he always did. He learned to push a wheelchair backward. He learned to turn himself in a hospital bed, grabbing the safety bar with his left hand.

When I finally found the cardboard box of family films in March 2009, my father had just come home from rehab. He couldn't tell me what he remembered.

That July, just as restoration of my grandfather's film was completed, my father developed pneumonia and went back into intensive care.

Every record—every word or memory or film or letter—is an eddy in time. It curls back against the current, persisting. Perhaps it lasts a few moments; perhaps it lasts a hundred or five hundred years. We can dream of preserving our experiences forever, of passing along our image, personality, or the stories and wisdom of our ancestors from generation to generation. But every act of preservation, whether intentional or accidental, cultural or biological, succeeds only temporarily. It is a brief swirl in the relentless flow of dissolution.

I was with my father at the hospital in Florida when my grandfather's restored film arrived at the United States Holocaust Memorial Museum. My father could not speak, but he responded with a sound that meant he understood. I told him this record of his parents' lives would remain at the museum, to honor them and to preserve their memory.

Milton Kurtz died a month later, in August 2009.

3

INHERITANCE

A WOMAN STANDS in a doorway. Stout, with black hair cut short or perhaps pulled back tightly in a bun, she's wearing a gray ankle-length dress that has large dark buttons running down the front. It may be a smock or an apron. She emerges from inside the building and leans out the door. Her right arm is across her breast, the hand grasping her left shoulder. Her left arm is bent sharply, her fingers at her lips. She peers out the door and down the street, as if waiting for someone to appear. Then she turns and retreats inside.

What does this moment of film preserve?

The month before my grandfather's film entered the collection at the United States Holocaust Memorial Museum, I spoke with Lindsay Zarwell, the archivist responsible for cataloguing it. Lindsay, who had been Leslie Swift's colleague for many years and was covering for her during her maternity leave, has a background in library science. She had launched the Film and Video Archive's public access database, and her job is to translate a film's visual information into a prose inventory, identifying every aspect of its content. She is preoccupied by the question "What are we looking at?"

"First round for me is to document the action," Lindsay explained

when we first spoke in June 2009. "What's going on, and the other critical details: the dates, if we know the place, what kind of camera it is, whether it's color, whether it has sound, adding a certain number of keywords to it so we can find it later on."

So, she asked, what did I know about my grandfather's film?

I knew the film was shot in 1938 during my grandparents' summer vacation. This was apparent from the title and was supported by physical evidence revealed during restoration. I knew—or at least, I inferred—that my grandfather shot it, since he is absent from all but one scene. From my sister's genealogical sleuthing, I knew when David and Liza had returned to New York, and from my aunt I knew the names of their friends, the Malinas and Essie Diamond. Thanks to the *Babette Gazette*, I knew my grandparents had visited my grandmother's hometown, Berezne.

Why did they go? Lindsay asked. Who were they visiting? How long did they stay?

I had no other information.

The practical goal of Lindsay's work is to make the film accessible. This means that the content should be findable in the catalogue database under the greatest number of potential keyword searches. "Last week I was looking at a film that was taken in the twenties and thirties, in Denmark," she explained. "Watching it over and over again, I suddenly noticed, after six or seven times, that I can now see a mezuzah on the door, which I hadn't seen before." She was elated by the discovery of this small ritual object, traditionally affixed to the doorway of a Jewish home. "Someone may be doing a project on mezuzahs, some documentary in years to come," she said, "and you wouldn't know to look here unless we actually wrote the term 'mezuzah' in our catalogue record."

In one sense, the content of a film, its visual information, is intrinsic to the images. Kids jump up and down in front of the camera. Yet to enumerate the visible facts demands extraordinary attentiveness. The clothing, its style, material, wear; missing front teeth; the color of the ribbons in girls' hair—unless it is explicitly noted, a detail may be technically preserved on film but buried in the archive, lost to view until a researcher stumbles on it by chance.

At the same time, when asked seriously and persistently, the question "What are we looking at?" is endless. A woman stands in a doorway. She presses her fingers to her lips, as if anxious, and peers down the street. What is happening? Unless you understand the context, her gesture is mysterious. You may imagine what it signifies. But you cannot know.

"Think about the kind of artifacts that we collect here," Lindsay said, "which could be as simple as a spoon. Well, that spoon doesn't really have meaning on its own without the story that goes with it. And so that's what we're paying tribute to, the life of that spoon, and how it got here. Because someone used it, it was their only means of getting food, and they hid it in their uniform, and it was the only thing that survived with them. So the stories are really, really important to us."

Part of Lindsay's job, she said, is "to badger the donor over and over, trying to grill them about whether they know anything more." She took down the little I had learned. But she asked me to keep thinking about the film. What is the story? What is the life of these images?

ıllıllıllıllıllıllıllı

In the spring of 1971, when I was eight years old, my Hebrew school held a book sale. The book I purchased, *The Yellow Star*, was about the fate of Polish Jews in the Holocaust. It was a small paperback containing mostly pictures. On the cover was the famous photograph of a Warsaw deportation: a German soldier, an unknown boy with his hands raised. The boy was also about eight years old.

I hated Hebrew school. Jewish culture was not emphasized at home. My parents went to synagogue three times a year: twice on Rosh Hashanah, once on Yom Kippur. They were not engaged in a struggle to find expression for Jewish experience in assimilated American culture. We were completely assimilated. We did not keep kosher and did not feel guilty about it. It never occurred to me that our Friday night dinners at Grandma Liza's were a way of celebrating Shabbat.

But as a child, you're always being forced to learn things no one else cares about. So I was sent to Hebrew school. From age eight through age twelve, five interminable years, I went to Temple Beth Sholom in Roslyn three days a week to be educated about what it means to be Jewish.

I remember very little of what we were taught, not a word of modern Hebrew, no Bible commentary, perhaps a prayer or two, the names of a couple of kings. What I remember most vividly is the feeling that our teachers hated us, spoiled children of postwar Jewish-American suburbia. In particular, I recall one teacher, a pineapple-shaped man whose pants hung on his belt like a shower curtain. I remember he had a nasal voice and a comb-over, which he smoothed with his palm while intoning Old Testament accounts of Jews failing to abide by God's commandments. A *jealous* God. A *wrathful* God. The purpose of these stories eluded me.

Still, I was bar mitzvahed in June 1975, enacting the traditional ceremony that signifies a Jewish boy's entry into the community. For me, the bar mitzvah signified my exit from the community. Its most joyous consequence was that I'd never, ever have to go to Hebrew school, or for that matter, synagogue, again. After the ceremony, my friends, my parents' friends, and my relatives all gathered for a party in our backyard. A yellow-and-white-striped tent had been erected to shelter the rows of round tables set with specially printed tablecloths, napkins, and matchbooks bearing my name and the date. My grandmother Liza attended the party, too, accompanied by Rosie Malina, both women long since widowed. The two walked through the den of the house in Roslyn on their way to our backyard and passed within a few feet of the film can stored in the cabinet beneath the TV containing moving pictures of their vacation to Europe thirty-seven years before.

In every religious and institutional sense, my supposed education in Judaism was a failure. Looking back, however, I can't deny that Hebrew school provided me with an education. I became acutely aware of an overwhelming power that ruled my life. Unfortunately, this power was death, not God. I no longer have *The Yellow Star*, but its gruesome, graphic images of torture, medical experimentation, and murder are seared into my mind.

In August 2009, a few weeks after my father's death, I received a DVD from the Holocaust Museum containing the restored footage of David Kurtz's film. David had filmed the street life in Poland, the local color, pleasant shots of more or less happy people. But each time I viewed the film, the images on my TV screen receded in my mind behind those from *The Yellow Star*. I wanted to reach inside the frame and shake these people, scream to them, *Get up! Run! Flee!* Some of them must be my relatives. I had no choice but to identify with them. I felt a visceral ache, a desperation to save them.

It did not feel like enough simply to preserve the film as a memorial. "Prewar Jewish life" may accurately describe the film's content, but its vagueness bothered me, as if these were not individual people but examples of a type. I had been working on a novel about a character in exactly this situation, compelled by the unknown faces in a film discovered by chance. Perhaps I was primed to follow a script I had already written. But with an urgency fed by grief over my father's death, I now wanted to know who these people were, the particular people who thrust themselves into the frame of my grandfather's camera lens while he held the shutter open; these people whose images therefore just happened to survive—by chance, by luck, by fate.

In Theo Richmond's book *Konin: A Quest*, he describes a similar compulsion to honor his family by uncovering the life of the town where his relatives were born. "What fueled my curiosity," Richmond writes, "was the wish to know more about one small corner of that world. I was interested not so much in the broad canvas of 'The Jews of Poland' but rather in the Jews of one particular community, in the daily life once lived by my family and by my family's neighbors in a town that held a personal meaning for me—a town on the river Warta. I wanted to explore its banks and meadows, its orchards and woods. I wanted to know my way around the town, every street, every corner, every building of the Konin I might have been born in, the Konin I might have glimpsed for the last time through a gap in the timbers of a railway cattle car." Collecting stories about the Jews of Konin, Richmond writes, felt like "a way of keeping them alive."

Looking at my grandfather's film, I too had wanted to save these people. But after reading Richmond's book, I realized how natural it is to confuse remembrance with reanimation.

In the months after my grandfather's film was restored, I was mourning my father. I also wanted to believe that remembering the dead might preserve them. "He lives on in you," I was told again and again by well-meaning friends. Each time I heard it, I felt the inadequacy of memory, its abject failure to keep him alive.

Nothing I learned about the people in my grandfather's film could prevent their deaths or bring them back to life. No film, no memorial, and no recollection could restore, retrieve, recover, or revive this world, though these words are so often used to describe the work of memory. To remember and honor the dead honestly, all I could do—all anyone could do—was to piece together the few fragments of their lives that remained, to show their edges and absences, defining the loss of that world by detailing the little of it that had been preserved. In this way, we might succeed in keeping the *memory* of the dead alive, remembering them, *despite the fact* that they are dead.

With a new sense of personal significance, I sought to understand what these images contained, what had been passed down to me. I had little interest in Berezne as a place of "orchards and woods," "banks and meadows." I did not want to imagine what might have been. I wanted to discover what we could know. This film had fallen to me to preserve. Its history was my inheritance, and I felt responsible for it.

||||||||||||||||||

A woman stands in a doorway. She does not appear to know she is being filmed. She steps from inside, looks worriedly down the street, and turns back. I don't know what she does next, because my grandfather lifted his finger off the shutter. The film leaps to a different shot, a few moments later, a few feet away. The woman's two seconds on-screen comprise a complete if abstracted gesture, like someone raising her arm to check the time on a wristwatch, then letting her arm fall again. I doubt my grandfather noticed her.

What are we looking at? What is it possible to know?

The woman stands in the doorway of a building on the corner. Next to the door, there is a dented drainpipe assembled from numerous pieces of greenish metal. Perhaps two feet farther to the left, the building ends in a sharp line. An unpainted slat fence extends from the building's side. Cumulus clouds mass in the distance.

A white, rectangular board hangs above the doorway. Three lines of lettering are visible, but only part of one line is easily legible: SPOZY . . . A handmade sign, with the word's first half printed boldly and its second half crammed into the remaining space.

I captured a screenshot of the image, enlarged it, and heightened the contrast. In Lindsay Zarwell's first draft of the Holocaust Museum's catalogue record, she identified the word as "*spozyncz*, possibly a society storefront." But looking at it in supersaturated black-and-white, I identified a few more letters and, playing with Google's translation software, I came up with *spożywczy*, a grocery. I called Lindsay at her office at the museum, and she consulted several native Polish speakers. Yes, they said. *Spożywczy.* The woman in the doorway stands beneath a sign that says "Grocery."

"That's part of why I love my job," Lindsay said before we hung up. "It's a puzzle that you're constantly trying to piece together."

Two other words on the sign remained illegible. But we had identified one word, one small fragment of my grandfather's film. It felt like a triumph, a beginning.

4

PEOPLE AND FACES

SAUL GERSHKOWITZ WAS born in Berezne in 1925, the youngest of Baruch Gershkowitz and Leah Kanat's six children. His father's family had lived in Berezne for at least three generations. His mother's family came from the nearby town of Sarny. Baruch Gershkowitz was a carpenter. In the wintertime, he built and repaired carriages, from the wheels to the fancy ornaments the wealthier people commissioned to distinguish their vehicles and themselves. In the summertime, Saul's father worked for the farmers in the surrounding countryside, building houses and barns, slotting hand-hewn logs into joints, stuffing the gaps with moss. As a boy, Saul often accompanied him on these jobs for the farmers, and so he was known to the non-Jewish Poles and Ukrainians who lived outside the town.

On September 17, 1939, in accordance with secret provisions in the German-Soviet Nonaggression Pact signed three weeks earlier, the Soviet Union invaded Poland, annexing the territory east of the Bug River. Berezne, located on the border between Poland and the Ukraine, was occupied immediately. On July 6, 1941, two weeks after the German invasion of the Soviet Union, the town changed hands again.

In the oral history Saul gave in 1996 to the Visual History Archive, part of the Shoah Foundation, founded by Steven Spielberg, he remembered hiding in a field as the two armies clashed, destroying almost half the town. In September 1941, German military command turned over administration of Berezne to the civil authorities in the Kostopol district, part of the regional government (*Generalkommissariat*) of Volhynia-Podolia. SA-Standartenführer Löhnert was the district commissar (*Gebietskommissar*) in Kostopol, and Lieutenant Wichmann of the Municipal Police (SchuPo) became the head of the district gendarmerie. They ordered the establishment of a Jewish ghetto on October 6, 1941. S.S.-Obersturmbannführer Günther Karl Pütz was commander of the Security Police (SiPo) in Volhynia-Podolia. It was likely he who led the detachment of German police, based about thirty-five miles away in Rovno, and local Ukrainian collaborators, who annihilated Berezne's Jewish population on August 25, 1942.

In her memoir of survival, Tzilla Kitron, who like Saul was a teenager at the time, described the scene that day. "[The Germans] ordered all inhabitants to leave the ghetto for work. To us Jews, it was clear that this had nothing to do with work, because we had already learned about similar *Aktions*. There was a great uproar going on. Screams, crying, and the shots from machine guns mixed together in a hellish inferno. The Jews were led in columns to the death pits, which had already been prepared outside the village."

That morning, Saul and his father were working at a neighboring farm. "He took me so he can send me back with the man, who he was working for, so I can bring some bread and vegetables home," Saul recalled in his oral history. "And this particular day, I set out in the morning to bring some bread and something to my mother."

Saul and the farmer, who was Ukrainian, arrived in Berezne as the destruction of the Jewish ghetto was already under way. Seeing the line of Jews being herded to the edge of town, the farmer kept going. "I saw the people were walking opposite, and that all the Ukrainians—the big, you know, the doctors, the pharmacist—they were standing outside and looking. And every time I saw somebody, I turned over, you know, they shouldn't see me. And he took me out on the other side of the city, and he told me, 'Run. Don't look back. Run.'"

Saul ran toward the village of Mokvyn, six miles away, where his sister lived with her young son. Along the way, however, he was spotted and chased, and he hid until late that night in a ditch. When it was dark, he started to walk. "I didn't know where I'm going, but I walked," he told the interviewer in 1996. "And that woman stopped me, it was maybe eleven o'clock at night, beautiful moon. And she said, 'Where are you going? You're Jewish?' And I said, 'Yes.' And I said, 'I don't know. I thought that I had a sister here, that I would like to find her.' This woman, I find out later, she used to live with a Jewish man. She was a Gentile, Polish, and she had a Jewish man as a friend. And she told me, 'Why don't you stay with me until the morning, and then I'll find out where your sister is.'"

The woman hid Saul in a haystack for two days. He doesn't remember her name. "A beautiful face," he recalled in 1996, "a nice, zaftig woman." On the third night, this same woman saw another boy walking along the road. "And she said, 'What's your name?' And he said, 'I'm Julius Gershkowitz.' And she said, 'I have one of your brothers here.'"

Julius Gershkowitz, Saul's middle brother, had hidden in a secret compartment in the family's root cellar, one of two hiding places built by their father during the occupation. The other, beneath a stair, where Saul's mother and his sister Channah had sought refuge, was discovered the day after the mass murder. As German police led Leah Gershkowitz and her daughter past the root cellar to the pit beyond town, she had said aloud, "*Zay mir gezint. Mir gayen shoyn,*" Be well, we're going. Julius, still in hiding, heard her and escaped that night.

The two boys remained concealed in the haystack several more days, during which time their sister Ruchel and her son were discovered and murdered in Mokvyn. Baruch Gershkowitz, their father, was still alive, having fled from the countryside into the woods. He survived for six or eight months before turning himself in, according to people Saul met in the 1960s in Israel. "They said that they know that he was alive then, and he couldn't stand being alone while his family was killed. He dug himself— they made him dig a grave, and they shot him."

A few days later, the Germans began to scour the countryside for surviving Jews. The woman told Saul and Julius to leave. During the night, they swam across the Sluch River to the forest on the other side. "We started walking for a few days, sleeping in the grass and finding whatever we can. We stole potatoes in the ground. And at night we used to make a hole and make a small little fire to cook the potatoes. Water was a creek water. One day I was drinking the water and I saw little bugs in there. But if you want to drink, you drink." In the woods, they encountered about thirty other Jews from Berezne and the surrounding towns who had also escaped the massacre. Among them were three sisters from Berezne, and very soon, Saul's brother Julius married one of them.

Eventually, this group established contact with the legendary Soviet partisan leader, Colonel Dmitry Nikolaevich Medvedev, whose unit was then operating in the forests around Rovno and Lvov. In his 1948 memoir *Stout Hearts: This Happened Near Rovno*, Medvedev writes of this time. "The Jewish population of Rovno and the surrounding districts was exterminated at the close of August in strict conformity to a plan. The nazis [*sic*] took large groups of Jews out of the town, made them dig graves for themselves and then shot them. Without stopping to see who was dead and who alive they pushed them into the holes and buried them. The vandals spared nobody, neither old folks nor babes in arms. Only a few escaped. But that was far from salvation. On pain of death, the Germans warned the population against assisting Jews. There were announcements of rewards for traitors: a kilogram of salt for every Jew betrayed."

Saul and his companions spent eight months with Medvedev before the partisans sent them away. Of the Soviet partisan leader, Saul said, "He was a very handsome, nice man. One of the women who, from our city, she was very friendly with him. And when he left, she couldn't go with him, because he told her that he's married."

The refugees survived in the forest for another eighteen months, until the Red Army reconquered the Ukraine. In the spring of 1944, Saul returned to Berezne, along with Julius's wife. Julius had left the group in 1943 to fight with the partisans. He was wounded and sent to a hospital in the Siberian town of Chelyabinsk. Their oldest brother, George, had been in the Polish army in 1939 and had spent the war as a Soviet POW. In 1945, by extraordinary coincidence, he was sent to work at this same hospital in Chelyabinsk. "My brother came in, and he looked at the names, and he saw 'Julius Gershkowitz,'" Saul recounted. After the war, the three brothers were reunited, the only survivors from their family, and among only 150 survivors from Berezne. They came to the United States in 1948.

Saul is a distant cousin by marriage of my grandmother's. In the early 1990s, my sister, Dana, had made contact with him while conducting family research. The following year, Saul and his wife, Irma, had joined my family for Thanksgiving in Florida. The VHS of my grandfather's film was sitting in a drawer in the living room where we had drinks and appetizers, but no one thought to look at it. We remained intermittently in touch, but by the time I found the film in 2009, it had been years since we'd spoken.

Now eighty-four years old, Saul responded cautiously to my suggestion that he view the film. "Let's take a look," he said on the telephone, managing to convey reluctance or resignation, as well as something I heard as hopefulness.

That November, I flew again to Florida to visit my mother, and we drove the thirty miles south to Delray Beach, where Saul and Irma had a small bungalow in a gated golf community. My mother and Irma sat on the couch beneath the family photos and discussed the weather, the children, the grandchildren. I tried to press the right combination of buttons to make my DVD appear on the TV. After a few minutes, Saul took his place in an easy chair. He had Einstein-wiry white hair and a bristly mustache, and he leaned back comfortably, with his feet propped up on a footrest. "Okay," he said. I pressed the "Play" button.

"That's not in Berezne," Saul said within a second. "No, because we didn't have porches like this," referring to the second-story balconies above the heads of the people in the picture.

Not Berezne?

"No, it's not Berezne. We didn't have too many people like this. My God. We had about three thousand Jews."

Children pranced before the camera.

"That's not Berezne. No sir. This is a city where they have lights in the streets. We didn't have it. They have posts and lights in the street."

He watched the rest of the film quietly. "All these people are killed," he remarked at the end. *"Az okh un vey,"* a misfortune, a tragedy.

We sat in silence for a moment. I had hoped he would recognize the town and some of the people, especially the children, who were about his age at the time. I thought he might even recognize himself. Now, after showing him the footage, I felt I had falsely raised his expectations. I apologized.

"Okay," Saul said, implying, *Yes, we're both disappointed. But what did we expect?*

So the town in the film was not my grandmother's birthplace, Berezne. Years of Kurtz family lore were wrong. And yet I knew David and Liza had visited Berezne. How had the wrong name gotten passed down?

Sitting with Saul Gershkowitz, I fumbled to recover from my confusion. This was not Berezne. What was Berezne like? I asked.

There was no electricity, no running water, Saul said with Polish-Yiddish diction preserved in his English. Of the streets, he remembered, "Some of them had sidewalks, and some of them were with . . . you know, packed sand."

Were there wooden sidewalks?

Yes, said Saul, confirming a stray detail that Shirley had remembered.

And the buildings?

"Some were brick, some were stucco painted. Some of them wood. Now my house, it's not far from the main street, was wood. And in the back, we had a big farm. Vegetables my mother used to grow. We had two cows. We sold milk. The man came down in the morning after the cows was milked, and he took the cows to pasture, outside the town. They used to have big markets once a week, not far from the church. And the synagogues was on the other side, not far from my house. There was two synagogues. Two rabbis. My rabbi was Rabbi Gedaltsche."

I had heard of Rabbi Gedaltsche. In 1937, he had traveled to Boston to raise money for the people of Berezne.

"Right," said Saul. "Now my father also got papers to emigrate to America. But he didn't want to leave the kids, the wife and kids, alone. He was making money. He was working. He had a good two hands. I remember when the wedding for my sister, Ruchel, there was the whole city. He spent over five hundred dollars. You know what that means, five hundred dollars? The whole city was invited."

Saul took a photo off the wall, a formal family portrait with the parents seated in the center and the children arrayed in size order around them. "That was one sister. That was George. And Julius. That was Channah. And I wasn't born yet. My dad was in the army at that time." The photograph was taken around 1921. It is Saul's only picture of his family.

I had brought a collection of digital photographs that Dana had found online, showing a recent "roots tour" to Berezne by a member of the Jewish genealogical community. The first image was of a woman, the tourist, posing beneath a blue highway sign that showed two roads converging. To the right, Berezne, to the left, Mokvyn, both names written in Ukrainian Cyrillic.

"Mokvyn! You see? That's where my sister was killed," Saul said, surprised to see the names on a modern sign. "That's where I hid myself with Julius. Till we were running into the woods." Saul pointed at the screen to the town straight ahead. "Sarny. This is where my mother was born."

We clicked through the images slowly, someone else's tourist pictures. "Is that the main street?" Saul asked. "Where was the church?"

I didn't know. I could only show him what the woman posing beneath the sign had chosen to photograph. An old one-story building with diamond-shaped decorations in the brickwork. Over the door, the date 1930.

"You see? They're all one story. This used to be straw. Now they put in metal." Saul tapped my computer screen to point out the building's roof, overlapping sheets of corrugated tin. "That's the street. That's the way it was."

The photos showed streets of single-story detached houses, very different in appearance from the two- and three-story blocks of buildings in David Kurtz's film. I could have noticed this earlier. But I'd believed the town in the film was Berezne and had assumed there must be another part of town, not seen in these tourist photographs. Now the discrepancy was obvious.

We came to a photograph of the river, a shallow, reedy stream bisected by a sandbar. "I remember crossing that river to go into the woods," Saul said. We looked at a photograph of an old farmhouse. "You see?" Saul tapped the screen again. "This is made of wood. They interlock." The building was constructed of rectangular wooden beams, fitted together like Lincoln

Logs, notched ends crossing over and under. "Yes, that's what my father . . . he used to work."

The final photos showed two black marble slabs, monuments in Russian and Hebrew commemorating the murders on August 25, 1942. For almost ten seconds, Saul sat silently, reading the inscriptions.

"So they killed thirty-six hundred and eighty people. I never saw that," Saul said, referring to the monument. "I know the old ones. I never saw that."

He asked me to send him copies of the photos, "Not on the Internet," he instructed. And he said he would like to go back, to visit Berezne now. "I wish I would have one of my boys go with us."

"We went to Europe, we went to so many of the different countries," added Irma, who had been listening attentively, only occasionally prompting Saul with forgotten details of his story. "We never went to Poland. We never went to Germany."

The four of us talked about the family for another ten minutes or so, but our interview was over. I could see that the town of Berezne had curled to the surface of Saul's memory. Names, places, physical details had come back to him, and with the help of other images, with the help of a film from that time, he might have remembered more. But the film and the survivor were mismatched, two unrelated sources of information. Now the town retreated again in Saul's mind, a wave receding.

"I don't know why you're going through all of that," Saul said to me as I extracted the DVD from the player, "but it was nice of you."

||||||||||||||||||||

Driving back to my mother's house on I-95 that day, past palm-shaded office parks and shopping malls, I tried to understand what had happened. Liza Kurtz had outlived her husband by twenty-five years. If she'd ever mentioned Poland, she probably would have spoken of her own hometown. Over time, Berezne must have become the name that Shirley and my father associated with the film.

But I realized that Saul had provided an essential clue. If the town in the film was definitely not Berezne, my grandmother's village, it was almost certainly my grandfather's hometown, Nasielsk. Dana had raised this possibility earlier. She had looked up the family histories of Louis and Rosie Malina and Louis's sister, Essie Diamond. The Malina family was also from Nasielsk. I had not paid much attention to Louis. But now, thinking about the film, it was clear. David was behind the camera, invisible. But Louis appeared in almost every scene, cigar in hand, talking with people, walking with a well-dressed family, escorting a distinguished gentleman down the steps. Nasielsk was his hometown, too. Naturally they would visit there. After my mother and I returned to the house, I texted my sister in San Francisco: "And the winner for best Polish shtetl in a 1938 home movie is . . . Nasielsk." Nasielsk, thirty-five miles northwest of Warsaw.

On the phone that night, after a few minutes of research on the Internet, Dana and I discussed the basic information. Like Berezne, Nasielsk had also been home to approximately three thousand Jews in 1938. But unlike Liza's hometown, which was a farming shtetl, Nasielsk was a commercial town. And while Berezne lay in Soviet-occupied Poland from 1939 until the German invasion of Russia in June 1941, the German army overran Nasielsk on September 4, 1939, three days after the invasion of Poland. Immediately, there were acts of terror and roundups of Jews for work details. On October 26, 1939, Nasielsk became part of the German Reich, annexed to East Prussia along with a swath of Polish territory renamed Bezirk Zichenau, the Ciechenów District.

Nasielsk's entire Jewish population was expelled in a single *Aktion* on December 3, 1939. They were put in cattle cars without food or water and shunted along different rail lines for days. Finally, they were deported to the towns of Łuków and Międzyrzec, about seventy-five miles to the east, in the Lublin region of occupied Poland. In the fall of 1942, the ghettos in both towns were emptied as part of Operation Reinhard. The inhabitants were deported to Treblinka and murdered on arrival. Only eighty of Nasielsk's Jews survived the war.

IIIIIIIIIIIIIIIIII

Lindsay Zarwell at the Holocaust Museum helped me search the databases of survivors and the lists of oral histories. We found five native Nasielskers who had recorded their stories. I searched phone books and the Social Security Death Index. Of the five, it appeared that three had died in the last few years. One I could not locate.

I met Susan Weiss, the fifth, at a reception for Holocaust survivors at the Park East Synagogue in New York City in December 2009. In her oral history, given in 1998, she said she was born Cesia Ajzenberg, or Eisenberg, in Nasielsk in 1930, coincidentally with the same birthday as my father. When I met her, however, she gave her birth year as 1932. She was either six or eight years old when my grandparents visited Nasielsk in 1938.

Wearing a bright red blazer and with neatly coiffed blond hair, Susan stood out among the sixty or so people, mostly women, assembled for bagels and coffee in the synagogue's basement. The first thing she said was that she was uncomfortable in the community of survivors. "I come here, but I feel I have nothing in common, because I was brought up living with the people from here," she said, meaning the United States. She arrived in 1947, the sole survivor of a family of nine, having passed through a series of ghettos and lived in the forest from 1942 to 1945.

"With us, in Nasielsk, the Germans told us—came in with guns—'get out!' And they brought us to a synagogue. And there they put us on the cattle trains for a week or two without water. And then let us off in a little town called Łuków, the first ghetto. And there were like six families in one room, or in a corner. And then they sent us to Parczew, Kock, all these ghettos," she said. "We tried to go to Russia. So my father and two siblings went to Warsaw and then tried to go to Russia. But they got stuck there. They got stuck—was how they died. Without food. And my sister died in Białystok. This was all told to me. I was not with them. I saw my mother die. My mother died. She was frozen. I remember. People put a match to here, like this . . ." She waved a finger beneath her nose. "This I just recalled the other night."

It was difficult to follow her. At first I tried to stop her, to clarify where and when her memories belonged. But after a little while, I let her remember how she remembered.

"I was hidden under the bed," she said. "My sister was working, taking care of the stuff for the Germans, and the killing of the people. They took the gold, the money, and clothes. And she was [sorting] that. And I was hidden under the bed."

This was a ghetto, I asked, not a camp?

"A ghetto. A ghetto," she said. And a moment later, "My mother, two sisters, and a brother. Two brothers. And one baby, we were—you see this?" She pointed to the food carts, trays stacked one atop another. "They look like beds? On top. The Germans came in and took my sister and two brothers, and they didn't see me. And they shot them. I was just laying there quietly. I came down, and I waited for my sister to came back from work. And then they brought me—you know, in Europe, everybody wore boots. They brought me the boots, and they were full of blood. But I didn't quite get it. I didn't understand. Now things are coming back."

Susan spoke without particular inflection, in a voice that mixed Yiddish and Bronx accents. If her tone expressed anything, it was a kind of amazement. "It's unbelievable," she said a few times as she jumped quickly between memory fragments.

"For me, after the war was worse than during the wartime," she said. "During the war you had to run, between the bombs and the shooting. But after the war where do you go? Who claims you? Nobody claimed me."

After the war, thirteen or fifteen years old, she had wandered to the Zeilsheim displaced persons camp outside of Frankfurt am Main, where by coincidence, a cousin was a U.S. soldier. He helped arrange for her to emigrate to America. Once here, she suppressed the memory of her experiences. "In order to live a normal life, you had to shut it off. Push it back," she told me. Although she gave an oral history interview in 1998, she did so reluctantly. Not even her children knew the full story of her survival.

I asked why she had started coming to survivor gatherings.

"Sixty years later, things are happening," Susan responded. "Now that I lose my husband and my kids are married, it's coming back. The way I survived, where I was chased. You know, when you get older, you can't sleep, so I say, 'Let me see.' I try to recall my siblings . . . I can't picture them. I can't picture my parents."

Having avoided remembering for so long, Susan was now afraid it might be too late. "What scares me, on Sunday I'm with some people. They're losing it. Dementia. It's very frightening. Because I can only say, 'That's me around the block.'"

What I sensed from talking with her, however, was not the onset of dementia. She was afraid of forgetting, but equally afraid to remember. The two fears collided, producing a jagged, halting kind of memory, reflected in the way she spoke.

"I was once hidden. Where the cows were. The Germans came looking for me. The woman would milk at night so that nobody saw me. And the Germans, the Gestapo didn't see me." She looked at me. "Do you know, when I say these things, it's like it's not real. Yet it happened to me."

Susan's first response to almost every question was that she didn't remember. "Nothing. I don't even remember the street I lived on. I have no recall." But when I asked specific questions, she sometimes responded with isolated images. Were there trees on the streets? "No trees. There were more patches. On one side Jews, on one side Gentiles, and the cows were in the back. I remember grass."

When I showed her the film, she commented immediately on the number of people gathered in front of the camera, just as Saul Gershkowitz had. "Maybe it wasn't so small. I thought it was a small town." She considered the people. "Certainly a lot of religious Jews."

We came to the scene where people enter what I believed to be the synagogue. "I don't even remember a synagogue," she said, even though she'd mentioned it before, as the place where people were confined prior to the deportation. "That's all from Nasielsk?"

But when I drew her attention to the buildings and asked about her home, she recalled playing hopscotch on the sidewalk. "I remember we had two bedrooms. The kids would sleep two in a bed. The floors were red. It was next to a big factory. I think they made buttons." This corresponded with a detail Shirley had mentioned, that Liza once referred to a button factory in the town, though she had implied it was in Berezne.

A detail Saul Gershkowitz had noticed also sparked Susan's most specific memory. I pointed out the balconies with their elaborate iron grillwork. "Yes, that's the way it was. That I recall," Susan said. "Little terraces.

I remember I used to go to the garden and pick out the weeds and put the prettier things in a pot on the terrace." This is the closest she came to identifying the town in the film.

I played the crowd scenes in slow motion, advancing frame by frame so Susan could study the images.

"Just people and faces," she said. "Even if it would be my brother and sisters, I would not remember."

In her 1998 oral history, eleven years before I met her, Susan had recalled much more. She remembered the names of her siblings, and those of her parents, Libo, her mother, and Mordehai, her father. Sitting at the Park East Synagogue, she had not been able to bring these names to mind. When I asked about her father, she said, "I think he was a rabbi. I don't know if you've ever heard of the Gerrer Rebbe, the big rabbi," referring to the leader of a Hasidic sect. "I'm a cousin. It was told to me. I don't know these things. So as a Jew, I'm very elite. So when I came here, they said, 'You have to date rabbis.' I said, 'Like hell!'"

In 1998, she had also been able to recount her experiences during the war with greater detail. The United States Holocaust Memorial Museum's *Encyclopedia of Camps and Ghettos* makes use of her testimony in the entry for the Polish town of Kock, located thirty miles south of Łuków and thirty miles north of Lublin. "Susan Weiss remembered that the reserve policemen stormed the ghetto one day, rounded up hundreds of nonworking Jews and shot them dead. Weiss likely was recalling the mass killing of 161 to 189 Jews on September 26, 1942."

Susan was probably transferred from the ghetto at Łuków to the one at Parczew, twenty-five miles south, in late 1940, and from there, west another twenty-five miles to Kock in mid-1941. The three towns form a triangle. It is also probable, though impossible to verify, that her sister and two brothers were shot during this massacre in Kock in September 1942. By that time, Susan was perhaps eleven, at most thirteen years old.

In 2009, seventy-nine or eighty-one years old, sitting in the crowded luncheon room at a round table with several other survivors, Susan was not able to gather her experiences or to connect her recollections with the scenes in my grandfather's film. Her memory was like a picture seen through a sieve. Individual points stood out, but the spaces between them were blank. The sieve kept moving, and the visible points shifted. Had she been willing, had we had infinite time, it felt as if we might someday be able to describe a coherent image. But her ambivalence was too strong. She remembered and she insisted she could not remember.

"You know, the pictures are vivid," she remarked when I let the film play a second time. "Like it's now."

Essie Diamond walks across what looks like the central marketplace. I pointed out the balconies on the buildings, the shapes of the doorways and their wooden shutters, the line of roofs with stubby chimneys. The marketplace was paved with cobblestones, I observed, hoping to free a memory that might help positively identify the town. Did that seem right?

"Yes, yes," Susan said, looking at the image on the screen and quickly looking away. "Quite right. But I don't recall."

When we said goodbye, Susan apologized for not being able to provide better answers. "Maybe for me I felt that it's good that I . . ." She paused, and I waited. After a moment, I helped her complete the thought. "That you don't remember?" "Yes," she said.

Several months later, I spoke with Susan again, and she said our talk had been disturbing to her. "I didn't realize what happens when you start telling stories," she said. "You lose yourself. For several days, I couldn't find myself."

In her oral history interview in 1998, Susan had also expressed this fear of losing herself to what had happened. She looks at the interviewer, maybe sadly, maybe defiantly. "In order for me to survive, to live, I made sure that all those things, since I lost them at such an early age, that I do not recall them," she had said. "Only in my dreams."

ııııııııııııııııı

Susan Weiss, the only survivor I had been able to locate, was unable to provide a positive identification of the town in my grandfather's film. In early December 2009, therefore, I turned to libraries and archives to seek confirmation and to learn what I could about Nasielsk.

At the New York Public Library, I found a privately printed book,

Nashelsk—A Name A City A People Eternal! This eighty-page commemorative booklet, which used the Americanized spelling of the town's name, was dated March 12, 1953, and celebrated the opening of an apartment complex called Nachlat Nashelsk, "New Nasielsk," outside Tel Aviv in Israel. Paid for by the United Nashelsker Relief Society, based in Los Angeles, the apartments were intended for survivors from the town. The book's cover pictured a simple two-story apartment house with four units, two on either side of a central stairway. The building stands forlornly on an empty lot, and three children play in the unlandscaped sand. Half of the book's pages were devoted to lists of contributors. David and Liza Kurtz are not included. But I noted "M. Malina," which may have referred to Louis and been one of the book's numerous typographical errors. Over the coming years, I would become familiar with the names of many Nasielsk *landslayt* who appear on these lists, "countrymen" from New York, Buffalo, Detroit, Chicago, Los Angeles, and elsewhere. But that day in the library, it was not the names but the pages of photographs that caught my attention: "Leaders of Aid Committee, Nashelsk. 1938." "Theater group in Nashelsk." Dozens of faces, often with names written in Yiddish beneath the photos. There were also two images of the Nasielsk synagogue.

The first photograph showed the building's grand Romanesque revival façade. A three-story central structure was supported by two massive columns, between which soared three gracefully arched stained-glass windows, topped by a rosette. Two smaller columns on rectangular bases flanked the entryway. Some of these features matched the building seen in my grandfather's film.

I copied the image and e-mailed it to Lindsay Zarwell at the Holocaust Museum. She wrote back, agreeing that we could erase the central question mark in the catalogue record. The building in the film was definitely the Nasielsk synagogue. We had confirmed the town.

Searching online, I discovered that the present city of Nasielsk has a website. From this, I learned that the first mention of the town was in 1065, the year before the Norman conquest of England, in a document prepared by King Bolesław Śmiały. In 1257, Prince Siemowit I of Mazovia—the name of this region in northern Poland—granted part of the territory

די שול נאָכן חורבן. פּויערים באַאַרבעטן
די ערד פֿון שול-הויף.
Nashelsker Synagogue — destroyed and deserted,
peasants using land for farming.

די נאשעלסקער שול (פֿאַרן חורבן).
Nashelsker Synagogue "in all its glory"
before Hitlerism.

to a religious order. Prince Janusz I presented the remainder of the territory as a gift to "his favorite knight," Jakusz (Jakub) of Radzanów, on November 11, 1386. The town remained the property of his family until 1647, when it was sold to someone named Wessel. In 1795, Count Stanisław of Lubrawiec Dembski became the town's owner. Between 1806 and 1812, Napoleon's army occupied Nasielsk and fought a battle there against Prussian and Czarist forces. In 1845, Józef Koźmiński, who had purchased the town a decade earlier, sold it to a man named Aleksander Kurtz.

This sent me to the New York Public Library again. Aleksander Kurtz, I learned from a Polish biographical encyclopedia, was born in Warsaw in 1814, son of a wealthy tannery owner. He was an Evangelical Christian, likely of Prussian descent, and in the 1830s, he studied economics in Berlin. This Kurtz was not a relative of mine. It was just a strange coincidence.

In 1877, a rail line connecting Warsaw and Gdańsk, then called Danzig, was opened, running through Nasielsk. This rail line put Nasielsk on the map of larger Polish history, making it a strategic junction on the road to Warsaw. The German army occupied Nasielsk during most of World War I. And in 1920, after the declaration of Polish independence, Marshal Piłsudski's army repelled the Russian Bolshevik units besieging Warsaw in a counterattack outside the town.

I had read about the Soviet raids on eastern Poland after the First World War, chronicled in Isaac Babel's masterful *Red Cavalry* stories, which take place in the area close to Berezne. The Battle of Nasielsk, by contrast, had a lesser muse. On August 20, 1920, A. A. Davidson of the *New York Times* wired a report under the headline "Bolsheviki in Panic Abandon Their Guns." "We are all busy rushing our little flags back on the map and Warsaw is breathing more deeply as the Russian grip on her is becoming relaxed," the reporter wrote. "The Bolshevist flood came up against a hardened wall on the Vistula and struck it, only to be forced to recede."

By 1921, according to the Nasielsk municipal website, the town had a population of approximately five thousand, and by 1939, it had grown to almost seven thousand. The final entry on the website's chronology covered the war years: "1939–1945: the city and municipality of Nasielsk are . . . incorporated to the German Reich." This is apparently as far as history goes in the municipal memory of the town of Nasielsk, which was highly selective in other respects, as well. In the chronology on the website, for example, there was no mention of the presence of Jews in the town, although by 1939, Jewish residents accounted for half the total population.

Searching historical news reports, I found two brief notices about Nasielsk that painted a grim picture of Jewish life there before the war. On June 13, 1923, the Jewish Telegraphic Agency published an article entitled "Another Blood Ritual Accusation Exploded." "A murder accusation which threw the entire Jewish population of the township of Nasielsk in turmoil was exploded today by the discovery of the alleged victim alive and sound." And on June 18, 1937, the *Washington Post* printed a brief Associated Press item, "Poles Beat Jews." "A crowd of Polish anti-Semites attacked a man who was buying from a Jewish merchant today, then turned on a number of Jews, beat them, and smashed windows. Seven persons were arrested."

Another website, Virtual Shtetl, run by the recently founded Museum of the History of Polish Jews, in Warsaw, offered a brief sketch of Nasielsk's history from a Jewish perspective, drawn primarily from the research of the Polish historian Janusz Szczepański. From these sources, I learned that Jews settled in the area around Nasielsk as early as the fifteenth century, with a small community in the town itself by the beginning of the sixteenth century. By 1650, Nasielsk had its own wooden temple. "Its constructor was Simche Weiss, the son of Szlomo from Łuck. It was one of the most beautiful synagogues in Poland," according to the article by Tomasz Kawski. This famous wooden synagogue stood for more than two hundred years until it either burned or was torn down in the 1880s and the brick structure, which my grandfather filmed, replaced it. A drawing and a scale model of the wooden synagogue were easy to locate online.

While this background information was important, it did not bring me closer to the kind of history I wanted to know, specific stories that might illuminate what appears in my grandfather's film. According to the historian Szczepański, Jews constituted 67.3 percent of the population when Napoleon marched through Nasielsk. By 1921, the percentage had fallen to 53.5. "In the period between 1830 and the 1863 uprisings significant changes occurred in Jewish society," Szczepański writes. "The Jewish intelligentsia started to assimilate the language, attire and habits of the Polish environment and more actively participated in its political and intellectual life." This must have been true for *some* of the Jews among the intelligentsia of the mid-nineteenth century, but certainly not for all. In historical writing like this, however, it doesn't make sense to ask, *Which ones? Who?* It seemed relevant to know that many Jewish workers joined the socialist Bund in 1905, and that after the First World War, the Bund was opposed by the conservative religious party, Agudas Israel, as well as by several stripes of Zionists. But I wondered what to make of the other, hard-won insights, in which historians of a certain kind seem to delight. "The biggest share in the expenses of a Jewish community constitutes the rabbi's salary, e.g. in Nasielsk it amounted to 48%."

David Kurtz's film offered an exceedingly narrow view into the life of Nasielsk's Jewish community. But at the same time, it was a unique and minutely detailed view. The film called out for a different kind of history, a microhistory, more personal and individual.

In the archives of the YIVO Institute in New York, devoted to the cultural history of Jewish life in Eastern Europe, I found documents from the

American Jewish Joint Distribution Committee's Landsmanshaftn Department. The JDC, universally referred to as "the Joint," was founded in 1914, at the start of World War I, to aid destitute Jews in Palestine, Europe, and, in time, around the world. The Landsmanshaftn Department coordinated activities with the many independent benevolent societies set up by American emigrants who sent money back to their Old World hometowns in Poland, the Austro-Hungarian Empire, and Russia.

In the files, I found a report that surveyed the Jewish social institutions in Nasielsk in the early 1930s. "The Jewish population numbers about 550 families, living mainly on small trade and partly on handicraft. The number of shops belonging to Jews is 150 and that of market-dealers is 50. There is a large Jewish factory of buttons, employing a certain number of Jewish workers as well." The report also noted the Beth Jacob (Beys Jakov) School for Girls, with 151 students, and the "Yesodey-Hathora," the religious school, or cheder, with an equal number of boys. The Joint subsidized both schools.

Archival sources provided a completely different scale of information than general histories. Here, instead of broad context, I gathered isolated details like those in my grandfather's film. For example, the files at YIVO also contained memoranda concerning the status of a free-loan association, called a *kassa* or *gemilut chesed*, literally "loving-kindness," sponsored by the Joint. "The Kassa writes to us that their American Landsleute are sending every year quite important sums to their native town which are distributed for individual relief," the New York office wrote to a Joint representative in Paris on March 11, 1938, a day before the German Anschluss of Austria. "Now the Landsmannschaft wants to transmit certain funds for relief along constructive lines—and there arose the question by which local organization or committee these funds have to be administered."

The sums involved were indeed considerable. An article published in the *Forward*, the Yiddish-language daily newspaper, on July 7, 1938, reported on the Second Annual Convention of Nasielsk *landslayt* or *Landsleut* in America, held in Buffalo, New York, hometown of the Relief Society's new president, Louis Silverstein. "Last year the sum of $2,000 was collected for relief from among the Nasielsk Landsleut," the report announced proudly. "This year, the new committee for Nasielsk has undertaken to raise $5,000." These sums are the equivalent of $32,600 and $81,500, respectively, in 2013 purchasing power.

There were, it appears, three rival loan associations active at the time in Nasielsk, including the one supported by the Joint, all seeking access to these funds. Deeper in the file I read a document detailing a fact-finding mission to Nasielsk by the Joint's Warsaw representative on August 7, 1938. This would have been within a week or two of my grandparents' visit. The mission sought to determine whether the two *kassas* competing against the Joint were trustworthy. It concluded they were not. The first, called the Achiezer *kassa*, "is subsidized by a wealthy Landsmann from London; he covers even the administration expenses. This *kassa* is not subject to any social control," meaning the Joint could exert no influence over his decisions. The second competing *kassa* "is entirely influenced by the 'Bund,'" the Socialist political party. "Loans are being given only to members of the 'Bund' or to such persons who sign a form to enroll [in] this party. Such a case happened recently to the local cabdrivers: only those of them received loans from the *kassa* who enrolled in the 'Bund.'"

These memoranda provided a snapshot of social life in the town, similar to that contained in my grandfather's film. Both sources captured unique details of ordinary life. Both provoked the question *What am I looking at?* My only answer seemed to be to dig deeper, to look for an even finer degree of detail.

On October 14, 1938, four days after the German occupation of the Czechoslovakian border region, the Sudetenland, another memorandum in the YIVO files noted the names of the new board members of the Joint's free loan *kassa*, elected to administer the funds arriving from America.

Mr. Salmon Kaczyński—landlord/grocer

Mr. David Kubel—artisan/tailor

Mr. Zelig M. Zilbersztejn—artisan/shoemaker

Mr. Mordchai Rajtszyk—baker/socialist

Mr. Abraham H. Drzyk—landlord

Mr. Mejer Wajngarten—timber-merchant

Mr. I. Rojtkopf—ironmonger

Mr. Aron Waks—landlord/dentist
Mr. Mojsze Cyrlak—drapery-merchant
Mr. Fajwel Lejbowicz—timber-merchant
Mr. Chaim Huberman—laborer
Mr. I. Sznajderman—tailor

These were the first individual names I discovered, people active in Nasielsk at the time of my grandparents' visit. I had no idea what to do with these names when I found them. Still, they felt like a major discovery, information on the same scale as the images in the film.

The final two documents I found at YIVO were composed after the war, brittle, yellowing photostats on A4 or legal-size paper. The first, dated March 2, 1946, announced the formation of a committee of survivors from Nasielsk in Warsaw. Stamped with the seal of the Jewish Committee in Warsaw, the page bore the signatures of the new officers: Chairman Mojzesz Tuchendler; Secretary Jankiel Jagoda; Treasurer Samuel Tyk. The second document listed the survivors. There were eighteen names.

For the first time, pieces of research began to connect. In the photo archives of the United States Holocaust Memorial Museum, Lindsay Zarwell had found a handful of images donated in the 1980s by Faiga Tick, born Fajga Milchberg in Nasielsk in 1917. Faiga Tick/Fajga Tyk: she appeared as number sixteen on the Joint's list of survivors, one line beneath her husband, Szmuel, Samuel, the treasurer of the Survivors' Committee. According to the information accompanying the photographs in the Holocaust Museum's archives, Faiga survived the war in a Soviet forced labor camp in Vologda province, then emigrated to Canada in 1948. Unfortunately, the address for her on the information sheet was no longer valid. Three of the photos she donated showed groups of schoolboys, among whom Faiga's brother Yehiel Milchberg was the only one identified by name. Another photo featured ten young adults, identified as members of a Zionist youth group. Among those pictured, according to the caption, were Leah Rutstein and Neshka Rosenberg, two of the three women in the photo. But the caption did not indicate which was Leah and which was Neshka.

Digging into the databases hosted by JewishGen.org, an online genealogical research community, I found the 1929 business directory for
Nasielsk, listing all the bakers, tailors, blacksmiths, grain merchants, and
other professionals and artisans in the town, their occupations printed in
Polish and French. Here were names slowly becoming familiar to me: Jagoda, "maker of soda water," the same family as Jankiel Jagoda, number six
on the survivors list and secretary of the Survivors' Committee. Kaczyński,
Z., grocer, who appeared on the board of the Joint's *kassa* as "Mr. Salmon
Kaczyński, landlord/grocer." Two men named Kubel were in the directory,
both tailors, undoubtedly from the same family as Mr. David Kubel, arti-
san/tailor, also one of the *kassa*'s directors. Mr. Rajtszyk, or Rajczyk, who
gave his occupation as "baker/socialist" on the list of *kassa* directors, appears in the directory simply under "Piekarnie (*boulangers*)," bakeries.

I had begun to accumulate names, to associate documents. I created a
spreadsheet, several spreadsheets. My career as a list maker commenced.

I viewed the five oral history testimonies of Nasielsk natives collected
by the Shoah Foundation for the Visual History Archive. Gloria Rubin,
born Gitta Piekarek in 1929, had been a student at the Beth Jacob School
for Girls, mentioned in the Joint's report on the institutions run by the
town's Jewish community. Her father owned a flour mill, and Piekarek,
M., is listed in the business directory under "Kaszarnie (*fabrication de
guru*)," grain, maker of gruel. In the video shot in Los Angeles in 1996,
Gloria Rubin recalled Nasielsk as "a nice little community, mostly Jews."

Czarna Ida Zimmer's maiden name was Kulas, and her father was
listed in the 1929 business directory as a butcher. Czarna was born in 1914.
As in most of these oral histories, her story of survival overshadowed the
impressions she retained of her childhood. She spoke for more than two
hours. But she spent less than five minutes describing her early life. At the
end of her interview, she showed photographs of her family, her brothers
and sisters and parents, all murdered. I copied these photographs from the
screen.

Studying my grandfather's film frame by frame, I searched for the boys
in Faiga Tick's photos, for Czarna Ida Zimmer's brothers and sisters, and
for the families of the other survivors who gave testimony, without success.

I flew over Nasielsk with Google Maps and culled recent tourist photographs of the town from the photo-sharing website Flickr. These photos showed two- and three-story houses, similar to the ones in my grandfather's film, with the same wrought-iron balconies. I found a current photo of Nasielsk's church spire, which appears in the background of three frames in the film, and compared the two images side by side.

After months of watching the film, I got to know the faces of the people in the movie quite intimately. I recognized the cast of characters whose expressions or gestures stood out and the people in the background, who did not know the camera had captured them. The tough boy who shoves the girl with braids; two older men with beards, one long and white, one short and gray, who stare placidly, thoughtfully at the camera; two young men in matching black coats, who stand calmly while their neighbors flutter around them.

In this way, a year and a half passed since I had discovered the film in a musty cardboard box at my parents' house. I had ensured its preservation and had identified the town. I had sifted through archival material and had learned a host of names. But by December 2010, I believed I had gone as far as was possible. Despite the few connections I had made, I had no way to relate the documents in the archives to the images in the film. They remained only names and faces. I feared I had discovered the film too late to learn anything of significance about who and what it showed. With no clear path forward, I resumed work on my novel about Vienna and more or less stopped researching the town in my grandfather's film.

5

A SEA OF GHOSTS

MAURICE CHANDLER STANDS in the former marketplace of Nasielsk, in front of the house where he was born. It is August 18, 2011, seventy-two years after he was forced to flee this town. The building is three stories tall, with plaster and stone now crumbling onto the sidewalk. Half of the ground floor has been refurbished, with a new window and new paint, a pearlish off-white. The other half, although it also has a new window, is a moldy tan with an undertone of pink. On the upper floors, the plaster façade flakes off to reveal a layer of rust-orange over a deeper layer of brownish yellow, like a lemon left too long on the counter. There is water damage along the roofline, beneath the windows, and under the upper of two balconies. In a few places, the brickwork is exposed.

"This is the bedroom I was born in," he tells his daughter, Evelyn, and her husband, Steve Rosen.

"That window?" Evelyn asks. She is pointing her phone at the building's façade, capturing the moment on video.

"Yeah," responds Mr. Chandler. "And this is the balcony that . . . as a little kid one time we . . . I don't want to say it . . . we peed on the balcony, and a policeman was walking by. It was right on him."

The bedroom window is half obscured by a yellow and red sign affixed to the balcony. The sign says "BAR. ORIENTAL CACH-CACH." A Coca-Cola bottle rises from a froth of white bubbles. The ground floor is now a restaurant.

"Turkish. They're everywhere," comments the young Polish driver who has brought Maurice Chandler and his family here in a Mercedes sedan, now parked in front of the building.

"We owned the one to the right, also," Mr. Chandler continues. "But this is the one, in the middle . . . the three stories."

Maurice Chandler is eighty-six years old. He is wearing a short-sleeved blue polo shirt, black Levi's, white sneakers, and sunglasses, a variation on the outfit common among older Americans on tour in Europe.

"And next door lived a Mrs. Wyszyńska. We'll go in and just ask some questions of the people. Okay?"

But instead of going in, the family lingers on the street in front of the house. This is Maurice Chandler's fourth visit to Nasielsk since leaving Europe after the war. The first time was in 1973 with his wife, Dorris. By then a successful American businessman, Mr. Chandler participated in a trade mission to Eastern Europe. After a meeting at the Jabłonowski Palace in Warsaw, the couple went back to their hotel and danced around the room. The way he had left Poland in 1946, an orphan, destitute, and the way he had now returned, successful, a husband and father.

He returned again in 1988 for the forty-fifth anniversary of the Warsaw Ghetto Uprising, and then twice more in the 1990s on trips with his children. Now, with Evelyn, his eldest child, the only one who has not visited Nasielsk with him, Maurice Chandler makes the trip once more.

"Since I'm getting younger every year . . ." he'd quipped to the driver earlier, on the hour-long ride from their hotel in Warsaw. "My house is still there. I call it 'mine.' It's not mine anymore. And I don't want it. People live there, and it's fine. I just want to show my children the room where I was born. And that's it."

Now they stand in front of the house.

"This was the bakery, here." He points to a boarded-up window at sidewalk level, peeking up from the building's basement. "This was the bakery. He used to pinch my cheeks. And I used to always run away from him. I must have been five years old. He drove me crazy. Every time. He had like a three-day beard, four-, five-day beard. It was like needles. And one time I fell on the floor and came into the house bleeding, you know, from my nose. I mean, that's what I remember. His name was Mr. Rajczyk."

They walk around the row of buildings to the back of the house and enter the rubble-strewn yard.

"See this building? It was attached to our main building, and this is where we had our dining room."

The low, single-story structure extends at a right angle from the house into the center of the interior lot. It is behind a fence, and an old sign leans against the wall where the brick is showing. Weeds and shrubs compete for scant sunlight. It is August, but the small rectangular lot is six inches deep in brown leaves.

"Mr. Perelmuter lived on this side," Mr. Chandler says, indicating the collapsed wooden shed to his right.

They enter his former home through the back door. The hallway is dilapidated to the point of ruin.

"Is it safe to walk in here?" Evelyn Rosen worries as her father climbs the wooden stairway past debris and crumbling plaster to the second floor.

All the doors are open. Mr. Chandler points to the doorframe. A gouge in the wood outlines where a mezuzah has been pried away.

The driver has come up the stairs ahead of them and is talking with the young Vietnamese man who now lives in the apartment once occupied by Mr. Chandler's family. The young man stands against a wall, bewildered, his arms crossed, as the Americans enter the room. His Polish is not very good, but the driver assures Evelyn he understands why they are there.

A white plastic patio chair and a small wooden desk occupy the dining area. Through a doorway, there is a mattress on the floor, piles of clothing, a white stuffed bear against the wall next to a two-tone wood-veneer dresser. Lace curtains cover the window.

"This was the bedroom," Maurice Chandler says. "But it was bigger. You see? This wall is new. It was a big bedroom. And there were stairs that led to the store downstairs."

"In this bedroom?" Evelyn asks. "Is there anything that you recognize from . . ."

"No. No."

It is the same building, the very room. But nothing has been preserved. If they were looking for something, some connection, it isn't here.

They leave the room and encounter an older woman in the hallway, brought out by the unfamiliar voices. Mr. Chandler speaks with her in Polish. He mentions the name Srul Skalka, his grandfather, the man who once owned this building. He asks about a family, Tomasiński, friends of his grandfather, and about other former neighbors. The woman doesn't remember or doesn't know.

They exit through the back door, past the former dining room. Standing out front again, Mr. Chandler looks down the street. He turns to look across the square that was once an open cobblestoned marketplace but is now a tree-lined park with a statue of Pope John Paul II in the center. He walks down the sidewalk alone, away from his family.

Evelyn Rosen stands in front of the building. She speaks into her phone, narrating the home video she is recording for posterity.

"So my ancestral home is now a kebab restaurant. We're not even going in, because my father said, 'What's the point?'"

A few minutes later, they're standing on the corner of the square.

"Outside of where I was born, in that building, that's it. The rest is all just . . ."

"None of this is the same?" Steve Rosen, Evelyn's husband, asks. "I mean, none? Like these buildings?"

"Everything is modern now," observes Evelyn.

"I'm looking for someone old," says Mr. Chandler. He eyes the passersby. "She's old enough." He indicates a woman with a shopping bag crossing ahead of them. "So how do you catch her?"

"We walk across the street," answers Steve, starting to go after the old woman.

"No, no," Mr. Chandler calls him back. "She'll be scared."

So they get back in the car and drive around in search of other old people. They drive past what Mr. Chandler remembers as the Jewish cemetery, which is now a field with crops. At the supermarket, they decide it doesn't make sense to try to find someone at random. Instead, the driver suggests they go to city hall. It's a good suggestion, and there, for more than an hour, Mr. Chandler sits and talks in Polish with the current mayor of Nasielsk.

Afterward, in the car leaving town, his mood has changed.

"He is a very fine man," he says of the mayor. "I mean, this is a fine gentleman. Because usually they are, what they call in Russian, an appa- ratchik. It means a bureaucrat. And they never have time for the 'common people,' for the 'peasants.' And he took the time. Came out, smiled, offered us a drink, and talked as long as you wanted. That was beautiful."

Evelyn wants to know what they talked about.

"Well, we talked about the people. His parents died. But the parents that died were my age. And they knew—he said he heard them talk about the So-and-Sos and the So-and-Sos."

Maybe Mr. Chandler says more, is more specific. But it's not captured on the video. In the next clip, they're still in the car, driving in silence along Route 632, a two-lane road bordered by linden trees, passing farms and small towns on the way back to Warsaw.

||||||||||||||||||

When Evelyn and Steve Rosen return home to Bloomfield, Michigan, in August 2011, they have recorded more than twenty gigabytes of brief, shaky, unedited video of Maurice Chandler in Poland. The clips are hard to watch in their raw form, and everyone agrees that something should be done to make them more viewable. At some point in the fall, the digital files end up with Marcy Rosen, Evelyn and Steve's daughter, a lawyer, a new mother, a vivacious, very busy woman. She discusses the task with her assistant and friend, Jeff Widen, and as they talk, their plans for the videos become elaborate. They imagine translations from the Polish and Yiddish, subtitles, an animated family tree, photos of all the family mem- bers. A keepsake for the generations.

Earlier that fall, just after her grandfather's trip to Poland, Marcy Rosen had surreptitiously recorded him telling his astonishing tale of es- cape from the Warsaw Ghetto. She had also shared this recording with her assistant, Jeff, and he had listened to it intently. He'd become a fan of Marcy's grandfather, occasionally even quoting lines to her from the recording. Jeff is a devotee of history, widely read, and a member of the Society for Creative Anachronism, which stages historical reenactments. Part of his job as Marcy's legal assistant involves combing databases for background information about clients and cases. The new project is just up his alley, so Marcy gives the job of organizing the travel videos to him. Jeff puts the files from Evelyn and Steve on DVD and, in the lulls of his workday, begins searching the Internet for information about the town where Marcy's grandfather was born, hoping to add "sprinkles and toppings" to the family videos. Online documentation is scarce. But over the course of several days, he keeps digging.

He comes up with a page at the Museum of Family History, showing a photograph of Samuel Perlmutter of Nasielsk. He e-mails it to Marcy and her parents. "Your grandfather's neighbor—yes?"

He finds a photo of the German Wehrmacht, soldiers on motorcycles with sidecars entering the town of Nasielsk in 1939. He finds images of the great wooden synagogue in Nasielsk, one of the grandest in all Poland. He finds a link to a family film about Nasielsk in the catalogue of the Film and Video Archive at the United States Holocaust Memorial Museum in Washington, D.C.

On December 7, 2011, he forwards the link to Evelyn and Steve Rosen, cc'ing Marcy. "You're going to flip when you see this little gem I found in the Steven Spielberg Holocaust Archive. 1938 home movie shot in Nasielsk. Town square . . . perhaps the family home/store in the background?"

He attaches the page from the catalogue. "David and Lena (Liza) Kurtz travelled to Europe from New York in 1938. Both were born in Poland and emigrated to the U.S. in the 1890s." The catalogue describes the film clip. "Several wonderful street scenes of people, especially children, in the Jewish quarter grinning and vying for the camera's attention."

Jeff's e-mail is stamped 6:32 p.m. It's not until the next morning that the Rosens open it and read his message.

Marcy is at her desk at the office, and she makes her morning call to her parents. She's on the phone with her father, who's sitting at home at the small desk in the kitchen, where the computer is. They click on the link and watch the film together, still talking on the phone.

Perhaps a hundred people crowd the street in front of a black sedan. Children jump up and down, making faces. They leap and swarm the cameraman as he pans across a row of buildings. He keeps the focus above the heads of the children, on the façades behind them. But the kids are too enthusiastic. They jump and wave their arms. The seconds go by, more and more faces make their way into the viewfinder.

At thirty-five seconds, Marcy Rosen, sitting at her desk in the office, and her father, sitting at home in the kitchen, both see a boy's face flash across the screen.

"Oh my God. It's Grandpa! It's Grandpa!"

Steve Rosen calls to his wife. "It's your father!"

They stop the video, drag the cursor back, view it again. Again. Again. They're laughing, crying, shouting, in shock. The face, the expression.

Maurice Chandler—born Moszek Tuchendler in Nasielsk, Poland, on November 16, 1924, middle of three sons of Chawa and Szaja Tuchendler, sole survivor of his family, now father, grandfather, great-grandfather—is thirteen years old in August 1938, when he appears for one and a half seconds in David Kurtz's home movie. A thirteen-year-old boy in his home village, amid his friends and neighbors, the shops, the homes, the bustle of life.

Seventy-three years and 126 days later, and eight hours after his daughter and granddaughter launch a flurry of frantic calls trying to reach him, he sits at the kitchen table of his winter home in Boca Raton, Florida, while Dorris, his wife of sixty years, plays the film on the computer.

"Look at you! You won't believe this!" she calls to him. "You're in a sea of ghosts."

||||||||||||||||||

On December 8, 2011, I spent the day working at the New York Public Library on Fifth Avenue and Forty-Second Street, the grand building with the lions out front. I was still researching my novel about a young woman who discovers an abandoned home movie in the Vienna flea market and becomes obsessed with discovering the fate of the people who appear in it.

I was almost finished with a draft of the book. But I needed to fill in more details about how the two brothers in this fictional film escape from Vienna in September 1940, and what happens to them on the dangerous voyage down the Danube and across the Black Sea.

By late afternoon, my eyes were tired, and the pink skies painted on the reading room's ceiling seemed as gray and dull as the real sky outside. I gathered my computer and notebook and left the building. As I pushed through the revolving doors to the street, I checked my e-mail on my phone. There was a message forwarded by my literary agent with the comment "Amazing."

> *Today I found videos that Mr. Kurtz donated to the United States Holocaust Museum and the Film and Video archives. There was video footage from 1938 involving a trip to a village called Nasielsk. As the camera panned across the faces of village boys, I recognized the face of my grandfather who was about the age of 14 at the time. This discovery was like a gift to me and my family. My grandfather is still living and we would like to contact Mr. Kurtz to thank him for donating these videos as well as to speak to him about his family who I believe my grandfather knew as a boy.*

The trip from Times Square to my apartment on the Upper West Side takes about twenty minutes, considering that on cold December days at rush hour, you might have to let a train or two pass before there is room enough to board. You have to stand in a crush of commuters wearing itchy wool coats in overheated subway cars. You have to endure the thumping from someone's cranked-up iPod. When you leave the subway there are stoplights and the taxis that ignore them; street corners and the jostling for position of people impatient to get home. Keys to fumble with, the elevator button to press, and the squeaky ride up as numbered lights slowly illuminate and blink off.

It was five thirty before I dialed the number at the bottom of the e-mail.

"I believe this is about the film of her grandfather," answered Jeff Widen, Marcy's assistant, who'd discovered David Kurtz's film online.

When we finally met, eight months later, Jeff told me he had been ex-pecting my call. "I knew instantly what the reason was and the impor-tance. And I knew I had to immediately get you two connected. Because I knew that there was more at stake. There were people in Florida that also wanted to talk to you."

Jeff gave me Marcy's cell phone number, and I reached her just as she walked out of the day care center with her nine-month-old son, Lev, in her arms.

"I have to call you back later," she said.

Even on life-changing days, a young mother still has to drive home from day care, greet her husband, and give their toddler his dinner.

||||||||||||||||||

Sometimes, when I told this story in the months that followed, I tried to imagine it from Maurice Chandler's point of view: You're a boy, a young teenager, growing up in a town where your family has lived for hundreds of years. The family is relatively well-to-do, among the most prosperous in the village, and you are the favored son. A rebel, a troublemaker, but clearly cherished. You go to cheder, to yeshiva. You are bar mitzvahed. You play games with your friends and tricks on your neighbors, you get into trouble. One day, a family from America comes to town, carrying a movie camera. It's a thrilling event in the life of your village. You join your friends, skip out of school, and crowd in front of the man to watch as he trips the shutter. A movie! Ten minutes later, your teacher collars you and drags you back to the musty classroom where you study Torah and Tal-mud, Yiddish and Polish, and the Wisdom of the Fathers. The Americans drive away. Life goes on, and you forget that it happened. And then every-thing stops. There is war. Unimaginable terror. The Holocaust. Your entire family is killed, and only you survive, miraculously. When the war finally ends, you're twenty years old and you have nothing, no one. What do you do? Where do you go? You find a job with a butcher. After two years, you finagle a visa to the United States. You have survived the war by your wits and by indescribable luck, and there is nothing in this new country that frightens you. All you have to do is make a living. So you work hard,

and after many years, you become a successful businessman. You meet and
marry your wife, and together you build a life. Four children grow up and
have children of their own. The grandchildren have children. And seventy-
three years go by, until one day, sitting in front of an iMac computer connected to the Internet, you see the town you grew up in as it appeared on
that forgotten day in 1938. You see yourself as a kid, when the worst thing
you had experienced was the bristly beard of an overly affectionate neighbor and a daily scolding from your pious Hasidic grandfather. Your village,
your childhood. And a few minutes later, the grandson of the American
who appeared and disappeared in your village seventy-three years earlier
and shot these three minutes of film calls you on the phone and wants to
know everything you can recall.

||||||||||||||||||||

"You know, my granddaughter is so happy, there's . . . ach! And how she
found me in the picture! You know, all these kids. It's unbelievable! I mean,
they've been on the phone all day. My daughter in Detroit, my granddaughter in her office, and my son in Chicago. My granddaughter was crying all day, she says 'Grandpa . . .' I mean, all of a sudden I'm somebody. I
didn't land from Mars. It's an unbelievable feeling."

I reach Maurice Chandler on the phone that night while he's still sitting at the kitchen table at his home in Florida, playing the film over and
over on the computer.

"Now you are the gentleman's, who took the pictures, you're his
grandson?"

"That's right," I answer. "It's my grandfather. He doesn't appear in the
film."

"Who is the man with the hat?"

"The man with the hat is named Malina, Louis Malina."

"Louis Malina."

"He was a friend of my grandfather's. Both my grandfather and Mr.
Malina were born in Nasielsk. My grandparents, Mr. Malina, his wife, and
Mr. Malina's sister, whose name was Essie Diamond, visited Nasielsk in
the summer of 1938."

"The Diamonds were Nasielskers."

"You knew a family named Diamond?"

"Yes, I remember there was a Diamond in Nasielsk. But we pronounced it Di-*AH*-mant."

"Diamant, of course."

"Right, Di-*AH*-mant. I remember that they used to come to our store. Somehow we had some business relations. I remember my mother used to talk about the Diamants."

Diamond/Diamant was the maiden name of David Kurtz's mother, my great-grandmother. According to Dana's genealogical research, David's father, Hyman, was born in central Poland. He married Leah Diamond of Nasielsk sometime before 1887.

"We were in the clothing business, manufacturing suits," Maurice Chandler continues. "We employed about fifteen tailors. We had a three-story building, right in the marketplace. We sold finished goods, yard goods, all kinds. I mean, the poverty there was so great. By those standards, we were considered the rich people. Because every Rosh Hashanah, I got new shoes at the shoemakers, Brawer's."

The shoemaker's name was Brawer. The baker's name was Rajczyk. The neighbor's name was Perelmuter. The school was run by Mr. Szmerlak and his wife. I hear these names for the first time with no idea where they will eventually lead, into what complexities of research and interrelation.

"You know in this movie I saw the shul," Mr. Chandler says, referring to the synagogue. "All these people, the kids are coming out of the shul. Now what was the occasion? I have no idea. But they're pouring out of the shul. Now, what they could have been, is, they used to have these preachers, you know, we called them *maggidim*. A *maggid* would come to shul, you know, he was sort of a holy roller, sort of a Jewish evangelist. He would chastise the people about sins and this and that. And I remember, as kids, we used to listen and be frightened about the souls."

I asked what he remembered of the shul, which I knew only from the fragmentary shot in the film and the grainy image from the 1953 commemorative book that I had found at the library.

"Well, it was a tremendous shul in size. The walls were built ten foot thick. And you don't know what happened with that shul, before they took the Jews out. They kept them at that shul for three days and three nights, and they made them scrape off all the paintings on the walls, all the . . . what do you call, on the walls? The frescoes that were done by Mr. Perelmuter. And then they took them away."

"Were you present during that?" I asked.

"No. I escaped a month before, with my older brother, to Russia, and then came back to the German side and wound up in the Warsaw Ghetto. It's a long story. But we . . . *Oy, yoy, yoy.*"

It will take weeks, months of talking before I begin to get it straight, before we both slow down enough to untangle the stories we want to tell all at once.

"You know, I'll tell you another little aside," Mr. Chandler said. "In London lives my only childhood friend who's still alive. He's ninety."

Wait! There's another Nasielsker? This is how I learned about Leslie or Lejzor Glodek in London, born in Nasielsk in 1922.

"He was in Russia, served in the Polish army, and served in Africa with the British forces, and wound up in England," Mr. Chandler said. "My kids and his kids are now connected and keep in touch with each other. They're going to come to visit us. Because we don't . . . I came out, you know, all alone."

He promises to send me Leslie Glodek's phone number and e-mail address so I can make contact with him, too, a second man who can remember the town as it appears in my grandfather's film.

"You probably wonder, where does a Chandler come to Nasielsk?" Morry asks—by now he insists that I call him Morry.

"Okay. My father came from a shtetl near Nasielsk, it was Nowy Dwór. There was a fortress right near Nowy Dwór, Modlin, a Russian fortress from three hundred years ago. He came from a family of people that supplied uniforms to the Russian army there, and he married my mother in Nasielsk. And his name was Tuchendler."

"Tuch-Händler," I said, "so a . . . a *shmate* trader?" It is one of the few Yiddish words I inherited, and I'm happy to use it.

"Yes. They were in the *shmate* business. So I came to America, and I

wound up in the Korean War, serving in Kansas. On mail call in the army, the guy that called off the mail, when he came to my name, he lost his teeth. *Tuk! Tak!* So when I got my citizenship in Baltimore when I was in the army, I decided to change it. And I took off the *t-u*, and I made it Chandler."

While we're on the phone, Marcy Rosen e-mails me two photos: a screenshot from the film, a boy at the head of a crowd of boys, wearing a black cap, his brow slightly furrowed against the sunlight; and a current photo of Maurice Chandler, a white-haired man with a steady, kindly expression, a large man, the rock of his family. The same face, the same nose and mouth, the same chin, the same eyes.

"You know," I say after a moment, "I look at this picture from the film, and I realize, you were standing just a few feet away from my grandfather. He died before I was born. And so, you met him, and I didn't."

The film gives Maurice Chandler a glimpse of his childhood. And in that moment, through some transitive property of contact, talking with him seems to give me a glimpse of my grandfather.

"I think that all the Jewish people say *bashert*," Morry responds. "*Bashert*. We have to believe in that."

Bashert, fate or destiny. Something meant to be, something so improbable, it feels as if only divine assistance could make it happen. Fate, or luck, or just an accumulation of uncanny connections. Because August 18, 2011, the day Maurice Chandler and his family visited Nasielsk, was also David and Liza Kurtz's ninety-ninth wedding anniversary. This has no bearing on the story, but it is one of the many, many strange coincidences that populate it.

"You know, first of all," Morry continued, "it's amazing, I don't remember ever, ever, somebody coming from America taking these pictures. But I'm right there, wearing the cap, and all this. You know, I was . . . We were all raised in a Hasidic home. My parents were very religious, my grandfather. I don't know if I told you, my grandfather's nickname was Kurtz."

Kurtz?

"I don't understand it. Because when I ran around, everybody used to go, 'Who was that?' they'd said, 'Oh, Srul Kurtz's *aynikl*.'" *Aynikl*, grandson. They were saying, *There's Kurtz's grandson*. "My grandfather's name was Skalka," Morry continued, "but now it was 'Srul Kurtz's *aynikl*.' So we might be relatives."

We have talked for more than half an hour. Morry's children and grandchildren want to get him on the phone. We agree to speak again the following day, and we make a date for our families to meet in Florida in January, to watch the film together.

In the meantime, there is a brief oral history that Morry gave to a professor in Michigan in 1993, and I'll stay up late reading the transcript. I'm impatient to learn all I can about his life and about the town. The third week of January feels like a long way off.

"Ach! I'm telling you," Morry sighs before we say goodbye. "I could tell you everything about Nasielsk."

PART TWO

6

IT'S GOOD TO BE BACK

FOR A FEW minutes in the summer of 1938, my grandfather stood on the
street in a small town in Poland and filmed a crowd of children. Seventy-
three years later, in January 2012, I flew to Florida to meet one of these
children, to learn the context of these few minutes of film, and to hear how
Moszek Tuchendler of Nasielsk had survived the Holocaust to become
Maurice Chandler of Boca Raton. We called it a reunion.

My sister, Dana, her husband, Rob, my sister-in-law, Cynthia, and my
nephew, also named David Kurtz, all flew down for the occasion. Morry
and Dorris Chandler's daughters, Debra Chandler and Evelyn Rosen, were
there, along with Evelyn's husband, Steve, and their children: Emily; Jason, with his wife and son; and Marcy Rosen, with her husband, David
Eisenberg, and their son, Lev. Leslie Swift came down from the Holocaust
Museum to record the meeting for the archive. We gathered to listen to
Morry talk of his life, an elder passing down stories, the oldest form of
preservation.

Morry and I had spoken frequently on the phone in the three weeks
since Marcy first recognized him in my grandfather's film. But I was
nervous as I rang the bell and waited for the door to open. On the phone,
Morry, too, had expressed trepidation about making such an event of
our first meeting. He would have preferred a quieter, more gemütlich

get-together. But everyone had wanted to share in the excitement, and in the end he'd relented.

Evelyn Rosen opened the door and greeted me like family. I had watched her home video of the visit to Morry's former home so often, seeing her in person was like meeting someone famous. She ushered me into the bright, spacious apartment, noisy with children, grandchildren, and two great-grandchildren. Leslie Swift waved from the den, where she and a camera crew were setting up. Morry was standing in the living room, a little overwhelmed by all the attention.

Meeting him for the first time, I could not fathom how one man's life could encompass a prewar childhood in small-town Nasielsk, the wartime horrors of the Warsaw Ghetto and the loss of his family, and this beautiful, boisterous, art-filled home in lush, semitropical Florida. How does someone make these transitions? He bore no mark, no obvious sign of this history, no tattoo. The experiences were internal, internalized, and when we shook hands and first looked each other in the face, his gaze was warm and open, yet with depths of caution and reserve.

We took our places in the den, Morry in an armchair with a plaid blanket thrown over it, and I next to him, perched on a dining room chair, the DVD remote control in my hand. Our families settled on the couches and the floor around us. After the introductions and some family banter, I pressed "Play," and my grandfather's 1938 film of Nasielsk appeared on the flat-screen TV.

Workers in torn shirts and gray caps and religious men in black overcoats hurry down the street, surrounding Louis Malina, just arrived in town. An indoor scene, dark and shadow-filled. Silhouettes around a table. And then a street scene bursting with movement. Children jump and wave. My grandmother and Rosie Malina laugh at the chaos. Boys mob the man with the movie camera. Moszek Tuchendler, age thirteen, darts to the head of the crowd.

Everyone sang out when he appeared on-screen.

"There he is!"

"The culprit," Morry Chandler said, laughing, his cheeks turning red. "I want to get to the front. It's amazing."

He first appears early in the panorama, in the back row. Marcy had not noticed him in these earlier frames, but on the bigger screen, it's plain that he is leaping up to see what's going on. The camera moves to the left, and Morry disappears from the frame. But then the camera swings right again, and there he is, in the first row of boys, just a foot or two from my grandfather, standing on his tiptoes and peering into the lens.

"On a day like this, when the word was out that an Amerikaner is in town, the kids wouldn't stay at cheder," Morry said. "I mean everybody would run off to see, and touch, and be near them, and so on. It was a major happening in the shtetl. So"—he laughed as he remembered—"all these kids probably ran away from the yeshiva, or from the cheder. They were AWOL."

We paused on Morry's childhood face.

Steve Rosen remarked on the resemblance to his youngest daughter, Emily. And Jason Rosen, her brother, agreed. "It's Emily's smile."

"It's almost weird for me to see it," said Emily, "because it's like déjà vu."

"That's why I recognized it immediately," explained Marcy, "because the face looks like—I mean, it doesn't just look like Grandpa. It looks like our family's faces."

Morry rubbed his chin. "I remember myself looking like that. You kids are all youngsters, but when you get to be a little advanced, my age, and I look in the mirror, I say, 'Who is this guy?'" He pointed at the face on the screen. "I remember this kid. I swear to you, this is what's stuck in my mind, this is how I look. But who's the guy that looked at me in the mirror?"

He teased Marcy, his eldest granddaughter, who's in her mid-thirties. "Wait until fifty years from now. You'll look and you'll say, 'Who is this girl?'"

"I do that already," she replied.

For Morry's family, this moment of recognition was joyous. Seeing the film allowed them to place stories they had heard their whole lives, to compare what they had imagined with how it actually was. All morning, as we went through the scenes frame by frame and Morry recounted stories and identified faces, his family called out for favorite anecdotes, adding details they remembered, if Morry forgot to include them.

For me, however, this opportunity to watch the film with Morry felt different. In my family, the town lay a generation farther removed. For me, it was the first time Nasielsk was more than a name in a document or a place in a few minutes of old film. Morry provided a bridge between two vastly different worlds. He was the film's Rosetta stone.

I asked how it felt to see himself back in Nasielsk.

"I'm trying to, you know, go into what I thought at the time. What my mind-set was," he said. "It was before, months before the whole Holocaust started. That we were happy kids, just running around. We had all the plans for the future. And how they just . . . how everything turned upside down. Right afterwards. We had no idea what was awaiting us."

He'd answered a slightly different question, not about how he felt now. And so after a little while, I asked again, "How does it feel to see yourself as a child?"

"It's like saying, *Was that ever possible?* I mean, I can't believe that we had this kind of a city, with kids and people and families and everything."

His grandson Jason picked up the thought. "Weren't you also saying, 'I was real. I really existed. This wasn't just a figment. This isn't just a story I've been telling my family all these years'?"

"Yes. That's right," Morry responded. "Because my kids were asking me over the years a little bit about the war, and I sort of doled it out in small portions. But what really bothered me was, they never addressed my mother or my grandmothers, or my grandfather. It's like it started with me. My kids, just lately they're asking, 'What was your mother like?' And I say, 'My God! I had a mother! And I had a grandmother!' But all these years, to them, I just walked in from Mars. I just came in, and it all started from me. Like there was no background."

In the whirl of the moment, we moved on to other questions. But now, as I review the video of that first meeting, I recognize something that would occur over and over in my conversations with Morry. As the sole survivor, he was the origin of his family, the Adam. To his children and grandchildren, he came from a *place*, and here, suddenly, that place was visible on the TV. Similarly, because I was interested in my grandfather's film and in learning what the footage shows, my questions focused on Nasielsk as it appeared on the screen. Morry's family and I easily overlooked the discontinuity of the images, their abstraction from their lived context. We were excited by what we saw because it was all we knew, and the images on-screen were so vibrant.

But Morry saw what was missing. When he looked at the pictures, he saw his home, his childhood, his friends and his family, the bustle of daily life. For him, the inward town—the felt, inhabited, experienced, remembered town—was the real one. *Yes,* he said, *that's me on the screen. But there was so much more.* None of us could see what he saw in these pictures, behind and around them. We asked about images of a place. But he told us about the people, about a community.

||||||||||||||||||

It is one of the peculiarities of this story that firsthand accounts of prewar Nasielsk necessarily come from people who were children at the time. And so we get a picture of the town from a child's perspective. These recollections take place mostly at home, at school, or in the secret places beyond adult supervision, where children are free. Often, these seventy-five-year-old stories are highly polished, worn smooth from retelling. It took me a long time to learn Morry's history well enough to ask for details not in these practiced versions, and longer still before I knew enough to inquire about Nasielsk's other inhabitants and to spark memories Morry had not known he possessed.

Moszek Tuchendler grew up in a house owned by his grandfather, Yisrael or Srul Skalka. The house stood on the main square or marketplace, in Polish *rynek*. Morry recalled the house at number 20 Rynek as "the only one that in the whole city was three stories," although a photograph of the marketplace I found later shows several three-story buildings. But this is how Morry remembered it; his way of expressing the centrality of his family.

The Skalka family business occupied the ground floor of the building, the place Morry showed Evelyn and Steve in August 2011, which is now a kebab restaurant. The Skalka store was well known in Nasielsk and the surrounding villages for its fine clothing—suits, coats, dresses, and yard goods. "Later on we went, sort of, I would call it 'interstate,'" Morry explained in January as we all sat together in his living room. Sometime in the early or mid-1930s, he recalled, a man from Nasielsk got married in Nowy Dwór, twelve miles to the south, and worked as a salesman there. "He gave us orders: so many suits, so many this, and this and that. And that caused us to have the only phone in the city. I remember it was a big thing with a handle and the post office answered, and we said, 'We want Mr. Cynamon in Nowy Dwór! Take your time!'" Morry didn't have many memories of the store, however, since it was part of the grown-up world, not shared with the children. "When I came into the store I was in the way," he said.

One of Morry's earliest recollections was of the death of his great-grandfather, Borris Yehuda Skalka, who was 105 years old. This would have been in the late 1920s, when Morry was four or five. Morry remembered only that Borris Yehuda had been conscripted into the czar's army as a young man and did not see his family for fifteen or twenty years. When he returned, he was a stranger. "I never saw anybody talk to him. He had a room on the third floor, a little Jew, you know, bent over. I remember when he died, people came to the house—people died at home. You used to put the body on the floor. And they put a black blanket on him, and they had two candles on each side. And people came to the house, and it was a whole procedure. So I remember as a kid, I was so happy, and I thought it was like a party. Everybody came in, everybody pinches my cheeks."

I asked Morry what he remembered of his grandfather, Srul Skalka.

"He would test me from the Talmud, every Friday. When I came home, I had to sit down, and he went over it with me. He was very, very serious and stern. I don't remember him as the type of grandfather that I am with my kids."

"Were you afraid of him?" I asked.

"As a kid, yes. He wore his glasses, I remember those old glasses, little glasses, and when he would want to take a look at me he would move his glasses to the tip of his nose, move down, he'd take that look—oh, my God, that was frightening! You know, like, if he wasn't sure if I davened that morning, or put on tefillin." To daven means to pray, and tefillin are the phylacteries, the small leather boxes containing Torah portions that religious men fasten to their forearms and forehead during morning prayers.

Srul Skalka was the patriarch of the family, and he ruled the household. "He sat at the head of the table, you know, on Saturday. Everybody sat around him, and my grandmother would cook, bring stuff from the kitchen, and my mother. Everybody came home from shul, and we sang the *zemirot*, the Sabbath hymns. I'll never forget, one story. You know, as a little boy, you want to sort of show-and-tell. So when we sat down, I—just to say something, because the kids were not allowed to talk unless asked—I couldn't wait to tell this story: 'On the way home from shul,' I said, 'I saw a dog as big as my father.' And that—I don't know from where—I got a *patsh*," a slap, a smack, "you know, in the face. *Comparing your father to a dog! Vey iz mir! Oy, yoy, yoy!* And I thought it was a big story! I had to compare it to something. I mean, I never saw an elephant or anything. *Away from the table!* I couldn't come back, and I couldn't eat. I remember my grandmother smuggling in food to the kitchen for me."

I asked about his grandmother, Dvora Skalka, born Friedman.

"She was like a Mother Teresa. When I look back at her, she was such a fine, fine human being. You never heard a loud word out of her. You know, what we call in Yiddish a *gute neshume*," a kind soul.

He remembered that as a small child, he would accompany his grandmother to the marketplace to buy meat at one of the small butcher stands, called *jatkis*, a Polish word adopted into Yiddish, meaning a hut or stall.

"They had about twenty butcher shops, one next to the other," Morry explained, describing the center of the marketplace. "It was one low, single-story building, and on all sides around, there were butcher shops, different butchers. And I was always frightened, you know—the knives, and the way they talked, and the way a side of beef hung from a hook."

Morry told me this in a phone conversation in February 2012, a month after we'd met in Florida. I asked whether he remembered which butcher his grandmother patronized. At that moment, he couldn't recall. But twenty minutes later, when he was talking about someone else, who also happened to be a butcher, the name suddenly occurred to him.

"Oh, yes! Wait. We had a neighbor, Kulas. Meir Kulas. And I remember his father, and the mother's name was Paja. It all comes to me now. Because we had a sukkah. We were the only people that had a permanent sukkah on the second floor. And we used to have sort of an electric handle that would open the roof. We would invite guests. You know, our family and the neighbors. It was a nice area, the Sukkus, a nice time of the year."

Memories, like artifacts, are tightly wound bundles of information. Pull one thread, try to identify one figure, and the whole bundle unfurls. I had asked about Morry's grandmother. But I learned about the butcher shops in the marketplace and about Kulas, the family butcher, who was a guest during the fall harvest festival, Sukkoth. And I learned that the Skalka family had a roll-away sukkah—traditionally, a reed hut constructed solely for the holiday—on the second-story balcony behind their home, with some sort of modern contraption to raise and lower the roof.

I could begin to knit the strands of these stories together with other strands I had found. Meir Kulas—Morry's friend and neighbor, the son of the butcher his grandmother frequented—was the brother of Czarna Ida Zimmer, who survived the war and in 1995 gave testimony about her life and family to the Visual History Archive, which I had viewed a year before meeting Morry. Czarna was born in 1914, and she died before I found my grandfather's film. But from her video, I learned that her father was indeed a butcher named Israel Kulas, born in 1880, and her mother was named Paja, just as Morry recalled. There were seven children in the Kulas family, including Czarna and her youngest brother, Meir, Morry's friend, whom the family called Max.

Morry's father, Jehouszua or Szaja (pronounced "Shaya") Tuchendler, married his mother, Chawa Skalka, daughter of Srul Skalka, around 1920, when they were both twenty-five years old. They had three sons: Avrum, born around 1921 (the same year as my aunt Shirley); Moshe or Moszek, born in 1924; and Dawid, born around 1928. Chawa's brother Jankiel Skalka, Morry's uncle, also lived in the family house on the *rynek* with his wife, Malka, and their three children, two girls and a boy. Morry could not remember the children's names—or he did not remember the first time I asked. But many months later, when we examined a photograph discovered in someone else's attic, he recognized a girl and a boy, his little cousins, and the names Brucha and Selig Skalka came to him.

Elia Applebaum, another cousin, also lived in the Skalka family home. He was Morry's mother's nephew, son of an older sister who had died in childbirth. Elia Applebaum became the chief clothing designer for the Skalka store. "If he had come to America, he would have been one of the top designers," Morry said. "He was so talented. He was a genius." Applebaum oversaw the workshop where ten or fifteen men sat over sewing machines, manufacturing the clothes that were sold in the Skalka store. This workshop was in back of the house, in the small building that now stands ruined in a patch of brown leaves. In 1938 or early 1939, Elia Applebaum married the daughter of a prominent rabbi from Radzyń, a town in central Poland, forty-five miles north of Lublin. "I remember all these things," Morry said, "because it was a great honor. Their last name was Fine. And she came to live with us. And I remember they had their first child as the war broke out, in the Warsaw Ghetto."

Applebaum and his young family did not survive. But in the Radzyń *Yizkor*, or memorial book, there is an entry by Sarah Achicam-Fine, another daughter of the Radzyner Rabbi Chaim Fine, and the only survivor from her family. She writes about her father in the first days of the war. "With great difficulties, and after experiencing attacks by anti-Semites along the way, we arrived at midnight in Warsaw, the place where my oldest sister lived. When the whole family gathered together at her place, my father turned to us: 'My children, the fire is spreading all over the world; I must go back home (to Radzyń), but you my dear children stay together.'"

It was to this older sister of his wife's that Elia Applebaum and his family fled after the German invasion of Poland in September 1939, and he may well have been at this meeting of the Fine family when his father-in-law decided to return to his congregation in Radzyń.

As the owners of a clothing store employing numerous tailors, the Skalka family was among the more prosperous in Nasielsk. They had a good reputation with the local people, both Jews and non-Jews, and within the Jewish community they were considered upper-class.

"Of course we had a caste system, you know, in every shtetl," Morry explained to me. "It was actually a dual caste system. One was financial, the other one was religious."

Higher up in the financial caste system were the more successful merchants, who were also better educated. Below them were the artisans and the workers, the *handwerker*, who did manual labor. The religious hierarchy depended on one's own convictions, and this, as in all shtetls in Poland in the 1920s and 1930s, gave rise to intense conflicts and rivalries between different sects and parties, and often, as I learned later, within individual families. Those observing traditional religious practices were divided among the Orthodox and the numerous Hasidic sects, which followed the teachings of charismatic teachers. The Gerrer Hasidim, like Susan Weiss's family, for example, followed the dynasty of Yitzchak Meir Alter (1799–1866), from Góra Kalwaria, then in Russia. Morry's family belonged to the Vurke or Otwock Hasidim, a small sect that adhered to the teachings of Yitzhak Kalish (1779–1848) and his disciples.

Each Hasidic sect had its own prayer house, called a *shtibl*, where they could worship together. The Hasidic *shtibl* where Morry's grandfather and father worshipped, and where Morry was bar mitzvahed, stood next to the main synagogue, just beyond the northwest corner of the marketplace. The congregation at the main synagogue, or shul, was primarily composed of workers, Morry said. "The shul people were not religious enough, and they were also mostly the *handwerker*. They were tailors, shoemakers, stuff like that. The Hasidim were more dedicated to learning and the Talmud, and they were the upper class of merchants."

As the grandson of a well-to-do Hasidic businessman, Morry spent his days receiving religious training at the Jewish elementary school, the cheder. "With us, in my house, it was de rigueur: you must be in cheder from morning till night. There was no escape."

So what was life like for a kid growing up in Nasielsk?

"In our way of life, religiously," Morry explained to me and our families when we met in January 2012, "you started with one hundred percent not allowed. Everything you want to do is not allowed."

For example?

"Well, especially on Saturdays, when we came home from shul, and we had the meal—we brought the *cholent* from the bakery—and everybody settled down," he said, referring to the traditional stew prepared before the Sabbath and kept warm in the baker's oven until after services. "And so my grandfather had his afternoon nap. I wanted to be out with the kids—we didn't go to cheder on that day. *Nothing doing.* I remember he would say, 'Will you come to bed?' And he put me against the wall, so I couldn't escape while he took his nap. And I remember hearing outside, the kids were throwing rocks and chasing cats and frogs. And I said, 'My God, why can't I . . . ?' I mean, these are things that I remember as a kid that were definitely not allowed."

And what else?

"Like, the terrible crime of riding a bicycle. *A bicycle! Did you ever see your grandfather ride a bicycle? Why would you ride a bicycle?*"

He laughed at the memory. "When I look at our kids, how we raised our kids, my childhood was just like the Stone Age, really. But that's what we were used to."

Bicycles must have been a particular temptation, whispering of mobility and freedom, especially because of their easy accessibility. The Nasielsk bicycle shop was owned by the family of Leslie Glodek, Morry's childhood friend who now lives in London.

"He was my brother's friend," Morry clarified. "I was a little younger. But I shlepped along with the older guys. And anyway, he was a friend. The shtetl was as big as, you know, ten by ten, and we ran around."

The Glodek family was not very religious. "On his side, it was a little laissez-faire. His brother had the bicycle shop. And they knew a lot of Poles, goyim, and stuff like that. We, on my side, were not allowed to ride bicycles. My grandfather decreed that this is too goyish. He said, 'The Talmud said: Don't adopt the goyishe behavior. Whatever they do, you're not allowed to do,'" and Morry laughed again at the recollection. "Of course, we were kids. So at night we used to sneak out. And that's how we learned to ride a bicycle. There was a lumberyard, around like an oval, where the lumber was in the middle, and we rode around, you know, and we fell off. It was the hard way. Anyway, one night, I mean it was sort of twilight, getting dark, somebody reported to my grandfather that I was riding a bicycle. And he came running out. It was like I committed murder. He yelled, *Goy! Goy! Goy!* I was afraid to go home. And I remember my grandmother hiding me in the back of the house until he cooled down a little bit."

Was there any other punishment?

"Well, I mean, what could he take away from me? They didn't give us any toys or anything. But what punishment? I mean, his look—this would have a devastating effect. When he looked, you knew that he was very, very mad."

The impression Morry gives is of a boy whose boyishness was continually at odds with the strict life he was forced to lead, a rambunctious, rebellious, but loved and talented kid, a kind of shtetl Tom Sawyer.

Months later, when I visited Morry and his family at their home in Michigan, he told me this story. "So Leslie and I and my brother—you know, I was always the . . . the instigator. We decided we were going to teach them all a lesson. You know? We're going to eat ham," an egregious violation of the strict kosher regulations. "So there was a Polish butcher on the way to the cemetery, because we didn't want to be noticed. Because these kids with the *peyes*," the forelocks that distinguish Orthodox Jews, "and they're going into a ham place? It would immediately—they would tear the city up. So we got to the edge of the city limit, and then we decided who's going to be the brave one. Guess who? Yes. So I remember walking in and the butcher said, 'What do you want?' And I said, 'Three small slices of ham.' And we got it on a white piece of paper . . . So I walked out, and the two of them were standing and shaking. I said, 'Well. We got to do it. Everybody will have the same amount, so you can't say, "I only took a little bite." Everybody's going to be guilty.' So we took—we thought it wasn't going to go down. We swallowed, threw the paper away. And then how did we go home? Everybody was sure that when we walked in, they'll know. So we snuck in. Nobody knew the difference. But this was of course such trauma."

His greatest, or worst, transgression, however, took place at the prayer *shtibl* one Sabbath or *Shabes*, while the men of the family were praying.

"I'll just as a little aside, give a little bit of an inkling of how bad I was—you know, by Nasielsk standards," he told all of us that January in Florida, clearly enjoying himself. His grandchildren bit their lips not to give away a story they had heard before.

"You know, kids collect all kinds of stuff. It's like a trend," Morry began. "This year they collect little stones, and then they collect these roasted chestnuts, little ones. We were trading, and so on. And one time, the idea was to collect buttons. We were trading buttons back and forth. Big buttons, little buttons. So one day we are in this Hasidic *shtibl*, and it was winter and everybody wore those heavy coats with buttons, this big"—he made a half circle with his thumb and first finger—"like Krugerrands in size. And I take a look and I see, and I say, 'There's a treasure of buttons hanging on the wall!' So, I called Leslie. 'You know what? We're looking for buttons? We're going to be the richest button makers in the city! We'll trade with the kids.' He says, 'Well, what are you going to do?' I said, 'We'll cut them off.' So we stood—I remember we had a razor blade—like this"—he mimed sawing behind his back—"and we were taking off all the buttons. They were beautiful buttons. Anyway, but we never thought—you know, criminals never think of the . . . retribution, what's going to happen to them. You only get the idea and you do it. Well, so, when they finished the prayers and everything, *Good Shabes! Good Shabes! Good Shabes!* And I see each one takes a coat off, and they go up and down"—he patted up and down his chest—"the buttons!"

Morry delivered the line deadpan, and everyone burst out laughing.

"A pogrom! First thing, they yell out, *Him!* Oh, my God. There was an outcry. *And on a Shabes yet!*—which you were not allowed to do, aside from the buttons. Well, I ran out, and I ran home. And my mother and my grandmother, you know, they were sort of our lawyers. But they never forgave us. We were in purgatory for a *long* time."

Although Morry's grandfather was rooted to a traditional religious life in Nasielsk, it was a time when many people, both Jews and non-Jews, were emigrating to America. Morry remembers a visit from a distant relative, Harry Gordon, who had settled in Nashville, Tennessee. Gordon encouraged Srul Skalka to join him in America. "'How am I going to be Jewish in America?'" Morry recalls his grandfather saying. "'The Sabbath . . . There's no Sabbath, there's no kosher, there's nothing. We can't live there.'"

It was also not uncommon for those who had emigrated to change their minds and return.

"I'll tell you another story," Morry explained in January 2012. "A man originally from Nasielsk went to America, and after a few years, he realized that in America, they're desecrating the Sabbath. He was very religious—they didn't have any kids—married to an American Jewish woman here, and he realized that, you know, it's not his cup of tea. So he made some money, and he came back to Nasielsk. Took all his money, and built a yeshiva. His name was Szmerlak. In America, he had the name Simon. But his name in Poland was Szmerlak, David Leib Szmerlak. And I remember, he and his wife were always a fixture around the kids in the yeshiva. When they wanted nobody to understand, they would talk to each other in English."

After Morry mentioned the name, I searched the Ellis Island database and found a "David Schmerlak," age twenty-seven, from "Nasselsk," arriving in New York on board the SS *Friesland*, on September 2, 1902. He carried one dollar with him. I could not discover precisely when he returned to Nasielsk, though it would have been around 1929.

I sent Morry the document, and he again recalled the Szmerlaks very fondly. "It's like I'm looking at them today," he said. Another time, months later, we returned to the Szmerlaks. "He had a little beard. He was so nice, he was so friendly. And the wife I remember as a heavyset lady, she wore Coke-bottle glasses. They were at the school every day, you know, saying hello to the kids. They're like angels, the two of them. All his money he spent—in those days, it was a fortune—to build this yeshiva. And he built from the bottom up. He started from scratch and put up a building with yeshivas, with teachers. He gave every penny to that. They had a little apartment probably in the building. And they were there till the beginning of the war, and that was the end."

Szmerlak's yeshiva in Nasielsk is the "Yesodey-Hathora" mentioned in the Joint Distribution Committee's survey of the town's social institutions, a school for 150 boys.

Although Morry remembered David Szmerlak and his wife fondly, his affection did not extend to the teachers at his school. "You know the teachers were very rough with the kids. They would try and lift you up by an ear." And if anything happened in class, Morry was the one to blame.

"I was always guilty," Morry said. "Automatically. Some of it we deserved, too." He told another story involving Leslie Glodek, his boyhood friend and accomplice, whose brother owned the bicycle shop. "We used to bring drills to the cheder. And while the rabbi would teach, you know, and go around the classroom, we would drill under the table."

Drill holes? I asked.

"Holes."

In the desk?

"Yes."

For any particular purpose?

"Just in spite. As kids, you gotta do something."

Despite his antics, however, it is clear that Morry was an unusual kid. Above all, his remarkable memory was already evident. "My father used to walk with me, in the afternoon—on summer evenings, you know, the dew would settle on the fields. I can still smell the aroma of all kinds of shrubs and trees and all this," Morry recalled in August 2012. "And he'd tell me, 'The rabbi tells me that all week you're a *mazek*,'" a troublemaker. "'Then you listen Friday to his lecture, and on Saturday, you're the best with the *prima*,'" the highest mark. "He says, 'Imagine if you would listen all week! You'd be a *tzaddik*,'" a saintly man. "'So promise me,' he says—he knew I was dreaming of a little watch, and he promised me he would collect money in the family to get me a gold watch if I would attain a certain height of learning. He says, 'I'll buy you a gold watch. If you could only'—you know, if I could . . . yeah, if I could just behave. So I said, 'Yeah, yeah, I'll behave.' Didn't do any good. I could not be what they call a 'good boy.'"

In the fall of 1937, Morry was bar mitzvahed in the Hasidic *shtibl* next to the main synagogue, reading from the Torah and delivering his commentary on a Talmudic theme. "It was like, you ask a question, 'Rabbi So-and-So says this, and Rabbi So-and-So says that, and Rashi says this . . . but *I* say . . .' I mean, I look back and I think, 'My God, how could I remember all that?' But they were serious, this was a serious dissertation. And they all applauded, and then they threw candy at me . . ."

Morry's rebelliousness only intensified with his entry into the community. After graduating from school a year later, he began agitating to go to Warsaw. At the end of 1938, his parents gave in, and that winter when he was fourteen, he finally left Nasielsk to attend the *szkoła rzemieślnicza*, a Jewish trade school, located on Stawki Street 5 in the Polish capital. "I was so happy that I got away from the *peyes* and all of it," he said.

The only photograph of himself that Morry had been able to save comes from that spring, May or June 1939, almost a year after a group of Americans visited town carrying a movie camera. In this photo, Morry is wearing a jacket and tie, not the long black coat of the Hasidim, and his school cap is jauntily tipped to the side. The face is very serious, in three-quarter profile, and mostly in shadow. The murkiness of the image in part accounts for its survival. "I thought it would not be recognizable as a Jewish face, that picture," he said when he first showed me the photo. "I was limited to what I could carry with me. So as a result I had nothing else. I had that picture, and that's about it."

⫿⫿⫿⫿⫿⫿⫿⫿⫿⫿⫿⫿⫿

Gathered in Florida in January 2012, with my grandfather's film still paused on Morry's childhood face, Morry's family and I began to question him about that moment. Morry immediately focused on the black, short-brimmed cap he wore.

"In the culture of the shtetl, everybody wears a hat. And some of us, like me, wearing what they call a *yidishe hitl*, you know, a Jewish hat."

This hat signified a cheder student, and it was a mark of distinction among the boys in the town. "That was an everyday hat," Morry continued. "For holidays, I had a velvet hat, and a kapote made of silk," a long black traditional coat. "Now"—he pointed at the boy next to him in the crowd, wearing a cloth newsboy-style cap—"that kind of hat, I would not

be allowed to wear. They call it in Polish a *daszek*." The *daszek*, which means "little roof," denoted the boy's low position in the shtetl hierarchy. "I couldn't associate with this kind of . . . ilk," Morry said, and he laughed. "These were more *handwerker* people, you know, a Hasidic boy didn't mingle with these people. Not allowed."

In the image on the screen, however, the hierarchy is scrambled by the excitement of getting into the picture. All kinds of hats are mixed together. We picked out the other boys wearing the little black caps that identified them as cheder students, boys who might have been Morry's schoolmates. Morry studied the screen, his brow tensed in concentration.

"There's another kid, the one on the right. You see his face. Yeah. I think his name was Piekarek." He sighed and seemed to second-guess himself. "I think. He had a sister that survived and lived in California. Somebody told me she just died a couple of years ago."

Later, I realized that Morry was referring to Gloria Rubin, born Gitta Piekarek, who had given oral history testimony in 1996. She died in 2007, but in her testimony, she names her family members, including a brother, Jankiel, who would have been about Morry's age. Unfortunately, no photos of her siblings have been preserved. When I reached Gloria

Rubin's daughter, a month or so after meeting Morry, she sent me photos of her mother's parents, Yitzhak and Frida Piekarek, as well as of the Piekarek flour mill in Nasielsk, which was still standing, as far as she knew, though the building was a ruin. But I could not verify whether Morry's visual memory of Jankiel Piekarek was correct. Indeed, the possibility of verification probably no longer exists. So Jankiel Piekarek, son of Yitzhak and Frida, brother of Gitta, entered the twilight of *might be*, is *thought to be* in my grandfather's film.

"Now, this kid"—Morry paused and considered as I advanced the film a few frames—"resembles my older brother. But I'm not sure. I'll show you a picture of him later. That might be . . ."

Avrum Tuchendler, Morry's older brother, was a gifted singer, and he studied violin with an older boy who lived next door. Morry has two photographs of Avrum, which he showed me later that day. Both pictures were given to him by other survivors after the war. The first shows a handsome, confident young man of seventeen or eighteen in modern clothes. In the photo, he leans on a stool, one leg resting on a rung, creasing his beautifully tailored pleated pants. His arms are folded across his chest, the sleeves rolled up, and he wears a black sleeveless sweater or vest over a white shirt and tie. As in my grandmother Liza's portrait at about the same age, the one with the big hat, Avrum's clothing fades into the background because of the striking expression. He has a broad, self-assured smile.

The contrast with the second photo could not be starker. This other image was taken in the Warsaw Ghetto, just a year or two later. Avrum is wearing what may be the same clothes, the pleated pants and a white shirt. But his eyes are dark and sunken; his posture and expression haunted, hunted.

I could not match the face in these photos with the boy Morry pointed to in the film, and Morry later threw the identification into question. "I'm trying to . . . It could be . . . He resembles my brother, my older brother. But I can't say for sure," he said again later about a different boy in the film. Over the course of the morning, as we scrutinized the film and all of us,

including Morry, hoped, perhaps ached for familiar faces, Morry pointed to three different boys and tentatively identified each one as his older brother, Avrum.

We came to the scene in the film where people emerge in a long procession from the synagogue. There was no question about the identification of the building, which Morry remembered vividly.

"Our neighbor, his name was Fishl Perelmuter. He was the town photographer, and he was also an artist, a painter. And he decorated the shul," Morry explained. "Somebody from America came and donated a substantial amount of money to decorate the shul and all the walls. I remember he worked for months. I remember the painting of the Leviathan, with his tail in his mouth. In Jewish lore, they say, if the Leviathan ever lets go of his tail, the world goes kaput. Also from Joseph and his brothers. And Jonah and the whale. And to give honor to the Nazis, when they put all the Jews in the shul, and they kept them there for three days and three nights, they made them scrape with their fingernails, all the walls had to be scraped clean of that, and then they led them to the train station. My mother told me that, later."

I asked Morry when the murals were painted.

"I would say, probably '35, '36. I remember it took months. He had the elevators and the stands, he stood, you know, like Michelangelo at the Sistine Chapel. It took a long time. One person."

The Perelmuters lived next door to Morry's family. Despite the similarity in last names, Fishl Perelmuter was not related to Samuel Perlmutter, whose photograph Marcy's assistant, Jeff Widen, had found online when he first began searching for information about Nasielsk. Samuel Perlmutter, a competitor of the Piekareks, owned a flour mill, which was located behind Leslie Glodek's house, in a lot where the boys played ball. Fishl Perelmuter, the photographer and artist, does not appear in the film. Nevertheless, his name would recur frequently in the coming years. Almost everyone I spoke with who remembered Nasielsk in the 1930s recalled Fishl Perelmuter with respect and affection.

"He was very prominent," Morry said in January. "He was so capable. And he had sort of a short leg, and he limped. We used to call him—not in his face—'Fishl *der lumer*,'" Fishl the Lame. "Fishl Perelmuter was sort of looked at with suspicion because he used to have clients come in on *Shabes*. The doors were closed, but he was taking pictures on *Shabes*, which was like, you know, smoking heroin."

In the film, as adults file out of the synagogue, two boys wave and hop from one step to another in an attempt to draw my grandfather's attention. One of the boys might be Jankiel Piekarek again, or the boy who tentatively bears that name. With this image paused on the TV screen, Debra Chandler, Morry's daughter, noticed something no one had seen before.

"Some of the kids do not have shoes on," she said. "You'd think that if they were going to shul for a service, they would put shoes on."

"No, that was not a holiday," Morry said, examining the dress and demeanor of the adults coming down the steps. "It had to be something impromptu. The Amerikaner are in town, and we're going to show them the shul, and everybody follows. Unless, maybe a cantor would give a performance there. You know, a special performance, maybe in honor of your relatives. They could have donated some money, before. And they wanted to show . . . Or maybe they paid for the murals that everybody went in to see. Definitely not a Sabbath or a weekend."

I advanced the film slowly, letting the faces remain on-screen long enough for Morry to examine them. Then he stopped me, suddenly pointing to a man descending the synagogue steps. "That guy with the jacket is Rotstein, I knew him. His father's name was Jankiel Hersz Rotstein."

In the next frame, Morry saw another familiar face. "Oh, him I know for sure. He was our neighbor. His name—with the goatee, the beard—his name is Kubel. And their store we called 'the sisters,' because he had three sisters. And they were selling tableware, pots and pans."

Rotstein. Kubel. Faces had names, names had faces.

Morry identified both Rotstein and Kubel again later in the film, where they stand in the background wearing the long black coats and black caps of yeshiva *bukher*, the older students. Rotstein, or Rotsztejn, with his hand on his hip, is looking to the side, not paying attention to my grandfather. Kubel, with a little beard, is smiling, and he seems to nod to my grandfather as the camera focuses on him.

In the following scene, with the footage now in color, we saw people sitting around a neatly set table with a vase of flowers on the sill. The neighbors poke their heads in through the open window. I said I believed this must be someone's home. Morry frowned.

"This could be either a house, or it could be a restaurant. Leibl Owsianka had a restaurant. It was a kosher restaurant. So, it could have been that they stopped there for lunch, and everybody looked through the windows."

As soon as he said it, I believed he must be right. The tables, the windows, the absence of any domestic fixtures. Above all, the bold design of the curtains, clearly visible in the image.

"Yeah, the curtains are sophisticated," Morry said. "I think it was a restaurant."

Like the photographer Fishl Perelmuter, Leib Owsianka, sometimes referred to as Leibl or Leibish, was a well-known figure in Nasielsk, and his restaurant became a focal point in my search to identify the scenes in my grandfather's film.

During the long, beautifully clear color panorama that follows this scene, Morry identified another of his classmates from school.

"The one at the far end, on the left, on top, with the hat, he looks familiar. He looks familiar." He paused for a long time, waiting for the name to appear. "Yeah, definitely. I know him. I knew him. He was in my cheder. But he was an orphan. His father wasn't alive. I think his name was Talmud. Chaim Talmud."

Just as Chaim Talmud disappears from the frame, we see the woman in a red, green, and black patterned dress, who has her arm on the shoulder of a girl with blond braids. In a later scene, this girl gets shoved by a boy whom Morry recognized as a town bully, but whose name he didn't recall, and with whom he was not allowed to associate. We paused on the girl's face, which seems especially bright and assertive.

Dana, who had been watching quietly the whole time, along with the rest of my family, said, "It's so strange. I remember seeing this film when I was little, and for whatever reason, that girl, who has a print dress on, and the blond braids—something about her felt recognizable to me. Even as a kid. And still to this day. There's something about her."

This girl appears frequently in the film, moving with my grandfather's lens to remain on camera, and popping up in almost every scene in the

color section. But her face was not familiar to Morry. Earlier, I had wondered whether Morry would recognize any of the girls in the film. "No, that would be beyond my scope," he'd said, "looking at girls." Another thing not allowed.

Certain faces seemed to stand out in the film, people who expressed stronger personalities than others. But these were not necessarily the people Morry remembered. Despite Dana's sense of recognition, we never learned this girl's name.

At the far end of the panorama, the camera lingers for a moment as a woman in a gray dress peeks out from a storefront. She views the scene and retreats. We examined the sign above her head, with its three lines of text.

"Does it say on top, S-K-L-E-P?" Morry asked.

Marcy and I got up to look closely at the screen. Yes, the top line said "Sklep."

"Well, *sklep* means store. *Sklep Spożywczy,* grocery store," Morry explained, reading two of the three lines. "On the bottom, it would probably say whose name . . . who it belonged to."

As hard as we tried, we could not decipher the word at the bottom of the sign.

I asked Morry about the woman standing in the doorway, who looks down the street anxiously, without being aware of my grandfather and his camera.

Morry recalled that Leslie Glodek's parents ran a grocery store at the other end of his block. "I think this could be Leslie's store. They called it a *spożywczy.* Yeah," Morry said. "Probably his mother."

The woman remains on-screen for just a moment before my grandfather lifts his finger off the shutter.

The next shot offers a new perspective on the street. We can still see the grocery store, but now from a different angle. In the foreground stands a pair of workers, shaven faces, torn work shirts, one of them wearing the distinctive worker's cap.

"Well, this guy, on the left, he was sort of bordering on the town dummy," said Morry.

"Grandpa!" Jason Rosen objected.

"Yes! He was a poor guy from a poor family. I remember he hung around our Hasidim *shtibl*, and he would recite the Kaddish. He knew everybody's name: 'So-and-So *ben* So-and-So.' That's what you say in Kaddish, you know, when you make a *mishebeyrekh*. So, this was his forte. He was impressing everybody."

For saying these prayers, reciting the names of the fathers and grandfathers, the man would earn a few coins or a piece of bread.

"Yitzhak, Yitzhak . . . His last name I don't remember. But his nickname was Boortz. What it meant, I don't know. He was a little bit of a poor soul."

So Yitzhak "Boortz" goes onto the list of people in some sense identified. Like images in the film, the identifications Morry provided might be sharp or fuzzy, in the foreground or background. Jankiel Piekarek's name emerged clearly, but his face in the film remained in doubt. Boortz is clearly seen in the film. But I was never able to learn his full name.

One of the clearest shots of Nasielsk's balconies with their elaborate iron scrollwork appears above Boortz's head. Both Saul Gershkowitz, the survivor from Berezne, and Susan Weiss, the first Nasielsk survivor I spoke with, had singled out these balconies when they viewed the film, and now we commented on them as well.

My nephew, David Kurtz, had recently graduated from college, where he'd dabbled in blacksmithing. He asked whether there had been a blacksmith in town.

"Yes. His name was Czarko," Morry answered, "Arieh Czarko. We had another *koval*," another blacksmith, "to fix the horses' hooves, and stuff like that. But Czarko was the one that did ironwork. And his son's name was Shimon, a friend of mine. He lived at the edge of the city."

I had not thought to ask about the balconies. To me, they were by now a familiar feature in the film. But my nephew, because of his interest in blacksmithing, wondered aloud who had done the work, and consequently,

Morry remembered Arieh and Shimon Czarko, the blacksmith and his son. Without my nephew, their names would have been lost.

Morry paused and expressed what I'm certain we were all thinking: "I don't know how I remember these names."

I advanced the frame. Once more, in the jumble of faces to the right of Yitzhak Boortz, Morry thought he saw his brother Avrum.

"It could have been. It could be," he said.

None of us could help him.

We came to the final two faces that Morry recognized that day, two men who stand in the doorway and stare back at the camera, one with a long white beard, the other with a short black beard.

"Okay," Morry said. "Here are these two people . . . The man with the white beard, he was sort of what they called the ascetic person. His name was Chezkiah. It's a biblical name, from the *Tanakh*. Nobody knew what he lived off. But he was dressed just like that, with that beard. And everybody fed him. He would walk into everybody's house. I remember, he used

to eat chopped liver with strong onions. And you knew he was coming before he arrived. A very simple life. And everybody thought he was, you know, the Jewish version of sainthood. He would come up and he would tell stories from the past, and so on. And then he'd leave. Nobody knew where he slept. Probably in the shul."

Morry also recalled the man standing to the left of Chezkiah the ascetic.

"Now, the man, the shorter man . . . His name is Chamnusen Cwajghaft. They called him the *matzevah kritzer*. He was the one that chiseled all the headstones for the cemetery. And I remember I used to watch him, he was next door to our *shtibl*, on the other side, you know, it's like within ten yards. And we used to watch him from cheder—we'd go out—how he chiseled the Hebrew words."

Morry laughed as another memory came to him about Chamnusen Cwajghaft, or Tsvaighaft, the man who carved the headstones for the cemetery, whom Morry referred to by a contraction of his two first names, Chaim Nusen.

"I remember an episode in *shtibl*. Chamnusen was obviously a talented man, that he could create all those markers, chiseling out from the marble. So he donated a painting with a section from the Friday night service, the Hebrew prayer, *Kegavna*. *Kegavna* is an Aramaic prayer, something connected with the Zohar, with the Kabbalah. So he had that written out, nice in oil, written in Hebrew, with the original, and he donated it. And he put it up in the *shtibl*, the *Kegavna*. It was big, this size"—Morry indicated a poster that hung on the wall next to him. "And he hung it there. And there was a controversy, because Leiser Horowitz or somebody else objected to where he placed it. And somebody moved it. And he was up in arms, and he threw a pitcher. You know, the water pitcher from the *kiyor*, where you come to wash your hands, before davening. He grabbed the pitcher and threw it, and it hit somebody in the head. And, *Oy! Gevalt!* With the blood! The doctors!"

Once again, everybody was laughing.

"*How could you do this?!* And this guy fainted . . . and Chamnusen was never—he was thrown out of the *shtibl*. I don't know where he was davening after that. For these people, you know, religion was life and death. I mean, there were no shortcuts. Either you is or you ain't. And you think back, in terms of American life—imagine, that's all they had to worry about. Who hung this, and where it's hanging, and—*ach*. And I was cutting buttons."

He shook his head.

"So these are episodes that stay in my mind."

We had been sitting for more than three hours talking about the people Morry remembered, about his family, his life. I asked him once again how it felt to watch my grandfather's film.

"It brings me back. Right there," he said. "I'm in Nasielsk now."

How does it feel to be back? I persisted.

"It's good to be back—knowing that I'm here."

Morry said it with a laugh. But a few moments later he continued. "It's like a childhood part that I never registered in my mind." He paused and became reflective. "I was never a child. I mean, right after this, the whole thing started, and I became an old man, of fifteen, sixteen, seventeen. I can't believe that I was really yet a kid, looking to get into the camera."

He thought about it, touching his forehead with his hand. "It's looking back and saying, *Yes, there was a world*. Other than what we have lived all these years, knowing what happened. It was a real world there. I mean, people were going about their business. Kids were running, and doing all the things that kids do. And here I look at myself, and I see it was a happy face."

7

LISTS

THE DAY AFTER meeting Morry Chandler, I finally gave up writing my novel about Mara Reshen and the fictional film she discovers in the Vienna flea market.

||||||||||||||||||||||

A few days later, before flying home from Florida, I visited Morry again to discuss some of the material I had already collected about Nasielsk and to view Morry's archive of photos and papers. After our big family gathering, Morry seemed relieved to sit together quietly, just the two of us. Once more, he expressed his amazement at how these moments from his past had suddenly reemerged.

We sat at a bridge table in the living room, next to sliding doors that opened onto a meandering pathway to the golf course. I spread out documents from the Joint Distribution Committee's Landsmanshaftn Department, which I'd found at the YIVO archive in New York more than a year earlier.

The first was the transcript of an incoming cable, received by the Joint office in New York from Warsaw on April 4, 1946. "NASIELSKI COMMIT-TEE IN WARSAW THANKS FOR EQUIVALENT OF $300 RECEIVED THROUGH

JOINT AND ASKS FOR FURTHER NECESSARY HELP." The cable was signed, "Tuchendler President. Jagoda Secretary."

"Yeah, that's me. That's me!" Morry laughed. "That's me and Jankiel Jagoda."

So you were the Nasielsk Committee in Warsaw? I asked.

"I was the Nasielsker Relief, a one-man society. Yeah," and he laughed again.

Morry remembered receiving relief packages from the Joint—"cocoa and coffee and honey and all kinds of tchotchkes from America"—and distributing them to the small circle of Nasielsk survivors in Warsaw just after the war. But he had no recollection of compiling the list of those present, which accompanied the telegram and was among the first documents I had found when I started searching in 2009. Later, we would go over this list of survivors slowly and carefully. But now we focused instead on the document, dated March 2, 1946, that formally acknowledged the founding of the "Committee of Jews of Nasielska, currently living in Warsaw and Lodz." This document bears the names and addresses of the officers of the committee. Their signatures appear at the bottom of the page.

"Chairman of the board!" Morry said, looking at his own handwriting from sixty-six years ago. "Oh *vey*."

As was often the case, this reminded him of a joke.

"Remember the story about the man that comes home with a cap on his head, and the father says, '*Vus iz dus?*'" What's that? "He says, 'Dad, I'm on a boat, and I'm a captain.' So the father says, 'Listen. By me, you're a captain. By your mother, you're a captain. By a captain, you're not a captain.'"

On my computer, I opened the folder of Faiga Tick's photos, which she had donated to the United States Holocaust Memorial Museum, and which Lindsay Zarwell had found soon after we identified Nasielsk in the film.

"Yeah, Szmul Tyk. I saw him after the war," Morry said, remembering Faiga's husband, later called Samuel Tick. "A very nice guy, and his wife, Faiga. Szmul Tyk already died. They lived in Hamilton, Ontario. And she might still be—no, no, you know, she's not there anymore. Faiga Tick. Her name was Milchberg, her maiden name."

Morry did not remember much about Faiga's brother, Yehiel Milch-berg, one of the few people identified in the Holocaust Museum's cata-logue entry for these photos. But he vividly recalled Faiga and Yehiel's father, Natanal or Sana Milchberg.

"Their father was a very hotheaded Hasid. We used to call him Sana Kommandant. He would start fights in the *shtibl* if somebody didn't daven right or something. A real hothead. They lived at the edge of the city, near the cemetery."

In another conversation that March, Morry told me more about Sana Kommandant. "Oh, yeah. He was all over the *shtetl*. There were two people, one was a real scholar. His name was Nusen Nuchim. And the nickname was, the kids used to laugh, they said Nusen Nuchim Patsher, meaning, for the slightest thing, you'd get a *patsh*, a smack, from him. These were like the guardians of the religion."

The boys had a little song about the two men, which Morry proceeded to sing for me:

> *Nusen Nuchim Patsher,*
> *Sana Kommandant,*
> *something, something,*
> *some-thing . . .*

"I don't remember what the rest of the song was," he said in March 2012. But one evening a year later, he suddenly produced the rest of the qua-train.

> *Nusen Nuchim Patsher,*
> *Sana Kommandant*
> *Gibt a groysn patsh,*
> *mit der linker hant.*

Nusen Nuchim gives a big smack with his left hand.

One of the photos donated by Faiga Tick appears to be a class por-trait. A large group of boys stands outdoors, younger, smaller boys sitting

cross-legged on the ground, older, taller boys assembled in size order in the middle and back rows. A round-faced man with a prominent chin, wearing a suit and a gray fedora, anchors the back row and must be the teacher.

Yehiel Milchberg, Faiga's brother, is in the back row, second from the left, with his hands resting familiarly on the shoulders of a shorter boy in front of him. All the boys are wearing long black coats, but there is a mixture of caps, both the short-brimmed Yiddish hats of the yeshiva boys and the cloth newspaper-boy caps of the less well-to-do.

I asked whether this class might be from the Szmerlak school.

"It could be. It could," Morry said, uncertain. "I remember we had a Polish teacher from Pułtusk," a larger town, about twelve miles east of Nasielsk. "His name was Gradsztein. And it could be him. These kids could probably be from that yeshiva."

It is also possible that the photo shows a public school class, where the social divisions were not quite as rigid as at the religious school that Morry attended.

"Okay, I'm looking, I'm looking," Morry said, leaning toward the image after my inevitable question about the boys, their faces, their names. "On the right side of that picture, from the rear, he's sort of very tall, number one-two-three-four. The tall kid. I think his name was Mottl Brzoza."

I had not yet heard the name Brzoza, and it took a few tries before I could pronounce the Polish *zh*, Br-*zh*oza. Apparently, there were at least two Brzoza families in Nasielsk. One, which sold farm equipment, was called the *ayzerner* Brzoza, the "iron" Brzoza. The other, which dealt in lumber, was known as the *hiltzerner*, the "wooden" Brzoza. Again Morry laughed. "They'd say, 'Which Brzoza?' 'Oh, the *hiltzerner*.'" Mottl Brzoza, the boy in the picture, belonged to the "wooden" family.

"And another one I recognize. The one in the middle, you know, the odd-looking one. Standing up in front. His name was Srebro. Yeah, yeah. He was a bad kid. He hunted after me. We were sort of the rich kids. Everybody was looking to be a friend."

In the photo, Srebro stands in the middle row, fourth from the left, his arms stiffly at his sides. He has a distinctively oval face, with small, close-set features sharpened by his lips, which are pursed in a doubtful expression. A month or two after this conversation, again examining my grandfather's film, I noticed a familiar face among the boys bunched together near Yitzhak "Boortz" in the film's color section. It was the same boy, Srebro.

After I returned to New York, I made a list of the people Morry had identified in the film, including Cwajghaft, Rotstein, Kubel, Boortz, Chezkiah, and Chaim Talmud. And I made a second list of those Morry had mentioned but who did not appear in the film: the photographer Perelmuter, the restaurateur Owsianka, the blacksmith Czarko, the schoolmaster Gradsztein. I extracted still images from the film of each person and began a file of other faces that had seemed familiar to Morry, but about whose identity he was still in doubt. I also made a digital copy of the class photograph donated by Faiga Tick and annotated it with the names Brzoza, Srebro, and the teacher, Gradsztein.

Yad Vashem, the primary Holocaust memorial and archive in Israel, houses the Central Database of Shoah Victims' Names, which collects testimony from survivors and other sources in the most comprehensive list available of the Jewish victims of the Holocaust. A complementary database at the United States Holocaust Memorial Museum lists the survivors, including among other data points their birthplace or residence prior to 1939. I began to sort through the material, to mine databases, in an attempt to build context, to learn the stories and the fates of the people Morry had mentioned.

In the victims' database at Yad Vashem, for example, I found several entries for Chaim Nusen Cwajghaft, the name variously spelled Cwajgaft, Cwajaft, Tzvighaft. These entries followed a formula, which soon began to sound like a prayer for the dead. "Chaim Cwajgaft. He was married. Prior to WWII he lived in Nasielsk, Poland. Chaim was murdered/ perished in Miendzyrzec, Poland." In other entries from this same source, Chaim Nusen Cwajghaft is said to have been the father of two children, Sara, born in 1933, and a son, Moti, born in 1931. This didn't seem like the Chaim Nusen (Chamnusen) whom Morry had recognized, who is much older in the film, more of a grandfather than the father of young children.

A second source also gave testimony. "Chaim Cwajghaft (or Tzvighaft) was born in Nasielsk, Poland. He was a Hebrew teacher and married. Prior to WWII he lived in Nasielsk, Poland. Chaim was murdered/perished in the Shoah." This second testimony bearing witness to Chaim Nusen Cwajghaft's murder seemed more accurate, though if it was the right man, some information was still incorrect. The Cwajghaft in the film was a stonecutter, not a Hebrew teacher. But he was very religious, very active in his *shtibl*, and his workshop was next door to the Hebrew school where Morry was a student. Someone who did not know him well might easily believe he had been a teacher there. An additional entry by this source names Abram (Avraham Isser) Cwajghaft, born in 1910, as Chaim's son, and identifies his wife simply as "Mrs. Cwajhaft, Tzvighaft." A photo that I would later find in an archive in Israel, showing the Nasielsk branch of the Zionist youth movement Hechalutz, includes an Avraham Isser "Cweikhaft," whose age and appearance would support his being Chaim Nusen's son.

In all, the woman responsible for this second testimony had entered forty-three records in the database of Shoah victims. Among them are Morry's father and grandfather. "Jehoszua Tuchhendler was born in Nowy

Dwor Mazowiecki, Poland. Prior to WWII he lived in Nasielsk, Poland. Jehoszua was murdered/perished in Międzyrzec Podlaski, Ghetto." Jehoszua's birthplace is correct, but the other details are not. Morry does not know his father's final fate precisely, but both his father and his grandfather were with him in the Warsaw Ghetto in 1940 and early 1941.

The Yad Vashem Central Database of Shoah Victims' Names contains 1,515 entries for people from Nasielsk. These testimonies, while sobering in their formality, contain inconsistencies and inaccuracies in birth year, occupation, spouse's name, number of children, place of death. I learned to read them with caution. Most of the victims' names are simply missing. When I combined duplicate entries, the number of victims from Nasielsk fell to just over one thousand, approximately one-third of the town's Jewish population in 1939; one-third of the people who were killed.

The blacksmith Czarko is not listed. Nor are the schoolmaster Szmerlak, the restaurant owner Owsianka, or Morry's classmate Chaim Talmud. This does not mean they survived, although they may have. It means only that they are not on a German list and that no survivor has submitted testimony bearing witness to their deaths.

In January, when we sat together in Florida, and in a phone call a month later, I asked Morry about the names I had collected, in particular, the list of directors of the Joint Distribution Committee's free loan association, or *kassa*, which I'd found in the YIVO archive. Most of the names were familiar to him.

Mordchai Rajczyk was a director of the Joint's *kassa*. He appears on the list with the profession "baker/socialist," which means he was a member of the Bund, the political opponents of the Hasidim. "He's the one who used to pinch my cheeks," Morry said. "You know, as a little boy, I had red cheeks, and every time I walked by in the corridor—I showed it to my daughter when we were there—he would grab me. I just hated him. He had red hair and a three-day beard. And he would grab me and hug me, and I would try to break loose. He was my nemesis."

David Kubel, on the Joint's list as a tailor, was a relative of the young man Morry identified in the film, but that was all he knew about him. David Kubel is not in the database of victims. But his family is, starting with his sons: "Avraham Kubel was born to David and Chana. He was a child. Prior to WWII he lived in Nasielsk, Poland. During the war he was in Parczew, Poland. Avraham was murdered in the Shoah at the age of 18." "Elazar Kubel was born to David and Chana. He was a child. Prior to WWII he lived in Nasielsk, Poland. During the war he was in Parczew, Poland. Elazar was murdered in the Shoah at the age of 14." And David Kubel's wife: "Chana Kubel nee Glodovski was born in Poland in 1896 to Alter and Rakhel. She was a seamstress and married to David. Prior to WWII she lived in Nasielsk, Poland. During the war she was in Parczew, Poland. Chana was murdered in Treblinka, Poland, at the age of 46."

Mojsze Cyrlak, on the Joint's list as "drapery-merchant," appears in the Database of Shoah Victims' Names. "Moshe Cyrlak was born in Nowe Miasto in 1893 to Meir and Brakha. He was a merchant and married to Dvora nee Srebro. Prior to WWII he lived in Nasielsk, Poland. During the war he was in Warsaw, Poland. Moshe was murdered in 1941 in Treblinka, Poland." This testimony was given by Moshe Cyrlak's son. Even so, the date of Moshe's death is probably incorrect, since Treblinka did not begin operation until the summer of 1942, when deportations from Warsaw commenced. Morry remembered the younger Cyrlak, who survived the war in the Soviet Union and eventually lived in Brooklyn. Later, I was able to contact one of Moshe Cyrlak's granddaughters, to share with her the information about her grandfather I had collected.

Zelig Zilberstejn, on the Joint's 1938 list of *kassa* directors as "artisan/shoemaker," also has an entry in the Shoah database: "Zylbersztajn, Mair, Zelig. Son of Elazar Yehuda and Khaia. Born 1892. Married to Henia (Miriam) Mirla. Merchant. Killed in Łuków, Poland in 1942."

"He's probably Louis Silverstein's *mishpukhe*," Morry said, using the Yiddish word for family, relatives. Morry did not know Zelig. But Louis— also known as Leibl or Leibish—he knew well. "Yeah, Leibl Silverstein. I knew him before he left Nasielsk. And he eventually moved to Buffalo."

Louis Silverstein was the president of the prewar Nashelsker Relief

Society mentioned in the *Forward* article from July 1938. It was he who helped raise the funds that the Joint's *kassa* directors would distribute. Louis Silverstein was born Lejba Zylbersztajn in Nasielsk in 1892. In the Ellis Island database, I found the ship's manifest for his immigration to the United States. He arrived from Antwerp on the SS *Belgenland* on November 10, 1923, with his wife, Leja, and their two young children. In the box listing "nearest relative," he had given "Unszer Swarcberg, father-in-law," living at Rynek 9, Nasielsk, just around the corner from Morry's family on the market square.

"And as a matter of fact, I have the number of his nephew," Morry continued. "His name is Richman now. His father worked for us in the shop."

A week later, when I contacted Keva Richman, who also lives in Florida not far from Morry, he explained that his mother, Idessa Schwartzberg Rycherman, was a sister of Laja (Leah) Schwartzberg Silverstein, Louis Silverstein's wife. Shmuel Usher Schwartzberg, mentioned in the Ellis Island document, was Keva's grandfather.

One thing led to another: When I finally met Keva Richman in Florida in April 2012, we spent two hours looking at the family photo album his parents had brought with them when they emigrated to the United States in August 1939, on the last ship to leave Poland before the outbreak of the war. One photo from this album made it possible to give faces to many of the names on the Joint's list of *kassa* directors, preserved in the YIVO archive, as well as to some people Morry had mentioned, and others whose names are entered, often inaccurately, in Yad Vashem's Database of Shoah Victims' Names.

Taken just before the Rycherman/Richman family left Nasielsk in 1939, the photo in Keva's album shows nine men—four sitting and five standing—with two framed pictures on the wall behind them. Before she died, Keva's mother annotated many of the photos in the album, mostly with the names of family members. The label on this photo, written in blue ink on a white adhesive tag attached to the plastic sheet covering the image, says, "Nasielsk Committee for the Needy. Shloma-front row—Leibish-pict. on wall."

Shloma Rycherman, Keva's father, who changed his name to Solomon Richman when he came to America, sits in the front row, second from the left, with his arms crossed over a white short-sleeve button-down shirt. He has a square face and muscular arms and looks like a boxer sitting for a portrait. "Leibish-pict. on wall": this is Louis Silverstein, Keva's uncle, who was already in the United States when this picture was taken in Nasielsk, and so he is represented in the photo by another photo, hanging in the upper right behind the men.

Chaim Nusen Cwajghaft, the *matzevah kritzer*, or gravestone carver, who threw a pitcher at the head of a fellow worshipper in Morry's Hasidic *shtibl* and who appears in David Kurtz's film, is standing in the back row, center, the only man in the black clothing of a Hasid. He has dark, intensely focused eyes and a high, rounded forehead. He seems dignified, with his immaculate overcoat and neatly groomed beard. His expression is serious but not unkind. It's hard to imagine this man throwing a temper tantrum, trying to break a pot over someone's head.

Moshe Cyrlak, the drapery merchant on the Joint's list of directors and in Yad Vashem's list of victims, stands next to Cwajghaft, wearing a striped tie, suspenders, and glasses, a very friendly-looking man, one of only two who smile for the camera.

Fajwel Lejbowicz, on the Joint's list as "timber-merchant," sits in front of Cwajghaft and Cyrlak. "He was right across the street from us," Morry recalled, when we discussed the members of the Joint's *kassa*. "One of his sons survived and became a lumber merchant in Chicago." Fajwel Lejbowicz is listed in the Shoah database: "Faiwel Lejbowicz was born in Pułtusk in 1895 to Schulen and Mirla. He was a lumber mill worker and married to Szeindla nee Waligura. Prior to WWII he lived in Nasielsk, Poland. During the war he was in Miendzyrzec, Poland. Faiwel was murdered in 1943 in Majdanek Camp at the age of 48." Fajwel's wife also appears among the victims, along with three sons and a daughter. They were murdered in Treblinka in 1942.

Chaim Huberman, whose profession on the Joint's list is simply "laborer," also appears both in Keva Richman's family photo album, sitting to the left of Solomon Richman, and on the Yad Vashem list of Holocaust victims, along with his wife, Feiga, born Kubel, another member of the Kubel family. In the photo, Huberman has his arms crossed, and his glasses seem to be sliding down his nose. Both Huberman and his wife are said to have died in Łuków.

Hersz Jagoda is seated in front, on the far right, wearing a colorful tie and suspenders. He was the father of Jankiel Jagoda, who became the secretary of the Nasielsk Survivors' Committee after the war in Warsaw. Hersz Jagoda is not listed in the Yad Vashem database, but he appears on a list of people who died in the Warsaw Ghetto, though the date given is November 2, 1939, a year before the ghetto was formally established.

Abraham Issek Wlosko, another man in the photo in Keva Richman's family album, would eventually become part of the story, though at the time I learned his name, I didn't yet know it. He stands in the back row, second from the left. He's the other man smiling for the camera, along with Moshe Cyrlak. Abraham Wlosko is the tallest of the group. He's slender and broad-shouldered and tilts his head slightly in a way that makes him seem gentle. Later, I would meet his granddaughter and her father, Abraham Wlosko's son-in-law.

A man named Figa stands on the far left, his hand resting on Chaim Huberman's shoulder. He may have been the driver of a wagon or bus that ran a regular route between Nasielsk and the larger nearby town of Pułtusk. An Aron Figa is listed in the Shoah database, along with a Mrs. Figa. No profession is given. There is not enough information to determine whether this is the same man.

The final man in the photo, in the back row on the far right, is Fishl Perelmuter, Fishl *der lumer*, Fishl the Lame, Morry's next-door neighbor, the artist and photographer who painted murals on the synagogue walls. He has a round face with a receding hairline. His ears stick out, and his head seems precariously balanced on his slender neck, which is accentuated by his collarless shirt. His eyes are set close together, and he squints at the camera with a half-smile. Maybe he shot this group photo with a self-timer or a cable shutter release. The setting is clearly a studio, and a vase with flowers rests on the table at the far left, a prop frequently visible in Fishl Perelmuter's portraits, which I will learn as I slowly assemble a small sample of his surviving work.

Living so close to Keva in Florida, Morry had a chance to view this photo before I did.

"I'm amazed," he told me on the phone that evening, having recognized Fishl Perelmuter. "I haven't seen him since the beginning of the war. They were in Warsaw. I saw them in the ghetto. They had one little girl, her name was Rizla. He opened a little studio on the Zamenhofa and Gęsia Streets. I visited once there. And that was the end. I never saw him again."

I was surprised to learn that Fishl Perelmuter was still taking photographs in the ghetto. "Yeah," Morry said. "He opened a studio, *az okh un vey*. You can imagine how much he made. But everybody—they tried to, to survive, whatever they could. You know? Who took pictures in those days?"

I searched the Shoah victims' database. There were two entries, one for "Fishel Pairlmuter" and one for "Fisl Perlmuter." The basic information was the same: Fishl Perelmuter was born in Nasielsk to Mendel and Riza.

He was a photographer, a painter, an artist, and married to Khaia or Sara. Fishl was murdered in the Shoah.

Morry said that Fishl had only one child, a daughter, Rizla or Raiza. She is listed among the victims as well. The database also contains entries for three other children born to Fishl and Khaia: Bila (girl, age four); Liba (girl, age six); Zeda (girl, age eight), all submitted by the same person, identified as a niece. But Morry recalled that Fishl's wife was sickly, and that she died in the early or mid-1930s. He said that Fishl had not remarried. These children would have been too young to be Fishl's daughters. Either their ages or the parents are incorrect in the testimony collected at Yad Vashem.

Surprisingly, in the Ellis Island database, I found a ship's manifest for a "Fischel Perlmutter" from Nasielsk and his wife, Chaya, both age twenty-three, on board the SS *Siboney*, arriving in New York on November 4, 1921. The manifest states they arrived on a transit visa, having visited "Friend: E. Edelstein, Obispo 84, Havana, Cuba." Although the age and names seem correct, other elements of the manifest cast doubt on whether this is the same Fishl Perelmuter from Nasielsk. The manifest gives Fishl's residence as Berlin, Germany, and his profession as "Engineer." Beyond this, the document offers only the standard information of importance to the U.S. government: "Length of time Alien intends to remain in the United States: 2 months. Polygamist? No. Anarchist? No. Carrying $6.50. Intended destination: Uncle—Charles Baum, Arverne, Long Island." A handwritten annotation states, "See letter attached." But the letter has not been preserved, and I could not locate a Charles Baum in Arverne, Long Island, in the phone book or in the 1920 census.

It is easy to suggest a story to make sense of these inconsistencies. As a young man, before discovering his passion for photography, Fishl Perelmuter went to Berlin to study engineering. At age twenty-three, uncertain of his future, he traveled with his young wife to visit relatives before returning to his hometown to start a family and open his photography studio. While in America, the promising young man met with other Nasielskers, who recognized his talent and eventually commissioned him to paint murals in the interior of the Nasielsk synagogue.

Spending so much time with lists, especially lists of the dead, I became ravenous for stories. I sought refuge in speculation, fictionalizing the few facts, pretending the pieces fit together better than they really do.

"The more information we are able to save," I'd stammered to Morry one night on the phone, after I'd kept him for more than an hour dissecting lists. "The more life that we can remember of the town . . ."

"In other words," Morry responded, "the more we can inject into these dead bodies."

|||||||||||||||||||

In 2010, before meeting Morry, I had discovered the 1929 business directory for Nasielsk at the website JewishGen.org. But I had not appreciated the value of this directory until now. The directory helped me cross-reference the people Morry remembered, as well as to spur his recollection of others. The directory was also an important link in the chain that led to other discoveries, beginning with the name of the famous button factory, the only detail about Nasielsk that had come down to me from my grandmother.

In one of our conversations, Morry remembered the family name of the button factory owners, Filar. There was no mention of a Filar in the business directory, but searching in the Warsaw telephone book for 1939, I found the company's address (Nasielsk, Warszawska 46), the phone numbers and telegraph address of the office in Warsaw, the telephone number in Nasielsk (19), and the names of its managing directors: Aron and Boruch Filar. It was also possible to learn the Warsaw bank account number for another member of the family, Lejb Filar. In the Pułtusk *Yizkor* or memorial book, I found the birth years of the Filar brothers: Aron Josek (b. 1871), Boruch Pinkus (b. 1880), along with two others, Gersz Chaim (b. 1880) and Abram Mordka (b. 1890), all of them originally from Nowy Dwór. According to the Pułtusk *Yizkor* book, a man named Eliezer Charka had originally founded the button factory. The name Charka was familiar to me from the Joint's correspondence concerning the competing free loan associations in Nasielsk. In the memo dated October 19, 1938, the Joint's representative had named "Cherkow" as the suspicious former Nasielsker, now living in London, who operated the independent Achiezer *kassa* without "social control."

Once I learned that the Polish word for "button" is *guzik*, I noticed the factory listed in the Nasielsk business directory after all, "Warszawska Fabryka Guzików." This led to a special edition of the Warsaw business newspaper, *Gazeta Handlowa*, from March 18, 1930, profiling "The Button-Manufacturing Industry in Poland." "There have been rapid advances toward the improvement of the button manufacturing industry in Poland, but the first years of development cannot be classified as successful, since consumers accustomed to foreign goods look only reluctantly at domestic buttons, believing them to be inferior," the article begins. It then provides an overview of the prominent button manufacturers in the country. "One of the oldest button factories is 'A. and B. Filar,' founded in 1897 in Nasielsk, and today employing 200 workers. The plant is used for making pearl buttons, galalith, Bakelite and buffalo horn." In particular, A. and B. Filar's company was known for making "French" buttons from mother-of-pearl. Previously, these had been imported from France and Japan. "In 1922, thanks to long-term development, the A. and B. Filar Company managed to manufacture this kind of so-called 'French' button, so that today, a factory with modern machines produces them to perfection."

The Filar Company spokesman seemed especially proud of their Bakelite products. "Buttons made from Bakelite are durable, have a nice sheen, are much cheaper than buttons made with 'coconut [*orzecha kokosowego*],' and even have the appearance of finer quality buttons. Bakelite buttons are sold in mass quantities and are not subject to special changes in style, as happens with more expensive buttons." This expertise in the use of Bakelite had also led the company to expand into electronics, producing Bakelite insulation for cameras, telephones, and a patented radio transmitter for the Polish army, under the trademark Filaryt. The *Gazeta Handlowa* carried a photograph of Aron Filar and of the factory building in Nasielsk.

As with the photographer Fishl Perelmuter and the *matzevah kritzer* Chaim Nusen Cwajghaft, the Filars were noted figures. They were the only large-scale employers and by far the wealthiest people in Nasielsk. Morry recalled peeking in the windows of the button factory as a boy to see the machines in operation. The names Aron and Baruch Filar were not familiar to him, but he recalled a Meir Filar, who also lived in Nasielsk, and who may have been the company's export director. "The *rakhmunes* is, of Meir Filar, that he went back and forth overseas," Morry recalled, meaning the pity of it, the tragedy. Much of the Filar Company's production was exported to the United States. "And his misfortune was, because he went to America quite often, that he came back just before the war started and got trapped," Morry said. "Later on, I read lists of people that were executed in the Pawiak," the Czarist-era fortress in Warsaw, used by the Gestapo as a jail, "and I saw his name. Filar."

I was unable to find Meir Filar in the book that compiled the names of those executed in Pawiak. Neither he nor any member of the Filar family appears in the Shoah database. In a different database, however, run by the Polish Center for Holocaust Research, I found a Majer Filar, born 1860, who died in September 1940. This database does not provide the cause of death. Citing the "*Gazeta Zydowska* 1940," the official German newspaper for Jews in occupied Poland, published from July 1940 until August 1942, it notes only: "80 years old, funeral organized by the Funeral Home 'Wiecznosc.'" *Wieczność* means "eternity" and was the name of the main Jewish funeral home in the Warsaw Ghetto. There is no way to tell if this refers to Meir Filar of Nasielsk.

<hr />

In the 1990s, while my sister, Dana, was president of the San Francisco Bay Area Jewish Genealogical Society, she had exchanged information with other researchers seeking family from Nasielsk and from Liza's hometown of Berezne. Shortly after we met Morry and his family in Florida, Dana reviewed her twelve years of correspondence with these family historians. One e-mail leapt out immediately. Written in 2007, it was from a woman searching for the Kubel and Diamond families. It seemed that Kubels and Diamonds had frequently married each other. The researcher and Dana had exchanged a few messages, since our families were very probably related, if distantly. But the exchange had petered out when the connections remained elusive. At the conclusion of one note, however, after attempting unsuccessfully to untangle the relationships, the woman had written: "Does the name Louis Molina [sic] mean anything to you?" In 2007, Dana had no reason to find this reference to Louis Malina important. In March 2012, however, it was astonishing. I contacted this researcher, Faith Ohlstein, immediately. Our conversation changed my view of David and Liza Kurtz's visit to Nasielsk.

In that first conversation, Faith informed me that Louis Malina, my grandfather's boyhood friend and traveling companion, had paid for her mother's passage to America. The Ellis Island database quickly yielded the ship's manifest. On November 26, 1938—just three months after my grandparents and the Malinas were in Nasielsk—Sura Kubel, age twenty-six, profession: corset maker, formerly residing at 10 Rynek Street, Nasielsk, arrived in New York on the SS *Piłsudski*. Her destination, according to the manifest: "Cousin: Louis Malina, 211 Central Park W. New York, NY."

A week later, I received a photograph from Faith of her mother's family. Sura's parents, Eliahu Kubel, a miller, and Frumet Haze Kubel, had both died shortly after World War I, perhaps of tuberculosis, perhaps in the worldwide Spanish flu epidemic. Consequently, the five sisters, including Sura, and one brother lived together in Nasielsk as orphans. The women, who lived two doors down from Morry's family and whom Morry's mother referred to as "the *maydlekh*," the girls, ran a housewares store. The brother was a student, a young man with a beard and a black coat. One day in 1938, he walked down the steps of the Nasielsk synagogue and was recorded in David Kurtz's home movie.

In the formal portrait that Faith sent me, the sisters all bear a strong family resemblance. Faith provided the names of her mother's siblings, but she was in doubt about some of these identifications. Shandl, apparently the head of the family, and the only one who was married, sits in an armchair in the center, her hands in her lap. She has a Mona Lisa smile, reserved, confident, inviting, and mysterious. Seated on either side of her are two younger sisters, Chaja on the left, with the same hairstyle but a much slimmer face, and Leiba on the right, clearly the youngest sister, her face still girlish and round. Mindl (or perhaps Rachel) stands behind

Shandl's chair and leans on the backrest. She closely resembles Shandl but seems somehow more direct. Next to Mindl, standing beside his wife's chair, is Josef Lederman, tall with dark eyes, a neatly groomed black beard, and the black coat and brimless hat of a Hasidic Jew. Sura, Faith's mother, stands on the far right, the only one not wearing black. Like her sisters, her dark hair is parted in the center and pulled back tightly, and she shares the facial features of her family. In every other respect, however, Sura Kubel seems inserted from a different photograph, almost from a different era, with her bold plaid suit and round glasses.

Avrum Kubel, the only brother, stands on the left, opposite Sura. He, too, is clearly a younger sibling, his face still forming, though he already has the beard of a yeshiva *bukher*. He is obviously the same man who appears twice in my grandfather's film, first descending the synagogue stairs, and then later, in color, standing with his friend Rotstein, amused by the commotion around him, giving a faint nod to the man behind the camera. Avrum has the same directness and self-possession as his sisters. Dressed like his brother-in-law, he rests his hands on the back of his sister

Chaja's chair. But his gaze is slightly lowered, as if in the instant the photo was snapped he was looking at the photographer's feet. This gives his expression an air of distance, dreaminess.

Sura was the only survivor. Testimony in the Shoah victims' database, given by sources identified as cousins, provides names and approximate birth years: Chaja, born in 1913; Mindl, born 1916; Abrahm, or Avrum, born 1919; Leiba, born 1922 (or 1914 in a duplicate entry, where she may have been confused with Shandl); and Rachel, born 1923. The dates or names may be inaccurate, since they do not follow the order Faith had identified. Shandl is not in the database at all, nor is her husband, Josef Lederman.

Faith knew very little about her lost family in Nasielsk. Sura Kubel had rarely spoken of her siblings. But after Sura's death, Faith and her brother, Jerry Goldsmith, found a bundle of letters and photographs that the Kubels in Nasielsk had sent to Sura in America between November 1938 and the spring of 1942. It would be almost a year before I saw these extraordinary documents, which provide a tender and terrifying glimpse into the life of a Jewish family in Nasielsk in the year before the war, and in the two and a half years of escalating suffering and systematic deprivation and humiliation that would end in their deaths.

Louis Malina obviously knew the Kubel family. Was Avrum's presence in my grandfather's film an accident, then, or did he have some closer connection to the visitors? There was no way to tell. But when we spoke in April 2012, Faith Ohlstein and I were both captivated by another moment toward the end of the film, a scene clearly shot in someone's home, in which a young woman fixes her hair. Her back is to the camera. We see the tweed fabric of her suit, the shoulders bunched because her hands are busy with a comb or a pin. For a split second, she turns. Her face is heavily shadowed, in three-quarter profile. "Like a Vermeer," someone would say to me later. Could this be one of Avrum and Sura Kubel's sisters?

"I had a funny feeling that it may have been my mom's place, where she lived," Faith said, examining the film online.

Just two months after the film was made, Louis Malina would sponsor one of these young women when she emigrated to America. He appears to

have been a cousin, at least by marriage. Surely he would have consulted with the family during his brief visit to Nasielsk, to make arrangements, iron out details. If the brother, Avrum, knew that David Kurtz was accompanying Louis Malina, this might explain his nod in the film, acknowledging some relation to David, however slight.

For days, I compared the faces in the Kubel family photograph with the shadowy image in the film. The woman fixing her hair has round cheeks, which disqualifies Sura, Shandl, and the slimmer-featured Chaja. But could it be Mindl (Ruchel) or the youngest, Leiba? The image is provocatively obscure. I could not determine the woman's identity.

The Kubel family photograph was not the only invaluable information Faith Ohlstein provided in our first contact that spring. In the course of her genealogical research, she told me, she had located a man from Nasielsk who might be a cousin by marriage, a man born around 1919, who came to the United States in 1935, and who, at ninety-three, still remembered the town where he grew up. Faith had not spoken with him, but she gave me his telephone number. Another Nasielsker—not a survivor, strictly speaking, but an emigrant—who would eventually share his memories of the town with me. As I might have guessed by this point, Irving Novetsky also wintered in Florida, not far from Morry. I called him immediately, but it was too difficult for him to hear on the telephone. It would be four months before we met.

Faith also gave me the e-mail address of a man who had contacted her a few years before, a Polish history teacher from Nasielsk who was interested in the town's Jewish community. He had obtained Faith's address through the Holocaust Museum in Washington, D.C., where she had filed a research request. Faith had not written back to this Polish historian. But she suggested that I might try, which I did. This man, too, would eventually become integral to the story of my grandfather's film.

IIIIIIIIIIIIIIIIIIII

My conversations with Faith Ohlstein, the daughter of Sura Kubel and the niece of Avrum, strengthened a suspicion I had been harboring. Perhaps Louis Malina, and not David Kurtz, had been the driving force behind the visit to Nasielsk. Louis's name appears among the donors to the postwar United Nashelsker Relief Society, while my grandfather's name does not. (David was a sponsor of the Berezne *Landsmanshaft*, undoubtedly at Liza's insistence.) Most of David's Nasielsk family, the Diamonds, including his mother and many aunts, uncles, and cousins, had come to the United States in the 1890s. Perhaps David did not know any of his distant relatives still living in the town. Perhaps his visit was not for family reasons but entirely a matter of curiosity. Perhaps the visit had not been his idea at all, and he and my grandmother had merely tagged along.

Viewing the film again, I had to acknowledge that the footage of Nasielsk differed only subtly from other, touristy scenes, particularly in Holland, where groups of people in traditional dress surround the travelers and wave for the camera. In Nasielsk, there are no obvious group shots of a family gathering, as you would expect from someone who had come so far to see his relatives. There are portraits of small groups, the shots of Chaim Nusen Cwajghaft standing next to the onion-exuding ascetic, Chezkiah, for example. David films with sympathy and, judging from the expressions of his subjects, with permission, even encouragement. But except for the one fleeting glimpse of the woman fixing her hair, David seems to capture "typical" people, rather than specific people. *This happened*, the film seems to say, not *Here are the cousins I visited*.

My suspicions may be wrong. David Kurtz may have filmed the

peripheral moments of his visit, when he was unoccupied, not otherwise engaged with the people he knew or had met. The woman fixing her hair—this intimate gesture, which only a friend or family member would have been permitted to witness, let alone film—may be David's relative, not Louis Malina's. When I asked my aunt Shirley, she told me with certainty, "His trip to Nasielsk was something he wanted to do. Fortunately, he had Louis Malina to back him up, because she [Liza] would do anything Louis said." Perhaps Louis Malina and David Kurtz had shared the costs of Sura Kubel's emigration. Both Louis and David were probably related to the family. But only Louis's name appears on the ship's manifest.

Shortly after speaking with Faith Ohlstein, I sent David Kurtz's film to the descendants of Louis and Rosie Malina and Essie and David Diamond. The film, after all, could be said to star their grandparents. David Malina, Louis and Rosie's grandson, and Faith's (and probably my) cousin by marriage, quickly responded to my e-mail. He was grateful for the information, since he had not known the name of Louis's hometown in Poland. He filled me in on a little Malina family history. "I don't know what Louis's earliest jobs were, but he eventually became a salesman in the textile industry. During this period he discovered a way to either dye or process textiles—particularly rayon—that was just as effective and much less costly than the prior method. The result was the Malina Company, which had almost a monopoly on that process. American Viscose was their primary customer and American Viscose was said to have had a more powerful hold on the textile industry than Standard Oil had on oil. Mostly what I remember was how marvelous both Louis and Rose were. Everyone loved them. They were both very funny, loving, generous, philanthropic, wonderful people. Also very modern New Yorkers rather than 'old country.' I remember the major textile magazine of that time put Louis on its cover and said, 'The name Malina was synonymous with integrity.'"

I met Jane Malina Levinson, another grandchild of Louis and Rosie Malina, a month later, in May 2012. According to Jane, Louis Malina "was very retiring. He didn't like the spotlight." Neither David nor Jane had known of their grandparents' trip to Europe in 1938. Nor were they aware of Louis's work on behalf of the United Nashelsker Relief Society. The names Faith Ohlstein and Sura Kubel were unfamiliar to them. No family photographs, postcards, or letters from before the war had survived in their family to shed light on the trip or the film.

According to a notice in the *New York Times* on November 4, 1928, Louis Malina had founded the Malina Company in 1924. As David Malina had said, Louis was an early manufacturer of rayon, and he was a founding member of the Rayon Yarn Association. He appears again in the *Times* on August 11, 1937, in an article entitled "Apartment Leasing Holds Active Level." "Included in the long list of rentals of residential space was one for a large suite in the Beresford, 211 Central Park West. There, Louis Malina leased a duplex apartment on the seventeenth and eighteenth floors, consisting of twelve rooms, six baths and a large terrace." This luxurious apartment is the one mentioned on Sura Kubel's immigration manifest.

A month or so after meeting Jane Malina Levinson, I received an e-mail from Ronnie Diamond, the granddaughter of Essie Malina and David Diamond. Since David Diamond was David Kurtz's uncle, Ronnie and I are cousins. "Wow," she wrote in response to the film, "that's my grandmother Essie Malina Diamond!" Ronnie passed along a story she had heard from another cousin. David Diamond, Essie's husband, was born in Nasielsk in 1878, she told me. He died in New York on March 2, 1927, which is why Essie Malina Diamond is traveling alone in 1938. According to Diamond family lore, Ronnie said, David had never given Essie a proper wedding ring, since he could not afford one when they married, and he died before making good the omission. By the time of the 1938 trip, however, Essie and David's son Fred Diamond, born 1909, had become successful. He bought his mother a diamond ring to wear on the trip, "so she would look respectable." The ring is visible on Essie's finger in my grandfather's film.

||||||||||||||||||

At the end of April 2012, four months after first speaking with Morry Chandler, I booked a trip to London, Warsaw, and Tel Aviv. First, I would spend two days with Morry's childhood friend Leslie Glodek and his family. Then I would continue on to Warsaw and its archives, and to Nasielsk, where the history teacher I'd contacted via Faith Ohlstein had agreed to help identify the streets seen in David Kurtz's film. Finally, I would fly to Israel to consult the archives at Yad Vashem and visit Nachlat Nashelsk, the postwar home to many Nasielsk survivors, now located in Kiryat Ono, a desirable suburb of Tel Aviv.

Very sweetly, Morry expressed concern about my travel arrangements.

"Have you prepared ahead of time, you know, the groundwork? So that you don't get *farblundzhet* as a stranger," meaning bewildered, befuddled, perplexed.

"A bit *farblundzhet*," I admitted.

Morry took the opportunity to instruct me a little. "You know, it so happens, *farblundzhet* is a Polish word that became a Yiddish word."

What does it mean in Polish? I asked.

"To be lost. But the Yiddish, it has more *tam*," he said, meaning taste or zest or, more generally, Yiddish soul.

In truth, I was more than a bit *farblundzhet*. Morry had given me so many stories, and I had amassed so many scraps of information, that I had had little time for synthesis. The only thing I could do was to make lists.

I had downloaded and organized a list of victims from the Yad Vashem Shoah database and a list of survivors from the United States Holocaust Memorial Museum. But people I knew had survived were not in the survivors' database, and people I was almost certain had been killed were not listed among the victims. So I made new lists of the people not present on the first two lists.

Because the Yad Vashem victims' database consists largely of survivor testimonies given by family, friends, or acquaintances of the victims, the data is messy. Sometimes the town is spelled Nasielsk. Sometimes it is Nashelsk, Naszelsk, Naselsk, Naschelsk. The spelling of proper names was even more confusing. I searched for exact, "literal" spellings, and I performed "fuzzy" searches, letting the search engine decide what range of variance would still count as the same name. I spent days trying to trick search engines into returning results the databases insisted were not there, hoping to find photographs, documents, names that lay hidden: present in the database, but excluded by the search parameters.

I made lists of the names Morry had remembered. I cross-referenced this list with associated documents. I made a list of spouses, children, relatives. I compiled a frame-by-frame inventory of the film. I reconstructed the itinerary of my grandparents' trip and the chronology of David's shots.

Dana had shared the names of all the family historians searching for relatives from Nasielsk. Dozens of names, hundreds of names. I didn't make a list of these names. They were stored in the genealogy society's correspondence. I figured I could consult the correspondence whenever I wished. There were too many people, too many possible connections. I couldn't pursue them all. The proliferation of names and family histories made me feel that my head would explode. I had to concentrate on the living survivors and their memories, before I became entangled in the endlessly expanding Diaspora of children, grandchildren, nieces, nephews, cousins, brothers- and sisters-in-law.

But not making a list had its drawbacks. Those names floated in my mind like debris. They bobbed, they swirled, they washed up on my shore. It made me anxious, because every single scrap of information might, at some unknown point in the future, become crucial. I had to remember it all, in case I later found a piece of data linking the fragments together. *Memory slips away, grows dim.* So I caved in and made a list.

And then there was the list of random facts I had accumulated that I simply didn't know what to do with.

- In the September 2009 issue of Marvel Comics' *Wonder Woman*, the supervillain Thomas Oscar Morrow ("T. O. Morrow") reveals that his real name is Tomek Ovadya Morah. "My family was from Nasielsk, a little town outside Warsaw," he says in a speech bubble above his darkened, kneeling form. "I can't be part of anything called *GENOCIDE*, Wonder Woman." In this case, however, "genocide" is not the Holocaust, but some comic-book version of a doomsday machine.

- The American artist Frank Stella created four works entitled "Nasielsk." These constructions are part of a series based on towns in the book *Wooden Synagogues*, by Maria and Kazimierz Piechotka. "Nasielsk IV" was completed in 1972 and now resides at the Art Institute of Chicago.
- In one frame of my grandfather's film, at 3:33:28 on the time code, two birds fly over the market square.

"The list is an absolute good," says Itzhak Stern in Steven Spielberg's movie *Schindler's List*. "All around its margins lies the gulf."

But the truth is more complicated than that. Like my grandfather's film, a list leaves out everything not falling within its narrow frame, which is both its glory and its terrifying limitation. And like my grandfather's film, every list also contains obscurities or errors, gulfs not only around its margins but within them.

8

NOW WE'RE ONTO SOMETHING

ON SATURDAY, MAY 25, 2012, I met Leslie Glodek and his family at his home in Cockfosters, London, the last stop on the Piccadilly line. Morry had cautioned me to expect a certain English reserve, but I was greeted with extraordinary warmth and graciousness. "Your name has been in the air for several weeks," Leslie told me as we sat down to lunch with his wife, Celia, and their daughter and son-in-law, Jennifer and Jonathan Benn. The Glodeks' son, Graham, could not join us. He was traveling in Eastern Europe, and a few days earlier, he had visited Nasielsk. As we sat down, I realized that when you are invited to someone's home to conduct an interview, you must be prepared to eat. Before Leslie and I began our formal conversation, Celia served a feast. The table was set as if for a holiday. As the guest, I was treated to especially generous portions, which began with two grapefruit-size mounds of chopped liver.

When I met him, Leslie was approaching his ninetieth birthday. He was slightly stooped, and his hearing and eyesight had been deteriorating for some time. But he exuded a boyish enthusiasm when telling stories. His voice would rise as he reached the climactic moments, and his face colored when he laughed, which he did often. He had prepared a list of things he wanted to tell me, which lay on the table next to his silver place setting. We would get to his "adventures," as he called them, after lunch.

But first, Leslie seemed to delight in table conversation, the anecdotes that came to him as he recalled his boyhood.

"When a circus came to town—the circuses did come at least twice a year, or more often than that—they would go to the town hall for permission to set up," he began. "In the early days, perhaps when I was very little, they used to get space in the market. But the people, the traders in the marketplace—there were shops all the way around the square, and those who came in twice a week, Tuesdays and Fridays, the farmers—they were all objecting to somebody taking up all the space. It disrupted their lives, you understand? So it was decided by the powers that be in the town hall, that when these people came, to send them to us. 'Go and see Mr. Glodek!'"

Leslie was born Lejzor Glodek in Nasielsk in 1922, the youngest of six children. If he was six or eight years old at the time of this story, that places it around 1928 or 1930. His family lived two blocks south of the marketplace, at the intersection of three streets, which formed a triangle. An electrical transformer in a little tower stood at the apex of the triangle and was a major landmark in the town. There was a water pump next to the property and a stand for horse-drawn carriages for hire, droshkies. Rather than a town house, like Morry's family had, Leslie and his parents lived in a freestanding building fronting the street, with an open lot in back. To the left of the house, Leslie recalled, there was a very tall willow. On the right stood two gates, a large double-door gate for horses and vehicles and a small pedestrian gate, through which you reached the house.

"We had the space available here, right behind," Leslie explained, continuing his story about the circus. "A large space, nearly as big as the market. Now, I used to get excited about it, because they used to make a fuss of me. There were two performances every day, and I was able to go in free. And I could even take a friend. I used to take Avrum. And they always made a fuss. They would give me ice cream, that sort of thing."

Avrum Tuchendler, Morry's older brother, was Leslie's best friend growing up. Most of the stories Leslie told me about his early years in Nasielsk featured Avrum and Morry, whom Leslie refers to as Morris, or they centered on the open space behind the Glodek house.

"Every boy of my age, at the time—*doesn't know what to do? No school today? Right! Go to the Glodeks'!"* Leslie clapped his hands at the table. "And they'll play football, or cricket, or whatever the games were. And they always wanted to be friends with me, because they thought I might put the bar up to some people I disapprove of." The game the boys played most frequently was called *palant*. "You know cricket? What's the American equivalent?" Leslie asked. In his magisterial history of Poland, *God's Playground*, Norman Davies suggests that baseball originated from *palant*, which was brought to America by Polish immigrants to Jamestown, Virginia, in the 1610s.

After lunch, when Leslie's family and I had settled on couches in the study and Leslie had taken his place in a plush reading chair in front of the floor-to-ceiling bookshelves, he pulled out the notes he had taken of things he wanted to tell me.

"I've made these notes because I wanted to talk in a chronological order, otherwise you'll be totally confused," he said. "So I've put down: Nasielsk, as a small town, was uneventful most of the time. You know, as small towns go."

I asked Leslie to tell me about the members of his family, to help me get oriented.

"My parents were elderly when I was growing up," he responded. "My mother was fifty-one when I was born. That gives you an idea. So I've never known what my parents looked like when they were young people. To me, being a teenager, they looked terribly old."

Leslie's father's name was Jacob, Jankiel in Polish. "He had another name, Shalom, but it was hardly used. And my mother's name was Chana. I spell it Hannah, with an *H*. But in Poland, we used to spell it with a *C-h*."

I asked for his mother's maiden name.

"Her maiden name is a bit tricky. I could find out, if need be . . . It could be Edelman . . . something like that."

It seemed strange that Leslie could not recall his mother's maiden name. But later, when he began to tell the story of his survival, Leslie gave a hint about why this detail, among others, might not be present to his mind. "You know that I cannot talk about my family, the final upshot," he told me then. "Nor can Morris. The information I have received was not firsthand. No eyewitnesses. People who had known people who had known other people, and so on and so forth. But he and I never discussed the subject. We leave the subject well alone, because it's too painful." Although his memory of other aspects of his life was remarkably detailed, Leslie had blocked out much that related to his immediate family. Even in the anecdotes he recalled, he often provided a small history lesson in place of personal traits.

Leslie's five siblings were much older. By the time he was a young child, they had married, and Leslie had nieces and nephews his own age. The eldest brother was Abraham, and Leslie told this story about him, set at the end of the First World War, when Poland fought for its independence: "Following the Armistice Day, Marshal Piłsudski then became active. And he took advantage of the Germans on one side and the Russians on the other side. He created a secret army. What was ironical about this was that my eldest brother, who was born in the year 1900, was then twenty years of age. And he, too, was a volunteer in Piłsudski's army. My father was a reservist in the Russian army. And when the war came—the First World War—he was called up, in the reservists. Piłsudski's army and the Russian army came face-to-face fighting. So I had my father on one side, and my brother on the other side. I wasn't alive yet."

The second brother, Leibl, operated a general store near the train station in a town called Pieścirogi, about four miles from Nasielsk. "He was actually quite successful in running the business," Leslie said. "But he had a competitor across the road, near the railway station. This competitor was a German national who lived in Poland. This German picked an argument with my brother. And just before the war, he threatened my brother. He said, 'You wait until the German army gets here.' So much so, that on Tuesday, about four or five days after the war started, my brother came into town, to Nasielsk, with his wife and four children. Locked up the place, because he was afraid what might happen to him when the Germans came in. And the Germans were not exactly gentle in dealing with people."

Before he opened the business in Pieścirogi, Leibl Glodek had run a small grocery store on the market square in Nasielsk, just down the block from Morry's family. When Leibl moved to the shop near the railway station in Pieścirogi, Leslie's parents took over the grocery store. This was the store that Morry suspected might be the *sklep spożywczy* in my grandfather's film.

Leslie's third brother, Herszek, owned the bicycle shop, located in one of the buildings on the family's large property near the transformer on Warszawska Street. "He was selling bicycles, he was maintaining bicycles, and he had at least several dozen bicycles for hire," Leslie said.

Almost a year after I first spoke with Leslie Glodek, I met a woman who had grown up a few doors down from his family. "Glodek had a food store," recalled Grace Pahl, whom I would meet in New York in January 2013, and who was born in Nasielsk in 1924, the same year as Morry. "They had a few children, and one of their sons had a *welodrom*, you know what that is? He had a bicycle shop. Him I remember. That's where I lived." Grace did not recognize Leslie's name or face. But his brother's bicycle shop was the site of a little family drama that had remained vivid in her memory. "My sister was the first one to tear her skirt there," she recalled. "She went to rent a bicycle, and she came home crying. What happened? She fell off the bike and she tore her skirt. And my mother said, 'You never go again to the *welodrom*! Forget it!' I never went. I was afraid. And my mother says, 'Look at Lila, what happened to Lila! She could have killed herself! She could have this . . .' You know how mothers are."

Herszek Glodek's bicycle shop, like Leib Owsianka's restaurant and even Srul Skalka's clothing store, was a landmark in the social map of Nasielsk. "That's why everybody always knew our name and they knew everything about us," Leslie Glodek remarked, sitting in his study in London. "From the circuses, and the bicycles. And apart from that, even at the very local level," he said, "if ever people just feel like talking, getting together, it was always in our place. I don't know why, but that's the way it was."

Leslie's fourth brother, Szlamek, born around 1918, had studied at a hakhshara, a Zionist training farm, in preparation for emigrating to Palestine. But his plans were interrupted by mandatory service in the Polish army. He fought and was wounded in the defense of Warsaw.

Gittla Glodek, Leslie's only sister, was closest to him in age. She had married and moved to Warsaw with her husband. Leslie did not share stories with me about her. But Grace Pahl recalled that she had a beautiful voice. "She sang very, very nice," Grace told me in New York in 2013. In the summer of 1938, when my grandparents visited Nasielsk, Leslie was living with Gittla in Warsaw, which is why he does not appear in my grandfather's film.

I asked Leslie what he remembered about Morry's family. For them, unlike for his own family, Leslie provided brief, personal descriptions. "Well, I remember his grandfather. He was an elderly man—elderly! Anybody over fifty was elderly for me. I remember him. He was very strict. If ever the two boys, Morris and Avrum, did anything untowards, he would immediately put his hand up: 'No way! Can't do it.' And in the presence of him, they had to be at their best behavior. I remember that distinctly. I would not have had any conversation with his grandfather, because they were so remote from the younger generation. Our generation were entirely ignored by the elders. But I do know that he was always well dressed, clean-looking, and he wore a good coat, a three-quarter-length coat or something like that. And Morris would always straighten himself up, if his grandfather appeared anywhere in close proximity. Nowadays, we would call him a tyrant."

Leslie had no idea why Srul Skalka should have had the nickname Kurtz.

"Morris's mother always had a smile on her face. And I came there very often. Not as often as they came to us. But when I did go there, she would smile and offer me a sweet, or something like that. She was a very kind person."

Leslie then returned to the first item on the list of things he wanted to tell me.

"Nasielsk, as a small town in Poland, it was not very exciting, to begin with. It was just sort of a modest place. There weren't many things to be excited about. But people used their own initiative to do something that caused some excitement and gave some satisfaction."

He began with an anecdote about Morry.

"Morris's neighbor was a photographer . . ."

"Fishl Perelmuter!" I interjected, to Leslie's surprise.

"I can't remember his name. The one thing I specifically remember is he had a lame leg. Now, he asked Morris if he could do an errand for him. This consisted of delivering some photographs to people in a place which was seven kilometers away from Nasielsk. Pomiechówek." In Leslie's memory, it was only seven kilometers distant. Google places Pomiechówek twice as far: fifteen kilometers, about nine and a half miles from Nasielsk. "He asked me first if I would accompany him. Moreover, we had cycles—there was no other means of transport. So I said to Morris, 'Yes, we'll go together.' And we rode out there to this place, Pomiechówek." The town was a popular destination for young people during the summer because of a large lake nearby.

"We stayed there for about an hour and a half. And when we were finished, and we were about to get ready to start going back, Morris said to me, 'Are you game?' And I said, 'What's on your mind?' And he says, 'Nowy Dwór'—in the opposite direction, where his father's parents, his grandparents, lived. He says, 'We're so close. I feel like going on.' 'Okay, if you feel like it, so do I.'"

Nowy Dwór, the birthplace of Morry's father, Szaja Tuchendler, is another four kilometers farther south in the opposite direction from Nasielsk. The boys bicycled there and visited Morry's grandparents. "They were pleasantly surprised, and they gave us some refreshments of some sort, and we spent a couple of hours. And then it was time to go. As we go riding back, about halfway through, the chain on Morris's bike broke. And without a chain, you can't ride a bike!"

Leslie's voice rose.

"We walk about a kilometer—maybe a kilometer, maybe two kilometers—and we went through a village, and we spotted a blacksmith. I said, 'Hang on a minute. We'll just go in and see if the blacksmith can help us.'" The blacksmith was too busy, but he offered to let Leslie borrow his tools. "Well, I didn't need much persuasion to attempt it. I am a fixer by nature, I fix things. Celia will verify this. So, he gave me some tools, took off the chain, and I said, 'Well, there is a rivet missing!'" Leslie found an old nail and fashioned a replacement rivet. "We thanked the bloke, offered to pay him. He said, 'No, no, no. This is not usual business. It's a good turn from one person to another.' And we thanked him, I shook hands with him—my hands were dirty, and his were dirty, and I didn't bother to ask him if he could give me something to clean my hands up. And off we went on the bikes. And it was still in the same village, but at the far end this time, we were passing a place, they were selling kielbasa. So Morris says, 'I'm hungry.' All of a sudden, I feel peckish, too—you know the term peckish?"

I said that I did.

"So we stopped, we went in there, and we bought a piece of kielbasa about *this* long—they still sell it here, from Poland, it's called *wiejska*. So we bought one, cut it in half, and we bought some nice, crusty rolls, and a drink. They didn't have kvass, but we bought something like lemonade."

The boys enjoyed a picnic by the roadside, then finally made their way back home to Nasielsk.

"When we told this—what transpired during the course of the day—to others, they would say, 'I wish it happened to me!' It was considered to be a big adventure!"

Kvass is a lightly fermented beverage made from rye or black bread and fruit. The leading manufacturer of kvass around Nasielsk was Leib Jagoda, from the same family as Hersz Jagoda, who served as a director of the Joint's free loan association, and his son, Jankiel Jagoda, who became secretary of the Nasielsk Survivors' Committee after the war.

It is also worth noting that kielbasa, made from pig, is decidedly non-kosher. In the time between Morry's accounts of secretly tasting ham and incurring his grandfather's wrath by riding a bicycle, it appears such transgressions became more commonplace for the boys. Or perhaps the difference in tone should be attributed to the different narrators, not to the experience. Perhaps Morry was grounded for months after he and Leslie returned from their adventure, these new unforgivable sins added to the long list of things Morry would have to atone for on Yom Kippur, while for Leslie it was just another day. It is also possible that the story has become so mild in its repercussions only with time and distance, become merely charming where originally it was also subversive.

Leslie told another story to illustrate his life in small-town Nasielsk.

"When somebody came from America, it was a big day," he said. "Everybody wanted to see them. Everybody wanted to know what this is all about."

One day, Leslie recalled, a relative of Morry's, who was staying at the house on the *rynek*, had to go out of town on business for the day. "So Morris or his brother said to me, 'Come up to us,' because normally, they come to me, to my house. So I went there. And they said, 'Well, come and see some of the things he has lying about.' And among other things, we found a drawer full of chocolate bars. *Funny, having all those chocolate bars.* So we decided amongst ourselves, he won't miss it if there was one short. And we opened up one and we started eating it. What we didn't realize is, these chocolates were Ex-Lax!"

Leslie's voice rose to the top of its range.

"We couldn't have known that! Soon enough . . ."

Leslie laughed, then added, "And we even gave a couple to other people that were not aware of . . ."

Leslie recounted the most extensive and controversial anecdote of his youth in Nasielsk the second day of my visit, over another sumptuous lunch. For reasons I don't understand, and for which I kick myself now, I didn't have my voice recorder running. As soon as I returned to my hotel that night, I wrote it down: "The Story of the Horse."

"Now and then, as you have heard," Leslie began,

a circus would come to Nasielsk. Occasionally, the circus would also have a menagerie with it, with wild animals that needed to be fed meat. Now, the menagerie owners would not go to the butcher for meat, because that was too expensive. Instead, farmers from the surrounding area would bring old animals that had lived out their useful life, and these would be killed and fed to the menagerie. One day, a farmer came into town leading an old, broken-down horse that he wanted to sell to the menagerie. But the circus had left town the previous day, and the man was unsure what to do. He didn't want to bring the horse back with him, because he feared it would not survive the trip. Since the menagerie had been in our yard, I saw the farmer's perplexity, and I had an idea. So Avrum Tuchendler and I and two other boys went up to the man and asked how much he wanted for the horse. Whatever the sum was, it was considerably more than we could muster. But we pooled all the money we had, and we came up with a sum, which we offered to the man. There was some conversation, some negotiation, and finally the man accepted the offer and went away satisfied. We led the horse outside of town to a wooded area, where we hid it. Well! What do we do now? First thing, we have to find food for it. So we took whatever we could scrounge from home, and we saved carrots and things like that from our plates at dinner. [Celia Glodek supplements the story here, invoking the mothers: Why are you so hungry all of a sudden?*] In the meantime, we had the idea to hitch the horse to a wagon. But you don't just find an extra wagon lying about! So we set about collecting cast-off wagon parts. I had access to my brother's tools, and there were enough places to conceal what we were doing. And after a few days or a week, we had managed to construct a cart for the horse to pull. The big day came, and we hauled the cart out to where we had hidden the horse, hitched it up, and the four of us climbed on board for a test drive. The horse pulled the cart perhaps fifty meters—then dropped dead! We fled in all directions! And when we met again later, we swore each other to absolute secrecy.*

And that's why Morris doesn't know about the story! Leslie concluded.

When I asked Morry for comment after I returned home, he was adamant.

"It never happened!"

He cast doubt on his friend's trustworthiness, blaming age. (Leslie is two years older.)

"You couldn't ride a bicycle in town without someone knowing about it," he said, incredulous. "How were you going to keep a horse?"

||||||||||||||||||

In the afternoon of my second day with Leslie Glodek and his family, we gathered again in the study to watch my grandfather's film. I hoped Leslie would help identify more faces, people who had not caught Morry's eye.

"It's the funniest thing," he said after watching the film. "I used to think that I knew everybody there. But I clearly don't." Leslie seemed genuinely taken aback. "I can't put names to them."

The only face he definitely identified belonged to his friend Moszek Tuchendler.

"The forehead now, and the eyebrows—now I can confirm it's Morris. Oh, yes! We're only seeing his forehead and his eyebrows. But I know for certain it is Morris."

As it did with Morry, the first thing in the film that caught Leslie's attention was the headgear. "You see? The youngsters there are wearing hats that I used to wear." But Leslie could not connect the faces beneath the hats with names. "He has a familiar face," he said, pointing out a boy standing on the synagogue steps as the community files out of the building. "It's quite conceivable that amongst them—I had a number of nieces and nephews, mostly nephews—that they could have been there. Yeah. Because it looks a bit familiar, and yet I don't . . ." He looked away from the screen to the curtained windows and tried to uncover the memory. "I just cannot place it. It's almost as if I were looking at one of my brothers when they were younger. But I can't put a name to it."

He remembered the synagogue building clearly. "I have never seen a synagogue this big, and with an interior of that sort. Quite elaborate," he said. Like Morry, he mentioned the murals on the walls, Fishl Perelmuter's artwork. "Twelve scenes, I think. Six on one side and six on the other side. Biblical scenes of some sort pertaining to the twelve tribes. They were quite sizable. But it was high up, and it was a big building. So it's deceptive, as to the size of it. But it was quite large. Wherever you were standing, you could see the details clear enough."

I asked whether he recalled any image in particular, but he did not.

"I was there once in a blue moon. If something, some big meeting were to take place, this was the place, because it could accommodate a lot of people. But I wasn't a shul person . . ."

"Even then!" emphasized Celia.

"Even if my parents insisted I go," Leslie continued, "I still managed to creep off to the back and clear out."

"Did you have a bar mitzvah?" Celia asked.

"No. I refused!" Leslie laughed. "I'll tell you—this was a touchy subject. Because one of my brothers, the one who lived near the railway station, he declared himself to be an atheist. Yeah. He wouldn't take part in any religious things at all. And the others were indifferent, this way and that. They couldn't care less. My sister, who was the one above me, to whom I was closest, she was also an atheist."

Being the youngest, Leslie was influenced by their views. "Whenever there was something going on at the synagogue, even if I couldn't refuse, I tried to make myself as scarce as I can, to get away and do something that I liked doing."

Recalling the synagogue, however, triggered another story.

"There was a place in addition to the synagogue—to the left, there was another place. A place for learning."

This was most likely the *bes midrash*, or "house of learning," a place for Torah study and interpretation, which Morry had also situated next to the synagogue.

"You could go there, you could study, read books, Hebrew books, and that sort of thing. And they used to have congregations as well. And moreover, that place never shut its doors fully. And if there were strangers milling about that didn't have a home, homeless people, they could go in there and spend the night. Just lie down somewhere. It was a well-known thing. They were wanderers, you know? That was part of the culture. And there was one who was permanently there, living that kind of lifestyle. And he was named as the town's idiot. And one day he went up to the place where they read the scrolls, which is the center of it all, and he banged the table. 'Will you give me attention for a minute?' And he said, 'You'd better get yourself a new idiot for this town! I'm leaving!'"

Leslie burst out laughing.

"Whether this is true or not, I don't know. Somebody said to me, 'That's what happened.'"

The synagogue, the *bes midrash*, the Szmerlak yeshiva, and Chaim Nusen Cwajghaft's stonecutting workshop were all in the same corner of town. When Cwajghaft appeared in the film, I waited for Leslie to recognize him, and when he did not, I said his name.

"I think something is beginning to register," Leslie said. "Because there was only one such family in town who provided the service. If you continue in that direction, a bit further, there used to be a *shtibl*, where my father used to attend." This accorded with where Morry had placed his family's *shtibl*, next to the *bes midrash*. For Leslie, it sparked another memory. "I remember something very silly, but it was something real." When electricity was introduced in the town, he said, it seems a cable ran into the Cwajghafts' home through a doorway that had recently been bricked up. "And that new piece of wall, when it was put in, if you touched it, you got a bit of a shock from the thing. And for us, it was heroic to touch it! You know what I mean? But in fullness of time, when it dried up, it didn't do it anymore. Only when it was wet, in the first day or two. It's a silly thing. But I remember. And you would say to somebody, 'You do it!' And you'd quickly get a shock. And you'd say, 'You do it now!' And they would be a coward, and say, 'Oh, no, I'm not touching it!'"

"Funny," Leslie said, surprised by this memory and the workings of his own mind. "I can remember these things I haven't thought of for seventy years."

From the information Morry had given me, I had narrowed down a few specific details about my grandfather's film that I hoped Leslie might help to confirm. In particular, I wanted to determine the street in the film's panoramas and the location of the indoor scenes, which Morry had suggested might be Leib Owsianka's restaurant. When the color pictures of this interior appeared on the screen, I asked Leslie whether he knew of a kosher restaurant in town.

"Oh, yes! There was one! They used to sell kosher things. There was a restaurant. I can't think of the name. But it wasn't exactly a restaurant as we recognize restaurants. It was, they were selling all sorts of things, delicatessen. And if you wanted to buy something to eat there and then, you could sit down at a table and eat."

Did you ever go in? I asked.

"Oh, yes. It was one of the favorites . . . in fact, it was not far from Morris's house, much nearer to his."

What was it like inside?

"Well, I don't know . . . There was a counter, where you come up to be served, but to one side or the other, there was a table or two. But I wouldn't call it a restaurant. People used to buy a piece of wurst with a crusty roll, and a drink of some sort, a soft drink, kvass. We called it—not a restaurant, we called it a *cukiernia*. *Cukiernia* was the word. *Cukier* actually means sweets and sugars, and things like this. You could go in there, you could buy drinks, and something noshy—if you know what I mean. You know the word nosh?"

I nodded.

"I can see the faces." Leslie leaned back in his chair. "I can tell you something else, associated with this. They had a good radio. And there was a certain amount of floor space available for dancing. And every Saturday night, the man would tune in to a broadcast of the BBC. And there was a famous band—famous for dance music."

He turned to his wife. "Maybe it was Joe Lawson. Do you remember Joe Lawson?"

"No, Joe Lawson was later," Celia said, "because the Savoy—"

"Ambrose!" Leslie called out. "There was somebody called Ambrose."

Later, I was able to confirm Leslie's memory. Bert Ambrose and His Orchestra were a popular dance band in England in the 1930s.

"He happened to be Jewish," Leslie continued. "And they used to—on Saturday night, it was dancing time, at seven or eight o'clock in the evening. So they would play this, and broadcast it through the BBC. But we picked it up there. And this man had a good radio, and you could dance to music. If we were dancing to any music, it was just a two-, three-piece band. And we were told on good authority that these people, this band—it's like Glenn Miller's band, you know? It could have been fifty, sixty people, with all the instruments available, and all the skill. So that was a special place to go to at any time. But on Saturday night, it was chockablock, because of the music coming over from London."

I asked whether he recalled the name of the owner.

"In Poland, a lot of people were known by their nicknames. And not in a derogatory way. In a friendly way, it was the way we were all referred to." The family that owned the place with the radio and that sold sweets, he said, were known in Yiddish as the *tsikerl makher.* "Do you know what it would mean, *tsikerl makher*? It would mean sweet-maker. You make sweets, chocolate, and they used to sell wholesale to whoever needed the service. And they themselves had a corner shop. We go in and buy a handful of sweets, whatever. I can't remember their name. The reason why I can't is because people always referred to them as the *tsikerl makher.*"

"Would there have been more than one sweet-maker in the town?" asked Jennifer, Leslie's daughter.

"If there were any others, I didn't know of them. They didn't amount to very much. I think they were the only *tsikerl makher*—as a matter of fact, I used to know—there was one about my age, and one or two others, a bit older than me. There were about five or six of them, brothers and sisters, and they were living not far from us."

That was all Leslie could recall of the owners of the small shop. I advanced the film. But a few moments later, Leslie interrupted himself.

"I just remembered now, to enter this place, that one we were just talking about, where they provided the goodies, and also the music coming from the BBC, London—there were steps, maybe four or five steps, to get to the entrance. Most retail establishments don't have steps going into them. The entrance would be at the level with the pavement. But this one had steps."

I rewound the film. There were no steps leading up to the doorway in front of the building. It seemed unlikely, therefore, that the restaurant in the film belonged to the sweet-makers.

Later, however, when I listened carefully to the recordings of Leslie's comments, it was difficult to tell how many different establishments he was remembering. A restaurant, a sweetshop, a dance parlor: Were these really all the same place? Or had he conflated memories of multiple locations into one? When I spoke with Morry, he recalled a café located on the edge of town run by a man called Yona Tancmeister, Jonah Dance-master. He thought this must be the place with music that Leslie remembered. Eventually I was also able to provide a tentative identification for the sweet-makers. If this identification is correct, their shop was on a different street than Leib Owsianka's restaurant.

With the film paused on the façades of the buildings, I asked Leslie whether he recognized the street.

"It would have been helpful if I knew what part of the town this is," Leslie said.

I laughed. This was what I hoped he could tell me. But then Leslie noted that the ground-floor spaces seemed to be both commercial and residential. Morry had been certain the façades in the film were on the north side of the *rynek*. But Leslie disagreed. There were shops all around the square, he explained. On the south side, where Morry's family's store was located, and on the north side, opposite, all the ground-floor spaces were commercial. "But on the right-hand side," he said, meaning the east side of the square, "there was certainly a mixture. A few shops, a few living accommodations. And I remember even people who lived there, we would call them *blacharzes*. Do you know, *blacharz* means roofing people, people who make roofs. *Blach* means sheets of metal. I can't remember their name. But one always referred to them as *blacharzes*. You know, roofers."

So Morry and Leslie disagreed over the street seen in the film. Later, Morry identified the family Leslie had mentioned: the Blaszkes, a name synonymous with their profession: tinsmith, roofer. They lived on the east side of the *rynek*, in the same building as Szmuel Usher Schwartzberg, the grandfather of Keva Richman, whose family photo album contained so many helpful images. Morry recalled walking past this building each morning on his way to school, smelling the acid and the freshly welded metal from the tinsmith's shop. This was the block Leslie felt was seen in the film.

At the end of the row of buildings seen in the film is the grocery store with the sign over the doorway. Morry thought this might be the store Leslie's parents had taken over from their son, Leibl, and that the woman in the doorway beneath the sign might be Leslie's mother. Leslie viewed it without comment. I finally asked whether he recognized the woman.

"No, no," he said. He was certain it was not his mother or his family's store. "But I wouldn't be surprised if this was on the right-hand side of the square," he persisted. If we could just read the name on the sign, he felt we could be certain. "You'd have to get closer to it to get the name. I have to tell you, that when we had a store, it might have said *Spożywczy*, but it also said Glodek."

Toward the end of the film, Leslie singled out a tall, very slender adolescent girl standing next to Essie Diamond. The girl seems dressed up for the occasion. Her black hair is neatly braided and she wears a green dress with white stripes. She also wears a wristwatch, which would have been a prized possession. Her careful grooming, and the fact that she stands next to Essie and Rosie, suggests that she belonged to a family the Malinas and my grandparents knew, people who were aware in advance of the Americans' arrival. In the film, she leans forward to catch the hand of a little boy, who darts toward the camera.

"I had a niece with a similar appearance," Leslie said. "My eldest brother had six kids: five boys and one girl. She was—she was older than me. She must have been about sixteen, seventeen. It might have been her." He tried to recall her name. "Rachel. Ruchla. Ruchel."

When we reached the end, Leslie expressed disappointment at not having been able to remember more or to resolve any of the mysteries in the film.

"I'm looking—wishful thinking, of course—for subtitles to tell me where it is."

|||||||||||||||||||||

Leslie had an easier time recalling names and identifying faces in photographs. His eyesight was not as good as it had been, and perhaps still photos produced less visual confusion than moving pictures. It was also easier to zoom in on a face in the photographs.

The first image I showed him was Faiga Tick's photo of the school class. The moment I brought up the image on my computer screen, Leslie pointed to the boy standing to the left of the teacher.

"This is Morris's brother, Avrum."

Morry and I had gone over this photo numerous times, and he had named several of the boys, in addition to Gradsztein, the teacher. He had not seen his brother among the students in the photo, and later, he felt that Leslie must be mistaken.

In the photo, the boy Leslie said was Avrum stands to the left and slightly in front of the teacher, who is a head and a hat taller. Like all the others, he wears a black coat, with either a scarf or a high-necked shirt beneath. His expression is neutral, neither smiling nor frowning. A slight squint against the light reveals a furrow in his brow, similar to the one Morry has.

Later, Leslie pulled out a photo that Morry had given him many years before. A formal portrait by Fishl Perelmuter, it shows four young boys, all elegantly dressed in long black coats with decorative scarves or cravats and the small black caps of cheder students. The two boys in front hold books open before them, although their gaze is at the photographer. One of them I recognized immediately. Morry at age seven or eight looks remarkably similar to the way he looks in the film, at age thirteen, and the way he looks now, in his late eighties. But in this photo, his feet don't quite reach the floor. His expression is serious, somewhat probing, a boy certain of his abilities. Behind Morry stands his brother Avrum, two or three years older than Morry. The two have the same shape face. But Avrum's gaze is less focused. He looks at the photographer a little absently, perhaps impatient for the photo session to end. Standing on the left is a ten-year-old Leslie Glodek. His face is narrow, tapering toward a soft, rounded chin. His eyes are hooded, and he peers at the camera with an expression of boyish skepticism. Leslie identified the fourth boy, seated in front of him, as Israel Ratovsky, who survived the war and settled in Israel. Ratovsky also appears in the class photo.

Leslie was not in the class photo. But since he also attended Szmerlak's school, I asked whether he recognized the occasion for the photo that Faiga Tick had preserved.

"There's a certain familiarity about them all," he said. "But it's a case of getting the memory cells in the right order."

I pointed to the boys Morry had identified: Faiga Tick's brother, Yehiel Milchberg; the boy Srebro, who was not familiar to Leslie; and the tall, skinny boy named Brzoza.

"Brzoza!" Leslie exclaimed. "Yeah, I know Brzoza all right! Actually, I have to tell you, they survived. Many, quite a few . . . because they went to Palestine just before the war. And when we were there, I wanted to see him. But somehow, it was impossible. They were in timber."

So Leslie must have known the *hiltzerner*, wooden, Brzoza, and indeed, Mottl Brzoza's name appears on the list of survivors in the Holocaust Museum's database.

"Actually," Leslie continued, "*brzoza*—it describes a tree, a name of a tree. I'm just trying to think, *brzoza*." Later, he recalled that the word means birch. This unlocked another memory. "He had a nickname . . ." Leslie drummed his fingers, looked around the room. "He was . . . *Szczapa! Szczapa!*" He almost shouted the word.

What does it mean? I asked.

"If you're a baker and you bake bread, you have to have an oven. And you have to heat the oven. And you can't just use any old sticks, wooden sticks. You have to have long ones that are about a meter long, and thin. That wood was referred to as *szczapa*. That was his nickname!"

Morry afterward said that *szczapa* meant a two-by-four: "You hit somebody with a *szczapa*. Before it's split, you know, it's a very thick piece of wood," he said. He had no recollection of Mottl Brzoza having had this very apt nickname for a tall, skinny boy whose family traded in lumber. But he said, "As kids, I remember we used to sneak out from cheder, and they let us use the hatchet and try to split it. We loved to do it because it was forbidden. It was very dangerous."

For Leslie, recalling this nickname released a thrill that enlivened, almost electrified him. The same thing happened a few moments later, when I showed him the names on the Joint's list of *kassa* directors and the photograph from Keva Richman's family album, in which many of the men on the list are pictured.

Leslie recalled the committee. "In those days, before the war, people who went to the United States and did well donated money annually. And those people who were administering the proceeds from these donations allocated them to people—buying matzos, various things like that—to poor people who were in need of it. Because there was no unemployment benefit, in those days. Nobody could get any help from the powers that be. So this was done on a private level."

He read down the list of names. "Salmon Kaczynski. David Kubel. Zelig M. Zilbersztejn. Abraham H. Drzyk." He looked up and asked, "You could not pronounce *Drzyk*, could you?"

I was forced to demonstrate that, no, I could not.

Leslie continued reading. "Mejer Wajngarten. Oh, the name Wajngarten rings a bell a bit. There were people called Wajngarten, and they were in the timber business. Rojtkopf. This Rojtkopf may well—my mother's surname, maiden name could have been Rojtkopf. Mojsze Cyrlak!!"

He almost leapt out of his chair.

"Now we're onto something!"

He slapped his knee in delight. It was as if he were six years old and had received exactly the present he'd been hoping for, this surprising reunion with a long-forgotten memory.

"Well, we're onto something! Cyrlak was a relative of mine. Yeah! I don't know whether his name was Mojsze. But it could have been. Cyrlak had a shop. They were in the same business as Morris's family. Textiles. And they were quite prosperous as well. They had a son and a daughter, and the daughter did not survive. I think the son—I don't know. Probably not alive now, anymore. But they— We once went to see them in New York, in Brooklyn."

He tapped the computer screen with his fingernail, identifying Mojsze or Moshe Cyrlak in Keva Richman's photo. "He I remember because he was quite an articulate man. And had a nice business. And he would have been a member of that committee. His son was Srulek Cyrlak. Israel Cyrlak."

Israel Cyrlak gave Shoah testimony for his father, Moshe, who appears in the photograph.

"Cyrlak! I couldn't think of it if I wanted to. Moshe Cyrlak! Now I'm convinced that I'm thinking of the right person. He was always a smart-looking man, with a small beard."

Watching the film, Leslie had puzzled over faces. He saw people clearly in his mind, he felt. But when he'd had to match what he saw in his mind with what appeared on the screen, the two did not overlap. In this moment, as he connected the face in the photo with the name Cyrlak, Leslie's pleasure seemed to be about remembering *successfully*.

But when I spoke again with Morry a month later, he recalled something Leslie had been unable to remember. Leslie had given his mother's maiden name as Edelman, or possibly Rojtkopf. But Morry was quite certain that Leslie's mother was born Srebro, from the same family as the "bad kid" in Faiga Tick's photo, who must therefore have been Leslie's relative. Srebro was also the maiden name of Moshe Cyrlak's wife, who was probably Leslie's mother's sister. Moshe Cyrlak would thus have been Leslie's uncle, and Israel Cyrlak, the son who survived, would have been Leslie's first cousin, his closest relative to survive the war. Perhaps Leslie's excitement also had something to do with the release of this name from the tight grip in which he held memories of his family.

"I'm glad you've shown me this," Leslie said about the photo of Moshe Cyrlak from Keva's family photo album, a comment he had not made about my grandfather's film. "It gives me something to think about."

He was also intrigued by Keva's family name, Richman, Rycherman.

"I do remember the name Rycherman. You know why? They happened to be living near us, the Rycherman family. Within about fifty meters. Not in the same street. It was Warsaw Street, Ulica Warszawska. There was a triangle. They were on the left-hand side. And I used to pass there and see them and talk to them, *good morning* and *good night*, that sort of thing."

Jonathan Benn, who had been listening very patiently and attentively to his father-in-law's stories, pulled up the map of Nasielsk on his iPad. Leslie pointed to the site of his former home.

"The Rychermans lived there. That's why I remember them. I used to go past them virtually every day. At this point, here, there was a transformer. A power transformer, at this sharp point here. And this is where the cab rank used to be. If anybody wanted a cab, they had to go here to get it."

He tapped the screen, indicating once more where his house had stood, at the intersection of Warsaw and Kilińskiskiego Streets, and inadvertently caused the iPad to zoom in on what is today a pizzeria.

"Now," Leslie said, "when soldiers came with vehicles or tanks, they generally made use of this triangle. And when they gave orders to pick people to do certain jobs, the first place, the first thing—they came into our house."

9

DARKNESS AND RAIN

"DO YOU EVER get nightmares?" Leslie Glodek had asked me on the first afternoon of my visit. We were sitting in his wood-paneled study with the curtains drawn. Leslie had asked his family to give us privacy so he could talk about his wartime experiences. As much as he relished incidents from his boyhood, those stories were not what he had written on his list of things to tell me.

I have bad dreams occasionally, I said, shrugging. I wake up frightened.

Leslie sat forward in his plush reading chair.

"Well, I can tell you that I will get nightmares. And the frequency of them will depend on what encounters I face. I might have read a book. I might have listened to somebody that made a speech. I may have seen a film. Anything on this thing will set it off," he said, anything about the war. "Celia is under instructions, that if ever she were to witness anything when I'm asleep, that I'm behaving in a hostile manner, like throwing my arms about, that she is to wake me *immediately*. Because I happen to be in a situation where I'm fighting for my life."

He paused to look at me. "This is the sort of thing I have to become reconciled with, and make the best I can of it. So there are some subjects that I cannot touch." Leslie sat back in his chair, then held up his notes for me to see. "What we need to talk about is . . . there was a ten-year slot, 1939 to 1949, which was eventful, and all the results, good or bad, stem from events that took place in that ten-year slot."

When I had first met Morry Chandler, five months earlier and more than two years after beginning my search, I hoped to preserve something of Nasielsk before the war. *Who are the people in my grandfather's film?* I had wanted to know. *What are we seeing in these images?* I had flown to meet Leslie Glodek motivated by the same impulse, to preserve this record that had chanced to survive and that only a Nasielsker could understand and explain.

But preservation is meaningful only in the face of loss. For Morry, for Leslie, as for Susan Weiss and the other Nasielskers I would later meet, unspeakable absences lay coiled inside every memory I evoked with my questions and photographs, with documents, newspaper articles, lists of names, and especially with my grandfather's film. Loss makes these otherwise ordinary images so important. Loss framed and sharpened every story I heard, or it displaced what might have been remembered and spoken of, but was not. "I was born into loss," the daughter of another survivor said to me, months later. Loss had shaped the survivors' lives, and it shaped the lives of their families. I may have understood this abstractly when I first discovered my grandfather's film. But only when sitting in the homes of people who lived with this loss did I learn what the film truly preserved, none of it present in the images.

Leslie Glodek did not talk about his years at school. We barely discussed his family's grocery store or his brother's bicycle shop. We could not examine his relationship with his parents or with his siblings or his friends, aside from the Tuchendler boys, Morry and Avrum. As Morry had said, at sixteen, he became an old man. After the war, childhood was a part of his life that he no longer registered. For Leslie, too, childhood seemed to be a distant, almost mythical time, a reservoir of charming anecdotes. The war, not childhood, had made him who he was, robbing him of everything except his life. This was the experience he wanted to remember and to pass on to me.

During his narration that afternoon, Leslie repeatedly said he did not want to tell me the worst things. He asked whether I even wanted to hear about them. At first I had been polite. "Only if you wish to tell me." On the third iteration, I realized the question was not addressed to me. He was asking himself, *Can I? Must I?* When I said yes, he accepted my response with an expression of resignation, *Very well*, yet it seemed to be the answer he had been waiting for.

Leslie took a breath and left behind his memories of childhood. It was a moment I had experienced earlier with Morry Chandler in Florida, and with Susan Weiss before that in New York, something I would witness again later with the other survivors I eventually met. The breath marked a boundary. After it, each began their history, the story of the war that they, among just a handful of Jews from Nasielsk, had survived.

||||||||||||||||||||

"The war broke out on the first of September," Leslie Glodek said. "It was a Friday. My father used to get up fairly early in the morning. Say six o'clock, something like that. On that Friday morning, he came into the house after he'd been for a walk, and he swore that he heard gunfire. At that stage, we didn't know we were at war. Because war wasn't announced on the radio till after, about eight o'clock. And he was aware of it between six and seven o'clock. He heard gunfire, aircraft shooting at one another, close enough in the vicinity for him to hear it, but not to be able to identify in detail what actually transpired. But after eight o'clock, there was an announcement on the radio that Germany had invaded, and all else followed accordingly."

When my family and I met Morry Chandler in January 2012, he had also recalled the first morning of the war. "I remember it was a Friday morning, the sun was shining, and suddenly everybody ran out into the street, and we saw maybe seventy, eighty planes flying over Nasielsk on the way to—later we found out they were bombing Warsaw. But I remember everybody in the street. The Polish people said *to nasze*, you know, 'They're our planes.' That's what they thought. Until we heard bombs falling. Not on Nasielsk, but further away. And then they announced the invasion started at five o'clock that morning. And the panic started, you know, everybody was looking—*Where's the mayor? Where are the police?* I remember Polish police captured some *Volksdeutsche*, Germans that lived in Poland for many years, but they considered themselves ethnic Germans. So they were arrested, because they thought they were spies. And then by that Friday night, the city was quiet. There was no administration; there were no police. Nobody was there. And it was an eerie silence that befell the community. You know the neighbors, everybody asked, *What do we do? What's going to be?*"

Leslie's family had remained sitting by the radio. "We kept the radio on all the time, but the programs were not as usual. They played music. I suppose appropriate music for the occasion. And from time to time, they'd stop and pass on messages which were coded. But late in the day it became apparent, one way or another, that the Germans were marching and they were on their way. That was Friday, Saturday, Sunday."

In her Shoah Foundation testimony, Czarna Ida Zimmer, daughter of Israel Kulas, the butcher whom Morry's grandmother used to frequent, described the second day of the war. She was a few years older and had been at school in Warsaw. But she fled home to Nasielsk soon after bombs began to fall on the capital. She arrived at the Nasielsk train station on Saturday, the day after the invasion. But Saturday was Sabbath, and the Jewish droshke drivers did not want to take her the seven kilometers, or four miles, into town. She hired a farmer to drive her to the outskirts, and then she walked.

"When I came home, people started, when they heard the war started, running away to Warsaw from the small city. They thought the big city is better. I try to stop everybody what want to run away, if they want to listen to me. Because I came from there. A whole night, the bombing, for the big city. And the small city was quiet."

That Saturday night, there was a meeting of the members of Morry's Hasidic *shtibl* in the Skalka home, Morry recalled. "Some people came over, they're going on the way to Warsaw, everybody was going round in circles. And I remember, it was the next day, I think, we saw people walking, carrying stuff. 'Where are you going?' 'Oh, we're going to Deblin, somebody said it's safe over there.' So I remember we all followed, a bunch of us. And about a mile out of the city there were people coming towards us. And they said that you can't cross. The bridge was blown. They were coming back already. So then, I remember, people said, 'Let's hide in the cemetery.' I mean, it's funny, you know, when you see grown-ups behaving like kids. The concept of a child is to look up to the grown-up. They can do everything, they know, they're smart. And it's the first time we saw all the grown-ups like little kids. Everybody was in shock. People were just going in any direction without knowing why. That was so frightening. It's a horrible feeling of helplessness."

Czarna Zimmer and her family had spent the night with friends at the apothecary, a building between Leslie's property and the apartment where Grace Pahl and her family lived, a block or so east along Warsaw Street. On Sunday morning, she said, her family and a group of neighbors were standing in front of the building when a bomb hit the town. "The Germans throw a bomb on, meaning on the factory," she recounted, referring to the Filar button works. "And this bomb doesn't fall where [they] wanted. It was in the back of our yard." Czarna's mother was injured in the blast. Their neighbors were killed. Two children playing in the yard were blown onto the roof of the building.

"They threw a bomb on our school," recalled Grace Pahl, who must have been at home with her family, next door to where Czarna Zimmer was standing. "That's what made us leave. They threw a bomb, that was the first thing they did. It came from an airplane. And hit the school. And my sister got hysterical. She was crying bitterly, and crying, didn't stop crying. 'Why are you crying?' 'Because they're going to kill us all.'"

The public school, the only building in Nasielsk damaged by bombs during the German invasion, was located just south of the Glodek family's property. "The school was a new school," Leslie said, "virtually in the back of our garden. It was a very formidable building. And in any case, the school was hit on Monday." Morry had placed the bombing two days earlier. "The war started Friday, and the bomb fell, probably on Saturday," he said. "And on Sunday, the German patrols already came in."

Friday, Saturday, Sunday. The German advance was swift. Nasielsk lay just forty miles from the border with East Prussia.

"I remember on Sunday morning," Morry said, "my mother told us kids, 'We stay in. Nobody go out in the street.' She remembered the First World War, when the Germans came in. And even though they were friendly later, the first patrols that come in are the most dangerous. They'll shoot at anything that moves. 'So kids, stay . . .' We were hiding, we won't look, the curtains were drawn, everything. Who was out there? I was out there. I had to take a peek and see what's happening. And then I saw the first motorcycles. They came in with the helmets and the goggles and with the machine guns and rode through the city. And I came into the house and said, 'Mom, the Germans are here. The Germans are here.' You can imagine what the feeling was. Everybody was lost and . . . The next day, the tanks came in. They occupied the city. And the fun began."

On Sunday, September 3, 1939, Britain and France declared war on Germany. Leslie Glodek and his family heard the news on the radio. "We knew about that, because it was announced. And we thought, 'Ah, good! They're going to come with airplanes . . .' And not a sausage came. Anyway. By Wednesday, the Germans were there in the flesh, taking over."

A month later, on October 5, 1939, the *Chicago Daily Tribune* ran an account of the collapse of the Polish army. On Tuesday, September 5, the reporter wrote, "Four Americans—I was one—were having our usual late Polish lunch in the courtyard of the Hotel Europejski in Warsaw." This is the hotel where my grandparents had stayed just a year before. "Suddenly from the east, from Warsaw's industrial suburb of Praga on the right bank of the Vistula opposite us, came the unmistakable dull roar of a heavy air bomb exploding. Then another and then five together. It was the first time we had heard such explosions without the preliminary warning wail of air raid sirens and without the accompaniment of the boom of heavy anti-aircraft guns and the rattle of light rapid-fire guns on the roofs in the center of Warsaw. We all understood what it meant . . . And then from an authoritative source came the news that a German column from East Prussia was at Nasielsk, only 25 miles northwest of the capital."

A motorcycle speeds through town. A truck with soldiers passes near the train station. A tank column crushes the pavement on the road to

Warsaw. An army unit arrives to hold the town and occupy it. What day did the German army arrive in Nasielsk?

In his 1993 interview for the Voice/Vision Holocaust Survivor Oral History Archive at the University of Michigan–Dearborn, Morry Chandler described what he witnessed the first night the Germans occupied Nasielsk, perhaps September 3 or 4 or 5. "It was a night that I will never forget," he said. "I remember, we used to look out the windows, and there were fires all over the city. They got into the shul and took all the Torahs and made a bonfire. And they were throwing them up in the air, and it was like you'd see sparks and all the books—all the Talmudic books and the siddurim," the daily prayer books.

In a phone conversation with me in January 2012, Morry added another detail to his recollection. "They kept bringing out the Torahs, and put them on the fire, and they were throwing them in the air. And they were yelling and dancing around. I remember we heard them, you know, it wasn't far from us. *'Wo ist der Moses?'*" Where is Moses? "And throughout the city," Morry continued, "they were breaking into houses looking for women."

The German army arrived in Nasielsk in the first days of World War II. Whether the Wehrmacht formally occupied the town on Sunday, September 3, or on Monday, Tuesday, or Wednesday, the soldiers immediately attacked the Jewish population, looting, desecrating the synagogue, committing rape, and seizing men for forced labor. Because of his home's central location, at the intersection of Warsaw and Kilińskiego Streets, where tanks and troop vehicles had space to maneuver and park, Leslie Glodek was among the first to be taken.

iiiiiiiiiiiiiiiiiii

"As soon as they were there, the next day, they announced a curfew, that no one is to be out of doors after dark," Leslie said, beginning the story of what he called his first "adventure." "I think it was on a Wednesday. But on Thursday morning, a soldier came in, or two soldiers, came into our house, and my brother, the one who used to live at the railway station, he and I just happened to be there as they came in through the gate. And, 'You! You! Come!' So it's a word you can't refuse. So we went."

Leslie and his brother were taken to the triangle in front of their house, where several dozen other Jews had been assembled. The soldiers then marched the group to the synagogue. "Now the synagogue had a lot of open space all around. The job that they put us to was to dig holes, put in posts. And there was a lot of wire. Big reels of wire. Barbed wire. And they were going to fence it off. We didn't know why. I think the rumor had it, that they were going to put prisoners in there."

After about half an hour of work, Leslie noticed that four forced labor-ers were being taken away for a different job, among them his brother. "So I walked up, because I thought, 'I want to stick together.' So somebody else was set aside, and I joined them." The boys were loaded onto trucks. Leslie recalled that another of the four was Michael Jagoda, the brother of Jankiel Jagoda, sons of Hersz Jagoda, from the family that included the kvass manufacturer Leib Jagoda.

"So we go," Leslie continued, "we drive all the way, till we got to Pułtusk. I thought, maybe this is the destination. No, it wasn't. At that point, we had to cross the river, to get on the other side, to the east of the town. But the bridge that was there, two sections had been blown up by the Polish forces when they were withdrawing. So a couple of hundred yards to one side, the Germans had laid on a pontoon bridge. We got to the other side, and we drove on further. We came to a town, and we were shocked. Most of the town was burned to a cinder. Hundreds of people lying dead all over the place. We didn't say anything, we just kept quiet. Then we saw, by virtue of road signs, that we were on the way to a place called Wyszków. We went immediately to the railway station, which was only about a few kilometers away from the town center. The railway station was completely, utterly bombed. But there were hundreds of wagons there, filled with coal. It was this coal that they wanted."

Leslie, his brother Leibl, Michael Jagoda, and a fourth boy worked all day loading coal from the trains onto the German trucks. "We had no op-tions. When you're told to do it, you do it. You know, if you refuse to do it, they shoot you on the spot."

At six o'clock, they boarded the trucks again for the thirty-five-mile return trip to Nasielsk. They passed through the bombed-out town again, bodies still smoldering in the street, and returned to the bridge east of Pułtusk, twenty-four kilometers, or fifteen miles, from Nasielsk. But during the day, orders had changed. No civilians were allowed to cross the bridge. The drivers continued on the road back to Nasielsk, leaving the boys on the far side of the Narew River.

Thousands of civilians crowded the river crossing, Leslie said, people who had been expelled from their homes in Pułtusk. "We spoke to some people," he recalled, "and we discovered what had happened the day before in Pułtusk. All the Jews were assembled by the means of loudspeakers—*Anyone who does not obey is going to be shot. Summarily executed.* And then, they were all marched across that bridge, the pontoon bridge, to the eastern side. And the Germans said, 'Go!'"

If Leslie met these refugees the day after their expulsion from Pułtusk, then he had been seized for forced labor a week later than he recalled. Pułtusk had been occupied by the German Third Army under General Georg von Küchler on Wednesday, September 6. Shortly afterward, the special SS killing unit known as *Einsatzgruppe* V, commanded by Ernst Damzog, arrived. The following Monday, September 11, the SS shot at least ten Jews and expelled at least three hundred across the Narew River, which runs east of the city. Women were allowed to cross the pontoon bridge over which Leslie drove with the soldiers the following day. The men, however, were forced to swim. Many drowned. Some were shot. The precise numbers are not known.

Standing on the riverbank surrounded by refugees on what may have been Tuesday, September 12, the four boys were stranded. "My brother immediately had to take charge," Leslie said. "He was the only adult. We were just boys, sixteen years old." They couldn't cross the river and continue west, toward Nasielsk. So the four walked east, away from the throng of now homeless Jews by the river. They spent the night in a barn. In the morning, they resumed walking in the opposite direction of their home, until they reached the town of Długosiodło, more than twenty-five miles east of Pułtusk. "I remember the name of the town because it was a market town," Leslie said. "My father used to mention it occasionally. He used to go there to a market and buy wheat." Here they encountered still more refugees. "The place was chockablock with people from Pułtusk. Every municipal building was taken up. A room, if there was a room like this, a schoolroom"—he motioned around the study where we were sitting, a space perhaps twelve feet square—"you could see twenty people in it." The boys continued walking. "We got into another town, and another town. So it's four or five days had gone. And we were still moving in an easterly direction," away from Nasielsk.

From other refugees on the road, they learned that many of the surrounding farms stood empty. These farms had belonged to *Volksdeutsche*, ethnic Germans who had been evacuated by the Wehrmacht. The four boys had entered the part of Poland occupied by the Soviet army after its invasion of the country from the east on September 17, perhaps on the same day Leslie, his brother, and the other two had arrived there. The boys took shelter in one of these abandoned farms. "A terrific house," Leslie recalled. "There were no utensils to speak of. But all the facilities were there. We went into the field and there were still potatoes and cabbages and everything, still in the field. They couldn't take it away with them. Good. We've got nowhere to go. We'll stay here for a while."

They remained for several days, until Leibl Glodek heard that the Russian army had arrived in the village a few miles still farther east. "We found soldiers walking about. You know? Russian soldiers. They didn't cut a dash, so far as presentation goes, compared to the Germans. But they were soldiers, and they were carrying rifles, and all the rest of it."

Leslie's brother could speak a little Russian and was able to communicate with the soldiers, who were friendly. Nevertheless, after a few days in this village, Leslie's brother announced they were leaving. "The other two and I were a little disappointed. My brother, he was the older one, and when he said, 'We're going,' I couldn't argue about it. And so we started to make our way back, town by town, avoiding major roads."

Leibl Glodek had learned of a place where they could cross the river with the help of a local man. Once back on the west side of the Narew, however, they were soon spotted by a German patrol. "One German was mounted on a horse. We looked in a terrible state. You could see straightaway that we were outsiders. So he came up with a whip. And we were running like mad. But he did manage to hit my brother somewhere around the ear. And then he just went off. We walked back to the main village. And then I saw my brother's ear bleeding badly. So when we got back, a woman brought out some iodine to stop the bleeding, bandaged it up."

The following day, they reached the town of Winnica, halfway between Nasielsk and Pułtusk, where Leibl Glodek had a friend. Still outside of town, however, a vehicle approached. "You could see it was a military vehicle. So my brother said, 'We'd better get off the road straightaway.'"

They hid behind haystacks, but the German patrol had seen them, or someone in the town had given them away. "Suddenly the man gets out of the vehicle. As soon as he was in the field, he takes out his revolver, and he's coming towards us. And my brother said at that point, 'Run like mad!' I remember him saying to me, 'Don't run in a straight line! Zigzag!'" The soldier fired six shots. But he was too far away, and the boys escaped.

"I want to digress for a moment here," Leslie said, leaning forward again in his chair. "Many years later, in this country, a man by the name of Roger Bannister, who was a student and also an athlete, he was the man who claimed to have broken the four-minute mile. The record." He paused and looked up at me. "They were wrong! I did that! In 1939!"

Twenty-one days after being seized for forced labor, Leslie, Leibl, Michael Jagoda, and the fourth boy returned to Nasielsk. "Of course, we had been given up for dead. A long time ago, because we had no way of communicating. And when they saw us, they just couldn't believe us," he said. "But all we needed was a good wash and a cleanup, and a good night's sleep!" Leslie laughed a little, still recalling his four-minute mile. "So I just thought, I'll mention it to you," he concluded, "because this was one of the big adventures."

<hr />

If Leslie had met the refugees from Pułtusk on the riverbank on September 12, 1939, then his return to Nasielsk would have been in the first days of October. By that time, Warsaw had surrendered and the German conquest of Poland was complete.

If, however, Leslie's "adventure" had begun the previous week, as he maintained, then walking home from Winnica a week earlier, at the end of September, he and his brother would have crossed paths with Julien Bryan, an American cinematographer who had filmed the German siege of Warsaw and who was evacuated from the capital with other foreign nationals on September 21, 1939. In his 1940 book about the German invasion, entitled *Siege*, Bryan writes about the evacuation:

> *As our caravan headed north, we passed a constant stream of traffic going in both directions; but most of it consisted of ammunition wagons, guns and trucks bearing soldiers on their way to Warsaw. Artillery and machine guns were on each side of the road. We passed Polish villages on the way. A few houses were still standing, but most of them were in ruins. German soldiers were on guard in these captured towns. After we had gone ten miles back of the lines, we passed even heavier streams of ammunition trucks and big guns going forward to destroy Warsaw. Darkness and rain. German soldiers furnished us with jute bags to put over our outer coats. The war seemed far away. There were no blackouts here. Houses and villages were fully lighted. An important bridge was down, but we crossed on a wonderful pontoon structure that had been made in less than 24 hours. Amazingly efficient and well organized, this Nazi army. There seemed to be little truth in all the earlier rumors of constant breakdown of German mechanical equipment, due to Ersatz. At Nasielsk we found ourselves on the platform of a railway station partly demolished by bombs.*

Thursday, September 21, 1939, the day Julien Bryan passed through the Nasielsk train station and noted it had been partly demolished by bombs, was the day before Yom Kippur, the Day of Atonement, the holiest day in the Jewish calendar, during which Jews traditionally fast.

On this High Holiday, Friday, September 22, Morry's father and his uncle, Jankiel Skalka, were seized by German soldiers in Nasielsk and marched the four miles to this same train station. "They were unloading artillery shells all day," Morry recalled. "And my father and my uncle came back at night so worn-out. And they didn't eat or take a drink of water, because it was Yom Kippur. It didn't matter. They would not . . . Yom Kippur is Yom Kippur."

In the September weeks that Leslie and his brother were wandering in the countryside, trying to return home, Morry and his family had remained in Nasielsk as the Germans consolidated their hold on the city. In his 1993 oral history interview, Morry had recalled, "My grandfather had his beard cut off with a bayonet. They came into the house. They cut his beard off. In front of the family. I remember my older brother, you know, wanted to jump them, jump these guys, and we all held him back because the guy was going to pull his revolver out. My mother spoke excellent German. She pleaded with them, 'Leave him alone. He's an old man.' My grandfather was eighty-seven years old."

As a prominent Jewish merchant in Nasielsk, Srul Skalka and his store were early targets for harassment. "It was like the town was turned upside down," Morry told me and our families in Florida, describing how Polish girls would point out Jewish stores to their new German boyfriends. "I mean, people that we knew. Don't forget, we were there for hundreds of years. It's like your neighbor all of a sudden doesn't know you. And everybody joined the fray. *Yeah, let's get 'em.*" German soldiers, acting on tips from Polish girls, plundered the store. "'*Wo hast du das Stoff? Wo hast das Gold?*'" Where is the stuff, the material? Where is the gold? "He'd pull out the revolver and say, '*Ich schiess dich tot. Du musst die Wahrheit sagen.*'" I'll shoot you dead. Tell the truth.

Czarna Ida Zimmer, in her oral history, commented on the same events. "Polish girls, [who] used to work for Jews, housekeepers or cleaning woman, they knew who has something, who is rich and who is poor. And they wanted to get it. So the soldiers need a girl, and she need the money. She brought them into the house where she wanted, where she will get something."

"They were all like there was never a Poland," Morry continued, describing the behavior of the Poles. "Everybody was fraternizing."

Gold was not the only thing the soldiers were after. "One night, the Germans were going around, breaking doors open, to look for women," Morry remembered. "And I'll never forget, to this day, I still remember, my grandmother, my mother, and my aunt, were all in one bed, all schmeared up with black stuff, and their hair in disarray, because they obviously knew what was coming. And I remember, I was in the room when the Germans broke in and they looked, and it was not attractive for them, and they left. My mother and my aunt, they were fairly young women, you know? They were like early forties." Two cousins, daughters of his grandfather's brother, however, were raped by German soldiers, who broke down the family's door with bayonets.

Morry told another story from these early days of the occupation of Nasielsk. "I remember standing in the market, and a German ran up and motioned to get to the square. And whoever he saw on the street, 'To the square!' So we all got there, and there was maybe about eighty people. And some of them are Poles, you know—they assumed that everybody there is Jewish. So they were saying, *'Mir, no Jude,'* 'I'm not a . . .' —Slap in the face. 'Shut up. We say you are, you are!' And then we looked and there was two machine guns on tripods, on the side, next to the road where we were standing. And everybody's scared, they were talking to each other, 'What's going on? What are they . . . ?' Later I realized what that meant. They were lining us up to mow us down." In this instance, however, an officer arrived in the square and sent the frightened people home.

In the last days of September or the early days of October, just as Leslie Glodek and his brother Leibl were returning to Nasielsk, Morry Chandler undertook the first adventure of his own.

"When the Germans just captured Warsaw," he told me on the phone a week after we'd met in Florida, "I, as a young boy, a fifteen-year-old, fourteen-year-old, hitchhiked through the German lines to Warsaw, stopped at the Landaus, and brought them a burlap bag with bread and meat."

Sura Landau was Morry's mother's best friend. She was the sister of the photographer Fishl Perelmuter, and had grown up next door to Chawa Skalka and her family. Sura had married Avrum Landau, owner of a knitting factory in Warsaw, and they moved away from Nasielsk before the war. But she frequently visited Morry's mother in Nasielsk. "They would stay in the same bed, you know, and they always talked and talked," Morry recalled. "My father used to complain, 'Don't you ever run out . . . ?'"

At the end of September, Morry slipped out of Nasielsk to bring help to his mother's friend and her family. "My mother says to me, 'You can't go.' I said, 'I'm going.'" And he went. "Warsaw was surrounded, they were dying of hunger. The city was besieged by the Germans. And the minute they opened it up, I got up with potatoes and meat and bread from the bakery. I liked the daring and the challenge."

The trip to Warsaw, Morry said, was "a nightmare." Sura Landau and her family lived on the corner of Bonifraterska and Muranowska Streets, he remembered. On that late September or early October morning, he arrived at their door at dawn. "I knock on the door, and Sura came out, she said, 'Moishe! *Vos tiste?*'" What are you doing? "'How did you get through the lines?'" In 2012, Morry did not recall the details of his journey, only that, like Julien Bryan, who was traveling in the opposite direction, he passed burned bridges, destroyed towns, and thousands of German soldiers.

||||||||||||||||||||

Shortly after returning to Nasielsk from his first "adventure," and within a few days of Morry's daring trip to Warsaw, Leslie Glodek and his father were once again seized and marched to the Nasielsk railway station for forced labor.

"I told you about—our house was vulnerable, because of the triangle," Leslie explained. "The Germans were always there, hanging about. They needed some people to be taken down to the railway station. Because there were things that needed leveling out after the bombs had been dropped on them. So two or three of them came into the house, and there was only my father and me. So we had to go."

Leslie and his father were taken out to the staging area, near the transformer in front of their house. There, perhaps twenty Jews seized for forced labor were ordered to line up behind three military trucks or lorries.

"And there was a man," Leslie continued, "a noncommissioned officer, a German, who looked more like a rottweiler. The way he behaved himself. Even with his own soldiers he was shouting. And he walked about with a whip. And when they were good and ready, we were ordered to get on those vehicles. We were standing in three lines. My father was in the first one, I was in the second one. And you were expected to get up there. But my father was sixty-eight, I think, at the time. He couldn't quite make it. So this rottweiler came up with a whip, and whipped my father two or three times until he fell to the floor. And when he fell altogether, he ordered two of his soldiers to pick him up, one at each end, and throw him into the [lorry]. I was standing there watching this. Riveted to the ground. Paralyzed. Because I didn't even move a finger, knowing full well, if I did, we would have been both shot dead. The upshot of it was—this lorry was filled up with whatever men were there, and moved on. And I was on the second one. I desperately wanted to be on the same lorry as my father, to see if I can say something comforting at least, if not anything else."

Leslie tried to explain what he had felt. "My father was none the worse for it. All right. So he was hit with a whip. But me watching it—was a thousand times worse. And when I talk about nightmares. This is it."

Leslie had never shared this experience with his family.

"I'm not going to tell you any more incidents. I've told you about this one. None of them know about this one. It's very painful to me. They do know about the one where we were being fired at and we were running. Because I can talk about that with a laugh. It doesn't matter. But it keeps coming back. From time to time . . . There were many such incidents. Some even worse than this. But I won't tell you about that. This is enough."

Leslie continued a moment later. "I developed an itch of running away." Like many of the younger people in town, he decided to try to escape to the Soviet-controlled half of Poland, east of the Bug River. "I had already had a taste of it," he said, "when I was once on the eastern side and saw Russian soldiers, and I was able to go up and talk to them." But Leslie's mother was against it. "She said, 'The family must stay together. It's the safest thing.' It made sense. Together we can help one another. And when you're on your own, who are you going to turn to? My argument wasn't very strong. So I conceded. And I made no attempt."

But a few weeks after the incident at the railway station, toward the end of October, Leslie was grabbed by a German soldier and again loaded onto a truck with a group of others randomly seized on the street. The truck was enclosed with a tarpaulin, but Leslie realized they were heading north and west, in the direction of Konigsberg, East Prussia. "Sometime in the middle of the afternoon, we finally reached this destination. There were lots of people coming from other directions as well. And what was the job? Building a prison for soldiers—for prisoners. A fence with barbed wire and all the rest of it. So, there was a twosome. We dug a hole, put in posts, and so on and so forth. And this chap I was dealing with—he might have been two, three years older than me—and he says, 'It doesn't look as if they're going to take us back tonight. They're going to keep us here until the job is finished. This could take weeks.' And he said to me, 'We can't do anything now, but under the cover of darkness, we've got to slip away.'"

Leslie doubted his courage that afternoon. But when the time came, he and the other forced laborer escaped from the camp. "He wasn't Jewish, by the way," Leslie added. "But these people, they were taking slave labor, and they didn't concern themselves with who you were. They just needed people to do these jobs. So, we got away—he went one way, I went another way, and I managed to get back home."

The following day, rumors circulated that people who had absconded from work details would be summarily executed, along with those giving them shelter.

"That gave me a weapon," Leslie said. "I said to Mother, 'I can't stay here anymore.'" He once more begged for permission to flee. This time his mother consented.

A few days later, Leslie, his mother, and his brother Szlomek, who had been in the Polish army and had been wounded during the defense of Warsaw, traveled from Nasielsk to the capital, to the apartment of Leslie's sister, on Franciszkańska Street 9. "By the way," Leslie said a moment later, "when I left Nasielsk, on that night, I wanted to say goodbye to family and friends . . . I had no voice. Gone. All I could do is mouth it."

In Warsaw, Leslie's mother and sister remained at the apartment while his brother accompanied him across the Vistula River to the Warsaw-Praga train station. "He had a ticket, just for a penny, to get on the platform. And he saw to it that I got on the train going in an easterly direction. Little did I know that I wasn't going to see anybody thereafter."

On the train from Warsaw-Praga, Leslie recalled, "I tried not to make contact, even by eye, with anybody. And there were some German soldiers on the train as well." The train traveled across northern Poland to the new German-Soviet border. "I got off the train, and I just saw some people going in a certain direction, towards a woodland . . . But. This is the crunch point. I got off the train, and I went in the right direction. Then there was a house. It was fenced on both sides. You had to go through this house to reach the no-man's-land."

A large number of refugees had gathered at the entrance to this building, which was guarded by German soldiers. Twenty at a time, they were allowed in, and the door was shut behind them. A dozen German soldiers were inside, waiting. "Each one was holding something equivalent to a baseball bat. And they were walloping us for about—I don't know how long for. Many people were screaming, they were hit very hard," Leslie said. "Now, I was pretty nippy. I was as nimble as anybody can be. But for some reason or other, my hat fell to the ground, in the melee of all this going on." The hat had been a parting gift from Leslie's sister, a fur-lined Russian hat for the eastern winter. "And I made this terrible mistake in trying to retrieve it. I managed to get hold of it, but at which point I was walloped on the head. So much so that I responded with a wobble in my knees. And I let go of the hat. But I still proceeded in the right direction, by which point they've opened the door, and you can run out."

Leslie escaped the house and fled across a field. "There was an officer there, sitting very comfortably, or standing, leaning against something, and he had a revolver in his hand. He just took potshots. I don't know whether he hit anybody or not. But I was aware a gun had been fired." Leslie finally reached the woods, which marked the boundary of no-man's-land. "I got deep into the forest. By which time, I realized I was exhausted. So I thought I must take a rest. I didn't want to join people in bunches. I thought, 'On my own, I'll be much better off.' So I sat down and got my breath back. And when I felt a bit relaxed, I said, 'Something terrible here . . .'" Leslie touched the back of his head. "I was full of blood. Then I realized, I was hit twice. The first time, I managed to take it in my stride, but the second time, the wallop came down. And all blood pouring down, a handful of blood, and I—I was unaware of this. Until— This is also one of the scenarios which keep repeating. And I don't think I wish to go into greater detail."

Morry Chandler may have passed by the same house between the German and Soviet occupation zones. He fled Nasielsk a few weeks after Leslie. "Remember I told you they used to bring Germans to our store?" he said when we were sitting together in Florida, recounting a day that was likely in October 1939. "So I figured, I had the shtick in me," the bravado. One day, he said, "I told a German, 'You're looking for *Stoff*? I'll take you.' I took him to our competitor . . . who was Polish."

It sounds like a joke, which perhaps to Morry, at the time, it was. "I didn't realize how much I risked my life." He shook his head. "So I took him there, and he went in, and they told him they were Catholics. Oh, my God! He ran out and he chased me, and I ran away. And he was looking for me, I was hiding out. That was a big mistake."

The German soldier Morry tricked had earned a nickname among the people of Nasielsk. They called him "*der merder*," the murderer. "A real mean, mean, sick killer," Morry said. "He was the one that grabbed ahold of my grandfather and with his bayonet cut off his beard. He had no mercy. And he was running around among only a couple of thousand people, looking for me."

Morry hid for a few days, but it had become too dangerous for him to remain in Nasielsk, as it had for his friend Leslie Glodek. At first his parents, like Leslie's, had been against him leaving. But by this time, Morry remembered, "everybody was sort of mentally decimated. You know, the old discipline was sort of loosened, because they knew they couldn't control every . . . And so when I said to my parents that we heard that the Russian side is open, and a lot of Jews are leaving, they didn't say anything." It was decided, then, that Morry and his brother Avrum would attempt to escape to Białystok, now in Soviet-occupied Poland.

In his oral history from 1993, Morry explained that someone in Nasielsk knew of a guide who could take them across the German-Soviet lines. "I remember we went to Warsaw, my brother and I and two other people. They were also a set of brothers, the Rotstein brothers—they were all from our *shtibl*—and we left by train about twelve, one o'clock, towards a city called Małkinia."

The brothers Moshe and Avruml Rotstein were several years older than Morry. They had another brother, Simcha Rotstein, who is most likely the young man seen exiting the synagogue and later standing on the street with his friend Avrum Kubel in my grandfather's film.

The town of Małkinia lies about sixty-five miles east of Nasielsk. This was the only point on the rail line where trains could cross into Soviet-occupied Poland, and it is therefore almost certainly where Leslie Glodek ran the gauntlet of bat-wielding soldiers and escaped into the forest. Later, Małkinia became the primary junction point where the trains headed from Warsaw to Treblinka separated from the main Warsaw–Białystok rail line.

Morry recalled the night he and Avrum escaped. "Around midnight, the train came to a halt, and it was something like in a bizarre nightmare what this place looked like at night, twelve o'clock at night. All the doors opened, and you could hear Germans running around with dogs, you know, German shepherds, and firing rifles in the air. '*Raus, raus, raus!* Everybody *raus!*' And we jumped out of the train, and they lined us up and they're searching for money. And somehow we were following—my brother and I—we lost the other two. It was in the darkness. All you could see was flashlights. And nobody knew where to go, but we're following the mob of people from that train. They were running like cattle, and here we heard somebody being beaten up and somebody being shot. I didn't see anything, you know, just running. And we ran through mud and obstacles and rocks. And then we come into a field, and in the field we see little fires, and we realized that there's people in the big field, and finally, we got to them. We see people sitting around, warming themselves. We said, 'Who are you? Where are we? What is this?' And they said, 'Don't you know? This is no-man's-land.'"

They camped in the fields for three days, waiting for the border crossing to open. On the fourth morning, the refugees attempted to cross into the Russian zone on their own. Soviet soldiers fired warning shots, but when the group did not disperse, the soldiers hesitated, and a mad dash ensued. "We started running—my brother and I—we started running through the forest. And I remember the first town on the Russian side that we came in was a little town called Zaręby Kościelne." Another time, Morry said, "I remember we had a pillow that my mother gave us to take. The pillow was so heavy because it was raining, and the water got into it."

From Zaręby Kościelne, Morry and Avrum traveled by train to Białystok, which had become a center for Jewish refugees from German-occupied Poland. Morry described it in his oral history in 1993: "The city is literally overflowing with refugees. So, we meet other Jews and *what do we do? Where do we eat? Where do we sleep?* Well, there's a kitchen the Russians set up, soup kitchens. And sleeping, well, we sleep in the shul on the floor. So we picked one shul and we went there, and literally at night the whole shul was wall to wall, people were sleeping on the floors. Here we came out of a home, we were looked after with maids and a governess and a mother and a father. We were the darlings of the house, you know, pampered. And we come in now, we're living on our own, we're eating at soup kitchens, and we're sleeping on the floors, with the dirt and with the lice and . . ."

It was late October 1939. Morry was fifteen, Avrum eighteen, and Leslie Glodek was almost seventeen. They did not see each other in Białystok; they did not apparently know of each other's presence. But they were there at the same time, along with numerous other Nasielskers, including Faiga Milchberg with her new husband, Szmuel Tyk, and his sister, Ruchla; a young theater actor named Avrum Moshe Lubieniecki and his wife, Manya Wlosko; Moshe and Avruml Rotstein; and thousands upon thousands of other Jews from towns like Nasielsk across northern Poland, running for their lives.

10

DAS VATERLAND DEINES GROSSVATERS

SEVENTY-FOUR YEARS after my grandparents' trip, I arrived in David Kurtz's birthplace, Nasielsk. I arrived by car after spending a day in Warsaw, as my grandfather had. I also carried a camera capable of capturing moving images, though in the age of YouTube, this was hardly noteworthy. From David's film, I knew he had visited on a bright, sunny day, with billowing clouds in the distance, a day very like the one that was beginning when I arrived in Nasielsk in late May 2012. My grandfather had been forty-nine years old when he emerged from the car and stepped into the marketplace of this small Polish town thirty-five miles north of the capital. I was the same age.

But waving, shouting children did not swarm around me, eager to grab my attention when I arrived. I was greeted by Zdzisław Suwiński, a sixty-two-year-old Polish historian and teacher, who stood at the door of his lovely two-story home with his wife, Anne.

"*Wilkommen in das Vaterland deines Grossvaters*," he said in German, our only common language. Welcome to the fatherland of your grandfather. I thanked him, we shook hands, and we nodded and bowed awkwardly. *Vaterland.*

I had flown to Warsaw from London on Monday night, after two days of talking with Leslie Glodek. The following day, I researched at the Jewish

Historical Institute, home to the collection of eyewitness histories, diaries, and official documents secretly assembled in the Warsaw Ghetto between 1940 and 1943 by Emanuel Ringelblum. There I met with Alina Skibińska, a leading Polish scholar of Holocaust studies, referred to me by Leslie Swift at the Holocaust Museum. Alina had offered to help me during my visit and to serve as my translator. She is the United States Holocaust Memorial Museum's representative in Poland and a member of the Polish Center for Holocaust Research at the Polish Academy of Sciences. She has published widely about the fate of Jews in Poland, in particular in the small towns.

On Wednesday morning, Alina had picked me up at my hotel, and we drove north on the country highway out of Warsaw. The two-lane road was lined with linden trees, and it wound past fields before bringing us to the Nasielsk train station and the final four miles into town. I had been to Poland in the mid-1980s while a student in Vienna. I must have known the name Nasielsk then, but it had not occurred to me to try to find the place. At twenty-two, I felt adventurous enough peeking behind the Iron Curtain, visiting Communist Poland in the age of martial law, Lech Wałęsa, and his banned and ubiquitous trade union, Solidarity. I retained moody mental images of Poland from that era, the dark apartment with drab, peeling wallpaper where my friend Janice and I had stayed in Kraków, and the dour faces on the long line at the bakery in Warsaw. Nasielsk in 2012 bore as little resemblance to the Poland I remembered as it did to the Poland my grandparents had seen. Alina and I drove past neat homes with carefully tended gardens; a grocery store with the sign SKLEP SPOŻYWCZY, fresh fruits and vegetables spilling off the display stand onto the sidewalk; a car alarm shop and a cell phone outlet. Somehow Nasielsk had stumbled into the twenty-first century. I could not make sense of it: that a place I had imagined being so distant and destroyed should be as easily accessible as any other place in the world.

Zdzisław and Anne Suwiński welcomed us warmly into their spacious, dignified home, bright with flowers and lined with books. The dining room table was set with china and linen napkins; there were serving plates of homemade cheesecake, coffee cake, chocolate cake, cups for coffee, a pot of tea, two red-ribboned gift boxes of Milka hazelnut special chocolates, sweets in the shape of little hearts. "Please," said Zdzisław in English as we took our seats at the table.

For most of his professional life, Zdzisław Suwiński has been interested in the history of Nasielsk, including the history of its former Jewish community. He had collected a folder of documents, photographs, articles, published histories, unpublished memoirs, postwar papers from the school where he had taught for thirty-five years and where he was now the director. He wanted to share these with me, he said, speaking half in Polish and half in German. A large man with very friendly, slightly mischievous eyes, white hair, and a bushy white mustache, he had a calm, avuncular demeanor. I could easily imagine him as a favorite high school history teacher. I had requested we visit the municipal archives, now housed twelve miles away in Pułtusk. This would be our first stop, Zdzisław said, since the archive closed at three in the afternoon. I also wanted to investigate the marketplace, to pinpoint the locations seen in my grandfather's film. We would do that later, in the evening. Zdzisław had already compared the scenes and identified most of the sites, he said. He had also heard stories from the local people, from his students and from members of his parents' generation, people who had been alive during the war. He wanted to tell me what had happened. He wanted to show me where it had happened.

Was this an acceptable plan? Zdzisław asked me.

Yes, I said, the plan sounded good. But sitting there, so suddenly in Nasielsk despite my weeks of planning, I felt pulled in a dozen different directions. The marketplace, with Morry's home, Fishl Perelmuter's studio, and with the storefronts visible in my grandfather's film, perhaps even the grocery store where an anxious woman stood beneath a sign, were just a few blocks away. The site of the synagogue, the Hasidic *shtibl* where Morry's family had prayed, his yeshiva, and the open lot where he and Leslie had learned to ride bicycles. The sweet-maker's shop, the tinsmith's building, the doorstep from which a bossy young housewife shooed away the neighborhood kids. Each of these exerted a gravitational pull. And I was disoriented by the Suwińskis' comfortable home, decorated with Anne's beautiful hand-painted religious icons. The Nasielsk of my imagination was dark and depressive. How had I gotten here? And how was I to understand Zdzisław Suwiński's interest in the history of Jewish Nasielsk?

A month earlier, in April 2012, shortly after first contacting Zdzisław, I had also written to the Nasielsk Board of Education, proposing to show my grandfather's film to students at the high school during my visit. I wanted to learn what the students knew of Nasielsk's history, and I could share with them what I had discovered about their town in my research.

I had received a polite response, vaguely accepting my offer, but devoid of specifics. And almost immediately afterward, Zdzisław had sent me a frantic e-mail in his rough German: *Caution! I write quickly. You do not write to other people. The people in Nasielsk are false. They say now that Jews come and will take back all houses. You understand? You write only to me.*

"There's a certain hidden animosity, don't forget," Morry had explained when I told him of this warning. "They're always, *The Jews are coming back.* Because the whole city was taken over by the goyim. They got it for free. So there is always that fear of when the Jews are going to come back and take it back from them."

You cannot grow up Jewish in America and not imbibe hostility toward Poles. It is a cliché to hear a survivor claim, *The Poles were worse than the Germans,* an assertion full of bitterness. The Germans were Nazis, it says, they hated "the Jews." But the Poles, for all their political anti-Semitism, were neighbors, customers, friends who turned against people they knew. Their betrayal was personal, intimate. *The Germans wouldn't have known who was Jewish if the Poles hadn't told them.* I heard this, in one form or another, from every survivor I interviewed.

Before leaving on my trip, I had braced myself for the anger and grief that I would inevitably feel, a fury at the stupidity of prejudice. I had braced myself for the casually anti-Semitic things even the most well-meaning people would say without realizing it, as they explained what "the Jews" were like or questioned me about what "the Jews" thought or felt. I knew these conversations from having lived in Austria, where even in 2013, 46 percent of Austrians polled considered the country a victim of Hitler's aggression. If some people in Nasielsk were anxious "the Jews" might repossess their homes, then they knew they lived in stolen property, I thought. I didn't mind if they felt nervous and guilty, or if my offer to speak to the high school students provoked a brief panic among the administrators.

At the same time, I harbored fantasies of reconciliation. In my offer to talk to students—which in the end did not take place—I imagined encountering a different generation, worldly, connected, free of the prejudices of their parents and grandparents. I had imagined they might crowd around, just like the kids in my grandfather's movie, *A visitor from Nowy York!* Maybe one or two would want to practice English or ask about life in the United States. My grandfather's film could become a medium of healing in the bitter history between Poles and Jews.

Two weeks before my trip, I received another e-mail from Zdzisław Suwiński:

> *In Nasielsk almost everything remained, as grandfather filmed. It changed only realities. Painted houses in the marketplace. Some locations, which I cannot find, because the film was made through a window. And, well, sadly not a single Jew is in Nasielsk. The Poles live in their houses. The Nasielsk Poles or the Magistrat took their belongings, while the houses stand. I will show you their cemetery—or rather, what remains of it. I will tell you what happened with their* macebami.

I had asked Morry about the word *macebami*, and he thought it might be a Polish rendering of the Hebrew word *matzevah*, meaning gravestone. The gravestones carved by Chaim Nusen Cwajghaft in his workshop next to David Leib Szmerlak's yeshiva, the gravestones Morry had said were used to pave the sidewalk on Warsaw Street after the Germans arrived, and which no one had seen since the war.

Zdzisław Suwiński had written to me, *This is a very serious message. Bring a hat*, meaning wear a yarmulke.

||||||||||||||||||||

After cake and coffee, Zdzisław drove Alina and me to the regional archive in Pułtusk, which houses the vital records for Nasielsk from the nineteenth century up to 1939. During the drive he and Alina talked in Polish in the front seat, and I listened uncomprehendingly from the back. But it was enough to know we were driving along the Pułtusker Weg, or what had once been the Pułtusker Weg, past (I would later learn) Wilczynski's blacksmith shop, along the bus route once served by a man named Figa, whose face may appear in a picture saved in Keva Richman's family photo album in Florida.

The Pułtusk archive occupies a decommissioned church. We put our bags in lockers in the dark, cramped hallway. Then we filled out forms to gain access to the collections. After half an hour's wait, we were allowed upstairs to the reading room located in the former nave. Honey-colored wood cabinets and long tables stood beneath the soaring arched ceiling. Three young Polish girls were busy doing something, chatting in hushed voices. We filled out more forms. One for each volume and for each person who was to view the volume. Then, when we were done, another form for each person, to certify that he or she had viewed the volume in question.

For the next four hours, we searched through the birth, death, and marriage records of Nasielsk, pages bound in oversize ledgers, written in flowing calligraphic script, in Russian before World War I, and in Polish after 1919. The archivist, who at first had ignored us, soon became solicitous, and by the afternoon, she was huddled over the documents with Zdzisław, helping decipher the bureaucratic formulae in which each document's information was encased. I collected photographs of documents with the names of people I had gotten to know: the birth certificate for David Leib Szmerlak in 1875. Documents witnessed in the 1920s by Fishl Perelmuter. The signatures of Morry's grandfather, Srul Skalka; Leslie Glodek's father, Jakob Glodek; directors of the Joint's free loan *kassa*, Hersz Jagoda and Chaim Huberman; and members of the families Kubel, Rotstein, Brzoza.

Dana had given me one genealogical assignment: to find Hyman Meyer Kurtz and Chaya Leah Diamond's marriage certificate, a document that might have helped clear up the mystery of who our great-great-grandparents were, and when, where, and why Hyman Kurtz had married into the Diamond family of Nasielsk. I could not find it.

In a dusty record ledger from 1888, however, I put my fingers on the birth certificate of Dowid Kurc. Dana had obtained a photocopy of this document in the 1990s. The page in the book I held in my hand contained nothing new to us. Yet holding the original record of my grandfather's birth while standing in the reading room of the Pułtusk archive felt different than looking at the photocopy in Dana's apartment in San Francisco. Like David and Liza's postcards and letters, the original handwritten document seemed to offer a kind of access that a copy did not. Of course, Hyman Kurtz did not write this document. But he must have been present when it was written, standing next to the clerk, providing him with names as he recorded the data in the baroque Russian then in use in czarist-controlled Poland. If I held the page in my hands, did this bring me closer to my grandfather, my great-grandfather, or any of the other people whose names I now knew but who had died long before I was born?

When the archive closed at three o'clock, we drove back to the Suwiński home for lunch: huge helpings of meat, potatoes, smoked fish, and greens of Jurassic proportions. After the meal, more cake and coffee. Then, once we had cleared the table, Zdzisław presented the stack of documents and photographs that he had collected. We sorted through them for an hour, until Alina had to return to Warsaw. In the early evening, Zdzisław and I finally set out to explore the *rynek*.

On the street, Zdzisław pointed out buildings where Jews had lived. But I was not really listening. This was the Nasielsk in my grandfather's film. I recognized the architectural style immediately, the two- and three-story town houses with wooden doors and shutters, the second-story wrought-iron balconies, many of which had now been replaced with concrete slabs, even if the ornate iron support brackets still jutted uselessly in rusted curls beneath them. The doors that had not been renovated all looked like the ones in David Kurtz's film. Entering the square, I recognized Morry's home, the Skalka residence, from Evelyn Rosen's videos of their trip the year before. The kebab restaurant was still there with its weathered wooden sign. The paint still moldered on the upper floors. The basement where the redheaded, bristle-bearded baker Rajczyk had lived and worked was still boarded up, a chunk of sidewalk missing in front of the window.

We walked down the south side of the marketplace, from Morry's building near the southeast corner to where the Glodek family had run a grocery on the southwest corner. The street and the square itself were much smaller than I had anticipated. Perhaps ten doors separated the corners. The west side of the square was entirely new. There was a tall, cylindrical billboard stand, the kind common in Europe, where announcements and advertisements are posted. One flyer announced a warehouse sale, another a cabaret, and a poster from April with the Playboy logo advertised an Easter dance party.

Previously, the *rynek* had been open space, paved with cobblestones, where the butchers had their *jatkis*, their stalls, and where on Tuesdays and Fridays, farmers from the surrounding countryside would gather for market days. Now the square was a park with trees and grass and an X of sidewalks, a bust of Pope Jan Pawel II mounted on a black marble obelisk in the center.

Zdzisław and I walked the twenty or thirty steps to the northwest corner. "This is the place where stands your grandfather," said Zdzisław in German. Morry had also identified this corner as the site of the film. We stood on the edge of the park, across the narrow street from the buildings, at approximately the same distance David Kurtz had stood when he pressed the lever and opened the shutter of his Kodak home movie camera.

The building on the corner, where the SKLEP SPOŻYWCZY sign would have been, was now covered in modern white stucco, with a metal door recessed in the façade. The building housed a driving school, and a blue-on-yellow plaque on the wall listed the different classes of driver's license available, from motorcycle to tour bus. But as with many of the buildings on the square, only half of the façade had been renovated, perhaps indicating the property line. The right-hand side still had the old shuttered windows and the double-leaved wooden door painted the same dark brown visible in my grandfather's film. A dented tin rain gutter, just like the ones in the film, ran down the façade from the roof, ending in an angled spout that would dump roof water onto the sidewalk.

I had brought an envelope of still photos from the film, shots that highlighted architectural details, doorways, windows, shutters, balconies. I hoped these would enable me to identify the precise location of each shot in the film. I held up a photo of the grocery, this very corner, this very building, if Morry and Zdzisław were correct. I looked through one eye, then the other, flipping between foreground and background, 1938 and 2012, trying to match the lines of the doors, the windows, the roof, the basement window, the thick band that separated the first from the second story. I shifted to the right a little, back to the left, forward a step, back, attempting to stand in the exact spot my grandfather had once occupied. Knowing the exact doorway in my grandfather's film would satisfy the obsessive strain in my historical curiosity. But if I could identify the building in the film, perhaps I could also identify the woman standing in the doorway or the people loitering on the street in front.

In one black-and-white movie still, Louis Malina stands surrounded by people. Above his head, an open window frames the cloudy sky. To the extreme right of the scene, for just a few frames in the film, the church steeple is visible, partially blocked by an A-frame roof with a square window just below the apex.

From the northwest corner of the *rynek*, where I was now standing, the church appeared in exactly the same profile. Almost exactly. An A-frame roof partially blocked the view in just the same way as in the film. Almost the same way: there was a slight difference in the roof's slope, which was sharper now. The building was in the same place, but it was a different building, or at least a different roof. In the film, the steeple is grainy, pixelated, yet it appears somehow slimmer than from where I was standing.

The foreground had also changed. In the film Louis stands on the edge of a warren of brick buildings, whose irregular roofs are visible to his right. None of that existed now. The buildings on this corner of the *rynek* had been entirely rebuilt, and where irregular roofs once undulated, there was now a vacant lot.

I held up another photo, showing the façades along the block to the right of the grocery store. Zdzisław suggested my grandfather had merely shifted his position between the two shots, turning his body to the right to change the view from the church steeple to the panorama with the grocery store at one end and a row of trees beyond the buildings at the other. I held up other photos from the sequence of shots, showing different doorways along the length of the street. I made then-and-now shots, holding the older photos at arm's length, trying to fit them into the buildings in front of me. I took a brief video with my digital camera, replicating as best I could the panorama that David Kurtz had made.

Most buildings had been modernized, or, like the Skalka home, partly modernized. Doorways had been moved, windows replaced. One building had been entirely rebuilt, diverging willfully from the otherwise consistent style of the block. The new building had an awning instead of a balcony and two pop-up dormers in place of the standard sloping roofs. Now there was no street life except a few loiterers in the park.

I stood for almost an hour in the tiny square, as the day became cloudy and windy. It began to grow dark. Moths and mosquitoes fluttered and buzzed. I believed Morry. I believed Zdzisław, who had lived in the town his entire life, just a few blocks from where we were standing. They had both said this was the spot. I wanted the photo and the space in front of me to match. But not a single still from the film could be definitively placed.

Even the following day, when Alina Skibińska joined me in comparing the angles and features of the buildings as they now appear with the images from the film, we could not finally decide. We walked around the block to view the buildings from the back. From this vantage point, Nasielsk still looked like a town from the 1930s. Even buildings with renovated façades were crumbling from the side facing away from the marketplace. There were chickens and roosters in wooden cages, cobblestones instead of pavement. On the corner, behind what might have been the grocery store, there was a stoop that looked just like the one in the final scene of the Nasielsk footage, where the young woman wags her finger at the shoving children. Alina and I compared the brickwork around the door. We looked for a gouge in the wooden frame, where in the film a mezuzah is visible. But a plywood plank obscured the doorway. Still, I thought it was the place. It *felt* like the right place.

I photographed the old doorway. If it was not in fact the doorway from the film, it was the doorway that now looked most similar to the one in the film. But this, of course, was the fallacy in my attempt at historical matching, trying to replicate an image rather than to discover a place. When on the first evening Zdzisław had shown me a modern door in a restored façade and said "Here," I had been disappointed. It didn't look the way I'd wanted. It had been ruined by restoration. The door I was looking for was the door in the film.

We'll come back tomorrow, when the light is better, Zdzisław had said that first night as I fought to make the present and past coalesce. I put away the still photos and my little digital camera, and we walked down the block and to the right, down the east side of the square, where Leslie Glodek had felt the film must take place, where the Blaszkes' tinsmith shop had been, where Keva Richman's grandfather, Szmuel Usher Schwarzberg, had once lived. I counted the doors and windows, most of which had been improved into irrelevance.

That night after dinner, I arranged for Morry to call the Suwiński home. While we waited, the Suwińskis' son, Tomek, joined us. He plays bass in a heavy metal band, and he spoke some English. I was eager to talk of something other than the film, other than the Jews' former presence in this town. Over an after-dinner digestif of homemade quince schnapps, we discussed music and instruments and recording equipment. I asked Tomek what he thought of the United States. He asked whether it was true that all Americans ate at McDonald's. I said it was as true as the American belief that all Poles ate sausage and danced the polka. He translated this for his parents, and they laughed.

Morry rang about thirty minutes later. He and Zdzisław spoke on the phone in Polish, comparing names and dates. When they were finished, I spoke briefly with Morry. "He knows about all the people I knew!" He was clearly excited. "I guess you can't paint everyone with the same brush," he said.

॥॥॥॥॥॥॥॥॥॥॥॥

When I woke the next morning, I had already spent more time in Nasielsk than my grandparents had during their 1938 trip. Zdzisław and I had agreed to have breakfast at eight o'clock, but by seven thirty I had spent half an hour on the Ellis Island website searching for information about

Zdzisław's family. His maternal grandfather, Stanislaw Tomaszynski, had emigrated to the United States at age forty-three, arriving in New York on July 17, 1923. I found the ship's manifest, along with an image of the ship itself. Zdzisław was delighted. He had never known the precise date before, and he went downstairs to share the discovery with his mother, who lived in an apartment on the ground floor.

Irena Victoria Suwiński, née Tomasińska, was born in Brooklyn in 1924, the same year Morry was born in Nasielsk. Her father, like so many Nasielskers, had gone to America. But as for many of them, including the schoolmaster David Leib Szmerlak, the New World had not appealed to him, and he returned to Nasielsk in 1926.

It was unnecessary for them to come back, Mrs. Suwiński said when I sat with her that morning. Speaking in Polish, with Alina Skibińska translating, she said her mother had missed *her* mother, who was in Poland. So that's why they came back. What happened happened, she said, so it has to be good.

Mrs. Suwiński evinced less interest in my grandfather's film than I had hoped or expected. She watched and seemed unimpressed. *Yes, that's the way it looked*, she seemed to say. *So?* Instead, she began to talk about her life. "She's telling her own stories," Alina informed me, deciding to summarize rather than translate. That story isn't relevant, Zdzisław said gently after a little while, in the way one speaks to one's mother when she strays. Talk more about the Jews and the relationship with the Jews, he told her.

There were more Jews in Nasielsk than Poles, Mrs. Suwiński said. They prayed a lot. They were very observant about their Sabbath. And they stuck together.

I asked Alina to inquire whether she recognized any of the stores in the film.

Stores were all one next to the other, Mrs. Suwiński recalled. There was a fancy store that was big. There was a grocery that was small. You must admit they were good at selling things.

I asked about the family names I had learned, and Mrs. Suwiński recognized Morry's grandfather's name, Skalka.

The Skalkas had a fancy store, she told us, where they would sew things. But they also had a store where they sold fabric. They had a workshop on the other side. But their store wasn't like one of these Jewish stores. They had a very Polish store.

What does that mean, a Polish store? asked Alina.

Well, a Polish store is very well kept.

So a Jewish store is ugly?

Well, you know, the Jews, they were salesmen. They didn't really appreciate presentation. But the Skalkas, she continued, their store was very organized and decent. When something cost something, that's what it cost. No one haggled or tried to change the prices. They were honest. They were very decent Jews. They were cultured. They were pretty Polish.

Mr. Perelmuter was also like that, Mrs. Suwiński added. When he got new film in his store, he would come and tell you. His store was also nice. He had a beautiful window display, and he would change it. He was a real photographer. He was really the best photographer in Nasielsk.

When I showed Mrs. Suwiński the photo of Fishl Perelmuter from Keva Richman's family album, she recalled other details.

Perelmuter had a limp. His daughters were the same age as me, Mrs. Suwiński said, maybe younger. She said she wouldn't recognize them now. I lived among Jews, she said. We were all like family.

Just like Leslie Glodek, Mrs. Suwiński recalled people by profession rather than by last name. She did not recognize the names Brzoza or Jagoda, but she remembered a lumber family and a family that made soda water. She remembered Rifka the sweet-seller, who must have been the *tsikerl makher*'s wife. She remembered Mordka the blacksmith, who had two sons and who owned property at the edge of town.

There were so many shops, Mrs. Suwiński said when Alina asked about restaurants. You could buy ice cream and drinks. Jews worked in basements. They had bakeries there, and an olive oil factory.

Mrs. Suwiński remembered the button factory, but not anything about it. And she remembered the synagogue, though she said she was never inside it, because her father told her she wasn't supposed to enter.

It was nice and big and well built, she remembered. The stairs were lovely, she said. And the windows were very colorful, like in church. It's a shame that it was torn down, at least as a historical building. It should have remained.

||||||||||||||||||||

A few years after the war, the Nasielsk synagogue was demolished and its bricks were used to build a dairy farm nearby. Zdzisław drove us there after we had finished speaking with his mother. It was Thursday, May 31, and Zdzisław now began the tour he had prepared for me, visiting the sites of significance to Nasielsk's Jewish community.

The synagogue had stood behind the square, to the north and east. An apartment building now cuts across where the entrance was, and where the large sanctuary had been there is now a dirt parking lot. A little shed occupies one corner, and a wire fence runs the length of the property down to the small creek on the north edge of the town, near where the *bes midrash* and the *mikva*, the ritual bath, had been. Morry had told me that people used to draw water for washing and cleaning from this stream. But when we stood there, the stream was clogged with soda bottles, cardboard boxes, food wrappers, and general slime. On the other side, a grassy meadow extended for several acres, out to a site of archaeological importance, a prehistoric settlement, now a large round mound that had been excavated in the 1990s. Nasielsk's grand wooden synagogue, predecessor to the stone building seen in my grandfather's film, had also stood in this field, and during the archaeological excavation into the mound, many massive foundation posts had been discovered, undoubtedly belonging to the wooden structure.

In 1941, the German archaeologist Otto Kleemann, who before the war had been an expert on the Viking presence in northern Poland, was serving as a reconnaissance pilot for the Luftwaffe. Sometime before November 28, 1941, perhaps in conjunction with the German invasion of the Soviet Union the previous June, he had flown over the territory surrounding Nasielsk and had snapped two photos, apparently for private purposes, of the prehistoric mound just north of the Nasielsk *rynek*. He published the images in the journal *Alt Prussia* in 1943.

Although pioneering in the field of aerial archaeology, Kleemann's photos of the site possess little scientific value today. One of them, however, is the only aerial photo of Nasielsk's stone synagogue and the buildings surrounding it. Among the documents Zdzisław had compiled for me was a scholarly article, "World War II Aerial Photo of Nasielsk," published in 2006 by Mariusz Bloński. Identifying the historical importance of Kleemann's image, Bloński refers to the 1885 *Geographical Dictionary of the Polish Kingdom*, which describes the building as "an extensive synagogue of brick, which will be supported only by iron." The reconnaissance photograph shows the synagogue from the north in a sidelong view. The massive entrance, a small part of which is visible in David Kurtz's film, can be seen in profile. Three arched windows tower side by side along the north wall. A side door is visible, and three rows of smaller windows toward the entrance. The building, finished in white stucco, dominates the surrounding area, overshadowing the dark-roofed two-story homes on the north and east sides of the *rynek*. The photo is not detailed enough to show whether the posts and fence that Leslie Glodek had been forced to erect in 1939 were still in place in 1941. Several of the other buildings that Morry had mentioned—the *bes midrash*, the *shtibl*, and the house where Chaim Nusen Cwajghaft lived and had his headstone-carving workshop—are not identifiable in the photo and may already have been torn down.

But a second, large building of significance, located a block farther east, behind the synagogue, is clearly visible in Kleemann's photo: David Leib Szmerlak's yeshiva, the Yesodey-Hathora where Morry and his brother Avrum, Leslie Glodek, Mottl Brzoza, the bad kid Srebro, and several hundred other Nasielsk boys went to school. This building is still standing. It now houses the Jarosław Iwaszkiewicz Public High School, the school at which Zdzisław Suwiński had taught history for more than thirty years and where he now served as director.

During the war, David Leib Szmerlak's school had been converted into a barracks, a *Lager*, for forced laborers working at the Nasielsk railway station. According to a postwar document, which was also in the folder Zdzisław had prepared for me, the *Lager* housed 150 occupants at any given time, the same number of students who had been enrolled when it was a school. Between 1941 and 1943, approximately 3,500 people passed through it. When the *Lager* closed in 1943, the prisoners were taken to the Stutthof concentration camp near Gdańsk. No information concerning their identities remains. Zdzisław had found this document in the school's files and saved it. He is endeavoring to have the building declared a historic site by the Polish Institute of National Remembrance.

Another letter contained in the school file, undated although almost certainly from late 1946 or early 1947, interested me even more. This letter, bearing a lawyer's name and address, concerned the effort by Ester Szmerlak to receive restitution for the German theft and then the Polish nationalization of this building, to which she and her husband had devoted so much of their lives.

"The applicant's husband, David Leib Szmerlak, was before the war through September 1939 the owner and occupant of the house in Nasielsk on Berka Josielewicza [*sic*] Street, number 20. In connection with the war, which began in September 1939, the applicant and the applicant's husband had to leave Nasielsk and thus the applicant and the applicant's husband lost their home. The applicant's husband died during the war in the Soviet Union and the applicant is his only heir."

David Leib Szmerlak, aka Simon, whom Morry had recalled so fondly, died in Soviet exile during the war. But his wife, Ester, who wore Coke-bottle glasses, survived, and after the war she lived in the town of Szczecin in western Poland, just a few miles from the current border with Germany. There is no evidence that she ever received compensation for the property that had been stolen from her.

Zdzisław gave us a tour of this solid two-story, perhaps thirty-room schoolhouse, which was busy with students, since for them it was a regular Thursday toward the end of spring semester. Zdzisław was greeted warmly by the office staff, all of whom shook my hand and said they were happy to meet me. We visited the classroom where Zdzisław held his history lessons, and we looked at an old map of Nasielsk that he had hanging on the wall. Then he brought Alina and me to the basement, where an unused back door led out to the grounds. A mezuzah had been mounted on the doorframe and, according to Zdzisław, had remained there until recently, when it was stolen. The eight-inch-long rectangular gouge had not yet been painted over, and the raw wood showed three empty screw holes.

Later, when I looked it up online, I learned that Jarosław Iwaszkiewicz (1894–1980), after whom the Szmerlak school is now named, was a Polish poet, dramatist, and essayist, who published under the pseudonym Eleuter. "He is mostly recognized for his literary achievements in poetry before World War II, but also criticized as a long-term political opportunist in the communist Poland, actively participating in the slander of Czesław Miłosz and other expatriates. He was removed from school textbooks soon after the collapse of the Soviet empire."

||||||||||||||||||||||

Why do some details become "history"—included in schoolbooks, in scholarly dissertations, or in personal narratives—while other details are forgotten? What scale of information do we accept when we say that we know something about the past?

Certain facts about the deportation of the Jews of Nasielsk are easy to determine from books about the Holocaust. In the reference work *A World in Turmoil: An Integrated Chronology of the Holocaust and World War II*, by Hershel Edelheit and Abraham J. Edelheit, for example, we can learn the following information: October 30, 1939: "Himmler orders all Jews deported from the annexed Polish western provinces within four months." November 15, 1939: "Nazi order blocks all Jewish bank and credit accounts in Poland." December 3, 1939: "*Umsiedlungsaktion* [resettlement action] in Nasielsk renders the town *Judenrein* [free of Jews]."

In the English-language summary to his *History of the Jewish Community in the Districts Pułtusk and Maków Mazowiecki*, the Polish historian Janusz Szczepański writes, "By the end of 1939 some 7,000 Jews had been expelled from Pułtusk, 5,000 from Wyszkow, 3,000 from Nasielsk and over 2,000 from Serock." Szczepański goes on to provide considerable detail about the events in Nasielsk. "On December 3rd–4th Jews from Nasielsk were displaced, and on December 5th those from Serock, who were driven to the railway station in Nasielsk . . . At first trains carrying the deported Jews were northwards bound. In Krolewiec, however, they were turned back, and after a 36-hour journey in sealed cattle-trucks, with no food or drink, they reached Międzyrzec Podlaski and Łuków." According to Szczepański, the trains first traveled north because the deported Jews were originally destined for a concentration camp in Germany. Only once they were under way was the decision made to send them instead to towns in German-occupied Poland, the *Generalgouvernement*, or General Government.

Szczepański based his account on a book by another Polish historian, Michał Grynberg, *Jews in Ciechanów 1939–1942*, published in 1984. In his version of the facts, Grynberg writes: "Once gathered in the market, the Nazis divided the Jews into two groups. One group of about two thousand people was hurried to the train station, about 4km from the city, and the other, also about two thousand people, was confined in the synagogue, and after twenty-four hours of waiting was also escorted to the train station in Nasielsk for deportation."

Grynberg, in turn, based his account on the only firsthand record of the deportation, which was discovered among the papers hidden by Emanuel Ringelblum in milk cans beneath the Warsaw Ghetto, and which are now located at the Jewish Historical Institute in Warsaw. I viewed this four-page water-damaged document the day before I arrived in Nasielsk. The account is attributed to someone named Lebensold, which is an odd name for a Polish Jew. It may have been Lebensgold, or the name may refer to the person who transcribed the account, or it may refer to something unknown.

On December 3, 1939, at 7:30 in the morning, the sound of a bell rang out through the village. The town official announced that all Jewish men, Jewish women, and children must gather in the town square within 15 minutes. No one knew what was happening. It could be sensed that something menacing hung in the air. At the same time, word spread that the Volksdeutsche *were barging into Jewish homes, looting them, and evicting their inhabitants. A terrible chaos arose. Frightened Jews began gathering in the square. Some brought with them small satchels, carrying them on hunched backs, and others brought their own carts, on which they had placed a portion of their belongings. In addition to the Jews, they were in the square.*

In the account, the author never refers to the Germans directly, instead using passive constructions and an indefinite "one" or "they."

Each of them held in his hand a braided whip, a horsewhip, a cat-o'-nine-tails, or a steel bar. This sight instilled terror. Right away, they "got to work." They chopped off beards, cut out sections of hair in order to disfigure; then, they photographed their victims. In the meantime, others were searching Jewish homes to see if, by any chance, anyone had stayed in the town. The 'fun' in the square lasted about 2 hours. Then the Jews were arranged in rows (all those sitting on carts had to get off them). The first four rows were ordered to march away, and . . . the few thousand Jews marched in the direction of the station (4 km from the city). The remaining few thousand were led through the city to the synagogue. It was already 11 in the morning. It was announced that the Jews were going to have to sit here until 6 a.m. of the next day. There was one huge room. Crowded, the Jews sat on the floor one on top of another. A guard stood near the door. Once in a while, they would come here to look, but they didn't beat. When one of the Jews had to leave to relieve himself, he had to report it. When he left, the guard would beat him with a leather whip, and the same happened when he returned. They sat like this until the end of the day, all night—without food, drink, in the dark.

At dawn someone noticed that in the hallway of the synagogue stood about 100 whips. At 6 a.m. it was announced that it was time to leave the synagogue. Near the door, everyone was whipped wherever possible, across their heads, backs, legs. In rows, they marched toward the station. The very ill were placed on plank beds that four Jews each would carry. Along the way, Polish neighbors stood on both sides of the rows, laughing. There were a few isolated incidents where Poles crept up to the Jews to give their close friends bread and money.

The Jews were not led to the station along a straight path, but a

circuitous one. There was a lot of mud here (swampy ground—1 km).
Along this stretch, for the entire length of the road, they stood on both
sides. The Jews were ordered to run (mud!) and sing. Whips hailed
down on the Jews' heads this entire time. The patches of mud were so
large that shoes sank into the clay, but it was necessary to run farther
and farther, because they kept beating. The screams of the women
and children were horrible. Blood streamed from heads, particularly
the men's. Backpacks were discarded along the way in order to con-
tinue running. The carts bearing belongings got stuck along the way.

Finally, the Jews reached the station. Here, they were arranged
into two rows. Now, a new Gehenna *[ordeal] began. Frisking. They*
looked everywhere. The better-looking ones were ordered to strip
down completely, and the naked women were particularly exam-
ined. Others' clothes were torn apart at the seams. Those who were
found to have something hidden, particularly the men, had to roll
naked in the mud. Those who had been searched were packed into
train cars waiting at the station, which were then sealed shut. There
were at least 25 people in each compartment. The cars were deprived
of water and light. The windows had to stay closed, and during the
day, obscured.

In these conditions, the journey lasted 36 hours. It went through
Ciechanów, Mława, Iłowo, Koenigsberg, Ostrołęka, Małkinia, from
there to the East Station in Warsaw. The train stopped at some of the
stations for a few minutes, but no one from the public was allowed
near it. From the East Station, the Jews were taken further, to Mińsk
Mazowiecki, Siedlec, and then to Łuków. Here, the train was stopped,
the cars were opened, and they came around asking how many corpses
there were. That day, everyone was still alive, but in the coming days,
a few people died each day.

Soon the local Jews came to the station in their company. The
newcomers were allowed to be given water. Then all the Jews were
ordered into the town. The local people distributed them among var-
ious empty buildings, and many of them took them into their homes.

The general attitude was very warm. They helped however they could. The first division of Jews from Nasielsk had been transported in an analogous way, but the endpoint was Międzyrzec.

If one pieces together the written sources with information from interviews and oral history, it is possible to know that Morry Chandler's parents and younger brother, David, his grandparents Srul and Dvora Skalka, his uncle Jankiel Skalka and his wife, Malka, and their three children, Brucha, Selig, and one whose name Morry does not remember, along with Leslie Glodek's parents and brothers and their families, were all among the people confined to the synagogue, and so apparently in this second deportation train that ended up in Łuków.

In Morry's secondhand account, told to him by his mother, and recalled now seventy-four years later, the ordeal in the synagogue lasted three days and nights, and while there, the Jews were forced to scrape the murals painted by Fishl Perelmuter from the walls with their fingernails. It is impossible to determine whether Fishl Perelmuter was a witness to the destruction of his artistic achievement.

Susan Weiss, the first Nasielsker I had spoken with, had also remembered being confined in the synagogue, although she could provide no specific details. She was a little girl, seven or nine years old. It seems probable that her parents and her eight siblings were in the same group of deported Nasielsk Jews. It cannot be determined whether the stonecutter Cwajghaft or Faiga Tick's parents, Sana Milchberg and his wife, Hendel, were among those in the synagogue or those sent first to Międzyrzec. A document that I discovered later in Israel would help add ten more names to the list of those who can be placed with relative certainty in the synagogue that day and, later, on the train to Łuków.

Another testimony in the Ringelblum archive describes the Nasielsk synagogue two days after the deportation of Nasielsk's Jewish community. On December 5, Jews from the nearby town of Serock had been marched the twenty kilometers to Nasielsk and were confined there overnight. According to this witness, the synagogue had been stripped of all objects and decoration, and a swastika flag hung over the Torah ark. The following day, the Jews of Serock were forced along the same muddy path to the Nasielsk train station.

Among the documents that Zdzisław gave me was an oral history by Father Tomasz Tomasiński, a priest and an uncle of Zdzisław's mother. Father Tomasiński was active in the Polish Home Army during the war, and among his duties was keeping tabs on the local administration in Nasielsk. In this testimony, which is available online, he also describes the deportation of the Jews of Nasielsk. "In order to mistreat, scare, and terrify them in the square, machine guns were shot above their heads," he states. Father Tomasiński then provides information that supplements what a Jewish eyewitness could have known. "The mayor made the Jews leave behind all the [valuables] . . . They were forced to walk through water, through the river, and they were forced to leave everything, and he looted all this and would send huge trunks. I was to confirm this. And I confirmed that he would send entire trunks full of valuables to his wife in northern Italy. I'm unable to say whether this was Merano or Bolzano, a small town in the mountains, in the Dolomites."

Another source in the documents Zdzisław gave me, a collection of essays on the history of Nasielsk, published in 1970, identifies the German mayor of Nasielsk from November 1939 to June 1940 as Otto Sperling. According to Father Tomasiński, the Polish underground assassinated Sperling in 1940 and left the body along the road north of town.

Further details about the deportation of Nasielsk's Jews can be found in German sources. In a recent book by the historian Wolfgang Curilla, the author cites a document found in the papers of the German army commander in Poland, General Johannes Blaskowitz. On February 15, 1940, Blaskowitz gave a presentation to the German General Staff, complaining about the behavior of Wehrmacht troops. In his presentation, the general cited thirty-three incidents of particular brutality that he found objectionable. Harassing the conquered population, he maintained, made occupation more difficult. Curilla paraphrases item number thirty-one: "Shortly before Christmas 1939, 1,600 Jews were supposed to be deported from Nasielsk, Zichenau Administrative District. The police locked them in the synagogue and beat the victims there with dog whips. Several Jews were shot next to the synagogue. As the majority of Jews were brought to the train station, they were driven by whip-blows through a particularly dirty area known as the 'red moor [*rotes Moor*].'"

But the document Curilla cites has garbled an important detail.

"Red moor" is a typographical error, or a transcription error by the clerk on Blaskowitz's staff. The area was almost certainly referred to as the "*rotes Meer.*" A little German army humor, forcing the Jews of Nasielsk to march through a muddy stream that the soldiers named "the Red Sea."

꜓꜓꜓꜓꜓꜓꜓꜓꜓꜓꜓꜓꜓꜓

Jews were gathered in the square, Zdzisław Suwiński told Alina and me on the morning of our tour.

We were standing in the Nasielsk marketplace, having walked the two blocks from his school and the site of the former synagogue. He spoke in Polish, and Alina translated.

A different group of two hundred left every two hours under German supervision, Zdzisław continued. They were marched along the road for four kilometers, until they reached a point where the road crosses a stream.

The three of us got into the car and drove out of the market square. We drove down Warsaw Street, past the small electrical transformer, onto Kościuszki Street and out into the countryside on what is now Route 571, or Kolejova. We drove about four kilometers, about two and a half miles, and stopped at a little bridge over a stream. Just ahead, a railroad bridge crossed the road on a stone embankment.

SS troops with machine guns stood on this bridge, Zdzisław explained when we got out of the car. They directed the Jews to go into the river to wash themselves, old people, children, everyone. Railroad workers witnessed this, local people who maintained the tracks and managed the movement of wagons and locomotives at the station. The workers knew the deportation was going to happen, because they had been repairing the railroad tracks. They knew the train cars had been assembled.

Four or five workers were on the bridge watching. Later, they told the people in town what they had witnessed. German soldiers surrounded the area. Each of the Jews had to bathe in the river. The soldiers undressed the Jews and forced them into the water. It was minus ten degrees Celsius, fourteen degrees Fahrenheit. Two cars or trucks were on the other side of the bridge, waiting for corpses. Small children or others who died were loaded into these cars and driven in the direction of Nasielsk, the workers did not know where. Out of each group of two hundred, between ten and twenty people died, according to the railroad workers who were there. Heart attacks, little children who died of hypothermia. This is the reason groups were brought every two hours, so the soldiers could remove the dead and collect the clothing and belongings left by the living before the next group arrived.

The reports from the workers on the bridge may have been embellished, Zdzisław admitted, but the fact is, this happened here. These stories were passed down. People repeated what they heard from other people. The railway workers said they heard horrible cries and screams. It was unbearable to hear their stories. This is all just what people said, grandmothers, word of mouth. After crossing the stream, those who were still able were marched to the train station, another two kilometers, about a mile and a quarter away.

Today, Nasielsk's train station has come down in the world. The station itself, a postwar glass-and-steel building with a red corrugated roof angled upward like a half-open drawbridge, is rusted and on the verge of dilapidation. Farther along the tracks, grass grows through cracks in the concrete landings.

Zdzisław drove us past the station another half mile to reach the freight platform. Paved in cobblestones, the platform is about thirty feet wide and perhaps a quarter mile long. A forty-car freight train loaded with coal was idling at the platform, a plum-colored locomotive with yellow stripes bearing the words *Rail Polska* at the head. The engineer held his cigarette out the window.

When we had gotten out of the car again and were standing on the platform from which the Jews of Nasielsk and many other towns were deported, Zdzisław resumed.

Nasielsk was first. All month until Christmas, other towns were emptied of Jews. Everyone left from the Nasielsk train station. They would load them onto the trains every two hours, and once a day the trains would leave. The one suitcase that they were allowed to take they had to abandon at the stream. And what were they carrying? Identification papers and money. Important things, otherwise you wouldn't take them.

The Germans stole everything, Zdzisław concluded. People were loaded into these cars with nothing left. And while the people were being loaded into the cars, German soldiers broke into all the houses in town. The week following the deportation, the Germans brought trucks into town and carried away all the Jews' belongings. They took the machinery from the button factory and transported it back to Germany. If they found any Jews in hiding, they killed them right away.

We got back into the car and drove back to Nasielsk. Just before we got to Zdzisław's house, we turned left onto a single-lane country road. A Soviet-era apartment building stood stranded incongruously in a field. We stopped at a weedy lot next to a grove of birch trees, the former Jewish cemetery.

These trees were planted here beginning in 1963, Zdzisław said. It was a municipal project that organized the schoolchildren, including him. At the time, four gravestones were still standing on the cemetery grounds. It is unknown what happened to them.

The little forest follows the boundaries of the cemetery. Forest paths now reproduce what were once the walkways. A gap in the trees marks what was formerly the main entrance.

From his pocket, Zdzisław pulled out a blue-velvet yarmulke. He placed it on his head as we walked between the rows of trees. I asked him where he had gotten it, and he said it had been a gift from his son's father-in-law, who had visited Israel several years before.

Places should be respected, he said.

We continued down the mossy path to the opposite end of the cemetery, which occupies several acres. Then we turned around and walked back toward the entrance.

I had brought a yarmulke with me, too, a black rayon giveaway that had ended up in the pocket of a suit after some wedding, funeral, or bar mitzvah. I thought about putting it on as we walked through the cemetery, but I did not. For Zdzisław Suwiński, it might have been a sign of respect. For me, it would have been a hollow gesture.

I had also brought with me a little blue booklet from the Riverside Memorial Chapel in New York, which I had received at the unveiling of my father's gravestone in 2010. This booklet had the Kaddish, the mourner's prayer, printed in Hebrew, English, and the transliterated, phonetic Hebrew for people like me, who cannot read and do not understand the original, but who are occasionally called upon to fake it.

I had not planned to say Kaddish. It would be pretending to something that had no meaning to me, I thought, and to which I felt no connection. My presence was the most authentic respect I could show to these desecrated graves. To find them, to know this was the cemetery, to record it.

Nevertheless, I had brought the booklet with me and had put it in my pocket with the yarmulke that morning. And when we had walked back up the central path, the path marked by the absence of trees in what is now a thick stand of birches, I asked Zdzisław and Alina to leave me alone for a few minutes. When they had left, I stood there quietly and looked at the blue booklet I had brought from New York.

In our conversations, Morry had frequently mentioned the *Pirke Avot*, the Wisdom of the Fathers, a collection of rabbinical sayings that he had been forced to memorize as a child, but which he now found to contain maxims of genuine wisdom. In the translation I had read, I found this line: "In a place where there is no person to make a difference, strive to be that person."

I read the Kaddish silently. I was there, and if no one else was left to say Kaddish, I ought to. I picked up two stones from the path, one for David Kurtz and one for my father, Milton Kurtz. I put the stones in my pocket and brought them home with me, to place on their gravestones in the Mount Hebron Cemetery in Queens.

⫿⫿⫿⫿⫿⫿⫿⫿⫿⫿

When I got back to the car, I asked Zdzisław what had become of the gravestones no longer present at the cemetery. In his e-mail a month earlier, he had said he would show me.

The ones that were still standing after the war were probably thrown into a ditch in the city, he replied, and buried along with rubble or debris from damaged buildings. But this is not what happened to the majority of the stones. The majority of the stones were taken to the airfield to make the runway.

The airfield at Chrcynno, five miles down the road toward Pułtusk, was the last stop on the tour Zdzisław had planned for me.

In early 1941, he said, all the horses and carts from the surrounding villages were requisitioned to move these stones. It took them all spring to move them. This was done in preparation for Operation Barbarossa, the German invasion of the Soviet Union. When the airport was being built, there was some German supervision, but not much. When the Germans took the stones, they used a truck with a driver and a soldier. But when the villagers were moving them, they would do it themselves in carts, without supervision. The truth is, Zdzisław said as we were driving, some of these stones ended up with the villagers who were transporting them. Not many, but some. And those ended up as doorways or in the pens where the animals are kept.

I asked whether any stones still existed.

He responded that he'd asked his students about it, and a boy came to him privately and said, *Mr. Director, I would be willing to show you, but I'm afraid someone will knock my teeth out.* Zdzisław had replied that he only wanted a photograph of it. He wasn't asking for it back. He just wanted to see that it exists. The boy promised that during the summer vacation, when he had some free time, he'd take a picture.

The road from Nasielsk's Jewish cemetery to the Luftwaffe airfield in Chrcynno leads past the house where Zdzisław Suwiński now lives, his father's and his grandfather's home, where I had spent the night. During the spring of 1941, he said, his father's family could see the procession of carts moving along the road toward the airfield. The airfield was strategically important, because it was located just forty-five miles from the border with the Soviet Union. They used prisoners to build the airfield, Zdzisław said, and the prisoners lived in the school. Exactly at six in the morning every day they would walk by the Suwińskis' house. People would stand by the side of the road and throw bread and pieces of fruit, he said, and the Germans tolerated this.

We turned off the main road and onto a gravel path that led through a gap in the trees. There was a sign saying AIRPORT: ENTRY FORBIDDEN. We drove through the line of trees and parked the car on the cracked, weedy asphalt. There had originally been a Polish airfield here, before the war, and when the Germans commandeered the site, they expanded it. Three new runways were built, accommodating fighter aircraft and a bomber group, which was stationed here. The nearby village of Chrcynno had been evacuated when the Germans took over, Zdzisław said. Fourteen houses were demolished and twenty-seven people were displaced. The main runway is fifty meters wide, twelve hundred meters long. Zdzisław is writing a monograph about the construction and operation of this airfield. He has been researching it for many years.

Today only a single runway is still in use. You can take flying lessons there. You can learn to skydive. A few weeks ago, in a field by the entrance, Zdzisław said, someone had been killed when his parachute failed to open. As we walked out onto the concrete, a single-engine plane practiced take-offs and landings in the distance, buzzing like a wasp, flying in circles. The abandoned runway stretched ahead of us, lost in weeds. The fields surrounding it are still under cultivation.

What happened is that water began to appear, Zdzisław explained. The ground suddenly became marshy. When the Germans retreated in 1945, they blew up the runway, which damaged the drainage system they had constructed. They drilled holes in the runway, alternating left and right, and then blew it up so the Russians couldn't use it. Ninety-six holes. These craters have since filled in, but circles of weeds mark their locations. The drainage beneath the airfield continued working for years until it stopped working. And then they had the idea they should fix it. This was in 1982 or 1983. They dug a small well nearby. And when they started digging, they found maybe one, maybe two gravestones. There's a ditch, a pit, where they buried them again.

We walked a thousand yards down the runway until we reached the hole left over from the repairs to the German drainage system. The pit was thirty feet in diameter and perhaps ten feet deep. The sides were muddy, but there were slabs of broken concrete all around. At the center, a foot or more of black, viscous water.

I climbed into the pit. Zdzisław cautioned he didn't have equipment to help me out if I got stuck, so I promised not to get stuck. Later, on my recording of his narration, I learned that he then turned to Alina and said that all the other Jewish people who come to Nasielsk visit the cemetery, ask for a street name, and then leave.

I started scraping around the sides of the pit, trying to loosen stones that were visible, gravitating toward anything larger or with an angular shape. Bugs, slime, broken stones. I saw nothing that resembled a gravestone. I slid around the outer wall of the pit and picked at the fragments. Finally, I held a chip the size of a cell phone. It was a piece of white stone that, to my untrained eye, seemed like marble. To my novice's fingers, it seemed to have been finished on one side. It was unnaturally smooth and flat, almost polished. I brushed off the mud. There were no markings, nothing to indicate it might once have been part of a gravestone, something carved by Chaim Nusen Cwajghaft in his workshop next to the synagogue and the Szmerlak yeshiva. It might have been a piece of a *matzevah*. It might have been just a muddy stone from a pit a half mile down an overgrown airfield abandoned in 1945 by the Luftwaffe.

I put it in my pocket with the stones from the cemetery.

As we walked back to the car, I noticed the paw prints of a dog embossed in the concrete. There were so many forms of preservation beyond the archive, I thought. A cemetery pathway preserved in a line of trees. Three centuries of gravestones preserved beneath a runway.

It would have been a one-in-a-million chance for you to find a gravestone from your family, Zdzisław said to me in Polish, and Alina translated.

If you have to climb into an irrigation ditch at an abandoned airfield in order to visit the graves of your ancestors, I replied, angry at him for the only time, anything you find feels like it belongs to your family.

IIIIIIIIIIIIIIIIIIII

That night, after Alina drove me back to Warsaw, I ate dinner at my hotel. The city was swarming with people. The UEFA European Championship was set to begin that evening, with Poland playing Ukraine. Shirtless men painted in national colors staggered down the street.

On the TV above the bar, President Obama was shown over and over again making a diplomatic faux pas. Two days earlier, he had awarded the Medal of Freedom to Jan Karski, the Polish diplomat and resistance fighter who had smuggled intelligence about the existence of the ghettos and the concentration camps to London and Washington in 1943. In describing this achievement, President Obama had spoken of "Polish death camps." Polish diplomats were outraged, insisting the president should have said "a German death camp in Nazi-occupied Poland," to distinguish the guilty perpetrators from the otherwise innocent location.

After dinner, I went back up to my room to look through the things Zdzisław Suwiński had given me. He had filled a briefcase with documents, photographs, and articles. He had also given me a small blue jewelry box, the kind that would normally hold a ring. Inside was a twisted metal object that at first I had not recognized. Zdzisław made a spinning motion with his fingers, and I understood. It was a crushed, dirt-encrusted pewter dreidel, a child's top, a traditional toy for Hanukkah.

"*Aus Platz wo steht Synagoge,*" Zdzisław had said. From the place where stands the synagogue.

11

A DIFFERENT STYLE OF TORTURE

I'M LOOKING AT a photograph of four young men. The photo is black-and-white, not quite three by five inches. The corners are bent and have begun to disintegrate; there are nicks in the surface and a few dark stains. But the four young men look at the viewer with a timeless teenage confidence, boys preening for the camera.

The four are all wearing buttoned-up jackets and open-collar shirts. Their pants are baggy and pleated. Two have on suits, while the other two wear the knickers typical for young men in Europe in the mid-twentieth century. Their hair is neatly combed. Their expressions are relaxed, playful, in one case provocative.

The man on the left, with an angular face, has a pronounced widow's peak. He seems in the midst of saying something, judging by his slightly opened mouth with deep lines at the corners. The man next to him is much smaller. He has dark hair, and his head reaches just above the shoulders of his companions. His smile is crooked, and his body is tilted away from the man on his other side, the tallest of the group, who has his hand on the smaller man's shoulder. The tall man is the one with the provocative expression. He smiles teasingly at the camera, as if he's about to pull a prank. He grasps his friend's shoulder with his right hand and reaches

toward him with his left, as if he's about to grab him, maybe throw him into a headlock, the way boys do. The fourth young man, at the right of the group, stands at an angle to the others. We see him mostly in profile. He squints against the light, and his jaw is set forcefully. He wears a white shirt and a double-breasted jacket, and with the steely gaze, the white collar against a black blazer, he looks almost like a young sailor scanning the horizon. At the bottom of the photo there are numbers handwritten in white ink, "4.7.43." July 4, 1943.

Of all the artifacts I have encountered in my search—the photos, the letters, my grandfather's film, even the crushed dreidel that Zdzisław Suwiński gave me from the site of the Nasielsk synagogue—this photo is the most complex and chilling. It contains the whole mystery of one man's survival of the Holocaust.

||||||||||||||||||||

In late 1939, after two months as a refugee in the Soviet-controlled city of Białystok, Avrum Tuchendler, Morry's older brother, begged him to take him home. "He came to me, and he says, 'Moishe, I'm not going to survive here,'" Morry Chandler told me on the phone in January 2012, a week after we had met in Florida. "If you picture what was happening in Białystok, with all the refugees from the other side. Every shul, at night, was like sardines in a can. People—you didn't know who—just lie down and sleep on the floor. Here we came from a nice home, with parents, and all of a sudden, this happens. He was yearning, he wanted to go back to my parents. So just like that, I'm going back."

I asked Morry whether he had considered sending Avrum back alone.

"You know the old saying 'Am I my brother's keeper?' Even though he was a few years older, I was his keeper. He was just not cut out for it. It took a lot of chutzpah to do all this stuff."

In the weeks in Białystok, they had heard from other refugees about the deportation from Nasielsk and had learned that their parents were living with relatives in Warsaw. Morry and Avrum hired another guide, who agreed to take them back across the Soviet-German border. They were briefly arrested as spies by the Soviet secret police, the NKVD, who could not believe that Jews would willingly return to German-occupied Poland. But proving their identities by speaking Yiddish, they were released, and once across, they took a train to Warsaw, even though this was forbidden to Jews. On the train, a German soldier slapped Avrum across the face. But he did not shoot them, and he did not throw them off.

So just like that, Morry and Avrum were in Warsaw. They went to the apartment of a family friend, the Neumann or Neimann family. Morry recalled they were relatives of his cousin Elia Applebaum, who had married the daughter of the rabbi of Radzyń. It is possible, therefore, that Mr. and Mrs. Neumann or Niemann were the sister and brother-in-law of Applebaum's wife, mentioned in the Radzyner *Yizkor* book. The couple told the boys where their parents were living. They may even have been the ones who helped the family find an apartment when they arrived in Warsaw after fleeing from Łuków, where the majority of Nasielskers remained as refugees. The apartment was at Kupiecka 8, near Zamenhofa Street, in what would become the poorest section of the Warsaw Ghetto.

In 2011, while in Warsaw with Evelyn and Steve Rosen, Morry told of arriving at his family's apartment in late December 1939. "I remember my mother, she greeted us at the door, she was so happy. She said, 'Oh, my God, my children, my children. Look how you look. You've got to eat something.' You know, like a mother. I told her, 'I brought you your oldest son.' And I said, 'I'm not staying here.' She said, 'I know, I know. Just in the meantime, look what you look like.' You know, 'some food, we'll see, everything will be fine . . .'"

Morry said he was determined to return to Białystok. But each day he waited, it became harder to leave, not only because he was reunited with his family, but also because the Germans were asserting control over the country. The border crossings tightened. The window for refugees to flee east to Soviet-occupied Poland closed. Then, on October 12, 1940, the establishment of a ghetto in Warsaw was decreed. The apartment on Kupiecka Street—occupied by Morry's parents, their three sons, his grandparents, his uncle Jankiel Skalka, Jankiel's wife, and their three children—fell within the boundaries of the new ghetto. They were fortunate and did not have to relocate again. But by November 30, 1940, the ghetto wall had sealed them in.

"It was very tough, just every day, to survive," Morry said, and only rarely said more. When I pressed him to describe his daily life, he responded, "It cannot be transposed. Just impossible. We can maybe understand it, like saying, 'This is what happened.' But you can't get the feel of it, or what it was really like. It's like a person that went through a hanging, and they dropped him, and he walks out. And they say, 'Well, what was it like to drop through the noose?' He can't describe it. We know what happens, but it's hard to transfer the feeling. It's just impossible to describe. The hopelessness. That people were walking around like zombies in the street, looking for—God knows, I don't know what people were looking for . . ."

Sometimes, in the course of other conversations, a few details emerged. When discussing the sudden independence he had achieved when fleeing to Białystok with Avrum, Morry said, "But on the other hand, when we were in Warsaw, in the ghetto, my grandfather said, 'The rules still apply.' And when he looked out the window and I took my hat off—you know, going around without a hat was a crime. *Ah!* And I came back, he carried on. Unbelievable. So there, they were still strict."

In one conversation, discussing Fishl Perelmuter, Morry gave additional details of his visit to the photographer's studio on the corner of Zamenhof and Gęsia Streets, near his family's apartment. I had asked whether Fishl had any customers. Morry groaned. "Who needed pictures? Who needed anything? People were dying from day to day. It was just hopeless," he said. I asked why he had gone to Perelmuter's studio. "Well, he had a daughter. A very pretty little girl. And I went to visit." It is almost a sweet scene. "And that same day—it's memorable—a woman threw herself down from the fifth floor into the courtyard. While I was there. I walked out. She was dead. You know, people committed suicide right and left. So, yes. He had a studio. Zamenhof and Gęsia. Right there on the corner."

Srul Skalka, Morry's grandfather, the patriarch of the family, died in the ghetto in 1941. "I remember going to the cemetery with everybody,"

Morry said in March 2013. "But there was no single burial. It was already in mass graves." Dvora Skalka, Srul's wife and Morry's grandmother, also died in the Warsaw Ghetto.

In his 1993 oral history, Morry provided a few additional scenes from this time. "I remember one beggar that I used to see every day. I would walk down on Zamenhofa Street. He was a blind man and he would stand up there begging. Nobody would give him anything. There was no way to give. And his voice, his begging, every time got weaker and weaker, you know, until one day, I saw him dead. Nobody even paid attention. He just dropped dead and people would walk over him." Scenes like this delighted the German soldiers who visited the ghetto as tourists. "They were on leave and taking pictures. Instantly they would stop their cars and sometimes we would have to pose."

He told a story about another man from Nasielsk, Saul Reingewirtz, who survived the war and later lived in Detroit, where he changed his name to Raimi. Saul was imprisoned in the ghetto at Mława, about seventy-five miles north of Warsaw. "I remember it was winter," Morry said. "He had a pass from his commandant to go to Warsaw. Over there you could bribe them. In a small town you were able to do that. So, when he came to Warsaw and I found out that he was staying at my uncle's house, I took his pass—the pass was good for so many days—and I became Saul Raimi and I would go out, I would hustle. I remember for two days I would go out one gate like I'm leaving—Saul was leaving the ghetto to go back to Mława. I'd buy up potatoes, come back through another gate, 'I'm just coming in from Mława to Warsaw.' Back and forth."

In the 1993 oral history, Morry also recounted this brief episode: "As kids, you know, my brother and I were always out in the street looking to see maybe a miracle would happen. I remember somebody was manufacturing tea, I don't know from what—little cellophane envelopes—and they were selling tea. I remember they called it 'Niko' tea. And we would—the kids—we were going out with these little envelopes to sell them—selling them in the streets and coming back with nickels and dimes, whatever we could do. There was the flea market where the Poles came in to trade. They took everything out of the ghetto—shoes, coats, suits, rings, jewelry, anything and everything. We were just trading, constantly trading."

In his oral history, Morry spoke about some of the forced labor he performed. "Every morning we used to have to show up at the *Judenrat*, which was where the shul is in Warsaw today—Nozyk shul. And we'd show up early in the morning and then the Germans would drive up in trucks and they would yell out, you know, *fifty pieces, Stück*."

He was assigned to break concrete at the Warsaw airport, extracting rebar from the broken slabs. He had to scrub the tile floor in the kitchen at Gestapo headquarters. "I remember a big fat German who was a cook, stirring the pot, and every time he walked by he stepped on my hands, and he would stay and waited for me to yell and I wouldn't— I didn't."

In 2012, Morry told me a story about a small hand mill his family had bought to grind grain. "To make kasha," he said. "And I remember my mother used to make soup out of it, with salt and water. There was no butter or fat, or other stuff like that. And it was forbidden, actually. I used to grind it like three o'clock in the morning, when everybody was sleeping in the building." In the earlier oral history interview, when he had mentioned this grinder, Morry had included another detail. "I remember we'd give a few grinds and stop and listen if somebody is moving, you know, outside in the hallway." And he recalled being constantly hungry and asking his mother, *Did you eat?* "She says, 'I already ate.' I don't know why these things stick in my mind. She fed her father, she was so devoted to him—my mother—and us."

Morry then reflected on his parents, on their fate in the ghetto. "These were people that were very, very gentle, fine people. They just didn't have it in them. They were fine businesspeople, you know, they knew their materials, their goods—in business for generations. But you come to being street-smart, they were nothing. There was no way they could survive. I mean, they were just sheep led to slaughter. They didn't know how to improvise, and how I got this in me—I don't understand it, honestly, because I'm a product of that world."

*   *   *

While Morry and Avrum were learning to survive in the Warsaw Ghetto, Leslie Glodek had remained a refugee in Białystok. There he had also heard about his family's deportation from Nasielsk. When we spoke, he mentioned the town of Łomza, about eighty-five miles east of Warsaw, not far from Białystok. As far as I have been able to determine, no Nasielskers were deported to this city. I suspect Leslie meant Łuków. "But I gather— it's purely guesswork on my part—that they made for Warsaw," he said. "And I just wish to mention to you, my eldest brother had six children and a wife. My second brother is the one I was away with on the twenty-one days' excursion. Four children. And there was my [third] brother and his wife. And my sister was pregnant." Leslie believes the whole family moved into Gittla Glodek's apartment in Warsaw. "How all the people got in there with all the children—I haven't the foggiest notion."

Leslie's longest and most dangerous "adventure" began seven or eight months after he arrived in Białystok. On June 28 and 29, 1940, Lavrentiy Beria, Stalin's commissar of internal affairs, chief of the NKVD, carried out the third of four mass deportations of Polish refugees and undesirable nationals in the Soviet-controlled borderlands of Poland, Ukraine, Belarus, and the Baltic states. In total, at least a million and a half people would be deported to Siberia, Kazakhstan, and elsewhere deep in the Soviet interior, among them approximately 350,000 Jewish refugees from German-occupied Poland. This number represents the vast majority of Polish Jews who would escape the Holocaust, including almost all the survivors from Nasielsk. Timothy Snyder, in his essential book, *Bloodlands: Europe Between Hitler and Stalin*, gives the number of those deported in June 1940 as 78,339, 84 percent of whom, or almost 69,000, were Jews. One of them was Leslie Glodek.

"After a time, we were gathered up, just like sheep, and sent away, used as slave labor," Leslie said. He would not give details of his time in the Soviet forced labor camps in Siberia, near the Arctic Circle. "The reason why I can't really go into any greater detail is because I became so depressed," he said. The prisoners were allowed to send a letter once every few months. Twice Leslie wrote to his parents' address in Nasielsk. He received no reply. Finally, in late 1940, he wrote to his sister at Ulica Franciszkańska 9, in Warsaw. "And lo and behold, I had a reply on a postcard." Leslie immediately recognized his sister Gittla's handwriting. Because of German censorship, she wrote simply that the family was well, and that she had given birth to a boy shortly after Leslie escaped. "That card was early in 1941. Now, during that period, I was so depressed with guilt. I felt I've let my family down, not being with them on the day of departure from Nasielsk. I was young and agile, and was . . . You know, I could do things that the others couldn't. And I felt so guilty about it. All that mattered was for the war to come to an end, and if they're still alive—so we start fresh. All I wanted to do was to remain alive. It wasn't easy. But I suffered from depression, mostly because I felt a failure. *I still have a chance. But what about them? What about family?*"

By deporting the Jewish refugees who had fled German-controlled Poland, Stalin inadvertently saved many of their lives. ("In misfortune they were fortunate," commented Morry.) Of the one hundred or so Nasielskers who would eventually survive the war, approximately ninety had fled east, like Leslie Glodek, and were deported to Siberia. Life in the labor camps was extraordinarily harsh. The historian Norman Davies writes that of the 1.5 million Poles deported by Stalin in 1940, almost 50 percent were dead by June 1941. But those odds were still much better than for the Polish Jews who remained in Poland, like Morry, his family, the Glodek family, and the rest of the Nasielskers who ended up in Łuków or Międzyrzec. Of the approximately 2,900 Jewish Nasielskers who remained in Poland, fewer than ten survived the war.

||||||||||||||||||||

It is obvious, but it must be said: The people who did not survive cannot tell their stories. There were thousands of residents of Nasielsk. We know the personal stories of just a few. By virtue of being preserved, each survivor's story, and each artifact, photograph, and document, is an almost impossible exception.

The remaining documents reveal a final few names. The archive of the Joint Distribution Committee in New York holds a list of Jews who had escaped German-occupied Poland and arrived as refugees in Vilna, now Vilnius, Lithuania. The list was received in New York on March 1,

1940. It is 157 pages long and contains 9,064 names. There are nine Nasielskers.

Moszek Rotsztejn, born 1913, and Abram (Avruml) Rotsztejn, born 1917, are numbers 7,030 and 7,033. These are the two sons of Jankiel Hersz Rotstein who escaped to Białystok with Morry and Avrum, but who were lost in the melee crossing no-man's-land. Mordko Wilczynski, born 1920, number 6,173, was the son of the blacksmith on the edge of town near where Faiga Milchberg Tick's family lived. (He appears twice on the list: Mordchaj Wilczynski, born 1920, is also number 6,308.) The Wilczynskis made and repaired horseshoes, and, according to Morry, it may have been at the Wilczynskis' that Leslie Glodek repaired the chain on his bicycle when they rode out one day to deliver photographs for Fishl Perelmuter.

Jakub Wajngarten, born 1911, is number 7,031 on the list of refugees in Vilna. He also appears on another list, compiled a year later, in March 1941, by the Jewish community of Kobe, Japan. The Jews of Kobe had undertaken to support a few hundred refugees who had crossed Soviet Russia and embarked for Japan from the port of Vladivostok using visas supplied by the Japanese consul Chiune Sugihara. Moszek Rotstein is also on this list, as is Jakub Gurfinkel, who also appears on the Vilna list as "Josek Garfinkiel."

At least some of these men would survive. Moszek Rotstein obtained a visa for the United States in April 1941. But the attack on Pearl Harbor prevented his departure, and he made his way instead to Shanghai and eventually to Calcutta, India. He came to the United States in 1946, settling in New York, where he became Mark Rothstein and ran a lumberyard, which had also been the family business in Nasielsk. Jakub Wajngarten became Jack Weingarten, resident of Brooklyn, and a member of the postwar Nashelsker Society of New York. There are four men from Nasielsk on the Vilna list whose names I do not recognize: Berek Melnik, Moszek Turner, Fiszel Wilamowski, and Belzalel Tauman. Of these four, I know nothing, except that Belzalel Tauman survived and moved to Israel. He gave testimony for his father, Meir, to the Yad Vashem database of Shoah victims.

Once the Jews of Nasielsk submerge into the mass of deportees in German-occupied Poland, it becomes almost impossible to identify individuals. In June 2012, however, after visiting with Leslie Glodek in London and with Zdzisław Suwiński in Nasielsk, I flew to Israel and consulted the archives at Yad Vashem. I found a single document about the dispersal of Nasielsk's Jewish community: a handwritten note on a torn sheet of nearly square, lined paper, which I viewed in digitized form. It reads in Polish: "On December 31, 1939, there was a meeting of the committee to help persons displaced from the city of Nasielsk to the city of Łuków." The committee consisted of ten members: (1) Mojsek Kuperstein, (2) Mordka Kozak, (3) Mendel Bergazyn, (4) Chaim Aron Błotnik, (5) Tuwia Blaszka, (6) Chaim Huberman, (7) Jankel Grynbienarz, (8) Mordka Rajczyk, (9) Mordka Ślubogorski, and (10) Suchar Kaftal. The memorandum is just a few lines long and reports the sole result of this first meeting of the committee to aid the refugees in the town to which they were deported. "It has been unanimously decided to select Mr. Mordka Kozak as the leader of the committee and Mr. Mojsek Kuperstein as secretary," which means the document is probably in Kuperstein's handwriting.

We know some of these men. Chaim Huberman, a director of the Joint's *kassa*, appears in Keva Richman's family photo, sitting next to Keva's father. Mordka Rajczyk, the baker and socialist with a prickly red beard, occupied the basement apartment in the Skalka family home and annoyed young Moszek Tuchendler with his affection. Tuwia Blaszka was a tinsmith who lived on the east side of the market in Nasielsk, where Leslie Glodek remembered seeing him and his family in the same building where Keva Richman's grandfather, Szmuel Usher Schwarzberg, lived. Mendel Bergazyn owned a restaurant, which after Leib Owsianka's place is the next most likely location of a scene in David Kurtz's home movie. Photographs of Jankel Grynbienarz, Mojsek Kuperstein, Mordka Kozak, and Mordka Ślubogorski appear in a Who's Who of Nasielsk's leading citizens, included in the United Nashelsker Relief Society's 1953 commemorative book, which I had found at the New York Public Library in 2009.

The presence of these ten men at a meeting in Łuków on December 31, 1939, confirms that they were among those confined to the Nasielsk synagogue on December 3 and marched either that day or the next through the stream by the railway bridge to the station and loaded onto the deportation train.

This is the final document from which it is possible to identify individuals among the Jews of Nasielsk who were deported. It is not clear to whom the committee sent its report or whether subsequent meetings took place. The precise fates of six of these ten men cannot be traced any further. There is Shoah testimony for four of them: Kuperstein, Kozak, Blaszka, and Huberman.

Chaim Huberman's name appears one last time. Among the papers assembled in the Warsaw Ghetto by Emanuel Ringelblum, there is a report from November 1941 on conditions in the Lublin district, which included Łuków. The document is signed, but the signature is illegible. The final lines read: "On October 15 our comrade, the Nasielsk councilor Chaim Huberman, was shot for giving something to Russian prisoners." Chaim Huberman is the only Nasielsker whose precise date of death I am able to record.

‖‖‖‖‖‖‖‖‖‖‖

Even the stories that have been preserved exist against a background of silence. Large swaths of each person's experience fall away and are forgotten. Other aspects, perhaps even the essence of each experience, may be vividly recalled, yet resist expression, like Morry's life in the Warsaw Ghetto. Finally, the reality of each moment, the one-moment-to-the-next of experience, has by now become subsumed in a story. Every remembered scene is a selection, a particular scale of detail, which compresses time and often leaps over emotion. Personal memory and historical narrative are two very different forms of preservation. In the story I now have to tell, attempting to join the two, we confront at each moment the edge of what can be expressed and what, so many years later, it is possible for us to know.

On May 20, 1941, just as the Warsaw Ghetto's population peaked at 445,000, Moszek and Avrum Tuchendler escaped with three other boys.

One of these three was a Brzoza. In April 2012, Morry said this boy was Mottl Brzoza, whom Leslie Glodek remembered by his nickname, *Szczapa*, the tall, skinny boy in Faiga Tick's school photo. But ten months later, in February 2013, Morry corrected himself.

"The Brzoza that I knew—as a matter of fact—was one of the five. We escaped the ghetto together."

"Right," I said. We were talking about something else, and I thought I already knew this information. "That was Mottl."

"No, Mottl is the *hiltzerner*," Morry responded, referring to one of the two Brzoza families. "And Shiye Brzoza was from the *ayzerner*, from the 'iron' Brzoza, the son of the machinery guy."

Later, I found records to show that Mottl Brzoza was deported to Siberia in June 1940, like Leslie Glodek. The Brzoza Morry escaped with, therefore, was almost certainly Shiye.

"He, my brother, and I, and Leibl Jedwab, and—who? Another kid. I don't remember anymore. I think there were five of us. Yeah, five."

In 1993, Morry had named Shimon Kaminski as the fifth member of the group. In 2012 and 2013, he could not recall the name. And sometimes he said he escaped with Leibl Jedwab, sometimes he said it was Avruml Jedwab. But Leibl Jedwab survived the war and afterward settled in Israel. The boy Morry escaped with must have been his brother or cousin, Avruml or Avraham Jedwab. All five boys were from Nasielsk.

Morry, Avrum, Shiye Brzoza, Avruml Jedwab, and Shimon Kaminski escaped the Warsaw Ghetto in the simplest, most dangerous way possible: they rode the streetcar. Because the Warsaw Ghetto occupied a central place in the city, tramlines available only to "Aryans" were introduced in November 1940, cutting across the ghetto territory. These "transit" lines had a police escort and did not stop in the ghetto. But sometime in the spring of 1941, Morry heard a rumor that the Polish policeman who rode on the steps of the streetcar would let Jews on for a bribe of five *złotys*. He and the other four boys decided to take a chance.

"My mother carried on," Morry recalled in 1993. "'No, no,' she says. 'We just got you back here. *Moshiekh vet kimen*,'" the Messiah will come, "'and the Germans can never win a war and it's just a matter of time. Just stay with us and we'll all together live to see Hitler go,' and so on. It was terrible. But really, honestly, if you asked me when we left, did I ever expect never to see anybody again—I never thought that this was how it was going to work out."

In his 1993 interview, Morry described the day of their escape. "I see that day like I'll see it all my life," he said. "I remember on that day a heavy snow fell on Warsaw—a blanket snow. The type of snow that falls in flakes this large, you know, and then eventually sloshes when it falls."

I was unable to confirm that a heavy, wet snow fell in Warsaw on May 20, 1941. There is no mention of it in Emanuel Ringelblum's diary, and in the diary of Mary Berg, a young American trapped in the ghetto by the war, the entry for May 20, 1941, begins: "On the other side of the barbed wire, spring holds full sway. From my window I can see young girls with bouquets of lilac walking on the Aryan part of the street." What weight does this one detail carry?

Morry, Avrum, and their friends paid the bribe to the Polish police-man and got onto the streetcar near the ghetto exit at Muranowska and Bonifraterska Streets. "We hopped on," Morry said in 1993. "He didn't care. Because he knew that the car will be inspected as it reaches the out-side. And if they take us off, so what else is new? We were told that they were shooting on the other side. You cross the Aryan side, you're dead. But you see, miracles happen, because that day with this big snow—I remem-ber we came to the end of the line. And a German that looked ten foot tall—he wore that big heavy parka, with a helmet and a rifle—instead of walking inside to look, he just walked on the outside. I remember we were all sitting—I was afraid to look—and he walked around and it was too burdensome for him to go in. And he just yelled out, 'Ab,' and the streetcar left and we were on the outside."

One moment he was inside the ghetto, and then the next moment he was out. Even though they were not shot immediately, the mortal danger of each moment did not diminish. It was still May 20, 1941.

"Now what? Now—it's like a whole new world. The cars are running, streetcars are moving, and people—it's a different world. *What—what's our next step?*"

The boys got off the streetcar at Żoliborska Street, by the Vistula River, and were immediately targeted by a band of Polish kids. "'Hey, Jews, where do you think you're going? We know you just escaped the ghetto.'" The gang searched the five boys and took whatever they were carrying, "odds and ends, a pocketknife, a few *złotys*." These bands of extorters were known as *schmaltzovniks*, from *schmaltz*, meaning lard. They made their living by blackmailing escaped Jews. And when the first gang left, a second one accosted the boys. "I was the spokesperson," Morry said. "I told them, 'We just gave. We just gave them there.' 'So give us whatever'— they searched our pockets. And one guy, he says, 'Let them go. They ain't going far.'"

Having escaped the ghetto, the next problem was to escape from Warsaw. They had emerged onto the street above the Vistula River, which separates the city from the industrial suburb of Praga. The nearest crossing was the Poniatowski Bridge. "So we went towards the bridge," Morry continued in 2012. "And we had a quick meeting: *Should we walk the bridge, or get in another streetcar?* They had German guards at each side of the bridge, you know, it's a strategic spot. But I said, 'If we walk, it'll look funny. Who walks a big bridge? So we might as well risk getting on the streetcar.'" In 1993, he had reported the conversation this way: "I said, 'If we're gonna play goyim, now we're goyim. Let's start realizing that we're not on the inside and let's start looking tough.'" They had been outside the ghetto walls for fifteen, perhaps thirty minutes.

"So we made it to the other end," Morry told me. "And we got off, and we started walking away from Warsaw. That's when we came to this farmhouse. And then we went further. And my brother and I got jobs as shepherds."

In another conversation, Morry said the boys walked to the town of Kałuszyn, about forty miles due east of Warsaw. The boys may have walked this far that first day. Or they may have walked all night. Or stopped somewhere else, arriving in Kałuszyn the next day. It is impossible to reconstruct the experience in finer detail.

Months later, Morry recalled more about the farm where the boys stopped on the road out of Warsaw. "It was the same day. We ate, she gave us—the lady from the village, she had just baked hot loaves of bread, you know, a big loaf like this . . . And, we were all five of us—and you asked for some bread. And she cut off pieces. Hot! You know, it was—the aroma was killing us. And we gobbled it up with cold milk, and it took us like a hundred yards, our stomachs went crazy." When Morry said, "We were all five of us—and you asked for some bread," he left something out, which should also be part of the story. After a year and a half struggling to survive in the Warsaw Ghetto, what is missing from this sentence is very likely, *And we were all five of us starving.*

"When we first left the ghetto, we wound up in that village, Wola," Morry told me at the end of January 2013, a year after we had first met, "and we both got jobs."

Wola Rafałowska is a village four and a half miles south of Kałuszyn. In May 1941, Jews were still permitted to live in the surrounding countryside. But the five boys could not find shelter together. Morry and Avrum found a place with the family of the village tailor. The other three boys set out on their own.

"Nobody made it," Morry told me. He believes they soon returned to the Warsaw Ghetto.

Avruml Jedwab, Shimon Kaminski, and Shiye Brzoza are all listed in Yad Vashem's Shoah victims' database.

"My brother was dating the village tailor's daughter," Morry remembered. In 2013, he told me the tailor in Wola was named Goldstein. In 1993, he had said the family was named Rothstein. But the daughter, who survived and ended up in Detroit, was someone known to Morry after the war. It seems probable, therefore, that the earlier interview is correct. "I think she had a brother. And the brother was sort of a Jewish unofficial policeman. He was able to get news items about the Germans, when they're coming, when they're going. But we spent that whole summer there. And my brother was dating her. He was like her age. And I was still a kid."

During this summer of 1941, when Morry and his brother Avrum worked as shepherds in Wola Rafałowska, postal service to the Warsaw Ghetto was still possible. Morry recalled sending parcels of potatoes to his family. The Polish post would not accept packages for Jews. But Skalka was a neutral name, and Morry shortened his uncle's more Jewish-sounding first name, Jankiel, to the generic Polish Jan. "My mother used to write me up until—oh, the beginning of '42. She says my little brother stands at the window every day looking out. When he sees the postman coming, how he dances from joy—*that my brother's sending the potatoes* . . . She says, 'What you're doing for us.' She says, 'There is no such thing as sin that you can commit because everything that you would ever do would be nullified.'"

In two years of our discussing Morry's wartime life, his extraordinary memory sometimes allowed me to determine what happened with some precision—memory and history coinciding to bring a date, a place, or an event into focus. Only rarely, however, did he express what it had felt like to live these days—not what had happened, but what he had experienced.

During a phone call in April 2012, just after we said hello and before we began our conversation, I made some small talk. I observed that it was raining.

"It brings me back to the time during the war, when I was a shepherd," Morry replied. "And I went out with the animals, the cows, and I think I would sort of dig up some potatoes, make a fire, and sit near the forest. The rain was falling, and I was covered, I had that— You know, they take a burlap sack and make it into like a hood. And I felt safe and sound. And why? Because I felt, on a day like that, the Nazis are not running around to look for Jews. And it was just a warm feeling. And anyway, it's stayed with me all these years. And every time I look out and it's raining, and I'm inside and sound and safe—it's just a good feeling. So. That's my memories. So, from the war."

||||||||||||||||||

A report by the Kałuszyn *Judenrat*, cited in the United States Holocaust Memorial Museum's *Encyclopedia of Camps and Ghettos*, states that at the end of September 1941, Jews in the area surrounding Kałuszyn were ordered into the town's small ghetto. The tailor whose daughter Avrum

Tuchendler was dating agreed to take him with the family into hiding near the town of Węgrów, about twenty-two miles northeast of Wola. "They had a lot of Polish friends," Morry said. "So they were taking him with them. And I was left alone." Instead of going to the ghetto, Morry walked to the town of Grębków, about halfway between Węgrów and Wola. There, he found work at the farm of Helena Jagodzińska, an unmarried woman of about thirty who lived with her older sister Fransziska, or Frania, and Frania's three daughters. Morry arrived there in late September or early October 1941. He would remain there for almost a year.

One night that winter, he was awakened by a knock on the window. "I came out, and the farmer said, 'This is your brother. Take him.' He was in such high fever, he didn't even recognize me. He was laid out on that wagon." The Rothstein family had taken Avrum into hiding. But when he fell ill with typhus, they sent him back to his brother. "So I gave the farmer some *złotys* to take him to Kałuszyn, to a hospital. That was on a Friday, and on a Sunday, I figured, on my day off, I'll go visit him. Well, by the time I got there on Sunday, nobody ever heard of him, nobody knew. I don't know what they did with him. They said that they used to bring people that died, and they would strip them and throw them out, and the garbage people would pick them up."

In the *Encyclopedia of Camps and Ghettos*, under the entry for Kałuszyn, it states: "Kałuszyn's Jewish Police was charged with maintaining order inside the ghetto. Its sanitary unit was responsible for cleanliness and also supervised an epidemic hospital that the Judenrat opened in the summer of 1941." This must be the hospital where Avrum Tuchendler died of typhus in the winter of 1941.

Morry remained a farmhand at the Jagodzińska farm until spring, when he too fell ill with typhus. "The sheriff came in. He was a mean, dumb anti-Semite. 'Turn the Jew away, he'll make everybody sick here.'" The sheriff ordered a farmer to take Morry to a Jewish clinic in Węgrów.

In a memoir about the destruction of the Węgrów Jewish community, Shraga Feivel Bielawski mentions this clinic, which was founded in the aftermath of the German invasion of Poland to treat Jews injured by the occupying forces. "It was staffed by Jewish doctors, nurses, and hospital aides," writes Bielawski. "The duties of the last group included getting patients to the hospital and supervising sanitary conditions. Patients who needed bathing were taken to the mikva. Usually, the mikva was for only ritual bathing, but Jews are practical about emergencies." The memoir contains a photo of the clinic's staff taken shortly after the outbreak of war, fourteen people, three in white lab coats, including one woman. They are smiling, confident, clustered around the director, Dr. Melchior. Morry recognized the building in the photo, but he did not remember the staff.

"I remember dreaming that I was tremendously thirsty," Morry said in 1993. "That whenever this is ever over, that I will buy a river and sit at that river and do nothing but drink."

When he woke up from his fever, Morry could barely walk. He had been in the ghetto clinic for four weeks. To remain longer increased the risk of becoming trapped there. He therefore convinced the doctor to certify that he was cured and made his way back to Helena Jagodzińska's farm. Helena refused to allow him in the house for fear of contamination. "I said, 'I'll sleep with the horse and the cow in the barn.' You know, on the straw. And then the sheriff came in, he says, 'The horses are going to die.' He says, 'It's very dangerous.'"

Later in our conversation, Morry returned to this sheriff. "The sheriff across the street was a *mamzer*, a very bad guy. He was one of those smart-aleck farmers. He knew everything. He knew that typhus can poison a horse. You know, this type of mentality. I was already working and shlepping pails of water from a well, you know, raising it by hand. It was very, very hard. He would come in and say, 'The Jew is still working.' He says, 'The horse is not sick yet, or the cow.'"

Morry continued working at Helena Jagodzińska's farm until late summer 1942, when once more the order came for all Jews in the area to move into the local ghetto.

That May, Jews from Węgrów had formed part of the labor pool conscripted to build the Treblinka death camp. In the *Encyclopedia of Camps and Ghettos*, the entry for Węgrów fills in the picture. "Suspicions about the camp heightened in July 1942 after forced laborers from Węgrów working there did not return home. In July, the wives of German military and police officials in Węgrów told Jews who worked for them to hide their valuables. Then, on August 24, 1942, posters were hung in Węgrów signed by [Ernst] Grams [Reich economic advisor and district leader (*Reichslandwirtschaftsrat* and *Kreishauptmann*)] restricting access to Jewish neighborhoods only to registered residents and voiding all Jewish travel passes."

In 1993, Morry described the scene this way: "Everybody was panic-stricken, because there was no place to go and that's it. This was the end. Everybody had to be in the ghetto and whoever by such and such date is not going to be in the ghetto, will be summarily shot."

Morry, too, prepared to leave. But on the last day, Helena spoke to him, calling him by his Polish name. "She says, 'Munya, what are you going to do? Where are you going to go?' I said, 'I think I've run out of places to go. I've been already all over. The roads are closed.' I say, 'I've got to go to the ghetto. I'm not going to go back to Warsaw, but I'll go to the Węgrów ghetto.' So she says, 'Well, we're not going to go to a ghetto.'"

Around midnight, Helena's nephew Stanisław Pachnik arrived. He worked at the county records office. He had stolen a *narodziny*, a birth certificate. Not fake papers, real papers, the original document from the files, the birth certificate of a Polish boy who had died. "*Be it known that* Zdzisław Pływacz *was born on* 21 January *nineteen hundred* twenty-three *of father* Bronisław *and mother* Janina *of the house of* Klaszka." Certified authentic, signed, stamped. Perfect, except for the warning in large print in the upper right: "Original Document. Do Not Remove." Morry and Pachnik tore off the corner. "We spent about an hour, folding it back and forth," he said in October 2012, recalling that night. "They said, 'You don't have to go to the ghetto. You'll have a new name. You don't look Jewish. Your Polish is excellent. Try and be that person.'"

In 1993, Morry provided more detail to this scene. "I was like a chameleon in every situation. I took on the coloring. I took on the mannerisms. I took on the mode of speech. I just blended right in. So we sat up until about three o'clock in the morning and they taught me the prayers of night, the morning prayers, and how to cross myself. And she says, 'This is it.' She says, 'Go.'"

In late summer 1942, Moszek Tuchendler disappeared behind a torn piece of paper and became Zdzisław Pływacz. Morry left behind the letters from his mother, a few photographs of his family, and anything else that might compromise his new identity. His survival now depended on maintaining a fiction.

It is impossible to determine the exact date Morry left Helena Jagodzińska's farm and went into hiding. It must have been after August 24, 1942, when Jews were forbidden to leave the Węgrów ghetto, and before dawn on Monday, September 21, 1942, Yom Kippur, when the Jews in the Węgrów ghetto were murdered in their homes or in the streets, or deported to be murdered elsewhere. Members of the SS, German and Polish police, and Ukrainian auxiliaries surrounded the ghetto. According to the *Encyclopedia of Camps and Ghettos*, "They went from house to house, ordering the Jews—approximately 9,000 people—to the town's square. Those who refused or were too old or infirm to comply were shot in their homes. By some accounts, the Germans murdered some 600 Jews in the first two hours of the roundup. More than 2,000 Jews perished from gunshots in Węgrów before this first effort to exterminate Węgrów's Jews ended."

By the time Moszek Tuchendler left Helena Jagodzińska's farm to impersonate a Roman Catholic Polish orphan in late summer 1942, he was one of only a few hundred Jewish Nasielskers still alive in German-occupied Europe.

Between July 22 and September 21, 1942, approximately three hundred thousand Jews were deported from the Warsaw Ghetto to Treblinka. Among them, most likely, were Morry's parents, his little brother David, his aunt, uncle, and their children; his mother's best friend, Sura Perelmuter Landau, and her family; Sura's brother, Fishl Perelmuter, and his daughter; Leslie Glodek's parents and his brothers and sister and their families; the four sisters and one brother of Sura Kubel; and all the other residents of Nasielsk who had fled to Warsaw before the deportation in December 1939 or who had made their way to the city afterward, fleeing the ghettos of Łuków and Międzyrzec. I am forced to say "most likely," because unlike at other death camps, no comprehensive records were kept at Treblinka. The pace of killing was too rushed.

It is possible, however, to learn the exact day on which the majority of Jews from Nasielsk deported to Międzyrzec were gassed at Treblinka: August 25, 1942, the day after a notice appeared in Węgrów forbidding Jews there from leaving the ghetto, and within a few days or a week of Morry's flight into a false identity.

It is a strange coincidence of historical documentation that, at the moment the Jews of Nasielsk disappear from the record as individuals with names, the names of the men who deported them to their deaths should have been preserved. In the summer of 1942, Łuków and Międzyrzec were turned into "transit" ghettos, funneling Jewish populations from all over German-occupied Europe to Treblinka, just sixty miles to the north. Both ghettos were guarded by Reserve Police Battalion 101, a unit of some five hundred mostly professional married men from the Hamburg area, who were too old for Wehrmacht service but who had been conscripted into the military police. The battalion commander was Major Wilhelm Trapp. Between 1962 and 1972, members of this unit were deposed by the office of the state prosecutor (*Staatsanwaltschaft*) in Hamburg, which was preparing to bring charges of war crimes against them. As a result, testimony from individual men was collected, yielding a rich portrait of the unit's activity. These documents form the basis of Christopher R. Browning's *Ordinary Men: Reserve Police Battalion 101 and the Final Solution in Poland*, and Daniel Goldhagen's *Hitler's Willing Executioners*.

"Unlike so many of the Nazi killing units, whose membership can only be partially reconstructed, Reserve Police Battalion 101's roster was available to the investigators," Christopher Browning writes in his introduction. "As most of the men came from Hamburg and many still lived there at the time of the investigation, I was able to study the interrogations of 210 men from a unit consisting of slightly less than 500 when it was sent at full strength to Poland in June 1942." These interrogations enabled Browning to undertake "detailed narrative reconstruction and analysis of the internal dynamics of this killing unit."

Both Browning and Goldhagen seek to answer how and why these men perpetrated the crimes they did. Here I rely on their accounts solely to describe some of the crimes themselves. The men of this unit took part in the two most intensive phases of the Final Solution, Aktion Reinhard, which began in the spring of 1942 and was named in honor of Reinhard Heydrich, head of the Reich Main Security Office, who had been ambushed in Prague by Czechoslovakian agents on May 27, 1942, and Aktion Erntefest (Operation Harvest Festival), which began in November 1943. According to Christopher Browning, by the end of these two operations, spanning just over eighteen months, Reserve Police Battalion 101 would be responsible for the death or deportation of at least 83,000 Jews. Among these 83,000 people killed or deported to death camps by the policemen from Hamburg were approximately 2,900 Jews from the small town of Nasielsk.

Those who had been deported to Międzyrzec were killed first.

"To receive more Jews from elsewhere," Browning writes, "the ghetto in Międzyrzec had to be periodically emptied of its inhabitants. The first and largest such clearing took place on August 25–26 [1942], in a combined action of First Company, Third Platoon of Second Company, and First Platoon of Third Company from Reserve Police Battalion 101, a unit of Hiwis and the Radzyń Security Police." "Hiwi" stands for *Hilfswilligen*, literally, "help willing," and refers to the Ukrainian, Latvian, and Lithuanian volunteers based in the town of Trawniki, near Lublin, whom the Germans had recruited from POW camps and employed as auxiliary manpower during killing operations.

The *Encyclopedia of Camps and Ghettos* provides a sketch of that morning: "During the Aktion, members of Reserve Police Battalion 101, Ukrainian SS auxiliaries from Trawniki, local Gendarmes, and SS from Radzyń, rounded up and forced 8,000 to 11,000 Jews onto trains destined for the Treblinka extermination camp. A surviving railway schedule indicates the deportation train of 50 wagons departed Międzyrzec at 9:30 A.M., only to return at 9:42 P.M. for another trip to Treblinka the next morning. Almost all the deportees were gassed on arrival. Another 960 to 1,800 Jews were shot dead in Międzyrzec."

Christopher Browning's description, based on the testimony of the members of Reserve Police Battalion 101, is much more detailed. "Some of the policemen arrived in Międzyrzec on the night of August 24, one unit accompanying a convoy of wagons bringing additional Jews. Most of the men, however, assembled in Radzyń in the early hours of August 25 under the supervision of First Sergeant Kammer. The initial absence of Captain Wohlauf was explained when the convoy of trucks stopped in front of his private residence on the way out of town. Wohlauf and his young bride— four months pregnant, with a military coat draped over her shoulders and a peaked military cap on her head—emerged from the house and climbed aboard one of the trucks."

Captain Julius Wohlauf, commander of First Company, was in charge of the operation. His new wife accompanied him merely as a spectator. "This," Daniel Goldhagen comments when reviewing the same events and data, "is how the pregnant Frau Wohlauf spent her honeymoon." The wives of other German soldiers, as well as a group of German Red Cross nurses, also observed.

Browning continues: "When the convoy carrying Wohlauf, his bride, and most of First Company arrived in Międzyrzec, less than thirty kilometers to the north of Radzyń, the action was already underway. The men could hear shooting and screaming, as the Hiwis and Security Police had begun the roundup."

For the next thirty minutes, the men of First Company waited for Captain Wohlauf to receive instructions. According to the testimony, the men of First Company had to seek shelter during this time because the security police and Hiwis were already drunk and shot their weapons wildly.

When Captain Wohlauf returned, "some men were sent to outer guard duty, but most of them were assigned to the clearing action alongside the Hiwis. The usual orders were given to shoot anyone trying to escape, as well as the sick, old, and frail who could not march to the train station just outside of town." Dispersing to their positions, according to one policeman, the men "'saw the corpses of Jews who had been shot everywhere in the streets and houses.'"

Thousands of Jews were driven from their homes to the marketplace. They were forced to sit or squat in the August sun without moving. Many fainted in the heat. Shootings and beatings were continuous. Frau Wohlauf was conspicuous, walking among the victims in her summer dress.

"About 2:00 p.m. the outer guard was called to the marketplace, and one or two hours later the march to the train station began. The entire force of Hiwis and policemen was employed to drive the thousands of Jews along the route. Once again, shooting was common. The 'foot sick' who could go no farther were shot and left lying on the side of the road. Corpses lined the street to the train station. One final horror was reserved to the end, for the train cars now had to be loaded. While the Hiwis and Security Police packed 120 to 140 Jews into each car, the reserve policemen stood and observed. As one remembered: 'When it didn't go well, they made use of riding whips and guns. The loading was simply frightful. There was an unearthly cry from these poor people, because ten or twenty cars were being loaded simultaneously. The entire freight train was dreadfully long.

One could not see all of it. It may have been fifty to sixty cars, if not more. After a car was loaded, the doors were closed and nailed shut.'"

Abraham Krzepicki, one of approximately seventy Jews who would eventually survive Treblinka, had been deported to the death camp that same day, August 25, from Warsaw. He was among the Jewish men selected for work upon arrival, and his first task was to meet this transport from Międzyrzec. In his memoir, "Eighteen Days in Treblinka," he recalled, "The cars contained only corpses. They had all suffocated on the journey from lack of air." Those among the eleven thousand Jews deported from Międzyrzec who had survived the transport were sent immediately to gas chambers, where they were asphyxiated with carbon monoxide exhaust from the diesel engines removed from captured Soviet tanks.

According to Browning, the first clearing of the Międzyrzec ghetto on August 25 and 26 was the largest deportation operation of Reserve Police Battalion 101's entire service. It was accomplished, he writes, with "an almost unimaginable ferocity and brutality," exceptional "even by the Nazi standards of 1942."

||||||||||||||||||||

The Jews of Berezne—my grandmother's hometown, 260 miles east of Międzyrzec—were also murdered on August 25, 1942. That morning, German Security Police and members of the Security Service (Sicherheitsdienst, or SD), based in Rovno, aided by the German gendarmerie and Ukrainian police, surrounded the ghetto and ordered the Jews to assemble for work details. As Tzilla Kitron described in her memoir, Berezne's Jews already knew of massacres in neighboring ghettos. They understood what would now happen to them. The German authorities ordered the Jews to form columns. They were marched out of town to death pits already prepared by the cemetery. There the Jews were ordered to undress. The German police and their Ukrainian collaborators shot them in small groups at point-blank range. According to the *Encyclopedia of Camps and Ghettos*, the number of Jews murdered that day in Berezne was 3,200. The official Soviet figure for this shooting is 3,680. The monument at the Berezne cemetery puts the figure at 3,460.

Saul Gershkowitz, who viewed my grandfather's film in November 2009 and whose memory of Berezne first pointed to the film's true location, evaded death that day with the help of a local farmer. He fled to the town of Mokvyn and hid in a haystack with his brother Julius. Three days later, they crossed the Sluch River and began two years of hiding in the forests.

One thousand miles to the east, the German Sixth Army had just reached the Volga River north of Stalingrad.

|||||||||||||||||||

On August 26, 27, and 28, 1942, Jews from Nasielsk were still alive in the ghetto at Łuków, though it is impossible to determine who or how many. They were certainly aware of what had happened to their families, friends, neighbors, business partners and competitors, religious and political allies and opponents in the ghetto at Międzyrzec. On the morning of August 25, the empty trains on their way to deport the Jews of Międzyrzec had stopped first in Łuków, provoking panic, before moving on to their destination. The president of the Łuków Jewish community, Hersz Lejzor Lendor, announced shortly afterward that the Jews of Łuków were safe. Most of them worked for German businesses. The German authorities had given him assurances.

The German authorities were lying. In truth, the volume of work in August and September had overwhelmed the death facilities at Treblinka, and deportations had been temporarily suspended. They resumed on October 1, 1942. On October 5, the men of Reserve Police Battalion 101, along with Security Police from Radzyń, Hiwis, gendarmes, and local ethnic German and Polish police, destroyed the Łuków Ghetto.

Again, the *Encyclopedia of Camps and Ghettos* provides a sketch: "After ordering the Jews assembled at the trading square on Międzyrzec Street, the German police and SS auxiliaries entered the ghetto and shot dead the patients and staff at the hospital and those who refused to leave the ghetto. At the square, men able to work were separated from women, the elderly and children . . . German employers read lists of those exempted from deportation. Eleven Jewish Council members were shot. They were among 500 Jews murdered on that day. Some 4,000 mainly women, children, and the elderly were marched to the railway station and sent from there to be gassed at Treblinka."

And again, Christopher R. Browning, drawing on the testimony of the men who performed this *Aktion*, describes the scene in far greater detail. "The men of Second Company who were stationed in Międzyrzec were awakened around 5:00 a.m. They were joined by [Lieutenant Kurt] Drucker's Second Platoon from Komarówka as well as a sizable contingent of Hiwis. Drucker's men apparently cordoned off the ghetto while the Hiwis and the rest of the Order Police drove the Jews into the main square. [Lieutenant Hartwig] Gnade and others used their whips on the assembled Jews to enforce quiet. Some died from the beatings even before the march to the train station began . . . A small contingent of policemen was already at the train station in order to keep Polish spectators away. Gnade supervised the loading of the arriving Jews onto the train. Shooting and beating were employed without restraint to maximize the number of Jews crammed into each cattle car. Twenty-two years later, Gnade's first sergeant made a very unusual confession, given the pronounced reluctance of the witnesses to criticize their former commanders. 'To my regret, I must say that First Lieutenant Gnade gave me the impression that the entire business afforded him a great deal of pleasure.'"

One hundred and fifty Jews remained on the platform when the final train doors were sealed. Lieutenant Drucker was ordered to lead these Jews to the cemetery, which attracted a crowd of "eager spectators," according to one of the men. A squad of twenty policemen was selected and supplied with vodka. "The Jews were brought in groups of twenty, men first and then women and children. They were forced to lie face down near the cemetery wall and then shot from behind in the neck. Each policeman fired seven or eight times."

Even at the end of October 1942, it is possible that some Nasielsk men remained alive in the Łuków ghetto. But on November 7, 1942, the final deportation of three thousand to four thousand people from Łuków began and continued for several days. With its completion, most of the Jews who had lived in Nasielsk when David and Liza Kurtz visited in the summer of 1938, just four years before, were dead. A few may have still survived as forced laborers in German factories. They would be murdered in 1943.

After their role in this stage of Aktion Reinhard, the men of Reserve Police Battalion 101 were given a rest. They would renew their participation in the deportation and murder of Polish Jews as part of Aktion Erntefest the following fall. During the winter of 1942–1943, their new assignment was to find and eliminate those Jews who had evaded the deportations and who were now hiding in the Polish countryside. The German policemen from Hamburg and their foreign and local helpers referred to these operations as a *Judenjagd*, or "Jew hunt." The people they hunted included Moszek Tuchendler, alias Zdzisław Pływacz, who was hiding in plain sight on a farm barely thirty miles from Treblinka.

||||||||||||||||||||

The question at the end of August 1942, as Morry put it to me seventy years later, was "How do I get the hell out of there?"

When he left the relative security of Helena Jagodzińska's farm in Grębków, he wandered from village to village, taking odd jobs. Even in 1993, he could not recall the sequence of events in these early days in disguise. "I don't remember where I went first. I went to another village someplace and found work for a day or for a night. I kept wandering," he said then. In that interview, the first job he recalled was near a town called Kostry Noski, sixty miles from Węgrów.

Morry told one story in April 2013 that seems to fall during these early weeks. "I remember I stopped off in one village and I asked for food. It was already cold, and I must have been worn-out. In those days, they were still moving Jews here and there, and hunting for them. The farmer must have known that I was a Jewish kid, because they must have talked among themselves. And I remember I was having soup with them, and I fell asleep at the table. And what woke me up is one of the kids sitting at the table saying, in Polish, '*Żyd śpi*.' 'The Jew fell asleep.' So I immediately caught what the conversation was. I must have looked the part, you know. I was supposed to stay the night, and I left immediately. I mean, I don't know where I went, I don't remember where I slept the next night. It's all, you know, in a fog."

Toward the end of this early period, when he escaped the area around Grębków, Morry may have sought shelter with a cousin of Helena Jagodzińska's who lived in Saska Kępa, on the Praga side of Warsaw. She turned him away, however, and he was forced to risk sleeping in a cheap hotel for a night. He likely remained in or near Warsaw until late September 1942. His next clearly datable recollection involves leaving from Warsaw's Central train station for the countryside.

"I make my way to the train station. There were no tickets to buy, trains were going without any rhyme or reason. I didn't even know where I was going. So I'm packed in like a sardine, with all Poles. And I hear conversation—every shtetl, as the train goes by. One was Wołomin, and they say, 'Oh, yesterday they took all the Jews out from here.' And the next city, the next city, the next city. And people are getting off. And I got no place to go, so I'm still riding, riding."

The reference to Wołomin places Morry's train ride in the first days of October 1942. The ghetto at Wołomin (aka Sosnówa), located twelve miles northeast of Warsaw, was destroyed on October 2, 1942. Killing operations had resumed at Treblinka on October 1. The first train from Łuków would be sent there on October 5. Morry was riding through the heart of *Aktion Reinhard*, on the same train tracks as the deportation trains.

"But anyway, I was on the train, going, going, going. And every town, people get off. And then there was one woman, I don't know if she was forty, fifty, and she was sitting, and I was left. So she asked me, 'Where are you going?' And I said, 'To tell you the truth, I'm looking for a job. I'm an orphan.' 'Oh,' she said, 'the farmer that I'm going to stop off, you know, at the end of the train, asked me if I could find him a shepherd, or something like that. Would you like that?' So I said, 'Yes.' So now I'm going already with her. See? I'm a known quantity."

The woman on the train, who was smuggling goods between Warsaw and the countryside, introduced him to a farmer in a village near Kostry Noski. I believe this is when Morry arrived in the area he mentioned in

1993. The woman transacted her business, and her contact at the farm hired the young man she had brought with her. In 2012, Morry recalled working in Kostry for a man named Wojno. It has been impossible to place this recollection. But he clearly recalled getting the job.

"He asked me what can I do? And I said I'll do anything. Plow. Milk cows. And the cows I milked, I learned earlier, when I first . . . I'm trying to fit in where I was earlier, when I escaped from the ghetto. The sequence of events. This is a puzzle for me."

But the sequence makes sense. By October 1942, when he arrived in the area around Kostry Noski, thirty miles from Treblinka, Morry, now Zdzisław, was an experienced farmhand, having already worked for almost a year at Helena Jagodzińska's farm outside Warsaw. Whether he stayed at this one farm or worked at different jobs, on different farms in the area, cannot be determined. It is probable that he moved around, safeguarding his identity. When asked, he said he had been raised by an aunt who had a fruit stand in Warsaw. She could no longer support him, and so he had left in search of work. He was cautious, offering few details, afraid of creating inconsistencies that might trip him up.

"I left a nonentity," Morry told me in January 2012. "I was nobody. I had to erase my past and start new." Another time he said, "In every village that I went and looked for a job, if I worked there two days, I went into the sheriff right away, and he gave me an acknowledgment that I was there this day, because the Germans kept track. You couldn't go from here to here without permits." These scraps of paper became his dossier, proof of his new existence.

In that same conversation, in January 2012, Morry recalled three scenes that show the dangers he faced in everyday life. These may belong to those first months, but some of them most likely occurred slightly later.

"I tried to erase in my mind every nuance and every behavior," he told me. "One time, the woman of the house saw me cutting bread. They had these big loaves, and I took a piece of bread, and I remember, like my mother used to cut challah. Like this." He sawed delicately back and forth. "And she says, 'Zdzisiu [a diminutive of Zdzisław], if I didn't know that you are one of ours, a real Catholic and a Pole, I would call you a Jew.'

And I got scared. And I said, 'Why do you say that? A Jew?' She says, 'The way you cut bread.' I wasn't even aware of that." The woman took the knife and plunged it in.

Later, Morry recalled being awoken from a nightmare by the farmer's wife. "She was standing over my bed, she says, 'You must have had a terrible nightmare. You talked, we couldn't understand what you were saying.' I was talking Yiddish. And from that night on, I slept with one eye open. I was afraid I'm going to babble something out, it'll give me away."

"And another time, I also had a faux pas," Morry added later. "What did I know about Christmas? So I ask a dumb question, 'By the way, when is Christmas this year?' She says, 'Zdzisiu, what are you talking about? You know Christmas is always the twenty-fourth, twenty-fifth of December.' And I quickly came back, I said, 'I didn't mean it by the date, I meant what day of the week?' And she says, 'Oh.'"

For other recollections, however, a precise date can be determined.

One day, Morry recalled, two men approached him in the field where he was working and asked whether the farmer was hiring. "Well, go in and ask him," Morry told them. The farmer hired them. "And that night, they slept in the barn, and I heard them talk in Yiddish. They were both from Warsaw. They just escaped Treblinka. They were sorters. One said he was a jeweler. And they hid in a car, a boxcar, with clothing that the Germans were taking to Germany." To speak a word of Yiddish would blow his cover. "I felt like telling them who I was, and I didn't," Morry said. Yet just hearing Yiddish made him homesick. He had been Zdzisław Pływacz for two or three months.

There was a small ghetto in the nearby town of Czyżew, and he decided to go visit the people there on Sunday, his day off. "I felt I had to go see Jewish people," he said to me. In 1993 Morry told the story this way: "I heard that there's a ghetto in Czyżew and so on my day off, I told the farmer I'm going to go into town. And I come into town, and the first thing I find where the ghetto is, and it's one little street—like a long street with barbed wire and a gate at each end. I came in there and I spent the whole Sunday talking to people. I told them who I am. I literally went from house to house and asked, 'Have you heard what's happening in Warsaw? What do you know? What's going on? I've been away and I'm living as a goy and nobody knows me, and I'm all alone.' And everybody poured their hearts out."

Having lost track of time, Morry remained in the ghetto past curfew. "I said, 'Could you put me up for the night? I'll sleep on the floor.' They said, 'No, nothing doing. You cannot stay here because everybody is registered. We're living here by the grace of the commandant, who knows us, and everybody's registered and we have designated work. And he lets us live and he lets us stay and we're going to be safe. And if a stranger comes in, God only knows what could happen. They'll shoot you. They'll shoot us. You must go.' I said, 'But I can't go. If I go outside curfew, they'll kill me.' So I went, literally, from house to house and begged and pleaded. Nobody would let me stay. I had to leave. I got out and made my way through the fields and got back to the farm."

He continued the story in 2012: "Early Monday morning, the farmer drives by, and he says, you know, 'Blessed be Jesus Christ,' and you're supposed to answer, 'Forever and ever, amen.' I answer that. And he says, 'Did you hear what happened to the Jews last night in Czyżew?' And I said, 'No.' He said, 'At three o'clock in the morning, the Germans surrounded them—and take a look,' he says, 'you can see them already . . . smoking.'" The man pointed to the horizon.

Morry's recollections of the ghetto at Czyżew—or Czyżewo, located forty-four miles southwest of Białystok—are confirmed by the documentation. An *Aktion* in August 1941 had reduced the town's prewar Jewish population of eighteen hundred to around two hundred. Those who remained were craftsmen, confined to a ghetto located on Polna Street with gates at both ends. "The Czyżewo ghetto resembled more of a labor camp, with its mostly young, single population," it says in the *Encyclopedia of Camps and Ghettos*. Those who remained in the ghetto worked primarily for the German administration. Carpenters made furniture for the German commander. Some men worked on construction projects, paving a road or completing the rail line to Czyżew. Others sorted captured Soviet weapons. Women worked as domestic servants or cooks. "Conditions were not as bad as in most ghettos, because the corrupt Amtskommissar, in exchange for bribes, eased material conditions."

Morry recalled, "It was a little ghetto. It was like a homemade ghetto." I asked whether anyone he spoke with had wanted to escape with him. "No, no. They were so intimidated. Because while they were there, they had a feeling of security. Everybody was working for the next day, *maybe I can see another day, and the war will be over.*"

According to the *Encyclopedia of Camps and Ghettos*, "In the fall of 1942, the ghetto residents learned of the mass killing of Jews at the Treblinka extermination camp from an escapee." This may refer to the same escapees who appeared at the farm where Morry was working. The *Encyclopedia* states that the ghetto was liquidated on November 2, 1942, which was a Tuesday. The Czyżew *Yizkor* book, however, gives the date as November 1, a Monday. October 31, 1942, was a Sunday. This must be the day Morry spent talking with the ghetto's inhabitants.

One day after Morry's visit or perhaps two, the ghetto's two hundred residents were deported fifteen miles north, to a transit camp in Zambrów, where they were confined with 17,300 to 19,800 Jews from the surrounding area. They were killed in Auschwitz-Birkenau in January 1943.

In 1993, Morry reflected, "So, I don't know if you call it a miracle or whatever. Somebody up there didn't want me there to be taken out. I pleaded, I wanted to stay and somebody didn't let me stay there. I mean, can you imagine? I was so mad. I said, 'Jewish people, how can you do this? You're throwing me out to certain death.'"

||||||||||||||||||||

On the same day the ghetto at Czyżew was liquidated, Nasielsk made a rare wartime appearance in the news. "A mass execution of fifty-five Polish hostages in one day at Palmiry was carried out on the order of Dr. Ludwig Fischer, Governor of Warsaw, it was learned here today. The action followed the derailment and blowing up of an ammunition train at the important railway junction of Nasielsk, north of Warsaw."

||||||||||||||||||||

The day after he learned of the liquidation of the Czyżew ghetto, Morry made plans to leave the farm where he had been working. "I decided it's getting a little too hot for me to stay. I think there were rumors that they were going to come after all the others, and I figured if I hang around, and they come after them, they'll come after me. So, anyway, it didn't take me long and I took off."

A handwritten note on the back of Zdzisław Pływacz's birth certificate, however, suggests that he remained at a farm in the village of Dąbrowa-Dołęgi, eight miles west of Kostry Noski, a few weeks longer than he remembered. The note says "*Zameldowany*," meaning "registered," with the place name, D. Dołęgi, and the date, November 11, 1942. It has a rubber stamp, "Mayor of," and a signature. This may be one of the many proof-of-residence stamps that Morry collected to certify his legitimacy. But as I worked out the chronology of his time in hiding, this note seemed to record something much more significant.

In the late fall of 1942, German authorities required all Polish citizens to obtain a German-issued identification card, a *Kennkarte* in German, or a *kennkarta* in Polish, as a way of combing through the population for Jews living on false papers.

"The farmer kept saying, 'If they come and find you working here without a pass, I'll be dead.' And then finally, one day, he says, 'Okay, that's the last day. It says, *Announced. No more. Whoever is found is dead.*' So I had to go."

The note on the back of the birth certificate probably records Zdzisław Pływacz's first appointment at the Gestapo office in Wysokie Mazowsiecke, the larger town where he had to register for his *Kennkarte*, four miles from Dąbrowa-Dołęgi.

I asked Morry to describe this day, which was probably Thursday, November 11, ten days after the liquidation of the Czyżew ghetto. "It was a building like a school building. And there were probably a couple of hundred people. Women, and old ladies, and they've all got their baptismal certificates. You had to bring everything you could. And there, I said, 'Ach! Here I come. What have I got? I've this, and I've got a little piece of paper. How am I going to make out, when all these guys have got, you know, priests' papers, everything.' And it reminded me, from my cheder. It says, 'We tell God, *eyle borekhev* . . . those that come with the chariots, *ve'eyle basusim*, and those that ride with the horses and the chariots. But *besheym adoshem*. Our strength is we come in the name of God.' So I said to myself, *eyle borekhev*, and *ve'eyle basusim*. I'm coming with a piece of paper, this is the word of God."

In his 1993 oral history, Morry had described the scene slightly differently: "There was a line all the way around the building. Old women, old farmers standing there with their baptismal certificates and the grandfather and all this. And I have my little piece of paper, you know, standing—acting very tough. I'm talking to them and trying out my best farm-type Polish, throwing in all the colloquialisms, '*Psia krew*.' It's like in English, 'God damn it,' you know, it's like 'jack rabbit's dog's blood' and, it's a word that you use if you're a tough guy."

But then the tough guy's turn came at the long row of desks. A girl is sitting at a typewriter. Behind her, an armed German officer keeps order.

Name?

"I pretended I didn't understand," Morry said in January 2012.

He hands the birth certificate to the secretary behind the desk. She examines it and asks for his mother's maiden name. "I was so tense, and . . . I knew the birth certificate by heart. Everything, the father, Bronisław, and everything. But I froze."

The girl looks again at the paper. "And she says, 'Klaszko?' I said, 'Of course.' She read it. It says, '*z domu*,' 'from the house of Klaszko.' She helped me."

The birth certificate, however, has a glaring flaw: a corner is torn off.

"And they asked me, 'What happened to that part?' And I said, 'It's just an old document, it fell apart.' It was all folded and folded and it just—'I lost it.'"

The German officer scrutinizes the boy standing before him. He scrutinizes the torn piece of paper in his hand. *Investigate, or let it go?* He hands the birth certificate back to the secretary, who takes down the information. Region: Łomża. Place of Residence: Dąbrowa-Dołęgi. Occupation: Worker. Nationality/Race: Pole. Religion: Roman Catholic. Citizenship: Polish. And the personal characteristics. Height: 1.67 meters. Build: Slender. Face: Oval. Hair: Dark blond. Eyes: Blue. Distinguishing marks: None.

"Ah. And that's the catch," Morry interrupted his recitation of the data. "Like, aka, circumcision."

They didn't check? I asked.

"No, sir."

And nobody ever asked you, the entire time?

"Never. So. And then . . ."

And then fingerprints, signature. "And at the end of the line, okay, they take a picture. And they said, 'Come back in four weeks.'"

In 1993, Morry had said, "So, I went home with that and I said to myself, 'Now, is that all I have to live, four weeks?'" If the German authorities were to check his papers, they would discover that Zdzisław Pływacz was deceased.

The *Kennkarte* still contains the photo taken that day, probably November 11, 1942, at the end of the line. Zdzisław Pływacz, a few months shy of his twentieth birthday, and Moszek Tuchendler, just a few days before his eighteenth.

And Maurice Chandler, on January 23, 2012, looked once more at the photo and said, "The fear. When I look at my face here . . ." He paused. "I remember what I thought about. This was life and death," he said. "I debated, whether I should just disappear and hide, or should I go back to pick up . . . and I did."

In 1993, he described what it felt like to receive the document that certified his existence as Zdzisław Pływacz in the eyes of the German occupation authorities. "If you live a hundred and fifty years, and you win all the lottos in the world—billions, everything that is available to you would never mean this much as what this piece of green paper meant to me the day I got it. And I went in—I had to go back again. And the second time was so frightening because I figured: took four weeks, they'll have had a chance to check the veracity of it and then I would be walking right into a trap. I don't think that any language is rich enough to describe what it means to take somebody, a human being, out of a furnace, and make him a live human being and say, *Yes, you have a right to live now.*"

When we sat together looking at the card at his home in Florida, Morry said, "I stepped out from the school . . . I don't remember walking. I don't remember feeling the ground. It's just like I was floating. My mind was . . . *Am I alive? Am I really alive?*"

The *Kennkarte*, a folded sheet of green cardboard with the Nazi eagle perched on a swastika, is dated 23 November 1942. Although it felt like a month, Morry's wait was probably less than two weeks. But this official identification document was valid only for one year. It had to be renewed on November 23, 1943, and again on November 23, 1944.

|||||||||||||||||||

Between November 1942 and April 1943, there are no documents. In that time, Zdzisław Pływacz left the farm in Dąbrowa-Dołęgi and wandered a few more miles farther east, to the village of Pułazie Świerze, eight miles from the Gestapo office in Wysokie Mazowsiecke, where he had received his *Kennkarte*. In the small village of Pułazie Świerze, Zdzisław Pływacz became a well-known figure, a boy from Warsaw who lived with the country people. "Every time the Warsaw smugglers used to come—they were the biggest danger," Morry recalled in 1993. Smuggling was a big business.

Traders from the city would bring clothing and manufactured goods to the countryside and exchange them for eggs and meat to take back to the city. "And every time a smuggler would show up from Warsaw, they would proudly tell them that they have a kid from Warsaw. *Go meet them!* Yeah, and I was always frightened because I figured what address I'll give, this guy might say, 'Well, it's not true.' It was a very, very frightening thing."

Because in a small town everybody knows everybody else's business, people ask Zdzisław Pływacz why he never receives mail from his relatives. It is suspicious: *What kind of boy has no relatives at all?* "They didn't say it sounded Jewish, but I wasn't going to let it get to that. Because I was afraid, once they think it sounds Jewish, then I'm dead. Then they won't ask me, they'll go to report me and then, you know, I can't stand a real test. So I decided in 1943—I remember it was Easter in '43—to go to Nasielsk."

The next document: A travel permit issued by the German construction firm Wolfer and Goebel. In the Kałuszyn *Yizkor* book, this company is referred to as "notorious" and accused of having employed forced labor. As a Pole, however, Zdzisław Pływacz became a regular paid worker, part of the crew building a bridge across a nearby creek. "It was a simple thing. You didn't have to go through any tax and so on," Morry told me. "So I applied, and I became one of them."

The document reads: "*Certification: Worker* Zdzisław Pływacz *from* Dąbrowa-Dołęgi, *Region* Łomża, *is employed by our firm at the construction site* Kostry Noski." Signed, stamped, dated 22 April 1943.

On what amounted to a weekend pass, Moszek Tuchendler traveled from the village where he was working and living in disguise back to his hometown. The sidewalks of Nasielsk were paved with stones from the Jewish cemetery, Morry recalled, Hebrew lettering facing up. The button factory stood empty. The synagogue had become a stable for horses, a ramp leading up the three steps.

The purpose of this visit to Nasielsk, however, was not sightseeing. The orphan Zdzisław Pływacz had come to find a relative. He asked around town for Mrs. Wyrzykowska, who had been a good friend of Morry's mother and was the wife of the man who had the liquor concession. She no longer lived in Nasielsk, but he located her in a village outside.

"She was ironing, I remember," Morry recalled. "I said, 'Mrs. Wyrzykowska, do you know who I am?' She says, 'No, who are you?' I said, 'I'm Chawa's son.' So she runs to the window, she closes the doors, she closes the curtains, says, 'Anybody chasing you?' I said, 'No, nobody's chasing me.'"

Morry calmed her down and made a deal. He asked her to write postcards to him, addressed "Dear Cousin Zdzisław," with news of his "family." In exchange, Morry promised to send her food from the village.

From there, Morry returned to Nasielsk to visit another family friend. Mrs. Wyrzykowska had advised against it, warning him that the man belonged to a Polish nationalist party, the Endeks. But Morry went anyway. "I mean, when I look back now, I think I was really stupid," he said to me.

The friend was a Polish merchant named Jan Tomasiński.

When I heard this story in January 2012, the name was unfamiliar to me, another in a long list of unfamiliar names. But when I returned home from Poland the following June and began to review my notes, I suddenly realized that Jan Tomasiński must have been the grandfather of the historian Zdzisław Suwiński's mother, Irena Tomasiński, who had shared her recollections with me during my stay at the Suwińskis' home.

"Mr. Tomasiński was my grandfather's age, and they were always close friends," Morry said, astounded at the connection. "They visited each other's shops and talked, you know how old men talk to each other, about kids, about this, about that." In the days following the German invasion, he said, "we gave them our stuff to hide if we ever come back."

On Easter Sunday, April 25, 1943, Zdzisław Pływacz knocked on Mr. Tomasiński's door. The older man immediately recognized the grandson of his deported Jewish friend, Srul Skalka. "He was that type," Morry said, "he was a big guy. 'Oh, you've got to stay for lunch!' Anyway, so what happens? We start eating, and who comes in? The daughter—with a German. I don't think he was a Nazi, he was just a soldier. And the first thing, he joins the table and said, 'Who is this?'" Once again, Morry's life hung in the balance. But Mr. Tomasiński, whatever his political affiliation, did not give away Morry's identity. "'Oh, that's my cousin's son from blah-blah-blah village.'" The daughter and her boyfriend were satisfied, and Moszek Tuchendler ate Easter dinner with the Tomasiński family and their German guest.

"I was craving for somebody to tell my story . . ." Morry told me, though his motivation for taking this unnecessary risk had to be more complex.

As soon as the meal was over, he fled Nasielsk once more. He traveled twenty-one miles west to the town of Płonsk. "I knew there was nobody there," Morry said. "But I just walked around—my grandmother's sister was married to Mr. Anzalevich there, and they had a leather store. They used to come for *Pesach*, you know, with a droshke . . . Anyway, from there I got to Warsaw."

It was Sunday, April 25, or perhaps Monday, April 26. The Warsaw Ghetto Uprising had begun a week earlier, on April 19, 1943, the eve of Passover, just as the final deportation from the ghetto was to commence. By April 22, the day Morry's travel permit was issued, the German commander in Warsaw, SS-General Jürgen Stroop, had ordered the ghetto razed building by building.

"What did I do? I remember I rode around in the streetcar."

From the streetcar, Morry could see the windows of the apartment where Sura Perelmuter Landau, his mother's best friend, and her family had lived. "They were on the second floor, and I rode around. It was the Bonifraterska Street, and they were— And I looked up, and I saw the windows. The windows were broken open, and the— Everything was empty. So from that, I knew—because my parents lived a little deeper inside the ghetto—that they were all gone already, to Treblinka. And then I said, 'Okay.'"

In Florida, in January 2012, Morry held the piece of paper, dated 22 April 1943, that had allowed him to make this trip. "That was the month that the Warsaw Ghetto was being destroyed. I was roaming around the countryside. I just—when I look back, *How is that possible? How was that possible, that I became invisible?*"

He returned to the village of Pułazie Świerze. Soon afterward, postcards began to arrive addressed to Cousin Zdzisław.

llllllllllllllllll

In the fall of 1943, Morry changed jobs again, this time arriving at the home of a wealthy farmer named Stanisław Miskowsky, who had once been a deputy in the Polish parliament. Morry described him as a "very articulate, bright man." He worked at this farm until shortly before the end of the war.

It may have been during this period, when he lived with the Miskowsky family in close proximity, that he had the nightmare in which he spoke Yiddish and when he almost gave himself away, cutting Polish bread as if it were challah. But Zdzisław Pływacz was resourceful, popular. He made friends with other boys in the village, in particular with the sheriff's son. "I was plotting constantly to get into the belly of the beast, so that there's no question of who you are. Because if you're right there in the midst, nobody would dare say, *Well, who's this? He's not one of us.*" Zdzisław Pływacz also had a girlfriend. In 1993, he described it like this: "Well, this girl, she was like my age, she was about fifteen or sixteen and she was a farmhand, too. In order for me to go to my room, I had to go through her room. Needless to say, every time I went through her room, I could never get out." This pleasant diversion, too, posed great dangers. "She's the one that gave me the ultimatum, *either I go to confession or else.*"

"It was a major threat," Morry said in 2012, though he also laughed at the memory. "So. Now. How do I find out how to confess? I mean, you can't ask. In cheder they never taught me." And so one day, at work in the fields, he confronted the young son of his boss. "'How are you doing with catechism?' 'Oh,' he said, 'I know catechism by heart.' I said, 'You know something? I'm older than you. Let's see how much you know.'"

The boy dutifully recites his catechism.

"'You know what? You're a good kid. But when did you last go to confession?' He said, 'I go every Sunday.' And I said, 'I bet you don't know how to confess. Prove it to me.' He said, 'What are you talking about, I go to confession—' I said, 'Start from scratch. You walk up to the confessional, you knock on the window, and what do you say?'"

The boy, now eager to prove he's a good Catholic, recites the ritual phrases.

"And then I had the Jewish chutzpah, and I said, 'Now, what do you confess?' And his face got red, and I said, 'Okay, I'll fill in the blanks.'"

A tough guy, a Tom Sawyer–clever guy, a very cautious, reckless, likable guy. A very frightened, traumatized guy.

"You know," Morry said when our families were sitting together in Florida, one of the rare instances when he described what this experience had been like for him, "this wearing a mask, that masklike appearance—inside I was Jewish, on the outside I was Catholic—it took a big toll on my mind. I was constantly thinking, to fix the breaks, to fix the paint if it chipped off, constantly worried that something will chip off, and they'll catch me. And I talk to people that were in the camps, and so on. And they went through a different style of torture, which was, you know, the privation of food and the hard labor. Mine was not physical. That mental strain was unbelievable. And many times, I used to think, *I got to talk to somebody.* And I would think about my friends, *Who can I tell my story? And what would they do if I told them?*"

Zdzisław Pływacz considered telling his best friend, the son of the local sheriff. The two boys attended church together, dated girls, discussed the progress of the war. "I felt very, very close to him," Morry said. Then one day his friend invited him on an outing. "He says, 'There are Jews escaping from Treblinka.' He says, 'My friends, they want we should go out on a hunt.'"

Morry told another story about the sheriff's son. "And one time, later, just towards the end of the war, he was telling me, 'People, my friends were talking that maybe you could be a plant here. A German spy.' And he says, 'I stood up and I said, "Over my dead body!"' I thanked him. I said, 'You saved my life.'"

Miracles, chance, fate, luck, talent, looks, cunning, friends, timing, chutzpah—everything had to be exactly right for Moszek Tuchendler to survive. So many other talented, good-looking, cunning, and bold young men and women in disguise were found out and killed.

We were sitting at the table in the kitchen in Florida two days after our families had met and spent so many hours looking at my grandfather's film. Morry had spread out his dossier of documents: Zdzisław Pływacz's birth certificate with the folded and torn corner; the German *Kennkarte* with the photograph of a terrified young man; the travel permit from Wolfer and Goebel; the scraps of paper documenting his presence in this little town or that.

And a photograph of four young men, dated July 4, 1943, just a few months before he found work at Stanisław Miskowsky's farm, when he was still working odd jobs in the village of Pułazie Świerze. Zdzisław Pływacz and three friends, tough guys, rough teenagers who work together at a construction site, now on their day off, horsing around.

"All these guys I remember—I'll never forget," Morry explained in 1993. "They used to imitate how Jews used to talk." And the toughest guy, the tall blond guy who's grabbing for the smaller man in the photo, he used to say to the others: "'Hey, Shasek is a *gantser yidisher*. Take a look. Doesn't he look like a *yidisher*?'"

A *gantser yidisher*, a total Jew, because their friend was small and dark-haired and so, to them, looked Jewish.

"And he was not," Morry said as we sat together, looking at the photo. He tapped his own face in the image. "But here, I was standing here."

PART THREE

12

SOMETHING GOES
FROM THE PICTURE

AT MIDNIGHT ON Wednesday, January 17, 1945, the Soviet press agency issued a communiqué from Moscow announcing the Red Army's broad advance across northern Poland and the liberation of Warsaw. "Following the artillery action, our assault battalions attacked the enemy's forward units and broke into his trenches. After that our main forces went into attack and broke through the first German defense line . . . Developing their offensive, the Soviet infantrymen, tank troops and artillerymen captured the towns of Makow, Pultusk, Ciechanow and Nowe Miasto. After two days of fierce battles, the Hitlerites were also driven out of the town of Nasielsk." Marshal Zhukov's forces captured the Polish capital. On his northern flank, Marshal Rokossovsky's Second White Russians had the honor to liberate a string of smaller Polish towns, which had lived under German occupation for five years, four months, and fourteen days. The war was over in Nasielsk.

Felix Rostkowski—Nasielsk's prewar and soon-to-be postwar mayor, and the brother of Zdzisław Suwiński's paternal grandmother—described the scene in his unpublished memoir. "When the armies retreated, the displaced villagers returned to their neighborhood, where for the most part they found ruins and ash. Despite all this, the people in Nasielsk were overjoyed with their reclaimed freedom and immediately elected a democratic council, from which emerged a presiding cabinet. Due to the work of this council, the following things arose in Nasielsk: a high school, two seven-grade elementary schools with a common room near the school building, a preschool, a narrow-rail train line from the Nasielsk rail station to Pułtusk, a children's home in what used to be the power plant, a public library, a public reading room, a cooperative bank." Among the council's accomplishments, Rostkowski also mentions a cooperative dairy; a fruit and vegetable exchange; cooperatives for blacksmiths, locksmiths, millers, and cobblers; and the renovation of "several dozen homes." Mayor Rostkowski neglects to mention that the dairy cooperative occupied the grounds of the defunct Jewish synagogue and was built from bricks scavenged from the ruin. The high school, the library, and many of the renovated homes were also formerly the property of his deported and murdered fellow citizens. But the war was over. It was time to look forward. The blacksmiths' workshops, the flour mills, the empty hulk of the Filar button factory, and several hundred homes and apartments—all these buildings and all this land now belonged to the municipality, presided over by the mayor.

||||||||||||||||||||

The war had ended almost five months earlier in the village of Pułazie Świerze, ninety-five miles to the east, which was liberated in August 1944. In the year since having his photo taken with his three friends, Zdzisław Pływacz had survived numerous close calls. One day in the fall of 1943, a patrol looking for partisans arrived at the farm of Stanisław Miskowsky, where he had recently begun to work. The soldiers searched the house and found a collection of German newspapers under the pillow of one of the farmhands. "This was my only lifeline to follow how they were abandoning city after city after city," Morry explained in 1993. "The *Oberkommando* of the Wehrmacht was announcing that they are moving forward. But when you watched the map, you could see that forward means backward." The German officer interrogated the young Polish worker. "'Do you read German?' I said, 'No.' He says, 'What are you doing with the German newspapers?' I said, 'I look at pictures.'"

Later, perhaps in early 1944, Zdzisław Pływacz had another, more seri-ous run-in. Once again, a patrol hunting partisans searched the farm, and this time, he was arrested with several others and brought to the commis-sioner's office (*Amtkommissariat*) in Szepietowo, three and a half miles away. "They bring us in and a German opens the door and an orgy's going on. There were a couple of girls running around without tops, you know, and their shorts, and the commandant is drunk and is chasing them around." The officer is not in the mood to interrogate Polish peasants. The boys are released.

Finally, in June or July 1944, with Red Army artillery already flying overhead, the retreating Germans conscripted the farmhands for forced labor. "Suddenly, the doors open up. German soldiers—SS—are yelling, 'Everybody *raus!*' Trucks are lined up. There are already people sitting on the trucks from other villages and we find ourselves on these trucks and off we go into the back. And I said to myself, *My God, is this ever going to end?*" They are brought to the city of Łomża, thirty-five miles away, where they are locked overnight in the courtyard of the city jail. In the morning, the four hundred local Poles are organized into work battalions to dig antitank trenches. They work for several days, and each day, when the workers line up to eat, a German guard stands beside the line carefully examining the faces of the laborers.

"Finally, about the third or the fourth day, I hear somebody yelling, 'Hey, Jew!' I knew who he meant. Nobody pays attention and he yells louder, 'Hey, Jew!' And he's squatting with his back to the fence and [holding] his machine gun like this. And finally he starts pointing, pointing, until every-body looks at me. And he yells, 'Jew, come over.' So I said to my friends, 'What is he talking about? How can he mean me? Jew? I'm not a Jew.'"

Zdzisław Pływacz and his friend, the sheriff's son, approach the soldier.

"'Let me see your papers.' So, I take out my *Kennkarte*, and he looks at it and he says, 'No wonder we're losing the war.' He says, 'A Jew issued a *Kennkarte.*'" The soldier demands to see the farm laborer's hands, which seem to him too soft. "So he starts moving his machine gun. He says, 'I'm gonna kill you.'"

Once more, Zdzisław Pływacz's friend stands up for him, vouching for his identity and begging the guard not to shoot. "The guy is still holding my paper, so he finally turns to the Ukrainian guard. He says, 'What do you think?' And he says, 'He's got the cross on his face,' meaning he looks like a goy. But he says, 'You want to check? We can check.' And at that moment, I let out a laugh and everybody laughed, 'Ha ha ha, check, ha ha ha.' You know? Because it had to be a moment like that where you nullify this idea, because if you let it hang in midair, then something had to happen." The soldier hands back the boy's papers. "He says, 'I'm still not happy,' but he says, 'I'll let it go,' and we walked away."

The next day, Morry and four or five others slipped away and hid themselves, digging a hole in the middle of a field. A few hours later, artillery and tank fire surrounds them, explosions. A female Russian soldier yells, "There is gonna be a big battle. Right now." She tells them to run to the forest. They run, and when they stop running, they are behind Soviet lines. They have been liberated. They dance on the bodies of the German soldiers, crushed beneath the treads of Red Army tanks. "This was the greatest sight that I ever experienced, you know, from the revenge—from the pent-up hate that I had in me."

But there are many different kinds of liberation. It would be five months before the Red Army reached Warsaw, and the war would continue for four more months after that. "I really had mixed feelings if I should go back or I shouldn't go back," Morry said in his oral history interview. "By that time, it was common talk already in the villages, they destroyed all the Jews. I figured, where am I going to go? Maybe I shouldn't even be going back. Maybe this is the only life. Maybe there shouldn't be any Jews."

For the time being, he remained Zdzisław Pływacz. He became the unofficial teacher in the village of Pułazie Świerze, offering elementary arithmetic and Polish grammar lessons. He befriended a Soviet army entertainment company and became their mascot, traveling with them to different villages in the area to sing Russian songs for the troops.

But after several months, probably in the summer of 1945 with the war in Europe over, Morry decided to travel to Warsaw, just to see. "I rode around on the streetcar, and there was a sign in Praga that Jews, survivors, should register there. And every time the streetcar stopped, Poles would come on. And they'd look out, and the conversation was, 'You see? We thought that Hitler killed them all.' And I said, *Oh, my God. What am I coming back to? Maybe I should . . . just disappear."*

At the entrance to the registration office, however, he overheard others talk about what they had lived through; he heard people speaking of their families and their communities; he heard Yiddish. "And I just— That was it," Morry said. He remained in Warsaw and never went back to the village.

Yet a mask so carefully cultivated and so bound up with survival could not be so easily or quickly shed. As late as October 30, 1945, according to another document preserved in Morry's dossier, he was still Zdzisław Pływacz, registering with the Republic of Poland Ministry of Labor, looking for work.

At the same time, however, he had begun to make contact with a few surviving Nasielskers, now living in Warsaw. And two weeks after registering for work under his alias, he was in Nasielsk again. Stopping at the post office, he noticed a letter pinned to the wall addressed to General Delivery. His friend Leslie Glodek had written from London, asking whether anyone was still alive.

ıııııııııııııııııı

On June 22, 1941, the German army invaded the Soviet Union with the largest military force ever assembled. Białystok, the city to which so many Jewish refugees had fled in 1939, was occupied five days later. Had Stalin not deported the majority of those refugees, including Leslie Glodek, to Siberia a year earlier, in June 1940, they would have suffered the same fate as the city's fifty thousand Jewish residents, of whom only about nine hundred survived.

"It was officially announced that the Germans had attacked. And we'd got to work twice as hard now, because we're going to need more material to fight the Germans with!" Leslie told me in May 2012, on the first day of my visit. It had taken two weeks for the news of the German invasion to reach the Siberian labor camp where he was interned. "I can't explain rationally why or how—but deep in my heart, I felt a little holiday for the first time. The depression I suffered suddenly was lifting." He felt that now something would have to change. Poland had become an ally of the Soviet Union. In August 1941, the Polish government-in-exile, led by General Władisław Sikorsky, made a deal with Soviet Premier Josef Stalin allowing military-aged men in Soviet captivity to join the Red Army or the free Polish forces.

"In August, out of the blue, the NKVD suddenly appeared on the scene," Leslie said. "They picked all those people like myself, Polish nationals—that was the only qualification. And we were given a loaf of bread, twenty rubles, and a ticket." This ticket would eventually take Leslie from Archangel, Siberia, by rail south across the entire continent to Kyzylorda, Kazakhstan, eventually reaching Tashkent, Uzbekistan, where the Polish army recruiting office promptly and repeatedly rejected him.

To survive, Leslie shuttled between Kazakhstan and Uzbekistan, riding the outside of the train, earning money until he could escape the Soviet Union and again attempt to join the Polish forces fighting Germany. "In Kyzylorda, most of the people were employed in breweries, and in places like that, where they make vodka," he explained. "I could go in there, for twenty-five rubles, you could buy a liter of vodka. But if you get this vodka to Türkistan," a city two hundred miles away, in Uzbekistan, "and you go on the *tolchock*," the marketplace, "you get a minimum of two hundred and fifty. So we exported rice to Kyzylorda, and we imported vodka to Türkistan." There were many refugees in Türkistan, including many Jews. In the marketplace, Leslie met a few people from Nasielsk, but seventy years later, he could not remember their names.

During one of these trips in early 1942, when he was staying in a mud hut occupied by a family from Pułtusk, Leslie fell ill with typhus. He was taken to a makeshift hospital in a schoolhouse, where he lay unconscious for days. His only recollection is seeing the dead being taken away. "I noticed that they were pulling people out by the legs. So if there were twenty people on one side, only about six or seven were left." He remained in the hospital for several weeks before regaining the strength to walk.

Soon after, Leslie and two friends, Jews who had also been rejected by the Polish army, formed a plan to escape on their own, sneaking aboard the train carrying Polish recruits to their training base in Persia, now Iran. "They couldn't afford to give them passenger trains, to transfer these soldiers. But when they came to a place like Türkistan, they stopped for an hour to feed them. Because the next stop is going to take twenty-four hours, and they've got to feed them, the soldiers. So when a train did come, the three of us were there." Leslie and his friends bartered for makeshift uniforms. When the whistle blew, they boarded the troop train. Its destination was Krasnovodsk (now Türkmenbaşy), Turkmenistan, a city on the Caspian Sea, fourteen hundred miles to the west.

But they were not the only ones to have had this idea. At each stop, twenty or thirty new stowaways boarded the train. Finally, the officials in charge announced that the train had become dangerously overcrowded. They halted at a station, where three additional wagons were added.

"Oh, we were so happy! We were delighted. We've got recognition! So what they did was, they picked all those stowaways and put them into the three wagons. *Right? Everything feel all right?* You know what the bastards did?"

In the middle of the night, Leslie noticed the train had halted again. "An hour goes by, and we're not moving. So we look out—and there's some daylight coming—there was no train. The buggers have disconnected the last three wagons." They had been abandoned without food or water on a siding in the middle of the desert.

"The crunch point will come in a minute," Leslie continued. "Now what do we do? We can't stop trains. They won't respond to us. So we decided to walk in another direction, which was the next-nearest village along the line of the railway."

Two days after being left stranded, Leslie reached a town. "Every small town and village had a commander of the NKVD. And whatever they said, this is the way it goes. They were the top dogs." Ordinarily, the NKVD were to be avoided at all costs. But Leslie had no other option. "I came in, and I said, 'I want to talk to the officer in charge. It's something very important.' So, while he's making inquiries, I could see from the distance, on the desk there was a name of Captain Goldberg. I says, *That would be a miracle if he happens to be Jewish!* And I said, 'There were all those hundreds of people'—they were not all Jews, but most of them probably were. And I said, 'This is what they've done to us.'"

There really was a Captain Goldberg. He arranged for the next train to stop and for the three abandoned wagons to be attached. To prevent the same thing from happening at the next rail siding, Captain Goldberg assigned two soldiers to accompany the train all the way to the Caspian Sea. From there, Leslie, his two companions, and several hundred other young Polish men seeking to join the army were transported by ship to Pahlavi, Persia (now Bandar-e Anzali, Iran), where they arrived on April 1, 1942. Leslie had been traveling for seven months.

It would take several months before he was accepted into the free Polish forces and transferred to Cairo, Egypt, where he was assigned to guard German prisoners of war, captured during the North Africa campaign. That summer he boarded the RMS *Queen Elizabeth*, which had been requisitioned by the Royal Navy in 1939, before it had entered passenger service, and which now ferried Leslie Glodek and four thousand German POWs to the United States. Leslie remained in the United States for six weeks, stationed at Fort Slocum, New York, ten miles north of Manhattan. During these weeks, the *Queen Elizabeth* was in dry dock, being converted into a troop transport ship, capable of carrying ten thousand American servicemen at a time to England, in preparation for the invasion of France. When the ship began its Atlantic crossings in the fall, Leslie Glodek, like all those American GIs, arrived in the United Kingdom.

On the final afternoon of my visit with Leslie in London, he showed me the few documents he still possessed from that period of his life: the photo of four boys—Leslie, Morry, Avrum, and Ratovsky—taken in Fishl Perelmuter's studio in Nasielsk; and the response he received to his desperate letter, written in June 1945, addressed to General Delivery, Nasielsk, Poland.

The response is dated November 13, 1945, six months after the end of the war in Europe. "Dear Friend!" it begins in a translation that Leslie had made for me.

Inadvertently I happened to call at the post office in Nasielsk, where I was handed your letter. From the tone of your writing, I get the

1 Warszawa-Praga dn 13.XI.45r.

Drogi Kolego!

Przypadkowo będąc w Nasielsku, doręczono Mi na poczcie list Twój do Nasielska. Śmieszny wydał Mi się Twój ton pisania, czy Ty sobie wyobrażasz co to u nas się działo. Ja Moszek Tuchendler Twój dawny kolega zostałem sam jeden z naszej całej rodziny, absolutnie nikt nie żyje. Mój brat Abram umarł śmiercią naturalną rodzice i najmłodszy brat że jak również reszta rodziny została spalona w Treblince. Twojego ojca brata Szlamę, Herszka widziałem jeszcze w początkach w Gecie Warszawskim. A później spotkał ich ten sam los co wszystkich żydów. Z Nasielskich żydów żyje niecałe 15 osób. Powinieneś 20 lat dłużej żyć, bo nie byłeś tutaj. Pamiętasz byliśmy razem w Białymstoku w roku 1940 wtedy jeszcze żyły nasze rodziny, a teraz?.. Jesteśmy odłamkami byłej całości, oderwanymi rękami bez radnych widoków na przyszłość

*impression that you have not been able to imagine what has trans-
pired. I, Moszek Tuchendler, your old friend, am the only survivor of
my entire family. Absolutely no one is left alive. My brother Avrum
died of natural causes and my younger brother like my parents and
the rest of the family have been burned in Treblinka. Your father as
well as your brothers, Shlamek and Hershek—I saw them in the early
days in the Warsaw Ghetto. Thereafter, they, too, met the same fate
as all the other Jews. From all the Jews in Nasielsk, barely fifteen persons
are left alive. You ought to live twenty years longer for not having
been here. Remember Białystok 1940, when our families were still
alive? But what now? We are no more than a tiny fragmented remnant of what was once a viable and formidable society—without any
prospects for the future. I am aware that my letter and its news will
make you unhappy, but we here are so accustomed to these conditions. You remember who I was, way back at home, but not anymore. I am now without any material means or anything else—but
taking one's life is strictly forbidden. I am not yet quite reconciled to
being the only one left alive. That is all for now. In future letters, I
will write in more detail. Please answer my letter.*

In a translation I commissioned, the imagery is more striking. Instead
of "a tiny fragmented remnant," Morry writes, "We are splinters of a
bygone whole, torn-off arms with no prospects for the future." And he
ends the letter, "Kind regards from me, only because there is no one else."

||||||||||||||||||||

In the archives of the Joint Distribution Committee in New York, there is
a cable sent from Warsaw to the New York office, dated February 26, 1946.
"TO AVOID MISTAKES WARNING AGAINST LANDSMANSHAFTN SENDING
CONTRIBUTIONS TO PRIVATE ADDRESSES," it begins. The Joint was attempting to resume its prewar activity, funneling aid from American Jews
to their destitute relations in Europe. It was also endeavoring to minimize
the hoarding and black-market profiteering that were rampant in postwar
Europe. The cable lists a number of towns for which funds have already

been distributed. Then it gives a brief account of efforts to find others in need. "NASIELSK NO JEWS . . . SEVERAL NASIELSK LANDSMEN RESIDING WARSAW CONTACTED WITH THEM."

When Morry returned to Warsaw under his own name in late 1945, he made contact with Idel Skornik of Nasielsk, a butcher whom he had known before the war. Skornik had hidden in Warsaw, behind a fake wall in the house of a former business associate ("his name was Janek," Morry remembered). Skornik's wife and two daughters were with him. The older daughter died during their ordeal, and after the destruction of Warsaw by the retreating German army, Idel Skornik had been captured and sent for forced labor to Germany. But after the war he returned, was reunited with his wife and their surviving daughter, and quickly found work at the Warsaw slaughterhouse. He offered Morry a place to live.

Now twenty-one years old, Moszek Tuchendler had nothing, and Skornik had a family and a job. But the prewar class distinctions remained in place. "To him, a Skalka was a big thing. He took me into his house. I had no place to go. You know, they had a little girl, she was probably seven, eight years younger. Maybe he thought someday we'll make a *shidduch*," a marriage contract. "I remember they used to beg me, 'Take her to the cinema!'"

Idel Skornik, his wife, Czarna, and their remaining daughter, Marysia (born 1935, so eleven years younger than Morry), are numbers 1, 2, and 3 on the list of survivors from Nasielsk that is preserved in the files of the Joint Distribution Committee's Landsmanshaftn Department, and which I found at YIVO in 2009. Mojzesz Tuchendler is number 4.

Number 5 on the Joint's list of survivors is Lejzor Finkielsztejn, Leon Finkelstein, also a butcher and Idel Skornik's brother-in-law. The list indicates that Finkelstein had survived "in the camps." In fact, Leon Finkelstein was one of the seventy survivors of the Treblinka death camp, and one of thirteen who gave testimony in 1946 to the Central Commission for Investigation of German Crimes in Poland. He had arrived at Treblinka with the first transport from Warsaw on July 23, 1942, and been selected for a work detail. "Word was, he was in the Himmelskommando," Morry told me when we looked through the Joint's list of survivors, compiled in

Warsaw in late 1945. "When they took the bodies from the gas chamber to the furnaces, he was one that stoked the furnaces with the bodies. And supposedly—I didn't hear it from him, but they were whispering, that he's the one that came across his wife, put her in the oven . . ." Morry's recollection may combine several different pieces of information, or it may accurately reflect an inaccurate rumor. There were no ovens at Treblinka, as there were at Auschwitz. The victims of the Treblinka gas chambers were first buried in enormous pits. In February 1943, in preparation for the abandonment of the camp, between 750,000 and 1 million bodies were dug up and burned on open-air racks. It is impossible to know whether or when Finkelstein saw his wife among those killed. But he was working at the camp during the murder of his fellow Nasielskers, transported to Treblinka from the ghettos in Warsaw, Łuków, and Międzyrzec. According to Finkelstein's 1946 testimony, he escaped from Treblinka during the revolt of August 2, 1943. He survived the remainder of the war in the surrounding forest, very near to the village where Morry was living in disguise.

In January 2012, Morry told me another story associated with Finkelstein from the period just after the end of the war, perhaps from the same visit to Nasielsk in November 1945 when he found Leslie Glodek's letter. The night before German troops had arrived in Nasielsk in September 1939, many of the neighbors brought valuables to the Skalka home for safekeeping. "We had the biggest house, so all the neighbors brought all their stuff, from generations, rings and chains and whatever jewelry they had. And we put everything in the basement, and sealed the basement. Including a lot of our yard goods," Morry said. After Nasielsk's Jews were deported, the Skalka house became the home of the new German *Bürgermeister*. This protected it from the ransacking that occurred in most other homes in the city. When Morry visited Nasielsk after the war, he spoke again with Mrs. Wyrzykowska, the woman who had written postcards addressed to Cousin Zdzisław. "I know you lost all your family," Morry recalled her saying, "but now you're a wealthy boy." She told him the basement compartment had remained intact. Morry took this news to Leon Finkelstein, who was traveling back and forth between Warsaw and Nasielsk, trading with the farmers. "He calls a couple of his Polish helpers, says, 'Let's go break it open.' So we did. We broke it open. I'm standing there, it opens up, it's all full, and before I know it, the whole town is behind us, breaking in, and they're pulling and . . . So I didn't identify myself. And I walked away, and that was the end of it."

Thirty years later, when Morry visited Nasielsk again, he heard from a woman at a clothing store how this story had persisted in town lore. Morry had asked the woman whether she recalled the Skalka family. "'Oh,' she says, 'Yeah. They were rich people and they had a big store and everything.' And she says, 'After the war, their grandson came and uncovered all this. People took everything away. You know, they robbed, they looted. But,' she says, 'the grandson didn't care.'"

Why was that? Morry had asked her.

"She says, 'He had a small box with diamonds. And he walked away with it.'"

This encounter infuriated Morry. He had walked away with nothing.

Number 6 on the Joint's list of survivors is Jankiel Jagoda, son of Hersz Jagoda, who appears in Keva Richman's family photograph sitting in front of Fishl Perelmuter. "He survived in Russia," Morry told me of Jankiel Jagoda. "He was quite a bit older than me, but he sort of became my guide, because he worked for us before the war." Both Jankiel Jagoda and Morry worked for Idel Skornik at the slaughterhouse. Mostly, he said, "we were just gofers." Morry and Jankiel also became the chairman and secretary of the Nasielsk Survivors' Committee, which had its headquarters at the Skorniks' apartment.

Szmul Borenstein is seventh on the list. "He was all by himself. He was sort of a poor soul," Morry recalled. On the survivors list, it indicates Borenstein spent the war in a camp. In Morry's recollection, he did not recover from this experience.

Four Buchman siblings survived the war in Russia and returned to Warsaw to be included on the list. Morry had encountered two of them, Icchok and Fajwel (numbers 11 and 12) in a farmhouse in 1939 while escaping to Białystok. Many years after the war, at a bar mitzvah in New York, Morry met the Buchmans again, and they reminded him of that meeting. "Icchok and Fajwel were telling me that when I was running on the Russian side, and I came in, they were in the attic someplace, and they were hungry, they hadn't eaten. And I had two loaves of bread, and I gave it to them. They said, 'We'll never forget you for this.'"

Szmuel Tyk, Samuel Tick, is on the list with his wife, Fajga, and their daughter, Maryla, born 1945 (numbers 15, 16, and 17). Szmuel Tyk became the treasurer of the Survivors' Committee.

Four others completed the initial list of eighteen survivors. Mojzesz Loboda had survived in Russia. In 2013, I found him still living in Los Angeles. He had suffered a stroke, which had robbed him of the ability to speak. He could no longer recognize faces in my grandfather's film. But his son sent me a photograph from the early 1930s, Mojzesz Loboda, age sixteen, in Nasielsk. Rywka Baharier, whose family lived on the opposite side of Nasielsk's marketplace from the Skalkas, with whom they were "unofficial competitors in yard goods," was also in Warsaw in late 1945. Hinda Szak, who had apparently survived with the underground, and Gittla Rzezak, who according to the list had spent the war "in Germany," are the final two survivors.

Despite the creation of a Nasielsk Committee, the survivors from the former Nasielsk were no longer a community. They may have helped one another when they could. They may have remained friends, as Morry and Jankiel Jagoda did. But each would now have to build a new life, and this they did more or less alone. "They were all remnants," Morry said, "human remnants. People didn't know where they're going to go, what to do."

In the spring of 1946, just a few months after its founding, the Nasielsk Survivors' Committee disbanded, and its members dispersed. Morry and Jankiel Jagoda obtained visas to France, and they left for Paris, where Jankiel eventually married a Frenchwoman and became Jacques Jagoda. Independently, the Skorniks also wandered to Paris, as did Leon Finkelstein, where he remarried and resumed working as a butcher. The others scattered, some going to Israel, some to Canada, some eventually to the United States, disappearing into the anonymity of peacetime.

The Joint's list of eighteen survivors in Warsaw in March 1946 is among the final documents in the history of the Jewish community of Nasielsk. Over time, the official list would be revised and supplemented with the names of those who had survived in the Soviet Union, until the final tally reached eighty-two. This is the number of survivors from Nasielsk referred to in the *Encyclopedia Judaica*. In fact, several people who survived were not included in this total. The true number of Jewish Nasielskers still alive in 1945 is probably closer to one hundred.

|||||||||||||||||||||||

Seventy years later, obsessed with my grandfather's few minutes of prewar film, I began to seek the traces of this lost community. I collected names, photographs, stories, pursuing the remnants of remnants, until almost without my realizing it, a faint outline of Jewish Nasielsk began once again to emerge. The film shows a small town. And a small town, even two or three generations after its destruction, is a network of relationships.

In February 2012, just after returning home from my first meeting with Morry Chandler and his family, I had written to a friend who lives in Israel. We had met fifteen years earlier in San Francisco but had lost touch until we became Facebook friends in 2010. Now I asked for her help contacting the community of Kiryat Ono, which was founded in 1953 by survivors from Nasielsk, with funding provided by the United Nashelsker Relief Society, based in Los Angeles.

A few days later, I received an e-mail from a man named Arie Yagoda. Yagoda or Jagoda was a familiar name to me. I wrote back to him. Like in a game of Jewish geography, the connections quickly began to emerge: Hersz Jagoda, the man in Keva Richman's family photo album, was the brother of Arie's grandfather, Leib Jagoda, who had owned the kvass factory near Nasielsk. Hersz Jagoda's son, Jankiel, who was Morry's friend in Warsaw after the war, was Arie's cousin, and Arie had visited him in Paris, where he was known as Jacques Jagoda.

Each connection was a small remnant of the web of interrelations that exists in any town. Before its destruction, the town itself—its culture, its gossip, its physical life—had held these connections. Now, in the absence of the town, my grandfather's film became the medium that brought the pieces together, unexpectedly creating a new kind of community. Slowly, I understood that the nature of my search had changed again. Nothing could revive Jewish Nasielsk. The isolated fragments that had survived would inevitably remain fragments. But perhaps, through the images in my grandfather's film, the fragments did not have to remain isolated.

|||||||||||||||||||||

I arrived at Tel Aviv's Ben Gurion Airport at 4:30 a.m. after an overnight flight from Warsaw. If only Tel Aviv were two hours farther, I thought, though the humid sea air already felt a world away from the inland chill of Poland. From the airport, I took the train into Tel Aviv and, exiting the station via the wrong elevator, found myself trapped inside a deserted shopping mall. A lone taxi idled in a parking garage on the other side of chained glass doors. I hammered on the glass, but the driver was asleep. It was 5:30 a.m. I rode the elevator back to the subbasement, stumbled through some passageway and up the ramp to the garage. The startled driver took me to my hotel and I slept for six hours. It was noon when I bought a bag of pastries at the Carmel market on King George Street and made my way to the sea.

From Warsaw to Tel Aviv. I sat on a bench, staring at the surf. For some, this journey was aliyah, "ascension," the return to *Eretz Israel* after two thousand years of exile. For many, the view I now enjoyed had represented a dream of freedom, a life that was not to be. For me and for my family, however, this land had remained distant, meaningful as a symbol, but not as a longed-for homeland. I don't think it had ever occurred to David Kurtz's parents to head to Palestine instead of to New York. But David and Liza had come to visit in 1953, five years after the State of Israel was founded. On my shelf at home in New York, I kept a photo dated May 23, 1953, showing David standing in an orchard near the Sharon Hotel, just ten miles up the Mediterranean coast from where I was now sitting. The housing complex built for surviving Nasielskers had been dedicated just a few months before, in March 1953. I wondered whether my grandfather, like me, had traveled to Israel to visit New Nashelsk, where his friend Louis Malina's name was stenciled on the wall of founders.

Later in the afternoon, Arie Yagoda picked me up at my hotel, and we drove the few miles from the city of Tel Aviv to Kiryat Ono, now a leafy suburb, home to the New Nashelsk synagogue.

The Yagoda family had lived in Nasielsk for generations, manufacturing soda water and kvass. Arie's father and his uncle were both born in Nasielsk. In 1936, Arie's grandfather, Leib Yagoda, moved from Nasielsk to the town of Jablonna, about twenty miles south. Leib Yagoda was killed there in 1942. His kvass factory is still standing, though it is now a dairy. Arie's parents survived the war in Siberia, where Arie's older brother, Natan, was born. After the war, the family emigrated to Israel, where they were deeply involved with the founding of Nachlat Nashelsk in Kiryat Ono.

We arrived as the sun was beginning to set. The stone walls of the synagogue glowed orange. Instead of ten-foot-high wooden doors, carved with the Lion of Judah, the New Nashelsk synagogue has doors of wood veneer. Over the doorway, there is a carved panel depicting a stylized impression of biblical Jerusalem. To the right of the door, a plaque in Hebrew and English reads "NASHELSK SYNAGOGUE."

Stepping inside, Arie and I interrupted a Bible study class, where a young teacher was instructing five older men. The interior was bright and pleasant, with space for a congregation of perhaps fifty. A modern, functional, simple place for worship. The young rabbi welcomed us and invited us to join the group, but we declined politely. Arie explained the reason for my visit, and the men shook my hand and thanked me. They did not offer information about whether their families had come from old Nasielsk, and under the circumstances, I did not ask. The class resumed, and I looked around the sanctuary quietly.

One of the men studying, however, pulled Arie aside and spoke with him. Later, Arie explained that the man was the caretaker of the synagogue and had sought Arie's advice. The housing complex of New Nashelsk was built at a time when the surrounding area was desert. In 1953, it might take three or four hours to get to Tel Aviv. Now Kiryat Ono is a ten-minute ride by car, twenty-five minutes from the city by bus. The land has become valuable. The survivors who settled there after the war bought their units for a nominal fee directly from the United Nashelsker Relief Society. The families that still own their original apartments do not necessarily have the proper paperwork to satisfy twenty-first-century real estate law. A developer is trying to buy the land.

The following day, I met with a small group of Nasielsk descendants at Bar-Ilan University in Tel Aviv. Second- and third-generation Israelis, most of them had grown up in Kiryat Ono. To them, the name Nasielsk had a mythological ring, the lost city of their ancestors.

Anat Aderet is the granddaughter of Ita Melman, the only survivor of a family of seven children. Ita had fled to Russia after the German invasion, and she and her husband ended up in Balqash, Kazakhstan. After the war, they had lived in the Altstadt displaced persons camp in Germany, where Anat's mother was born. In 1949, they moved to Israel. Anat showed me a hand-drawn map of the buildings where her grandmother lived. "My grandmother told me what the house looked like, and I drew it," she said. The drawing depicted a block of Warszawska Street with a bicycle repair shop, which may have been Herszek Glodek's place, a tannery, a grocery, a shoemaker, and a café, which might be the Owsianka restaurant. Anat's grandmother must have lived very near the families of Leslie Glodek, Keva Richman, and Grace Pahl.

Yaniv Goldberg's grandmother was Peril Skornik, daughter of Moshe Skornik, from the same family as Idel Skornik, the butcher, with whom Morry had lived in Warsaw after the war. We tried to work out how Yaniv was related. It took about twenty minutes. We finally determined that Yaniv's grandmother's grandfather was a brother of Idel Skornik's father. So Idel Skornik's grandfather was Yaniv's great-great-great-grandfather. And yet somehow, because I knew someone who in 1946 was friends with Yaniv's second cousin three times removed, we felt like family.

The grandchildren of Old Nasielsk were excited to see my grandfather's 1938 film. But they had not known the town.

"You should have come twenty years ago," said Anat, something I heard frequently, both from survivors and from their descendants. The older people lamented their failing memories, and the descendants all regretted that they had not asked more questions when they had had the chance.

"You didn't know what to ask," said Chani Levene-Nachshon, whose husband's father was from Nasielsk. "They didn't want to talk."

We discussed the names of people who had been the friends of their grandparents. But I had arrived too late to talk with all but one of the survivors.

Two days later, Yaniv Goldberg and I drove back to Kiryat Ono. Yaniv is a lecturer in Yiddish at Bar-Ilan University. He had offered to introduce me to Rachel Laks, born Rosenthal, who had been a friend of Yaniv's grandmother. Rachel's late husband, Chaim Laks, was born in Nasielsk in 1919, and Rachel had lived in Nachlat Nashelsk since its founding. We hoped she would know how to find the man we were looking for.

Now in her nineties, Rachel is still very lively, with a playful nature. She teased Yaniv about a deal they had apparently made years ago, that she would dance at his wedding.

"*Du muzst nokh a bisl vartn,*" he said. You have to wait just a little longer.

Rachel pointed at the small plate she had hastily prepared after our unannounced arrival and said to me in Yiddish, which Yaniv translated, "Have a cookie, or I'll be a bad Jew!"

Rachel had never been in Nasielsk, but she became acquainted with many Nasielskers after the war, through her husband.

"*Shayne yingele,*" she said as we watched David Kurtz's film together. Beautiful children. "*Shayne yidishe mentshn,*" beautiful Jewish people.

"It hurts the heart," Yaniv commented in Yiddish.

"Yes, of course," Rachel responded. "What can you do? Give thanks that you're not with them."

I asked whether she recognized the children.

"I wouldn't recognize any of them," Rachel said. "They were all older by the time they came here. But maybe Koprak will know. Koprak is smart."

Mordechai Koprak! That was the man we wanted to find. As far as I had been able to determine, he was the last Nasielsk survivor in Kiryat Ono.

Did Rachel know where he lived?

"He's not home," she told us. "If he were home, I'd hear his footsteps on the ceiling."

Koprak lives in the apartment above Rachel Laks.

Yaniv raced upstairs to knock on the door. Mordechai—or, as he introduced himself, Mikhail—Koprak was at home. But he was due at the hospital in fifteen minutes. He had just a moment to talk. Yaniv came running back down the steps. "Now is better than sometime," he said, and we grabbed the computer and the video camera and bolted back up to Koprak's apartment.

Mikhail Koprak was born in 1922 to Itzhak and Channa. There had been seven children, four boys and three girls. Only Mikhail survived the war. At first he was very reluctant to speak with us. A mostly bald man with a round, soft face, he was wearing a green T-shirt bearing the likeness of Bettie Page. But Mikhail Koprak had larynx cancer. He had a gauze bandage around his throat, and he breathed with a rasp through a hole in his chest. His voice was not even a whisper, but an inflection of breath in his throat.

I opened the computer and clicked on two photos from Keva Richman's family album. Both images show the same man. In the first, he sits in military uniform, with a high, tight collar bearing the insignia of his rank. The face is very narrow, with a sharp, pointed nose and protruding ears. He looks about twenty years old. In the other photo, the man, perhaps five years older, stands in a suit, holding a violin. He has the same sharp features and narrow face, and the same patient, curious expression as in the first image. In Keva's photo album, his mother had provided a caption for the photos, which was why I had opened them first, "Cousin Yitzhak Kopruk, Grandpa Shmuel Usher's nephew."

"*Mayn futer!*" Mikhail Koprak's pale face lit up. My father.

When we had walked in, Mikhail had been a sickly old man. Instantaneously, it seemed, he became an excited boy. He could not sit still. He bounced on the couch, half stood up, sat down, and looked again at the image on the computer screen. He tried to say something to Yaniv, but he could not. He pointed at the photo and at himself and said again, "*Mayn futer.*" No pictures of his family had survived. This was the first time he had seen his father's face since 1939.

After the German invasion, Mikhail Koprak had fled Nasielsk. Like many of the younger, politically active people in the town, he escaped to the Soviet zone. His parents and siblings remained behind and were killed. Like Leslie Glodek, Mikhail had been deported to Siberia in June 1940, and like Leslie, he had eventually joined the Polish army, although in a unit under Soviet, not British, command. He was released from the army in 1947 and went to Israel.

Mikhail told us his father had been a *balagula*, a horse-drawn taxi driver, the kind who waited for customers in front of Leslie Glodek's home near the triangle in Nasielsk.

"My family lived in poverty," Mikhail continued in Yiddish. "My father knew to make children, but he didn't know how to provide. All the Jews in Poland knew how to make children, but not how to provide for them."

Mikhail looked at the photo again. He grabbed my arm to thank me, and I promised to make a copy for him.

"I have a cousin living in America," he said to Yaniv, who translated for me, "but I don't know where he lives."

If Keva's grandfather was Itzhak Koprak's uncle, then Keva is Mikhail's second cousin. I could not determine if the Richmans were the family Mikhail meant. But they were family.

Mikhail canceled his doctor's appointment. He spent almost an hour with Yaniv and me, intently examining my grandfather's film, telling us what he could, gesticulating when he could not speak.

"I probably knew all of these people," he said. "But I can't remember them."

As with Leslie Glodek, or even with Susan Weiss, general questions and scenes crowded with faces provoked only a vague, frustrated sense of recognition. But when I asked specific questions or pointed to specific people, Mikhail's memories were sharper.

"Do you remember a restaurant?" I asked, with Yaniv's help.

"Yes," Mikhail recalled. "There was a big Jewish restaurant. Kaczyński. And a smaller one. Owsianka."

Mikhail peered at the tables, the curtains, and the windows visible in the film's dark color images. Morry had said the restaurant in the film was the Owsianka place. But I had not been able to confirm this, and I now knew of several restaurants in Nasielsk. I had hoped to narrow down the field of possible locations. Instead, it only grew larger. Mikhail could not identify which restaurant this was.

I asked whether he had known Morry's family, the Tuchendlers or the Skalkas.

"Skalka, yes," Mikhail answered. "It was a big firm, one of the richest. A clothing store. Skalka was a very famous person in Nasielsk."

I pointed out Morry's face in the film. Mikhail did not remember him. But he tapped on the screen when Avrum Kubel appeared.

"Kubel!" he said. He had known Avrum Kubel, and he recalled another Kubel who was a tailor.

I determined that he meant David Kubel, the cousin of Avrum Kubel in the film. David Kubel, who was a director of the Joint's *kassa* in 1938.

"All of them were religious Jews," Mikhail explained. "I was in the Hashomer Hatzair, I wasn't religious. So these were not my friends."

Mikhail shook his head as we watched the procession exiting the synagogue.

"He says he probably knows most of them," Yaniv related, "but he doesn't recognize them. He's really sorry."

But Mikhail remembered the synagogue proudly.

"There was a painting," he said. "There were paintings of a lion and a deer, with a saying from the Bible." He tried to recall the phrase. "*Be a light . . . a hero is a lion . . . pray to God, and walk with God.* It was a small village, but the synagogue was as big as the Warsaw shuls." And he provided additional insight into what had happened to the synagogue under the German occupation. "The Germans ruined the stairs," Mikhail said, meaning the three steps that led up to the main entrance. "It was about a meter high, and they made a ramp, and they parked the cars in the shul, the Germans. Next to the shul, there was a *shtibl*." This would be the *shtibl* where Morry's family prayed. "The Germans made it a . . . house for the horses."

"A stable?" I clarified.

"Yes, a stable. And they took the Torah, and they made from this a carpet, so the Germans won't have to stand in the, in the . . . mud. The mud from the horses. The shit."

The film moved forward. Chaim Nusen Cwajghaft, the stonecutter, appeared.

Mikhail held up his hand. He could not remember the name, but he recognized the face. He rubbed his forehead. I waited a moment, and then I said the name Cwajghaft.

Yes. He nodded vigorously. "What was his profession?"

"*Matzevah kritzer,*" I attempted in barely comprehensible Yiddish. Gravestone carver.

I knew it! Mikhail indicated with a gesture, and then said, "*Matzevah makher, ja!*" Excitedly, he told a story, which Yaniv translated.

"Cwajghaft had his workplace. All day long he clapped on the stones . . . to make *matzevahs.* It was near the shul. He lived there and made the *matzevahs.* The young children, the kids, they taunted him, made a fool of him. He said to them, 'I'll send you to your death!' He wanted to scare them. And it worked! They thought . . . because of his profession, he must have a close connection with the Angel of Death."

When we had finished watching the film, Mikhail wanted to see the image of his father again.

"He knew his father only with a beard," Yaniv explained. "And with a hat, so he almost doesn't recognize him. But he sees that something . . . something goes from the picture . . ."

Mikhail gestured from the computer screen to his chest, tracing the path that this something traveled.

Mikhail grew quiet and I could tell he was exhausted. But there were still so many things to ask. He had said he was in Hashomer Hatzair, so I pulled up another photo, one that Faiga Tick had donated to the United States Holocaust Memorial Museum, an image showing several members of that youth group. In the catalogue entry only two of the people in the photo were identified, Leah Rutstein and Neshka Rosenberg. Mikhail's eyes opened wide, and he mimed embracing someone.

"*Neshka! Wow!* Neshka Rosenberg was my teacher," he said. "She was a beautiful person. And she was smart like Einstein. Her family had a flour mill in Lelowo, a village near Nasielsk."

He put his hand to his mouth and rocked back and forth.

It was clear that Mikhail Koprak had been a little in love with Neshka Rosenberg. He made me promise to make copies of the photos for him, images of people he had never expected to see again.

"He really wants it," Yaniv translated. "He says *please*."

||||||||||||||||||||

During our brief visit, Mikhail Koprak had kept patting my arm and thanking me. On the bus back to Jerusalem that evening, however, I thought about what had transpired. All I had done was to carry the photos in Keva Richman's family album from one place to another, setting these fragments in a new context where they suddenly became meaningful. It occurred to me that this had been my role all along: to carry fragments; to establish relationships among them. I felt like a switchboard operator, connecting long-distance messages from one end of the Nasielsk Diaspora to another.

In the days that followed, I spoke with more descendants of Nasielsk and visited numerous archives. I met the son of Mottl Brzoza, the boy nicknamed *Szczapa*, of the "wooden" Brzozas. The son quickly recognized his father as a boy in Faiga Tick's school photo.

At Yad Vashem, I found the 1939 memorandum documenting the formation of a committee to aid residents of Nasielsk deported to Łuków, with the names of its ten members. This artifact related to documents from the Joint's Landsmanshaftn Department, held at the YIVO Institute in New York, as well as to the group portrait in Keva Richman's photo album.

Before traveling to Israel, I had paged through commemorative booklets from the annual meetings of the United Nashelsker Relief Society, preserved in the archive at YIVO in New York. The Nashelsker Relief Society in America had continued to raise money for New Nashelsk in Israel well into the 1960s. One of these booklets contained a letter from Arie and Natan Yagoda's uncle, Yisrael Yagoda. I shared the letter with Arie and Natan, a piece of their family history previously unknown to them. The text also offered me a glimpse of how David Kurtz might have appeared from the other side of his camera lens. In an English still sticky with Yiddish, Yisrael Yagoda had written, "Pre-war Nashelsk used to come on a visit to relatives, Jews from America, and they were always resembling each other. A middle-aged man, inclined to corpulence, getting bald, wearing spectacles in a golden frame (always gold) with a pocket watch suspended on a golden chain on the vest. A type of 'uncle Moses,' an 'Alrightnik' who is always going about with a smile and an Okay."

At the Ghetto Fighters' House Museum in the Western Galilee, I inspected three photos, two of which showed the Nasielsk synagogue. The first image was a close-up of the building's elaborately carved wooden doors, showing the lion resting on its front paws. The same lion is clearly visible in David Kurtz's film. The second photo showed the synagogue's façade, the most detailed photo of the building that I had found. In this image, the building's brickwork is exposed, revealing chips and cracks. Only the uppermost portion, surrounding the rosette, has been finished with white stucco, a corner of which is not yet complete.

From Morry, I knew that Fishl Perelmuter had painted murals on the synagogue's interior walls in the early 1930s. Apparently, Fishl's artwork was part of a comprehensive renovation of the building. Examining the photos with a magnifying glass, the archivist detected Hebrew letters carved into a lower panel of the wooden doors. These letters represented a year, 1926.

Another photo at the Ghetto Fighters' House Museum showed members of the Hechalutz Zionist youth movement, photographed in 1932. The people in this photo were identified in the catalogue, and many of the names supplemented information I had gathered elsewhere. Dvora Tyk is in the photo, a sister of Szmuel or Samuel Tick. Tova Jagoda appears, too, an aunt of Arie and Natan Yagoda, and a cousin of Jankiel Jagoda. Sara Srebro, who must be related to both Leslie Glodek and Moshe Cyrlak, is pictured, as is Avraham Isser Cweikhaft, most likely the son of the stone-cutter Chaim Nusen Cwajghaft.

ФРАГМЕНТ ворота

*   *   *

On my last day in Israel, back in Tel Aviv before an early-morning flight to New York, I visited Beit Hatfutsot, the Museum of the Jewish People. There I met with the curators of the film archive and showed them my grandfather's film. I told the story of how I had discovered it, and how I had learned that it documented Nasielsk. I explained that at first I had thought the film might show my grandmother's hometown in eastern Poland, Berezne.

"Berezne?" The curator interrupted me. "In the Ukraine?" She consulted the database of the museum's holdings. "We have a film shot in Berezne," she said.

She pulled a digital tape from the shelves. "Kutz Family in Poland. August 15, 1932." The Kutz family bears no relation to the Kurtz family.

The film of Berezne is four and a half minutes long, and it shows an American family visiting relatives in the town, viewing the synagogue, touring the countryside from a horse-drawn cart. Children gather in front of the camera to shout and wave.

The curators at Beit Hatfutsot had no information about this film or about the Kutz family, just as there had been no documentation for the photos of the Nasielsk synagogue at the Ghetto Fighters' House Museum. All these artifacts were isolated fragments of lost towns.

I asked for a copy of the Berezne film to bring home. I knew a survivor from Berezne, now living in Florida, I said. He might still be able to identify the town. He might recognize some of the faces.

13

A TOWN OF MEMORIES

OF THE ONE hundred Jews from Nasielsk who had lived to see the war end in 1945, I found eight still alive in 2012. I found them—or they found me—by research, by chance, by word of mouth. Susan Weiss had recorded her oral history for the Shoah Foundation's Visual History Archive. Her name was listed in the Foundation's directory. Marcy Rosen recognized her grandfather in my grandfather's film, discovered online by her assistant, Jeff Widen. Watching the film, Morry recognized a young man named Kubel. My sister helped me find Avrum Kubel's niece, Faith Ohlstein, the daughter of Sura Kubel, who had emigrated to the United States in 1938 with Louis Malina's help. In her genealogical research, Faith had come across the name Irving Novetsky. Irv Novetsky arrived in the United States in 1935 at the age of eighteen. He is not counted among the survivors. But he remembered Nasielsk; he remembered seeing Morry running around in the Skalka family store.

A few weeks after meeting Irv Novetsky, I received an e-mail from his daughter-in-law. She had been discussing my visit with a friend at the Jewish Community Center where she works. *Nasielsk?* her friend had said. *My mother was from Nasielsk. My father grew up there. He's ninety-three.* Morry and Dana led me to Faith; Faith led me to Irv Novetsky and his family; and Irv's family led me to Andrzej Lubieniecki, whose wife, Manya Wlosko, was the daughter of a man in a photograph I had collected.

Morry had been lifelong friends with Leslie Glodek. But recently he had also become acquainted with Keva Richman. Morry had known Keva's father, Szlama Rycherman, and his maternal grandfather, Szmuel Usher Schwarzberg, in Nasielsk. Keva was three years old when his parents caught the last boat out of Poland in August 1939, arriving in America just as the war began. Like Irv Novetsky, he is an immigrant, not a survivor. But his family's photo album supplied crucial pieces to the mosaic of fragments that preserves Nasielsk in memory, fragments such as the sole surviving pictures of Mikhail Koprak's father.

In December 2012, a year to the day after we had first spoken on the phone, I was visiting Morry and his family in Michigan, outside Detroit. "You really should talk to Grace," Morry said to me after dinner.

"Grace?" I asked. "Who's Grace?"

"She's going to be important. Because she lives in New York. She might be able to identify a lot of people in those pictures."

"You mean there's another survivor? We've been talking for a year, and you didn't mention her to me?"

Morry was sheepish. We'd had so much to discuss, he said, though he may have had other reasons, too, for not revealing her name sooner.

So in January 2013, I met Grace Pahl, born Gittla Gutman in Nasielsk in 1924. We lived just a subway ride away from each other in Manhattan. Grace had been a member of the postwar Nashelsker Society in New York. She had known Jack Weingarten, who had fled to Vilna and eventually to Kobe, Japan. She had known Israel Cyrlak, Moshe Cyrlak's son and Leslie Glodek's first cousin. She had been close friends with Neshka Rosenberg, the woman Mikhail Koprak recalled so fondly in a photo that Faiga Tick had donated to the Holocaust Museum. Neshka, whom Grace referred to as Neshkie, had survived the war and settled in the Bronx. "She was a wonderful girl," Grace said. "You could just love her. Which everybody did." Grace remembered Andrzej Lubieniecki and his wife, Manya Wlosko. Andrzej, Grace said, was the handsomest boy in Nasielsk. She remembered Moszek Tuchendler, grandson of the famous Skalka family, a very cute boy, too, she recalled, with round apple cheeks. She remembered Leib Owsianka, the restaurateur, and Sana "Kommandant" Milchberg, the religious zealot, and Sana's daughter, Faiga. Grace had run into Faiga and her husband, Samuel Tick, in Miami in the 1950s. Through the children of survivors Grace had known, I found Morris Loboda, born in Nasielsk in 1917, now living in Los Angeles. He had suffered a stroke and could no longer share his memories.

Faiga Milchberg Tick was also born in 1917. Both Morry and Leslie Glodek were certain she was no longer alive. But in October 2012, while researching at the Holocaust Museum in Washington, D.C., I found a note from Faiga's daughter in a file. I e-mailed her, and within a few minutes received a reply. Faiga, at ninety-five years old, was still very much alive. In December 2012, I spent two days talking with Faiga about Nasielsk. She recognized several people in my grandfather's film, including her husband. A week later, studying the film more closely, Faiga's daughter spotted Faiga herself in the crowd gathered on the street in Nasielsk in the summer of 1938.

When I first viewed my grandfather's film, I imagined it might still be possible to identify a few of the individuals who appeared in the beautiful color images. But my conversations with survivors quickly spilled over the frame of the film, running from individual identifications into much larger networks, encompassing dozens of names. It was far more than I had dared hope, and yet only a faint glimmer of what had once been a vibrant community of three thousand.

What is remembered? What is passed down? Jewish Nasielsk survives only in memory. But the Nasielsk that exists in memory now is the chance artifact of those who happened to live longest. The memories themselves are equally artifacts of a ruthless process of selection, what is left over after seventy-five years of forgetting, suppressing, reworking, and smoothing out through repetition. And from all the impressions that might still be remembered, how much could be shared? Among the people I met, there were many shades of memory, many different forms of preservation. Morry Chandler remembered names, places, and dates with astonishing accuracy. Faiga Tick, suffering from a slight dementia, remembered her childhood experiences with emotional immediacy, though people and places and eras metamorphosed in the course of her narration, as they might in a dream. A town of memory is ephemeral. Now the town is fading.

||||||||||||||||||

"Moishele!" Irv Novetsky exclaimed as soon as Morry, Marcy Rosen, and I walked in the door of his home north of Detroit in August 2012. Irv and Morry had met sixty-five years before, when Morry was a twenty-two-year-old refugee, working at a Yiddish bookstore in Detroit. But the impression Irv had retained was from much earlier, in Nasielsk.

"I remember you two boys so well," Irv said. "Those two little boys were just running around."

"My brother and I." Morry nodded.

"You wore a *kapote*, I think, a long—"

"A silk *kapote*," the long coat worn by religious Jews.

"You and your brother."

"With the *gartl*," the belt or sash used to fasten the coat.

"Yeah. And you wore a *yidishe hitl*, too," a cheder cap.

"Yes, yes."

"But you were so young. Seven, eight years old." Irv turned to me. "They had such a beautiful store. I remember it. Men's clothes, wasn't it?"

"Right, right," Morry responded.

"Men's clothes. But fancy! Not everybody could afford it. I certainly couldn't afford it. I was in the *Poalei yiddish yisrael*," the religious political party, also known as the Agudas Israel or simply the Aguda. "I was a member there. I was teaching the kids Hebrew, and all that. Anyway, so another fellow and I came into your store and talked to your father for a donation. Your father turned around, I don't know where he got the money, he came over, says, 'Here's one for you, one for you.' No problem."

Morry seemed a little embarrassed. But Irv turned to me again and continued.

"He's a landsman! I can say things about him!"

*   *   *

Irving Novetsky was born in Nasielsk in 1917. His father was a baker who emigrated to the United States in 1922. The rest of the family was supposed to follow in 1930, but Depression-era quotas prevented their arrival until 1935. "I got out just in time," Irv had told me when we first spoke on the phone in May 2012. "When I went to the Polish minister of affairs, he says, 'We need you here. Gotta go in the army!' I was eighteen years old. If I was a year older, they wouldn't let me out."

Irv and Morry had not seen each other since the late 1940s. But all this time they had been neighbors. It turned out Marcy Rosen, Morry's granddaughter, had gone to Hebrew school with Irv's grandson, and when Evelyn Rosen, Marcy's mother, was in the hospital giving birth to Marcy's brother, she shared a room with the Novetskys' daughter-in-law, there giving birth to another Novetsky grandchild.

The two men sat together all afternoon and compared recollections, catching up on Nasielsk gossip. It was like a seventy-fifth high school reunion.

"You remember Boyes's droshke?" Morry asked.

"Boyes? The droshke? Yes!"

"He used to go back and forth from Nasielsk to Pułtusk. Boyes's droshke."

"Was there a Meilich droshke?"

"Yeah! Meilich Shvitzer!"

"Meilich Shvitzer. He had a son?"

"Yes."

"A strong boy? *A gezinte yid?*"

"Yes."

"We used to meet!" Irv said. "He and I used to meet near the shul . . . We played soccer, football—we called it football, here it's soccer—on the mill. We also played soccer with this Boyes's son. He lives in Canada. Or did live in Canada."

"Yeah, Scheinbaum. Scheinbaum was their name. They live in Windsor."

"Windsor. Right! Oh my God! But I don't know if he's still alive or not, because he was older than me. And I'm not alive anymore."

The two men laughed ruefully at time, age, and memory. But so much of what they said added to the picture of Nasielsk, connecting stray pieces of information I had collected. Boyes Sheinbaum or Szejnbaum, the droshke driver, had parked his horse and wagon in the triangle in front of Leslie Glodek's home. His grandson, who grew up in Canada, as Morry recalled, had posted photos to a website of family history—Boyes the droshke driver, wrapped in a thick black coat, sitting on the bench of his wooden carriage, seemingly from the nineteenth century. Meilich Shvitzer was also a droshke driver, though his real last name was Hochman or Hokhman. His nickname, Shvitzer, means "one who sweats." On January 27, 1927, the *Jewish Daily Forward*, the Bundist newspaper published in New York, ran a photo of Moyshe Hokhman, part of an ongoing series of images from the Old World. I had seen the photo in the archives at YIVO. It shows an older man with a long white beard and a high black cap, standing proudly with his hand on the tire of a truck. The caption reads, "Before, Moyshe Hokhman transported merchandise and passengers from Nasielsk to Warsaw and back with his team of horses, and to-day . . . with an automobile." The mill where Irv had played soccer with the sons of Boyes and Meilich had belonged to Samuel Perlmutter, and was located next to the Glodeks' property. There was a fire there in the mid-1930s, for which a competitor, the father of Jankiel Weingarten, who survived and became Jack, was blamed, though apparently no proof was ever offered.

"Wasn't there another clothing store, where the droshkes are . . . right on the corner?" Irv asked. "Near the *markt*?"

"Moishe Pel."

"Moishe Pel? Oh! Bless your heart! You remind me that. It was your competitor."

"Exactly. And next door to him was my uncle, David Skalka."

"David Skalka. Yeah. On the corner, on this side of the building, there was a man, had a little grocery, Jedwab. Did you remember his name?"

"Sure, sure."

"Well, his son was my friend. Leibl Jedwab was my best friend! And in back of the market was a hardware store."

"Oh, Goldbroch. Sucher Goldbroch."

"Sucher Goldbroch! He had a son, Gedalia, I think his name was. Several boys . . ."

"His son was my— We went to cheder."

Months later, through the son of another Nasielsker who had survived but who was no longer alive, I received a photograph that showed a gathering of the Agudas Israel, and Morry identified one of the men as Goldbroch, though he could not say whether it was Gedalia or another one of the sons of the family Irv Novetsky remembered. Leibl Jedwab had survived and moved to Israel, I knew. He was related to Avruml Jedwab, with whom Morry had escaped the Warsaw Ghetto.

The conversation leapt from person to person, flitting through a town mostly unknown to me. Like at a high school reunion, if you were not part of the class, most of the time, you have no idea who the former classmates are talking about. The Nasielsk both men remembered was far larger than anything I could grasp. I was acutely aware in each moment that, small as the town's remembered population had become, I could only make it smaller. The passage from Morry's and Irv's memories to my notes, and from my notes into the story I would be able to tell, represented another ruthless process of selection, narrowing the town of memory still further, even as I tried to save it.

"Do you remember . . ." Irv was looking at the ceiling, as if the name he sought were inscribed in the plaster. "Hasidim . . . Sana . . ."

"Sana Milchberg!" Morry and I shouted almost together—the father of Faiga Tick. "That's Sana Kommandant!" Morry said.

"And there was another one with a red beard," Irv continued. "A real hard Orthodox. Like a damn fool!" He drummed his fingers. "What was his name? Sana's friend. A real fanatic."

"There was a song about them," Morry responded. "Nusen Nuchim *patsher*—he used to *patsh* everybody."

"Sana—you could at least talk to him. There was another guy, he was a real fanatic." Irv was still trying to find the name, his hearing not as good as it had once been. "Nusen . . . anybody Nusen?"

"Nusen Nuchim."

"Nusen Nuchim? That's the guy!"

As happened so often, one recovered memory led to another. "And do you remember the Radzyminer Rebbe came to visit Nasielsk?" Irv asked, referring to an important Hasidic rabbi from the nearby town of Radzymin.

"Sure. Oh, yes! And the whole city went out with candles. To the railroad."

"I was there! I was there when the Radzyminer Rebbe came."

"Oh!" Morry exclaimed. "So it was probably around '34?"

"Could be," said Irv. "I remember that, yeah," and he laughed with pleasure. Pointing to Morry, he said to me, "He reminds me of so many things. The Radzyminer rabbi. I remember we used to walk—the goyim didn't bother you, because there was a lot of Jewish people meeting the rabbi." He sighed at the recollection. "Such a *fanatishe mentshn*, I swear." Such fanatical people.

Later, Morry was talking about his home, the building that still stands on the *rynek* in present-day Nasielsk. "There was a store, a store near our building," he said. "They had porcelain and stuff for the house. And their name was Kubel."

"Kubel!" Irv bolted upright in his seat.

"They had a couple of sisters."

"And one boy," Irv added. "Avrum Kubel. And his sisters. Only one girl, Sarah, Sura—she escaped. She's in New York."

Sura Kubel, Faith Ohlstein's mother. I searched in my files for the photograph of the Kubel family, while Irv continued reminiscing.

"Avrum and I used to sit in Gerrer *shtibl* and learn together. Avrum was my age. He was the only boy. And his sisters, they treated him like he was a diamond."

I showed him the photo of Avrum Kubel and his sisters. "That's it!" Irv tapped on the screen. "But he didn't have a beard when I knew him. Looking at his eyes, I can see that. He had three, four, five sisters. One was sort of a hunchback, a little bit. Then they had that store, like you said. They sold housewares. Had a big store. Was Shandel the oldest?"

I pointed to the woman seated in the center of the photo, whom Faith had identified as Shandel.

"She used to go to Warsaw and buy merchandise. She was the brains," Irv said.

"We called them—I remember my mother always said, 'the *maydlekh*,'" Morry said. The girls.

"The *maydlekh*, yeah." Irv laughed. "Avrum Kubel. I can't get over, you have a picture of the girls. He was sitting in Gerrer *shtibl*. And his sisters treated him like he was Jesus Christ." Avrum Kubel, who appears twice in my grandfather's film.

Morry asked Irv about his father, and about where he had lived in Nasielsk. Irv responded with a story that wandered in the way that stories wander, with interruptions and digressions.

"Well," he began, "my father worked—there was a *spółka*," meaning a warehouse or, simply, a company. "Not far from me, actually. A couple of blocks down, on the Varshava Gas," the Warsaw Street. "A big *spółka*, like a wholesale . . ."

"There was David Bergazyn." Morry had closed his eyes for a moment and looked at the picture of the street in his mind. "David Bergazyn had a restaurant. Then Moishe Borstein had a restaurant."

"Yes, that's a—a fancy restaurant," Irv said about the Borstein place. "They served nothing but duck—roast duck, and things like that."

The conversation took a sharp turn toward the restaurants of Nasielsk. We never returned to the *spółka*, where Irv's father had worked, but in exchange, we came perhaps a step closer to confirming a location in my grandfather's film.

"And then there was Leibish Owsianka," Morry continued.

"Leibish! Now, there we go! Leibish Owsianka had a *shenk*!" Irv said, meaning a little café, a joint. "That's the man! Leibish Owsianka!"

The Owsianka restaurant was directly in front of where the Novetsky family had lived, and so the story turned in that direction.

"There was a shacklike building," Irv recalled. "You couldn't call it a building—next to the apartment building. We lived in that shack. We separated the living room and the kitchen, the dining room, by hanging a curtain. My grandmother—my mother's mother—stayed with us, after my grandfather died, naturally. Where's she going to go? And there's five or six people living there, in that shack. I mean, I thank the good lord every day what we, what I have achieved . . ."

Then Irv drew a diagram in the air, showing the Owsianka restaurant fronting Warsaw Street, with an apartment building next to it, and his family's shack behind.

"In the back, there was two doors to go in the court—and the outhouse was there in that corner." He laughed. "Anyway, that big apartment building was there, and we lived right behind."

I asked once again about the restaurant, about whether he remembered the inside, the front, whether it had curtains.

"It was big," Irv said at the same time that Morry said, "It was small." They debated what constituted big and small while I dragged the cursor on the computer screen, advancing the film to show what Morry had identified as the Owsianka restaurant.

"That looks like curtains." Irv pointed to the most clearly identifiable feature of the room's dark interior. "That's what it was. Yeah. I remember now. You could see the curtains."

Irv confirmed that the Owsianka restaurant had curtains. But did this confirm that it was the restaurant in the film? In the moment when Irv said it, I thought, *Aha! We've got it!* But of course I realized later that the fact that Owsianka's joint had curtains didn't mean that Bergazyn, Kazyński, or Borstein did not.

"My father was a baker at Hauptman bakery," Irv said, now talking about his father's profession in the United States, in Detroit. A new story, with a few digressions, eventually leading back to Nasielsk. "On Twelfth Street. Hauptman bakery. Before the unions came in, my father, he worked fourteen hours a day. Worked at night—naturally, as bakers have to work at night. And when my father came home, he put on his tallis and tefillin, and he *shuklt zikh*," meaning he davened, rocking back and forth while praying. "And before I knew it, he fell asleep while he was *shukling zikh!* How tired he was, working so hard! Anyway, what I want to tell you about—this man Hauptman came to visit Europe, Poland, came to visit my mother and me, of course. I was in the yeshiva in Pułtusk. They tried to make a rabbi out of me. If that didn't work, they tried to make a *shoykhet* out of me," a ritual butcher. "A *moyl*," a man who performs circumcisions. "Anything! Anyway, there are certain things . . . you remind me. Owsianka. This man, my father's boss, visited us. And where did we eat? Leibish Owsianka!"

The Owsianka restaurant was located on Warsaw Street near the transformer, near where the droshkes and the horses were, in front of the shack where Irving Novetsky and his mother and brothers lived, just next door to a big apartment building, which led to another flash of memory.

"There was a big apartment building. There were— The doors were closed, like a court. You know?" Irv said, again describing where he had lived. "So inside there was a big apartment building, and a woman lived there—well, with a man, of course. He was a *shoykhet* with the farmers, about cattle, horses. He was very seldom home. But she had a boyfriend who had a *knepl* factory, a button factory."

"Filar!" Morry and I said. But Irv did not recall the name Filar.

"And this young man—he was a young man at that time. I was, what? Twelve, thirteen? He was, must have been thirty-five, forty. She was about that age. She had two little girls dressed beautifully all the time. But anyway. There was stores in the front, including the *shenk*. There was a grocery story over there. And he came to visit every day while her husband was gone, which was okay with me. There's little things I remember," he said.

Irving Novetsky remembered a lot of things. But after two hours, the memories began to blur together and repeat. He was getting tired. I asked him to write down any other recollections that came to him. And a week later, Irv called to tell me he had remembered something in his dreams. As a boy, a year or two before he left Nasielsk, he had stolen a loaf of bread from a baker, the *shtimer beker*, the mute baker, whom Morry also remembered. He had felt so guilty, Irv recalled, that after he came to the United States, he sent the man a letter of explanation and a five-dollar bill.

IIIIIIIIIIIIIIIIIIIIIII

Like Irving Novetsky's father, Andrzej Lubieniecki's father, Yitzhak Leib, was a baker who had come to the United States, arriving around 1910. The older Lubieniecki was successful, and he returned to Europe to bring his family back to America with him. But they were trapped in Poland by the outbreak of World War I. Andrzej was born Avraham Moishe in Zakroczym, thirty miles south of Nasielsk, near the czarist-era fortress of Modlin, in 1919, one of seven children. Two of Andrzej's older sisters married men from Nasielsk, and the family moved there around 1930 or 1931, when he was eleven or twelve. Around 1935, the year Irving Novetsky left Nasielsk, Andrzej moved to Warsaw, where he lived with his older brother Hershel and studied theater, which would become his career. But he visited Nasielsk often. His father died in 1937, but the rest of his family was still there. And by the time he was sixteen or seventeen, Andrzej had a girlfriend in Nasielsk, Manya or Maria Wlosko, the daughter of Abraham Itzhak Wlosko.

I met Andrzej Lubieniecki in Windsor, Ontario, in December 2012. He was ninety-three years old and had lost most of his vision. He was unable to view my grandfather's film. But his memories of Nasielsk remained sharp.

Andrzej arrived at the train station with his daughter wearing an array of Polish and Soviet military medals. Like Mikhail Koprak, he had joined

the Red Army after fleeing to Soviet-occupied Poland in 1939, ending up in Białystok, at about the same time as Morry, his brother Avrum, and Leslie Glodek. But Andrzej Lubieniecki's path to Białystok was different. A few years older than the others, he was in the Polish army when the Germans invaded. He took part in the defense of Warsaw (as attested by one of his medals) but was captured by the Germans early on, around September 6, 1939. He was transported to a POW camp in East Prussia, but he and a fellow soldier managed to escape before the prisoners were registered. "I went right away from Warsaw to Nasielsk," he told me after we had eaten dinner at a local Chinese restaurant and were back in his apartment with his daughter. "I know my mother is there. My sisters are there, and children, and husbands. This was probably eighteen or nineteen of September. Probably. Probably. And I come to Nasielsk. And they told me the family from my girlfriend is in the synagogue. Other Jewish people is in the synagogue. They prepares them to transport them somewhere. Why do they make this, the Germans? Everyone has got something in the house, you know? And they want to take all these things."

After Leslie Glodek and others had been forced to build a barbed-wire fence around the synagogue property, and before the building was turned into a stable or a garage, it appears the synagogue was used as a detention center.

"But in the house where I live, upstairs, lives a German officer," Andrzej continued, his English still heavily inflected by Yiddish and Polish. "And he is an anti-Hitlerist. He don't likes where they arrest Jewish people. And I say to the officer, 'Can you help me to take from the synagogue my girlfriend?' He says to me, 'I personally can't make this. But I give you my *Mantel*,'" his coat. "'Go to the synagogue. Say to the guy what he is there, and tell him you want to arrested Maria Wlosko.'" So the young actor Andrzej Lubieniecki dresses himself in the coat of a German officer and marches to the synagogue to arrest his girlfriend. "I come to the synagogue, and soldier stays with a gun. And I say to him, 'I come to arrest'— first of all, I, *Heil Hitler! Heil Hitler!*—'I want to arrest a girl, her name is so-and-so. She is the head of the library, the Jewish library, and she has the keys.' And he calls her, *Maria Wlosko!* And she cames, and he says, 'An officer want to talk to you.'" Andrzej takes his terrified girlfriend into custody and leads her to the apartment where he is staying with his sister. Only then does he remove his disguise. "I take off the hat. She say"—he clapped his hands as he spoke—"'*Mayn got! Ikh hub dikh nisht derkent*,'" I didn't recognize you! They married that night, and the following morning, they fled Nasielsk for Białystok. "The parents was very happy I take her," Andrzej concluded, "because you know what the Germans were doing with Jewish girls."

In Białystok, the situation was so chaotic that the young couple moved to a village farther east. Perhaps three or four months later, sensing that the refugees' position was precarious, they moved again, much farther inland. In this way, they escaped the mass deportation that would scoop up Leslie Glodek and all the other Jewish refugees in Białystok that June. The Lubienieckis ended up in Chelyabinsk, Siberia, which became famous in February 2013 when a meteor exploded in the sky above the city.

In October 1941, six weeks after the birth of the couple's first child, Andrzej was drafted into the Red Army. He fought the Germans for two years, until he was wounded. Andrzej did not speak about this period, although the quantity of medals on his chest testified to his service. The family remained in the Soviet Union until the war ended. They returned to Poland in 1946, now with three children, and settled again briefly in Nasielsk.

Andrzej's wife, Manya Wlosko, belonged to a prominent family in Nasielsk. Their home was just down the block from the Szmerlak yeshiva. According to Andrzej, theirs was the only brick house in town, the biggest house, the nicest house, just as Morry had said of his home. Abrahm Itzhak Wlosko, Andrzej's father-in-law, who stands next to Chaim Nusen Cwajghaft in Keva Richman's photo, owned a furniture factory, which was large enough to export products to Britain. He was also, according to Andrzej, a partner in the Filar button factory, producing the wooden crates in which the buttons were shipped from the factory to America and elsewhere.

"The father of my wife, Abrahm Itzhak Wlosko, was a very good man," Andrzej recalled. "In Nasielsk was a man, got a wife, four children. He didn't got what to make a living. And the father from my wife says to him, 'I borrow you money from my bank. Buy a horse, and go with the water to people. Sell the water.' The man start to kiss him! Years he was working with this. He didn't got money to buy bread. Now he has."

It is possible that Abraham Itzhak Wlosko's business connections in England came through his brother-in-law. His wife's sister had married a man named Cherkow, who had fled Poland before the First World War to escape service in the czar's army. This may be the Cherkow mentioned in the Pułtusk *Yizkor* book, who had helped found the button factory in Nasielsk in the 1890s. In London he had prospered, and some of the money he earned he sent back to Nasielsk in the form of a free loan association. Mr. Cherkow, Manya Wlosko's uncle, was the director and sole sponsor of the Achiezer *kassa*, which the Joint Distribution Committee's representative had regarded with such suspicion in the correspondence from 1938 that I first read at YIVO in 2009. "Mr. Cherkow was every two or three years or four years visiting Nasielsk," Andrzej told me, beginning a story that may have involved Boyes Sheinbaum and Meilich "Shvitzer" Hochman, the droshke drivers. Each time Cherkow visited Nasielsk there would be intense competition among the droshke drivers who ferried passengers the four miles from the train station to the town. "You know what he says?" Andrzej asked me, before continuing in Yiddish. "He says, *All the droshkes should come to the station. They'll travel with us, and I'll pay them all.*"

Andrzej related another memory of Nasielsk that also involved a droshke and that located him in the same place on the same day as Irving Novetsky. "In Nasielsk was a lot of religious people," he said to me. "And the Radzyminer Rebbe, he comes to visit Nasielsk." Morry had placed the rabbi's visit around 1934. Andrzej continued in Yiddish. "*The pious Jews formed a path, and they carried the droshke by the axles. With the rabbi!*" He was rocking with laughter at the recollection. "I was a young boy! I see this! I wasn't lying! *They carried the droshke! With the rabbi!*"

His earliest recollections of Nasielsk concentrated on its thriving amateur theater scene. "In Nasielsk was a drama *krayz*," a drama group. "When I was very young, before I finish drama school, we make *Der Dybbuk*," he said, referring to the play by S. Ansky, made into a movie in 1937, about a young woman possessed by the spirit of her deceased lover.

There is a photo of the theater group in the 1953 commemorative booklet about Nachlat Nashelsk preserved in the New York Public Library. Andrzej is not in the photo, but he recognized many of the names, in particular Avrum Styczen, who was also a baker, related to the *shtimer beker*, the mute baker, from whom Irv Novetsky had once stolen a loaf of bread. Nasielsk's amateur drama groups, Andrzej recalled, performed in a theater located above the fire station on Warsaw Street. When I conveyed this recollection to Morry Chandler and to Leslie Glodek, both remembered seeing their first movies at this theater. Morry even recalled the names of two films, *Chu Chin Chow*, a musical version of *Ali Baba and the Forty Thieves* from 1934, and *The Garden of Allah*, starring Marlene Dietrich, from 1936.

Andrzej also remembered the synagogue, not because he was religious but because it was an appealing place to sing. "Nasielsk got a beautiful synagogue," he said. "I was in the synagogue every Saturday. Very famous *khazndls* comes to Nasielsk, sings in the synagogue. The paintings and everything, was a very nice synagogue." Morry, too, had recalled a concert in the synagogue by one of the leading cantors of the era, Moshe Koussevitzky, whose cousin, Serge Koussevitzky, later became the conductor of the Boston Symphony Orchestra.

After the war, Andrzej Lubieniecki returned to Nasielsk with his wife and three young children. He found no one from either his or his wife's family. While in Nasielsk, however, he spoke with the newly reinstated mayor, Felix Rostkowski. "I talk with him about the *matzevahs* from the cemetery," Andrzej told me. "I told him, 'My father was buried there, and I can't find this. And now the animals eat the grass from the cemetery.' And he told me, 'The Germans make this.'"

Shortly after returning to Nasielsk in 1946, Andrzej visited the office of the Bund in Warsaw, where an official told him to leave Nasielsk immediately. "They told me, 'Don't be there longer. Come back to Warsaw with the children. Because they kill you. Because they think you come to take back everything,'" he said. After moving his family to Warsaw, Andrzej made contact with other surviving Nasielskers, including Idel Skornik, the man who had given Morry a home. He remembered visiting Skornik's apartment. "I come with my younger daughter. She was in this time maybe three years old. And this man got a daughter, his daughter was twelve year old. She likes my daughter very much. And she says to me, 'Can you leave her?' I say, 'No! I don't leave my child!'"

In Warsaw, Andrzej also became friends with a man named Berl-Bernard Mark. Mark was a historian and scholar, born in Łomża, who had survived the war in Soviet exile. In 1949, he would become the head of the Jewish Historical Institute in Warsaw. In the fall of 1946, Andrzej recalled, Mark received a letter from a survivor of the Warsaw Ghetto who revealed the existence of the documents collected between 1940 and 1943 by the historian Emanuel Ringelblum.

"The ghetto was destroyed. It got rubble just. But we went to the street. And we find this house, and we went downstairs in the basement. I saw this time a big, long basement, but in one side the bricks was new. All others was old ones. I bring an engineer, a specialist. And he says to me, 'Something happens here.' He takes off a few bricks, and he puts his hands in-side, and he finds something. He takes off more, and takes a can from milk, a big one. He opens this. Papers. And he takes all of them what was there, in the wall, and we take this to the Historical Institute. And in this was written every day in the Warsaw Ghetto, what happens in the day."

Andrzej Lubieniecki assisted in the discovery of the Ringelblum ar-chive, which included, among thirty thousand sheets of paper, four pages of testimony describing the deportation of Jews from Nasielsk.

After several years struggling in Warsaw, Andrzej eventually joined the Jewish State Theater of Poland, under the direction of Ida Kamińska. Twelve years after the end of the war, in 1957, he met a man on the street in Warsaw, also a former Nasielsker, now living in France. The man had just come from a visit to Israel, where he had met another man named Lubie-niecki, he said. It was Andrzej's younger brother, Shimon, who had sur-vived Auschwitz and after the war had emigrated to Israel, where he fought in the War of Independence and was wounded in the Sinai War of 1956. This was the first news of his brother Andrzej had heard since 1939. "After twelve year in Poland I went to Israel and went to my brother. I didn't know absolutely nothing about him!"

In 1957, Andrzej held a theatrical recital at Kiryat Ono for the other Nasielskers. He stayed at the home of Yisrael and Elke Yagoda, the uncle and mother of Arie and Natan Yagoda, whom I met on my first day in Tel Aviv. "I was in the house a few times," Andrzej told me. "He makes the ar-rangement for me to perform there. Kiryat Ono. I performed for the peo-ple. With poems. Was a very intelligent man," he said of Yisrael Yagoda. "Yes. I like him very much."

The Lubieniecki family remained in Israel until 1978, when they moved to Montreal, Canada, and Andrzej began to work in the Yiddish theater there. "When I went from Israel to Canada, I went in a store to buy a coat for me and for my wife. Because we come from Israel, and wintertime in Canada is very cold." At the coat store, the salesman kept eyeing him strangely. "And he looks at me, and he looks, and looks, and looks. And I said, 'What you look on me like this?' He say, 'I was in a concentration camp. And with me was a guy, his name was Henry Lubieniecki.' I say, 'My brother!'"

Andrzej's older brother, Hershel, had also survived, escaping from German captivity and joining the Jewish partisans in Poland. He had come to the United States after the war and changed his name to Lubin. He was living in Chicago. The three surviving brothers were reunited in 1979.

 |||||||||||||||||

Faiga Tick was close to ninety-six when I met her at her home in Toronto in December 2012. She was energetic, even flirtatious, and she enjoyed having company.

"I see the street where there was an American . . . from Nasielsk," she said soon after I arrived, when I had again explained the purpose of my visit. "There was a sickness going, a children's sickness. They became, like paralyzed. Polio. That's right. And I don't know if this child lived through or died."

An American from Nasielsk in the street, polio. Faiga remembered specific scenes with great clarity. But often the threads between them had fallen away. Moving from image to image, she sometimes arrived at a thought that surprised her.

"I have a picture from boys from Nasielsk. Lots of boys. But where is the picture?"

On my computer, I brought up the school photo that she had donated to the United States Holocaust Memorial Museum, showing her brother Yehiel, perhaps Avrum Tuchendler, Brzoza, Srebro, and twenty-two other boys whose names I did not know.

"That's my picture!" Seeing the image made Faiga begin to cry. "That's my brother." She rubbed her eyes. "It's okay. I'm a crybaby." She pointed to the man wearing a fedora in the center of the photo. "And he's the teacher from Pułtusk." Morry had identified this teacher as Gradsztein.

Faiga remembered David Leib Szmerlak, the man who had founded the school her brother attended. "Yes, he gave the money for it. He was a rich man then. A rich man—for America, maybe not. But in Nasielsk. I remember he came, and everybody danced around him, *Amerikaner geki-*

men," the American has come. She then pointed to a boy in the photo. "This is a Zlochiewski," she said, indicating a tall boy on the far right, whom Morry had thought was named Kahan. Later, Faiga used the name again to identify a different boy in one of the photos, and she pointed to a third boy in my grandfather's film and thought he, too, might be named Zlochiewski. There was a Zlochiewski family in Nasielsk. But for Faiga, I think the name had come to be an endearment, meaning "a boy I recognize."

Faiga had a sense of humor about her confusion, or at least a charming way of describing it. "I'm very upset that I didn't make notes," she told me. "Now, if I have something on my mind, I write it down. I don't know where. But I write it down."

Yet Faiga's memory was quite exact in some ways. She remembered family scenes very clearly, even if the connections between them were fluid, images floating in a cloud of images. I began by asking about her father, Natanel "Sana Kommandant" Milchberg. I told her I knew her father was very religious.

"Yes. Orthodox. I wasn't allowed to comb my hair. One time, he went to sleep. After *Shabes*, *darft men aynshlofn*. In the middle day, *Shabes*. So I went out on the steps outside with a comb and combed my hair. And he heard it. How could he? He ran out, you know? And I had to run away. He would pull my hair out."

Faiga had some lovely childhood memories of her father. "We lived on the outskirts, so the window went out to a garden. And he went out somewhere there, on the *Shabes*, and he prayed, or he read the Bible. You have to know how to sing it. And he knew it. And I liked it very much. I used to lay there and listen. He came in, and if he sees that I'm up, he wanted me to *makh a brukhe*," to say a prayer, "and wash my hands. So I knew if I do that, he'll give me a piece of cake. So that's what I did. I say the *brukhe*, and he gave me this piece of cake. Piece of sponge cake that till today I remember it. I eat it now."

But it was clear from Faiga's stories that Sana Milchberg was a difficult man to live with. "Actually, he had no profession," she said later. "And he did everything for the *Agudim*, for the Hasidim." Then she recalled a story that combined a sweet childhood memory with a scene of parental conflict. "My mother went to the shul, Saturday morning. And he went to his group, a very religious one," she said, referring to a *shtibl*. After praying, Faiga's father brought members of his prayer group to celebrate the Sabbath in their home. "He came home—I liked it very much, because I danced in the middle of them, holding my father by the legs—and they ate up all the food. And my mother came home and said, '*Vos zol ikh gebn di kinder tsu esn?*'" What should I give the children to eat? Sana and his dancing friends had eaten the Sabbath meal Faiga's mother had prepared for the family. "She was very mad," Faiga recalled. "He got from my mother a lot to hear, but he didn't care. He went to sleep, and that's all. *Shabes*."

Later in the day, when the conversation returned to her father, I asked Faiga about Nusen Nuchim, the man in Morry's childhood song who gave the kids a *patsh*, a smack.

"Nusen Nuchim? Yes!" she said. "He was the best friend my father's. And I don't know. There was— The girls used to tease me, that my father probably flirts with him."

With Nusen Nuchim? I asked. Because they were such close friends?

"Yes! They were always together and talked. *What are they to talk about?* they said."

Irving Novetsky had remembered Nusen Nuchim as a religious fanatic with red hair. Faiga recalled, "He was double-fat from my father. Because he has no children. And he didn't need money for them. And his wife was doing everything." The two men spent all their time together, Faiga said. "In the market, walking here, walking there. And I didn't like it either. I wanted him to be home and help Mother. She had a very hard time in life, my mother."

Hendl Nordwind Milchberg, born in 1890, ran the family grocery store, located at the edge of town, near the cemetery, on the extension of Warsaw Street known as the Pułtusker Veg (Pułtusk Way).

"I think a container, what was here flour, here was something else similar, a different kind of flour. And then it was for horses, you know," Faiga said when I asked her to describe the inside of the family store. "So, and . . . on the end is *gestanden*, a round barrel, this big, with herrings. Herring was our daily food, you know? In the morning, or for lunch—there was a song," and Faiga remembered a fragment of a childhood song.

—iz zingn—iz zingn
a zeml roll, a zeml roll.
Boser iz flaysh;
Tugend iz fish.
La-la-la-la-la.

—is singing—is singing
a sesame roll, a sesame roll.
Meat is flesh,
Virtue is fish.
La-la-la-la-la.

"*Ikh gedenk nisht,*" I don't remember, she said. "My mother used to complain that she gives my sister food, so she has something for it. She's big. And me she feeds, and she can't see it."

In the afternoons, Faiga worked in the family store after school, helping her mother. If a customer came in, asking for something they did not have, Faiga would run to another store to get it while her mother talked with the customer to keep him from leaving. "Because outside was a Polish store, not far away, and he would go there—and he wouldn't come back anymore."

Faiga's memories compressed whole situations into a string of moments.

"Customers came in. It's groceries. This one wants ten gram of sugar, and half a kilogram of flour. And I was good, and they liked me. My sister wasn't good. She didn't want to be good. She stayed in school and she made her work. And she had good marks, and I don't. I had some homework at night, and she wasn't home to help me. Because at night, she ran to Hashomer Hatzair. And then she got hit from my father, for why she goes there. *What business do you have to be out late?* Yeah. And I was in the middle."

Pesa Milchberg, Faiga's older sister, had been a member of the Zionist youth organization Hashomer Hatzair. For Faiga, the tensions this produced in her family, with her strict Hasidic father, were still painful. "She used to go the Zionist organizations. And my father didn't like it. So I was sitting up at night—to wait for her, because she used to come home twelve o'clock at night, and I knew that Father would hit her." The recollection made Faiga cry again. "She suffered a lot from Father. The Aguda Jews used to bother my father: *Your daughter is a Zionist, and you should wait until God will take us there.* And she went away, and he said, he won't let her in the house. But then she came, and she stayed with friends. So he told me to bring her over. He wasn't that bad."

The bitter divisions among rival ideologies within the Jewish community played out in the Milchberg family. To religious Jews like Sana Milchberg, only the coming of the Messiah could sanction the formation of a Jewish state in Israel. To them, the Zionists, who sought a political path to statehood, were anathema. Sana Milchberg was thus trapped between his orthodoxy and his family. He banished his daughter from the house, and then he broke his own decree, telling Faiga to bring Pesa secretly back home before she emigrated with her Zionist youth group to Palestine in 1936.

"My father was doing lots of things between the Hasidim, to get money for the Hebrew school," Faiga told me on the second day of my visit, referring to the Beys Jakov School for Girls, mentioned in the Joint's survey of social institutions in Nasielsk. "We had a teacher, I think she was the last teacher. From Grodno. Perla Tch, was her name. Perla, like pearl."

Faiga was a student at the school, but even this produced conflict within the Milchberg household. "I remember—I have to have fifty cents a week. And my mother said that she can teach me this. And I shouldn't go. And my father didn't want it. And they fought about it. And so he used to tell me, when my mother doesn't see, to take out money from the drawer—to pay the teacher."

Faiga clearly remembered the teacher, Perla Tch. She had inspired a powerful schoolgirl crush in Faiga, which apparently worried her mother, Hendl Milchberg. "I was in love with her!" Faiga told me about Perla. "In *love* with her! My mother—I told her that I like her so much—she used to give me scotch." The strong emotions in Faiga's stories made them feel immediate to her, and she then said, "She lived in Grodno, I heard. She must be alive somewhere. No?"

Faiga's younger brother, Yehiel, appears in three of the five photographs she donated to the Holocaust Museum. "In Hebrew, they say 'Yehiel,'" Faiga explained. "But we called him Hiele." She recalled another scene of family conflict, this time involving her brother. "I remember when the mill was burning," Faiga said, describing how Samuel Perlmutter's mill, located behind Leslie Glodek's house, had caught fire. "So my brother—he was very strong. He was saving the flour from the mill on his back. Why I remember it? Because my mother screamed at him, 'Let it burn up!'" Their mother was afraid Yehiel would become trapped in the burning building. "He was proud of himself, that he was able to take it out and save it. So she said, 'I'm not proud of it, if you break a leg there, and you're laying, nobody will help you.'"

The child of a difficult father, a child in a household laced with conflict, Faiga was attuned to the undercurrents of emotional strife around her. These were the things she recalled, even when they showed an ugly side of life in the small town. On the second day of my visit, we were sitting at the dining room table, and Faiga's daughter Heather, who had helped arrange our meeting, requested a story she knew.

"Tell the story about when you were little," Heather said. "With the horses."

"When I was little?" Faiga asked. "When I was little, I remember only this. In the wintertime, the stove was in the kitchen. And I was sitting here, with my back to the wall. And here was the hot oven. And I— I wanted to say something else about that." The image of the stove caught her attention, and whatever she had meant to say about horses was forgotten. "I was sitting in the kitchen. That's right. That's not—it's not a nice story to tell. The owner from our apartment was a—I don't know if you call this a womanizer—he didn't care that much about his wife. He was a mean, mean man. He liked to grab women. So I was sitting in the kitchen. He used to came in unexpectedly. But I didn't think—I was little, so I didn't have a lot to think. But he told me, to pick up one of my foot. And then my mother was screaming at him. That he—to see me. But I didn't understand it, even then. Later on, when he—when I grew a little older, I wouldn't listen to him. He had a daughter. A beautiful girl. The daughter's name I remember now, Aurela. Yeah. She got— Oh, oh, oh! I remember something. She was very beautiful. And a very rich man in the city was— he made her pregnant. And what happened?" Faiga paused and tried to answer her own question. "And she went to Warsaw to have this child. And she came back sick. And we knew she was dying. She got probably tuberculosis. She came back. I shiver now, you know? And my sister, Pesa, came from Warsaw. She was helping—my mother had a sister in Warsaw, Masha. She had a store with, they call it in Polish, 'white things'— eggs, cheese, butter. And sometimes—what was it?"

I asked Faiga what it was like to be a young woman in Nasielsk, what she did with her friends.

"We walked from the mill outside the city till the post office, back and forth," she said, probably referring to the Piekarek flour mill, owned by Gloria Rubin's family and located near Faiga's home, and the post office not far from Leslie Glodek's house. "We'd talk about the people."

I asked who her friends were.

"Who were they? Usually the brave girls who didn't listen what the fathers or mothers . . ."

Walking around was forbidden?

"We shouldn't go," Faiga said, "because the men were going. We always told Father we didn't see any men. They'd sit in the synagogue, or somewhere. And here were a few soldiers behind us. And we were four girls. And they made jokes with us. They said, 'The fifth one is a beautiful girl.'"

Later, Faiga showed me a photograph of the four girls posing on what looks like a pile of cinder blocks. Faiga, perhaps eighteen years old, stands on the left, leaning her arm confidingly on the shoulder of her friend. All four girls face the camera boldly. Faiga identified them from left to right as Zelda Beharier, Heike Goldwasser, and Manya Goldwasser. Recalling the names made Faiga cry again. "They're not here," she said. Of the three, I

found Shoah testimony only for Manya Goldwasser, who died in Rostov-on-Don, in the Soviet Union, in 1942.

I asked Faiga how she met her husband, Szmuel Tyk, or Samuel Tick.

"I knew him my whole life, almost," she said. The Tyk family lived across the road from Faiga. "When I was older already, when I was going out at night, till ten o'clock, and it was dark, I was afraid to go home. He used to wait for me. We ran together to Russia."

In October 1939, after the German occupation of Nasielsk, Faiga wanted to join a group of young people fleeing east to Soviet-occupied Poland. "My father was there. He said to me, 'You can't run away with a man.' So I told him, 'He's a neighbor, and everybody's running.' And he said, 'No, I insist you get married. Or else you stay here.' So I said, 'I don't even have a ring.' So he took out a ring from his bosom. And he said, 'Here's the ring.' And he married us right then and there. And then we were together."

Like Andrzej and Manya Lubieniecki and many other couples, Faiga and Samuel Tick married the night before they escaped. Faiga's friend Manya Goldwasser fled at the same time. "She was with me, together. I remember sleeping on the floor, where the Christian woman gave us place on the floor. I don't remember any more about what happened. It was raining. Some women were crying. They were having babies. And children were crying."

Later, at the Holocaust Museum, I found a brief note about Faiga indicating that she and Samuel had fled to Świsłocz, Poland, now Svislach, Belarus, about forty-five miles east of Białystok. "I had some money. My mother gave me whatever she had. And that gave me sleepless nights. I thought, *I shouldn't have left her.*"

Like Leslie Glodek, Faiga recalled crossing the new German-Soviet border. "I hide a watch. A cheap watch, a little one. So I had it here. I was lucky why he just let me through," she said.

Who let you through? I asked.

"The German. We went in, one after another, into the Germans, and they searched us. And before me, I was standing, and a woman was screaming. I don't know, they probably—put her arms out, they made a mess of her. I don't remember if she made it even, after the screaming like that. And I went in after, and they were very good to me. I had the watch hidden on my foot. He could have hit me, too. He didn't. He said, 'Why did you do it?' I said, 'Because I was afraid that the boys would take it away from me if I put it on my hand.' He didn't take it. Maybe he did take it. I don't know. I don't remember. But this was not important. *Ikh bin adurkh leybedik,* you know?" I came through alive.

Once Faiga was on the Soviet side, Samuel Tick apparently returned to German-occupied Poland and helped his sister, Ruchul, cross the border to safety. According to Faiga's daughter, Samuel had also tried to convince Faiga's parents, her brothers, Yehiel and Efraim, and Efraim's young family to escape. They refused to leave Nasielsk.

Faiga, Samuel, and Ruchul remained in eastern Poland until the summer of 1940. In a database of Victims of Soviet Oppression hosted by the Polish Institute of National Remembrance, I found records indicating that all three were deported to Wołogodzka, in the Vologda Oblast, on July 9, 1940, which was probably the date of their arrival, ten days after the mass deportations that also brought Leslie Glodek to Siberia. From Faiga's family, only she and her sister Pesa, already in Palestine, survived.

*   *   *

On the first night of my visit, Faiga, Heather, Faiga's older daughter, Malca, and Malca's husband, David, all gathered around the TV to watch my grandfather's film.

When she saw the synagogue, Faiga recalled several stories. While her father had prayed in the Hasidic *shtibl*, her mother had gone to the synagogue on Shabbat, sitting upstairs in the women's balcony. "In top there. The women, with curtains covered. And in the bottom is men," she described. "Yeah. They made jokes from it. That they're flirting, the *vayber mit di mener*," the women with the men. "Behind the curtains. All the women looking down—like this," and she arched her neck forward and looked down toward the ground.

Faiga also remembered that her mother had led a small group of women in reading the Torah. Hendl would read aloud, and the women would repeat. One time, during the winter, when it was drafty in the room where they were sitting, Faiga's mother had said, "*Nem a shmate un farshtek dos lokh*," take a cloth and stuff the hole, and the women had repeated this, too, thinking it belonged to the Torah portion. The phrase became a joke, something of a dirty joke, that the women repeated among themselves.

Faiga also remembered the little creek behind the synagogue, and a joke the girls had told about this. *The water is so deep*, she said in Yiddish, *you have to stand on your head to get wet.*

A few moments later, in the scene where the townspeople exit the synagogue, Heather told me to stop. "Hold on," she said. "I think I just saw my father. Just coming down the stairs." I rewound the scene. Yes, Heather and Faiga agreed, there is Samuel Tick. He comes down the steps just ahead of Avrum Kubel, wearing a white shirt and a gray worker's cap. It is his chin, Heather said, his ears. It's just the way he walked.

Later in the film, in the color section, Samuel Tick appears again. This time, he is standing with his hands on his hips, observing the scene on the street as my grandfather pans across the people's faces. We didn't notice it as we were sitting together in Faiga's apartment that night, but just before the camera passes Samuel Tick, a woman emerges from the background to

stand next to him. She has on a dark blue or black dress with white polka dots and a white collar. She appears to say something, and Samuel Tick seems to say something in response. The image is blurry, the camera is moving swiftly. A week after my visit with Faiga and her family, Heather and I spoke on the phone, and she said there was no doubt: the young woman is Faiga Milchberg, age twenty-one.

Samuel Tick and Faiga Milchberg are also among the people peering in the window of the restaurant where Louis Malina is smoking a cigar. The man behind Samuel Tick wants to be noticed, so he removes Samuel's hat and waves it above his head. Faiga, bareheaded as in all these shots, seems to be standing on her tiptoes, her forehead bobbing above the heads of the children in front of her.

Faiga had required a moment before she recognized her husband in the earlier scene in front of the synagogue. But as we were scrutinizing the sequence, she suddenly called out, "Oh! Miriam Myrla!"

Standing in front of the synagogue, her head tilted quizzically to the side, is Miriam Myrla, who also survived the war and was later a close

friend of Faiga and Samuel Tick's. In fact, in Keva Richman's family album, there is a photo taken in the 1950s at Crystal Beach on Lake Erie
showing Keva's parents with Faiga and Samuel and Miriam Myrla, all five
Nasielskers sitting on the sand in their bathing suits.

After the war, Miriam Myrla married a man named Sadik. Their
daughter, Carla, and Faiga's daughter, Heather, were friends growing up.
A few days after meeting Faiga, I sent Carla these moving images from
my grandfather's film. "She died over thirty years ago so there are many
things as an adult I never got to talk with her about," Carla wrote to me.
"Seeing her face alive and young was amazing."

In the film, Miriam stands to the right of a woman who wears a bold,
floral-print dress. In the few seconds they are both on-screen, the second
woman turns to reveal long black braids. Then she faces the camera again.

"Czarna was a little younger than Miriam," Faiga said in Yiddish.

Czarna was Miriam Myrla's sister, and she also appears in my grandfather's film. Czarna Myrla did not survive the war. Testimony in the
Shoah victims database indicates she died in the Majdanek concentration

camp, where Miriam had also been a prisoner. Of the six siblings in the Myrla family, only Miriam and her youngest sister, Malka, survived.

"She was a popular girl," Faiga recalled of Miriam. "Ran around with lots of boys. God forbid anybody should see me talking to her, they told my father."

But by 1938, when my grandparents visited Nasielsk, Miriam had married a man named Josef Skurnik, and the couple had a young son.

"She had a little boy," Faiga remembered. "And then she had to make a choice. The Germans told her she can have only one."

Heather corrected her. "I think that's the movie, Mom."

Faiga had folded her friend's history into William Styron's 1979 novel, *Sophie's Choice*, made into a film in 1982. It was a sign that she had grown tired after a long day of remembering. We let it go, and soon after, we said good night.

Perhaps it was just a poignant mistake, tangled threads in Faiga's memory. But after spending time with her, I sometimes felt that Faiga's memories were like poems, images with a potent emotional core. Rather than names and dates, she recalled situations and strong feelings.

Miriam Myrla's first husband and young son both were killed in 1942, as was Czarna, and most of Miriam's family. Perhaps Faiga did not recall—or perhaps she never knew—what Miriam had suffered during her time in Majdanek, or what choices she was forced to make there. But I believe Faiga was expressing what it *felt like* to remember her friend's suffering. The reference to *Sophie's Choice* was like a metaphor. It was *as if* Miriam had been in the situation described in the novel and pictured in the film. But in Faiga's memory in this moment, the "as if" had fallen away.

||||||||||||||||||||||||

"First of all, he was a very *frum* boy, from a beautiful family," Grace Pahl told me when we met at her apartment in lower Manhattan in January 2013. Morry had belatedly introduced us, and Grace was now describing the first time she saw him, a very religious, observant boy, who came to her school one day in 1936. "So they brought Mr. Chandler. And they introduced him, 'This is Mr. Morris Chandler'—at that time, it was Mr. Tuchendler, and now he changed his name, good luck to him. But he didn't talk to girls. I don't think I spoke to him two sentences. But I remembered him, because he was a cute boy," and she laughed a little in embarrassment. "He had a face like an apple."

Grace also remembered Andrzej Lubieniecki. I told her I had just visited with him and his daughter in Canada, and I showed her a few photographs of young Avraham Moishe Lubieniecki in Nasielsk.

"That's Monek Lubieniecki?" Grace asked, using his Polish name and looking a little disdainfully at one of the photographs. "I want to tell you one thing. That's not a good picture of him." She shook her head at the computer screen. "He was the most handsome boy in town. And I'm not kidding." I flipped through the other photographs, until we reached the one of him striding down the street in Nasielsk holding a stack of newspapers over his arm. "Oh, you see here? Here he looks more like Monek. Here I recognize him. That's right. That's Monek," she said. "He did everything to make a dollar! Very poor boy. But every girl loved him."

When I reported this to Andrzej, he laughed and said that Grace and her sister, Lonia or Lila, were the prettiest girls in Nasielsk. Morry, too, recalled Grace and her sister as town beauties, comparing Lonia to Elizabeth Taylor. A month after Grace and I met, she spoke with Andrzej

Lubieniecki for the first time in perhaps seventy-five years. According to Grace, after an hour's telephone conversation, Andrzej said to her, "You forgot something." "Everything I remember I told you," she said to him. "You forgot to say how handsome I was," he replied.

Grace remembered Sana Milchberg, Faiga's father. "Yes, the principal from my Beys Yakov was Mr. Milchberg." Grace continued in Yiddish, saying Sana Milchberg was a very respected Jew. Very learned, Yiddish, Hebrew. A scholar. But Grace did not know him. "To me he was just the principal. So we all were afraid of him. You know? If he's going to scream at me? Or if I didn't make my lesson right?"

She recounted the one time she had seen Faiga after the war, at a hotel in Miami Beach. "She couldn't get over it, that I remembered her father. She said she never saw me, she never knew me. I used to see her, because she went for a *shpatzir* on our street," a stroll, the kind Faiga had to hide from her father. "On a *shpatzir*, all the young girls with their boyfriends used to come on our street, the Varshava Gas."

What was Faiga like as a young woman? I asked.

"Faigele Milchberg," Grace said in Yiddish, "was *a zayer fayne maydl*," a very nice, fine girl. And Grace asked me, "You know what a nice girl was in Nasielsk?"

No, I said. I did not know.

"She didn't go with non-Jews."

I could not resist asking whether Grace had been a nice girl, too.

"I was too young not to be a good girl," she said.

Grace Pahl was born in 1924 to Chaya Finkelstein and Abram Gutman. Grace's mother had been married before, to a man from Pułtusk. A son from that marriage emigrated to the United States with Chaya's parents in 1922, and Grace only met him after the war. "I am from the second marriage," Grace said. "I, and I had a sister. She's not here. Yeah. Life go on. From my family, nobody survived." Because her parents were in America, Grace's mother had desperately tried to leave Poland in the mid-1930s. "I remember how my mother was sitting at night, and put down a lamp, a kerosene lamp, and closed up the light on the ceiling, and nobody should bother her," Grace said. "And I remember my mother sitting and crying and crying to her family, they should at least take me and my sister."

Because Grace and I lived so near each other, we had the opportunity to meet on numerous occasions over the course of several months. We sat on her living room couch or around the small table in the dining area, together with Grace's two daughters and the woman who was her care-giver. Each time, Grace urged me to eat the cookies or chocolate she had set out, and each time she commented that I had not eaten enough.

The first person she mentioned when we began to talk was Fishl Perelmuter. "Mr. Perelmuter I know and I remember, because his grand-child was a friend with my cousin," she said, although it was probably Fishl's daughter, not his granddaughter. "Mr. Perelmuter, he was crippled on one leg. I believe so. He used to tell us, or maybe he told just to the chil-dren, that he was wounded during the First World War. And he had a very big boot. I remember that. He loved all the kids."

Grace also recalled the centerpiece of the murals Fishl painted in the Nasielsk synagogue. "He painted beautiful pictures," she said. "And one picture he made—*Avrum Avinu mit bayde froyen*," Abraham with his two wives. "Like I would see it now. I remember that Abraham was dressed like—in a long *shmate*. You know? A robe. And it was painted in, where the holy rabbi was sitting there. It was the most beautiful painting that people could wish to see."

As with Faiga Tick, Grace's memories sometimes crowded each other. "I must tell you what happened with that painting," Grace continued. "My mother loved that painting. But you couldn't buy it. This was made for the temple, and that's it. But the man who got it finally—not a Jew. He was a Polish man. This was a Polish man who got it. He put his hand on it. My mother went to Mr. Perelmuter, and she told him, she would love to buy the picture. And he said, 'This picture is not for sale.' But my mother was very good in handwork. You know? Some women do handwork? So my mother had made a picture—not a picture . . ."

Did she sew a copy of this picture? I asked, misunderstanding.

"Right," Grace said. "And then, when the years started to go a little more by, and the war started to come closer from Germany—so what did my mother do? She told that Polish man, 'If you going to let me have that portrait'—the portrait was made on linen, painted."

So the Polish man had a painted copy of Fishl's mural?

"Yes, yes, yes," Grace said. "And my mother gave it to him, he should keep it. When the war will end, she wants to come back and get it back from him. It was the most beautiful thing I have ever seen."

So Grace's mother gave a copy of the mural that she had painted to the Polish man for safekeeping?

"And he promised," she concluded, referring to the Polish neighbor. "He's not going to sell it to anybody. So my mother hoped, all during the whole war, she said, 'I'll go back to Nasielsk, and he has to give it back to me.' So she took it out of the frame, and she rolled it up, because it was linen, she rolled it up, and she said to him, 'Remember, you promised. You give me your word.'"

Grace enjoyed seeing the photos I had collected. In Faiga Tick's photo of the Hashomer Hatzair youth group, Grace immediately recognized Trana Kohn, a tomboyish girl standing behind Neshka Rosenberg. "Those were my friends' sisters. So how can I forget them?" She singled out another older sister of a friend, Leah Rotstein, in a photo from Keva Richman's album showing a large group standing in the Nasielsk marketplace. And she identified Malka Myrla, the younger sister of Miriam and Czarna Myrla, in a photo of Manya Wlosko Lubieniecki and her friends.

When we watched my grandfather's film, Grace's memory was equally sharp. I put the film on the TV, and as soon as the scenes began to unfold Grace looked at the black-and-white images of the town and said, "It was yesterday." She quickly focused on the son of the blacksmith, or *koval*.

"Oh, you know this boy, where you hold your hand? No, no. To the left." Grace pointed at the TV while I kneeled in front of the screen, moving my finger from face to face. "Wait, I'll tell you who he is. I know for sure it's him. What was his name? There were two brothers. Oh my God, how can I forget his name? He loved my sister, he was crazy about her. But he's not alive a long time ago. They lived on the Pułtusker Veg, and the father was a *koval*. He made for the horses, he made shoes."

I mentioned the name Czarko, since Morry had said he was a blacksmith. "No," responded Grace firmly, and then continued in Yiddish, *"He is not Czarko. Czarko lived out in the fields.* There were two young boys, and they belonged to the Hashomer Hatzair." Fifteen minutes later, Grace remembered. "Oh!" She stopped herself in the middle of a sentence. "The guy that I told you that his father made the shoes for horses? Wilczynski." She tapped her hand on her leg. "Did you ever hear that name?" I had not heard it before, although I had read it on the Joint's list of Jewish refugees in Vilna, Lithuania, in 1940. "Well, you check out with somebody else, and you see, it was Wilczynski. Two boys, two brothers." A few weeks later, watching the film again, Grace pointed to another boy and thought it might be the second Wilczynski brother.

The Wilczynskis lived on the Pułtusk Way, past the button factory, just across the street from where Faiga Milchberg lived with her family. The blacksmith's house is still there, and when I visited Nasielsk, I saw it, a few steps down the street from the home of Zdzisław Suwiński, the historian and my guide in Nasielsk. Mrs. Suwiński, his mother, had remembered Mordka the blacksmith. Faiga Tick had also remembered two Wilczynski brothers and said their names were Valek and Tadek. "And Tadek got killed," Faiga had recalled. "Where did he get killed? From the Germans."

Mordekhai Vilchinski, the man on the Joint's Vilna list, survived the war and gave Shoah testimony for his family: Abraham, his father, the blacksmith; his mother, Leja (Leah); and his brother, Yitzkhak, who was ten years old.

In one instance, Grace's powers of recall directly contradicted Morry's. We were sitting in front of the TV again in Grace's apartment in March 2013. Morry had identified a boy in the film as Piekarek. Grace identified the same boy as Jedwab, perhaps Leibl Jedwab. When Morry had first said the name Piekarek, I recognized it from one of the Shoah Foundation oral histories about Nasielsk. Gloria Piekarek Rubin was no longer alive, but I had sent the boy's image to Gloria's daughter and told her it probably showed her mother's younger brother, Jankiel, who had been killed. So I asked Grace whether maybe the boy was Piekarek. She was not convinced.

She had known Gloria Rubin in Nasielsk when she was Gittla Piekarek, and had known Gittla's six siblings as well. "To me he looks like somebody else," Grace said. "I think he looks like Jedwab."

But often, the memories I heard from different sources proved to be complementary. In another conversation, when we were talking about the postwar Nashelsker Society in New York, Grace helped identify a family that Leslie Glodek had spoken of, though he had been unable to recall the name. In the 1960s, Grace recounted, she had worked in a jewelry store in Brooklyn, and a man came in to buy a watch. He bought the watch on layaway, Grace said, so he had to give his name, Pludwin. Grace remarked that she had known someone from her hometown named Pludwinski. The man was startled. Where was she from? Nasielsk. It was the man's family. "Pludwin should be known by everybody," Grace said to me, speaking of all the young people who had lived in Nasielsk and were now old, "because they were the *tsikerl makher*, they made candies."

Pludwinski, the *tsikerl makhers*! When I e-mailed the Glodeks' daughter in England, she reported that her father thought it sounded right. Morry, too, recalled the shop as soon as I said the name. "Yes, yes . . . you're right," he said. "I remember we used to stand there, outside the window. We watched them pressing the—like a plate with teeth that would separate pieces of candy from a whole plate. In the summer, it was hot, and the windows were open. So we went there and we looked in. To get rid of us, they would give us a couple pieces of candy."

I asked Grace whether she had gone to the Pludwinskis' store.

"Oh, all the time, sure," she said.

What did it look like?

"What do you think, every store has a different face? No. All the stores in Nasielsk had one face. But this building belonged to them, so it was nicely made. You know, bigger. And they were, how many? Maybe four daughters, I think. And the youngest daughter was my good friend, we went together to school."

The memories that I asked for to help identify a place were not the memories that had been preserved, not the facts important to those who had lived in Nasielsk.

"Her name was— Wait." Grace sat motionless and concentrated. "What was her name? Faigele! Faigele Pludwinski was my good friend. We went together to school. You see?" she said. "Little by little it comes back. Otherwise I would be a loser in this game."

It was an odd coincidence that three of the Nasielskers I met, three who also happened to live particularly long lives, should have been neighbors. Leslie Glodek, Irving Novetsky, and Grace Pahl all lived on the same block of Warsaw Street.

"The house was the newest building in Nasielsk," Grace had explained when I first asked where she had lived. "Because they built a drugstore—it wasn't ours, it was a Polish family who built a drugstore, Mrs. Machnikowska. In my eyes—when you're young, you think this was the biggest building in the world. So this big, big building, when I went and I took my daughter with me, she said, 'Ma, *that's* the big, big building?'"

A big building, by Nasielsk standards: two stories, perhaps six apartments. Grace showed me a photograph of the living room of this apartment, which was among the very few pictures of her family that had survived. Her mother had sent the photo to her parents in Brooklyn before the war. It appears to be staged, with three middle-aged couples posing around a fancy table in a fancy drawing room, playing cards. A grandfather clock in the corner shows that it is five minutes before eight o'clock. The photograph has severe water damage on one side, and it is impossible to make out the faces of the couple on the left. In the center, a woman with black hair parted in the center and a coil of pearls around her neck holds up what looks like the ace of spades. A man leans over her with his arm around her shoulder. Grace recalled that his name was Mr. Cytrin. Her mother and father sit on the right, her mother in a striped dress with a shawl. She is looking to the side, pretending to spy on the cards in the hand of her friend. Next to her, her husband looks doubtfully at the fan of cards in his hand. He wears a suit and has a little mustache of a kind popular in the 1930s but never seen today, a little square mustache that Morry said was called a *shmektabak*, literally, a "taste tobacco." His daughters huddle next to him, sharing a hand of cards.

"I want you to know, all Nasielsk women used to come past our window to see the curtain," Grace said, describing the elaborately decorated curtain in the background. "Look at the flower that was worked out in those curtains! My mother went specially to Warsaw and buy them. I don't know if she saw them in a magazine or someplace and brought them to Nasielsk. I can assure you, that nobody else in our hometown had such beautiful— it looked like a bouquet of flowers. I would recognize them in the dark. Would you believe me? After so many years?" These curtains were among her mother's prized possessions. "She loved them her whole life," Grace said. "That was my mother."

The family's apartment was on the second floor, above a store that sold books and paper supplies. "A *księgarnia*—a bookstore," Grace recalled. "And his name was Mr.—wait one minute—yeah, Horowitz. Yeah, he had a bookstore. The kids for school needed books. We lived upstairs, and downstairs lived Mr. Horowitz." When I asked Leslie Glodek, he also remembered Mr. Horowitz's store for paper and writing materials near where he lived. Mr. Horowitz also figured in a story Morry had told when we first met in January 2012. Leiser Horowitz had been a member of the same Hasidic *shtibl* where Morry and his family prayed, and it was at Leiser Horowitz's head that Chaim Nusen Cwajghaft hurled a pitcher when the bookseller objected to the placement of the stonecutter's painting of the Aramaic prayer *Kegavna*.

Next to Horowitz's bookstore, Grace remembered, was a restaurant, just as Irving Novetsky had recalled. Leibish Owsianka's café, or *shenk*.

"Oh, sure," Grace said when I asked whether she knew the Owsiankas. "I called him my *zayde*," my grandfather. "You know why?" She looked at me until I said no, I did not know why. "You know what he gave me to drink? Fish oil! Because I was a very bad child to take a medication. Because this medication—excuse my expression, it stunk. I have never drink anything worse than fish oil." Grace stopped and looked at me again. "Why are you laughing?" she asked.

It was true, I had begun to laugh.

"Did you ever drink it?" Grace demanded to know. "It was a terrible, terrible medication. And we had to drink it. And I said, 'I will *not* drink it.' I cried. And I said to my mother, 'If I *die* I'm not going to take it.' So my mother remembered him, they had a restaurant downstairs, and so she said, 'I'll call up Mr. Owsianki, and he'll help me.' Because he was a strong, older gentleman. And when he came up, he held my legs, and kept my nose closed. So I drink it. So I called him the *zayde*. That's right—when I came from school, they gave me soup, vegetable soup. And I loved these people. His wife I really loved, because she didn't give me medication."

Leib Owsianka, owner of the restaurant where David and Liza Kurtz, Louis and Rosie Malina, and Essie Diamond may have stopped on their visit to Nasielsk in 1938—now, at last, I had met someone who knew the people and the restaurant well.

"It was as narrow as half of this room," Grace said, waving her arm around the small living room. "And you could sit down, you could order whatever you want to." The restaurant had a few small tables. "Not too big, but there was a counter. Yeah. I think that was the only restaurant that I knew in Nasielsk. Leibish Owsianka. And she was Faigele Owsianka."

Later, I found two photographs of Leib Owsianka, a distinguished man with a long white beard coming down to two tufts, in the style of Theodor

Herzl. When I showed the photos to Grace, a month or so after our first meeting, she recognized him immediately. "I didn't have to sit and think," she said. "He looked identical, the way he looked."

On a subsequent visit with Grace, her daughter showed me a booklet from the eighteenth annual convention of the United Nashelsker Relief Society, held in March 1963. Among the pages of advertisements purchased in honor of individual families was one dedicated "in loving memory of our mother and father, Leibish and Faiga Owsianka." The text stated that Leibish Owsianka had been a lifelong Zionist and president of the Mizrachi organization, and that he had "lived to see a free state of Israel established, which was his lifelong goal." Leibish Owsianka survived the war. But in the fifty years since the Nashelsker Society convention, his descendants had dispersed, and I was unable to locate them.

Since Grace had known the Owsiankas well and had eaten lunch at their restaurant, as she said, every day after school, I felt hopeful she would finally identify the restaurant seen in my grandfather's film. When Grace, her two daughters, and I sat together and watched the film that first afternoon in January 2013, I paused the frame and said that Morry Chandler had identified this as a restaurant.

"Maybe he ate in restaurants in Nasielsk," Grace responded.

"He said he thought it was the *Owsianka* restaurant," I persevered.

"I couldn't say this, because I wouldn't know."

"But you just said you ate there every day," I said, a bit crestfallen.

Grace shrugged. Her daughter pointed out the most striking detail of the interior space. "Do you recognize these curtains?" she asked.

"I tell you," Grace said finally, "I don't remember one fancy restaurant from Nasielsk— Wait a minute. Then came another store, a restaurant. One restaurant was not far from Owsianka, from our house. And that was a restaurant called Borstein. Yeah, that could have been. Small. Smaller than Owsianka. Because Owsianka was on the main street, the Varshava Gas. But this store was going into a smaller street. That was Borstein."

I asked what she remembered of Borstein's restaurant.

"Also, small place. Small. I think Owsianka was the biggest, in my time. It could be that this was Mr. Borstein's. And then was— Ah, slowly it comes back." She raised her finger and made a point in the air. "Because now I remember there was another restaurant, and his name was Mr. Segal. Yeah. Sure, I remember now three: Owsianka and Segal and Borstein."

Instead of confirming the location, the possibilities had again multiplied. I now knew the three restaurants Grace had named, plus one more that Morry recalled, Bergazyn, and the one Mikhail Koprak had named, Kazyński. But I could not learn which of the five was seen in the film. Finally, I asked Grace what the Owsianka restaurant had looked like from the outside.

"What do you think, it was a restaurant like here?" she responded, not angrily, just trying to set me straight. "Or it was elegant? Or one restaurant showed a difference between the two? Never. It had four people. Who built up in Nasielsk a nice restaurant?"

Grace's memories of her wartime survival were both exact and, a little like Faiga's, fragmentary. She distinctly recalled listening to a speech on the radio in the weeks before the war. "In our hometown, who had a radio to listen? Only a very well-to-do man," she said. "He had a store of materials, not far away from us, where we were living. And he opened the windows, and he opened the door, and everybody who wanted to listen to Hitler's speech could come in front of his building and could listen."

Do you remember the name of this man? I asked.

"Suwiński," Grace said, naming the historian Zdzisław Suwiński's paternal grandfather.

"I ran and I stayed behind the window, underneath—right? And listened what [Hitler] said. And he told what he's going to do. And I believed, but our parents didn't believe. Parents did not believe that this is the end of Polish Judaism."

After the German invasion, Grace's father tried to flee east, while she, her mother, and her sister sought shelter in Warsaw. But after a short time, they all returned to Nasielsk, probably in late September. "Unfortunately, when we came from Warsaw, there wasn't a piece left in our apartment," Grace said. "Nothing. They threw everything out, made a hospital for the soldiers." The house was destroyed, and the experience appears to have devastated Grace's mother. "My mother loved her belongings," she said. "When we came back from Warsaw, I want you to know, in 1939, none of our neighbors even recognized my mother. She lost so much weight. She thought that she lost her whole life."

The family stayed with neighbors, but conditions in Nasielsk were terrifying. "They started right away with us. They didn't wait even a week," Grace said, referring to the Germans. "They hit. They killed you. They just ran out and [committed] cold murders. *You are a Jew?* They came into your house. They took everything away from you. You had nothing left to stay in Nasielsk. And then they were talking about that they are going to liquidate every one of us. You didn't know which way to go. Who knew where is right, where is bad? The Polacks used to say, 'Go, leave Nasielsk, because they're going to kill you all.' So we started to leave Nasielsk, and that's how my family left Nasielsk and went to Warsaw."

They fled the town again before the deportation on December 3, 1939, although Grace's grandmother and aunt were on the transport to Łuków, as they heard from friends shortly afterward. Grace, her mother, and her sister remained in an apartment in Warsaw for a brief period. Then they were deported to the ghetto in Jablonna, twelve miles east of the capital, where Leib Jagoda had once had his kvass factory. Grace's father was sent first to an associated forced labor camp, Legionowo, adjacent to the Jablonna Ghetto, and later, after perhaps a year, to a labor camp called Piekiełko, east of Warsaw.

The family was in the Jablonna Ghetto for almost two years. Grace recalled seeing a girl she had known in Nasielsk, perhaps a cousin, named Rifka Finkelstein. "We went to school together. And she came—she ran away from the ghetto, from Warsaw, and she came to us. I was in the Jablonna Ghetto," Grace said. "And I want to tell you something. As long I'll live, I could never, never forget this girl. Never. I have seen bad—girls who didn't survive. But what I saw on her, nobody should ever see it. What they did to her, the Germans, God should never forget that. Forgive that. How you could make an animal from a child. So young. When she came to us from the ghetto. How she looked. This picture I always have in front of me."

The German *Aktion* that destroyed the Jablonna Ghetto took place on

October 4, 1942, three days after the resumption of killing at Treblinka, and within a day or two of Morry Chandler's ride on the train from Warsaw, when he encountered a woman smuggling goods to the countryside. That night, Grace, her mother, and her sister escaped.

"I tell you what happened," Grace said. "We were running all at night, and it was dark. And here you don't know where you're running even. So I looked around, and my mother was near me, and so was my sister. And my sister said to me—I was the more athletic girl than my sister—and she said to me, 'Look, we have to jump over that—that fence.' So I—like a stupid one—jumped over. I climbed up and jumped over. And when it started to get light, a little daylight, I said to myself, 'My God, I'm all alone.'"

Grace searched for hours before she found her sister again the following morning. But their mother was gone. Hiding in the field, the girls could not agree on a plan. Lonia decided to seek shelter with a Polish woman, Mrs. Grochowska, a friend of the family's from Nasielsk, who had moved out of the town and now lived outside Warsaw. Mrs. Grochowska had provided the family with a little help while they were in the ghetto, and she had told the girls to come to her if things got too "hot," as Grace recalled. Grace, however, decided to go to their father at the work camp in Piekiełko. The sisters separated. Grace did not see her sister or her mother again.

Alone, or perhaps with another Jewish girl she met at this time, Grace boarded a local train heading south. The conductor recognized immediately that she was on the run. "He knew right away when he saw me," she said. "Not combed my hair. Not dressed like a human being. You run out in the middle of the night, where it's dark. No light in the house, and you don't know where you're going. You don't know what to wear. It was a shirt laying on a stool. I grabbed that shirt, and I put it on, and I ran out of the house. And that's how I lived through three years, with that shirt." She still has the shirt.

The conductor confronted Grace, who was then eighteen years old. "He says to me, 'You are a Jewish girl, aren't you?' And I said, 'No, I'm not. What do you think of that? I am not a Jewish girl.' And believe me, I looked not like one Jewish girl, but like ten. I had long braids, black." The conductor persisted, and eventually Grace broke down. "I told him my life story, how good my life story is. And he has somehow a little pity, and he says, 'You know what? I could take you to Warsaw.'" But Grace was cautious. She said she first had to go to Piekiełko, where her father was in a labor camp. The conductor gave her a ticket. Grace found a way into the camp and spent a night there, hidden by her father.

"So my father cried like a little baby," Grace said. "And he says to me, 'I'm telling you, my child, you are naïve, you are young, you don't understand. He'll promise you that he'll take you to Warsaw. He'll never take you to Warsaw. You'll never see Warsaw. Don't go.'" And Grace replied, "'Daddy, you're telling me a hundred times, Don't go, he's going to kill you. Do you have a better place for me? Where should I go?'"

Grace may have spent more than one night at Piekiełko, or she may have hidden for a night in the woods around the camp, because she recalled lying in the bushes, waiting for the conductor to return, as they had arranged. During the night, Grace said, a German patrol with guard dogs searched the perimeter of the camp. "And this dog—like would be sent from an angel. I don't know how other to say it. And he jumped over my feet. I was so afraid. I was terrible afraid. Because if he would give one bark, such a big German shepherd." But the dog simply leapt over her legs and kept going. The following day, the conductor returned precisely on time, and eventually he took Grace to Warsaw and gave her a place to hide.

"You see?" Grace said to me. "Sometimes you don't have to listen to parents. That was my only time that I didn't regret . . ." The conductor hid Grace in Warsaw in a tailor's shop that had been abandoned by a Jewish family when the ghetto was created. "He didn't touch me, didn't hit me, didn't hurt me," Grace said. "The only thing that he was looking [for] was money. Money—not from me, because he knew that I don't have the money. Because I told him right away. I did not want him to think that I lied to him. So when he met me, he said he's going to take me to Warsaw, I said, 'But I don't have any money to give you now. I could promise you one thing,' I said to him. 'I have relatives in America, and if God wants me to live,' I said, 'if I should survive this war, then I'll send you money from America.' That's what I told him, and I kept my promise."

The conductor used Grace as an advertisement and a character reference to lure in other Jewish families who could pay immediately. "So they asked, 'Did he do something to you? Did you give him a lot of money?' I said, 'No. He didn't hurt me. I didn't even have money to give him.' I told the truth."

Grace lived in hiding in this store with several other people for two years, until the German army crushed the Polish Home Army's uprising in October 1944. With the city destroyed, Grace fled and survived the remainder of the war using a Polish birth certificate that her sister had given her when they were still in the ghetto in Jablonna.

Lonia Gutman hid with the Grochowska family for two years. In 1943, their father escaped from Piekiełko and hid in a barn, which also belonged to the Grochowskas. He was denounced by Mrs. Grochowska's sister-in-law and shot. Lonia fled to the nearby town of Henryków. She was killed there in 1944.

Grace is still in touch with the conductor's daughter and her family.

‖‖‖‖‖‖‖‖‖‖‖‖‖

It is impossible to learn "everything" about Nasielsk. It is impossible even to learn everything that one person remembers about it. Inevitably, then, individual stories and details come to represent the whole, both for the people who remember the town and for those who grasp at memories of it and try to make sense of something they never knew. But which stories? Which details? What governs this final selection in the long series of ruthless selections, which narrows the town's life to isolated moments and single images?

I heard so many stories. Often, during the years of my search, I would not recall specific details or memories until much later, when I listened again to the recordings of my conversations with the survivors. So it was two months after I first met Grace that I put together the pieces of a scene that, if true, would constitute one of the most bizarre coincidences in this story built on coincidence.

When I first met Grace, I had asked her father's profession. "My father— may he rest in peace—he bought cattle and sold cattle for the army, the

Polish army, which was in those years a very good profession," she said. "But later on, they took it away from the Jews. They said the Jews cannot bring this to the Polish soldiers, because they making too much money."

Weeks later, after learning some of Grace's history, I listened again to the recording of my visit with Irving Novetsky. Suddenly, a pattern of details leapt out: Irv recalled a woman with two beautiful daughters who lived in the apartment in front of the Novetskys' shack; her husband, who traded in cattle with the farmers, and who was often away from home; and a daytime visitor, a man from the Filar family, owners of the button factory. It seemed possible that the woman in Irv Novetsky's memory was Grace Pahl's mother.

The next time I spoke with Grace, I asked whether she remembered the button factory.

"Oh, sure. The Filars? What questions," she said. "I would describe it as a tremendous building," and she laughed because of how the "big, big" apartment building of her memory had later shrunk. "We thought that the factory of the Filars from the buttons took away the whole block. It was a building built from brick. It was a beautiful garden inside, when you walked down. Beautiful."

I asked what she remembered of the Filar family.

"He was described as a millionaire. I don't know if he was a millionaire, but he was considered as such. Listen. All town of Nasielsk make a living from that factory. All the goyim went to work there. Jews they didn't give so much work. And I visited inside the building because Salke Korn was my best friend, and that was her grandmother who was a sister from Mr. Filar. We went in, and her grandmother baked cookies for *yontif*, you know, for the holidays. And we always had a good time, because they were good people to us, whenever we came. They were very well-to-do people. And they were charitable people. And they made beautiful buttons. What else can I tell you?"

Grace could not recall the names of the different family members. But she remembered that one of the Mr. Filars did not have children, perhaps Boruch Filar. The other brother, perhaps Aron Filar, however, had a family, and at least two of his children also had families. In addition, there was a sister, who was the grandmother of Grace's friend, Salke Korn. I asked Grace whether she remembered the names of the Filar sons.

"Wait. Let me see." Grace thought about it. "Avrum? No. I knew one son that they had. And we moved together with them, when we left Nasielsk in 1939."

The families had left Nasielsk together, after the German invasion?

"This was—Avrum? Maybe it was Avrum Filar. I can't remember. If you had come ten years earlier, I wouldn't say 'I can't remember.'"

During another conversation, Grace said she thought that her family had fled to Warsaw after the invasion with Yossel Filar, who may have been the son of Leibl Filar. In that conversation, she said they had met Yossel Filar on the road to Warsaw by accident. But she clearly recalled that the Filar family had helped her mother find an apartment in Warsaw, in the period before they were sent to the ghetto in Jablonna. "Gliniana," she said, naming a street on the western edge of what would become the Warsaw Ghetto, near the Jewish cemetery. "A very run-down neighborhood. That's where they gave the people, the emigrants who came in from smaller towns. Because it was such a mishmash."

I asked Grace about the Filar family in various ways, and I spoke directly with Grace's daughters about the memory Irv Novetsky had retained all these years. They questioned their mother. They said she did not know anything about it. Like so much gossip, this piece of eighty-year-old hearsay proved impossible to pin down.

The sons of a wealthy family are often the subject of gossip and rumors. Leslie Glodek had remembered the Filars in almost hostile terms. "As a family, they were very remote from the rest of us," he had said at his home in London in May 2012. "The only time you could see a Filar was if he was driving through in an open car—and women were always present, hats and very fashionable, that sort of thing. All you know is that, if you saw a jazzy car, it could be one of the young sons."

Irving Novetsky easily recalled specific names and incidents when he reminisced about Nasielsk with Morry. But he was a twelve- or thirteen-year-old boy around 1930, when he saw the woman who had a boyfriend who owned the *knepl* factory, the button factory. What he saw, or thought he may have seen; what he believed or imagined the relationship to have been—this is impossible to verify, material perhaps for a novel.

What struck me about these coincidental details, however, more than any ancient scandal they might imply, was the extraordinary improbability of their survival. That Irv should have remembered this story, among all the others that make up daily, messy life in a small town; that we should have made contact by chance when he was ninety-five years old, and that he should have told me this story, in particular, in the few hours we spoke; that I should have met Grace and learned enough of her family's history to locate Irving Novetsky in a shack behind the apartment building on Warsaw Street where Grace and her family lived. And, to me, the strangest coincidence of all: the added improbability that my grandfather's film also should have survived. Without the film, I would never have been in a position to connect these stray details. The fragility of this gossip overwhelmed me. It was so slight, and nevertheless it had been preserved.

14

FAMILY HISTORY

WHEN I RETURNED home from London, Poland, and Israel in June 2012, more than three years after I first asked my aunt Shirley what she knew about her parents' 1938 trip to Europe, she sent me a present: the envelope of postcards and letters from her parents, spanning forty years, that she'd rediscovered a few months earlier. There were postcards from a trip to the American Southwest in 1935 that I had never known about; a tantalizing hint of a cruise to the Panama Canal Zone in 1936; and letters and postcards from two trips to Europe, in 1937 and 1938.

On their first trip to Europe in 1937, David and Liza Kurtz had traveled alone. Perhaps for this reason, David wrote numerous letters, while he sent none at all in 1938. These letters are maddeningly vague about the things I wanted to know. But they provide the only insight I have into my grandparents' thoughts. David and Liza left New York on July 3, 1937, aboard the Italian liner *Conte di Savoia*. On July 9, David sent a long letter to Shirley, who spent this summer, like the summer of 1938, at Camp Oquago for girls in Andes, New York. "The high spot of the trip so far was the night Mother won $40," David writes. "Yes, sir—was she excited. We played Lotto and Keno, and sure enough Mother, lucky guy, wins the pool of $40. She gets acquainted with a nice California lawyer and he advised her not to turn over the money to our general fund, but to keep it herself." David is chatty and excited. He continues, "Then who do you think were fellow passengers—Mrs. James Roosevelt, the President's Mother—and the President's son John Roosevelt, and several of their family and friends. Young Roosevelt danced with every girl on board the boat—Shirley, you missed it."

David gives a day-by-day account of the crossing: seeing the Azores; a midocean meeting with the *Conte di Savoia*'s sister liner, the *Rex*; sighting the coast of Portugal, the Rock of Gibraltar, the Balearic Islands, where he mentions "a Spanish airplane with a machine gunner in front," a reference to the ongoing Spanish Civil War. It's a warm letter, and David closes it, "Well, so long kids and here's hoping you have a healthy summer and write regularly. Our love and kisses to you and to all our friends. xxxxx Dad."

They arrive in Naples on July 10. David sends a postcard from Capri, one from Sorrento, and another from Rome. The postcards are sweet and exasperating. "Enjoying the art of Ancient Rome. Love Mother & Dad." They go on to visit Florence and Venice, where David stops to write a letter. From this, I learned that Shirley was the editor of her camp newspaper. David writes: "How are the editorials? Are you a communistic paper or are you for the plutocrats? . . . I am your European Correspondent who believes that America is still tops." I asked Shirley about this newspaper. "I spent a lot of time up there," she said, "because, one thing, the boys' paper was written up there, too, so that I liked."

David and Liza toured the highlights of two thousand years of European culture. But my grandfather's commentary betrays little of his response to this ambitious trip. By July 18, they had crossed the Alps and were in Vienna, visiting Schönbrunn Palace. Then, on July 23, David sends a postcard from the Hotel Europejski, in Warsaw: "A quaint old town—with a tremendous Jewish population," he writes. It is the only direct reference to the Jewish community of Poland in all of David's surviving correspondence.

Three days later, on July 26, he sends another postcard from Warsaw: "Darling, your letter of July 11th just rec'd in Warsaw and so happy to learn you are well and busy. We visited Brezna that town in Poland where the folks come from and will have lots to tell you." This is how I learned that my grandparents spent the night of July 24, 1937, in Berezne, Poland, now in the Ukraine, birthplace of Liza Kurtz née Saltzman. The postcard solved the mystery of my grandparents' visit to Berezne, but it did not explain why Berezne had supplanted Nasielsk in the family story about my grandfather's film, and it did not shed light on what my grandparents had experienced while there.

"I remember my mother saying it was so hot, she had to get out of there," Shirley had recalled in June 2009. We were sitting in the little den of her summer house in Pittsfield, Massachusetts, surrounded by posters from the nearby Tanglewood music festival. While I had been questioning Shirley about her parents' travels for a few months already, this was our first opportunity to view the film together. The original footage was still undergoing restoration at Colorlab, so we viewed a DVD of the old videotape. An interior scene, apparently shot in a private home, was paused on the TV screen. We still thought David's film documented Berezne, and so we both believed this shot must show the Saltzman family home, the house described by Liza's older sister, Rose, in her brief article published in the *Babette Gazette* in May 1939. Viewing the image in 2009 had jogged Shirley's memory. And even though we were wrong about what we saw in the film that day, Shirley's recollection would be the only description from this 1937 trip to Liza's hometown passed down in my family.

Writing to his daughter from Europe in 1937, David has nothing to say about the family, the house where his wife was born, or his impressions of rural Poland. His next letter is dated July 28. "Shirley Dear, Well here we are in the Soviet Union. The red flag adorns the public buildings and the hammer and scythe and five pointed star with pictures of Lenin and Stalin are everywhere in sight." On July 27, 1937, at 9:00 p.m., after returning to Warsaw from a side trip to Berezne, David and Liza Kurtz boarded the overnight express to Moscow from Warsaw's Central train station, where five years later Moszek Tuchendler would embark on his first journey under a false identity. "It is exactly 12 noon at the New Soviet Hotel," David writes on stationery with the hotel's letterhead. "It is modern, clean and inviting. The streets are crowded with people all seeming busy and having some place to go. Everyone carries a brief case and I wonder what's in them. Can they all be officials carrying documents—or do they contain a ham sandwich—I wonder."

Here, for the only time, David Kurtz describes what he sees for his fifteen-year-old daughter at summer camp in upstate New York. "The women do the same heavy manual labor as the men—swinging heavy axes and handling heavy railroad tools—ties—rivets. They work along the R.R. exactly as the men do—and in fact are important parts of the entire scheme. Just as many women are officials and workers as the men. The dress is terrible, everything the poorest. The women are—streetcleaners, painters, motormen on streetcars, and in fact are doing men's work, besides you see them in the fields since daylight, in bare feet. There seems to be no lack of children either. All along the road we saw plenty. What a life. Not an idle moment. Regarding small cities in Poland and Russia—the life is so primitive. We'll tell you more later on. It would fill a book."

Oh, David! I am struck with admiration for my grandparents, who were so adventurous, traveling to Moscow in 1937. And I am seized by a furious, futile curiosity. How could they go to Moscow, to Berezne, and say so little? These experiences might fill a book. But that book never got written.

David's sense of the Soviet Union quickly changed, but only in casual asides does he reveal how he felt about this extraordinary journey. "From that horrible nightmare Russia we landed this morning in Germany (of all places)," he writes on August 2 from the Hotel Adlon in Berlin. Of all places, indeed. I already knew my grandparents had stayed at the Hotel Adlon, one of Berlin's fanciest hotels, just steps from the Brandenburg Gate and Hitler's new Reich Chancellery, then under construction. I knew this because Liza apparently stole a notepad from the hotel, which Shirley remembered seeing on the table next to the telephone at their home in Brooklyn. When we spoke about it in 2009, Shirley also recalled that in Berlin the hotel staff had called my grandfather Doctor, "Doktor Kurtz." At the time of this conversation with Shirley, I assumed David and Liza had stayed in Berlin in 1938. Didn't they find it uncomfortable to be in Germany then? I had asked.

"I don't think they knew what was going on in '38," Shirley answered. "Because I don't think they would have gone to Europe if they had known in one year that Europe would be overrun. Did anybody know?"

From Berlin they ride to Paris ("What a dream of a place. Frankly—

we've been dizzy since arrival"), and from Paris on to London. On August 14, David writes a letter from Stratford-upon-Avon and takes a rare moment to muse on the trip. "Of all the places we've been to, Paris is the most artistic, London is the biggest. Naples the prettiest. Moscow the filthiest. Vienna the quaintest. Rome the most religious. Florence the most intellectual. Berlin the craziest. Of course our short stay in each city qualifies us as experts in everything concerning politics—economy—both political and social. But that is the beauty—the wonder—the miracle of the ages—of our own country—that you can think and SAY what you like and here in England they have the same measure of Freedom. But in Italy—Germany—Russia—*ah* that's another story. So thank God for the good old U.S.A."

On August 16, David concludes his narrative of this first trip to Europe from the Hotel Savoy in London. "We can appreciate our beautiful country only when we see the others."

If David's correspondence in 1937 is notable for its breezy vagueness, the collected postcards from 1938 are almost comical in their brevity. On August 1, 1938, he writes from Amsterdam: "Holland is a swell place. Lots of outdoor sports. The girls and boys have a swell time. I hope you are too. Mother and Dad." On August 2, 1938, from Brussels: "Just visited this art gallery in Brussels. We saw Belgium. Many cities occupied during the world war. Hope all are well. Mother and Dad." And on August 6, 1938, from the Linden Restaurant, located on Unter den Linden 44. "Here we are in Berlin, enjoying a nice glass of beer. Only here for a few hours waiting for a train to Switzerland."

In all, there are only six postcards from this summer in Europe, a total of 120 words, including six repetitions of "Mother and Dad." Nevertheless, I was profoundly grateful to Shirley for having saved these artifacts, which provided me with invaluable information. In addition to helping me reconstruct my grandparents' itinerary, the dates and cancellations allowed me to narrow down when they had visited Nasielsk: between Brussels on August 2 and Berlin on August 6.

The postcards also enabled me to pinpoint numerous other locations seen in my grandfather's film. On the seventy-fourth anniversary of David and Liza's departure for Europe, I identified the Grand Place in Brussels and the Grand Hotel National in Lucerne, which still exists today. I e-mailed a still image of a scene in Holland to a Dutch friend in Amsterdam, and he wrote back, "My bet would be it's Volendam, still a touristic place, a small village on the seaboard not too far from A'dam." A few minutes later, he wrote again. "I searched for hotels in Volendam, and indeed there is an old-looking hotel with the name Hotel Spaander." In the film, Louis Malina and Essie Diamond sit on a bench beneath a sign that says "HOTEL SPAAN . . ." the final letters cut off. "Funny, no?" my friend concluded, "You now know precisely where your grandparents went, and you should probably go to this cute little town one day yourself!"

From the August 11 postcard, sent from the Jungfraujoch, Switzerland, I quickly determined that my grandparents had ridden the Lauterbrunnen–Kleine Scheiddegg small-gauge railroad, which passes the Staubbach Falls, the highest waterfall in Europe, and culminates at the Jungfrau. Here David shot the longest panorama of the film, with the exception of the street scene in Nasielsk, showing the glacier-covered ridge that leads from the Jungfrau in the west, across the saddle of the Jungfraujoch, to the Eiger on the eastern edge. Just three weeks earlier, a joint German-Austrian team had completed the first successful ascent of the north face of the Eiger, the last unclimbed peak in the Alps. It was a propaganda triumph for Nazi Germany. There is no evidence of it in the film. In the foreground stands the Hotel Jungfrau, which also still exists today.

An August 17 postcard sent from the Villa des Fleurs, Cannes, helped me to identify the scene in the film where my grandmother helps Rosie Malina with her sunbonnet. They were in Nice, France, standing in the Parc Municipal du Mont Boron. In the next shot, they view the red-roofed palaces of Monaco. Louis Malina waves his cigar to indicate admiration. Several months later, another friend sent me a matching photo from the Jardin Exotique of the same view today.

After August 18, 1938, however, when he writes from Menton, France, en route to Paris, David goes silent. One scene in the film shows Liza and the Malinas feeding pigeons in a Parisian park near the Louvre. I was unable to determine which park. Nor could I learn how long they stayed in

Paris or when they left France for England. The film's final shots show the voyage home.

ıııııııııııııııı

In January 2012, after I met Morry Chandler, I realized that I knew much more about his family history than I did about my own. My aunt Shirley and my cousin Bernice were the exact contemporaries of the Nasielskers I met. Morry, Leslie, Mikhail, Faiga, Andrzej, and Grace were all born between 1917 and 1924. Shirley and Bernice were both born in 1921. Yet I knew very few of my family's stories and nothing of the town where Shirley and Bernice had grown up, a world away from Nasielsk. What could be retraced of the childhood memories they had preserved?

"My mother's sisters were all kind of . . ." Shirley paused to reframe her answer. We were speaking on the phone in February 2012. "I mean, they had a good time together. I think maybe they had inside jokes and family jokes and gossiped about the family. But they weren't warm and loving, like my father's family. I mean, it was no big deal to throw my arms around my grandmother, my father's mother. But it would not be seemly to do with my mother's mother." My cousin Bernice, who has been lifelong friends with Shirley, agreed. "None of the sisters was really nice. I've really got to tell you, they were all *farbisene*. You know the Jewish word?" Shirley had used the same expression, *farbisene, farbisene punim*. Bitter, biting, or just plain mean.

Bernice shared one story that her mother had told her, which shows Chaim Saltzman, the patriarch of the family, father to these seven sisters, to be a strict, religious man, like so many Jewish men of his generation. "Before my mother got married," Bernice told me at the end of February 2012, "she had a friend who lived on the same block, on Throop Avenue, who ended up being a movie star. She was a silent star, Lillian Tashman. A beautiful blond woman. She was always in the movies with Kay Francis. And my mother always wanted to be a blonde. So Lillian Tashman and her brother poured peroxide on my mother's hair. And when my mother came home to Throop Avenue, Grandpa wouldn't let her in. He called her a *kurve*. You know what that is?"

"It is the Yiddish word for 'whore.'"

"Yeah," Bernice continued. "So she went back, and they had to put shoe polish on her hair. Because Grandpa wouldn't let her back in the house again until her hair was black." This story might easily have taken place at Sana Milchberg's house in Nasielsk, and not at 137 Throop Avenue, in Brooklyn.

Bernice, who often spent weekends at the Kurtz residence in Brooklyn visiting Shirley, also said that Liza had inherited this Old World stubbornness. "Your grandmother ruled the house. Without a doubt." Liza achieved this dominance, Bernice recalled, less through words than with silence. "She wasn't nasty to me at all, ever," she said. "I mean, she always, she *always* told me what to do. And if I did it, I was a good girl. If I didn't do it, she wouldn't talk to me."

Yet despite this controlling streak, or perversely, perhaps because of it, others were captivated by Liza Saltzman Kurtz. "My mother was crazy about her," Bernice told me. "My mother didn't love her for what she had financially. My mother talked about her even when they were on the boat coming over. She told me that nobody was as beautiful as Lena. Everybody on the boat couldn't stop looking at her. My mother was enthralled with her sister."

Hyman Meyer Kurtz, David's father, died in 1924, when Shirley was only three years old. But Shirley remembered David's mother, Leah Diamond Kurtz, who was born in Nasielsk around 1866 and who didn't speak any English. Shirley recalled her grandmother gave the children chewing gum. Because it had become that kind of search, I asked whether she remembered what kind of chewing gum her grandmother had brought her. "I think they only had one kind then. Wrigley's Spearmint."

About her Kurtz family relatives, Shirley recalled, "They all had a warm personality. But as they got older, they developed problems." She mentioned Uncle Willie, William Kurtz, David's brother, born in 1893 in New York, who "was in the millinery business, and business wasn't good." And Harry, the youngest Kurtz brother, born in 1903, who "was a gambler, and business wasn't good." David Kurtz was the only one who flourished financially, Shirley said, "and that's because he had my mother to push him. Did you ever hear the phrase 'Behind every successful man is a woman with nothing to wear'?"

Shirley recalled her father working all the time when she was a child. "My dad used to go to work six days a week. And he went to 'the Place,' that's what we called it. The Place. What was done at the Place, and where the Place was, we didn't know. But he went to the Place, and he came home with like three newspapers. You know, there were evening papers, the *Telegram*, the *World*."

Even though Bernice was frequently at the house, she could not recall hearing any stories about David's and Liza's childhoods. "Dave and Lena never spoke about when they were little. We used to sit around and talk a lot, nonsense. But they never talked about themselves when they were little." But she shared an anecdote about David Kurtz that offered a glimpse of him at the Place, where he worked. In the fall of 1939, Bernice, then age eighteen, was briefly employed by the David Kurtz Company, manufacturers of boys' blouses. "I hated it," she told me on the phone. "Because, in the car together, he was Uncle Dave. As soon as we got to the office, of course, it was Mr. Kurtz. And Mr. Kurtz used to send Bernice down to the Automat. There was an Automat on Thirty-Second Street and Broadway. They were at 1239 Broadway. And he would send me down every morning to the Automat to get him some cold cereal. And invariably, I'd bring back the wrong one. *Invariably.* And he yelled at me. So after I worked there four days, and he yelled at me four days, I walked out, and I went to an employment agency. I said to myself, 'I'm not going to work for him, he yells at me all the time.' And I got a job."

So, I asked, was David Kurtz a difficult man?

"He was a very nice guy!" Bernice said, laughing. "He really was. Your grandfather was a nice guy. It's just that I irritated him."

On one occasion, when I visited her at her home in the Bronx in the fall of 2012, Bernice shared a story about David Kurtz's business that must date from either 1937 or 1938. While David and Liza were traveling, Bernice said, the husband of another of Liza's sisters was left in charge of the company factory, which was then located in Elizabeth, New Jersey.

"A very bright man," Bernice said of Louis Karpf, husband to Fanny Saltzman. "And he was a real Lefty, you know?"

A member of the Bund? I asked.

"I don't think he was a Communist. I think he was a member of the union. And the story that I heard is, while Uncle Dave was away, Louis got the place unionized."

David fired Louis as soon as he returned.

Leslie Glodek recalled the circus coming to Nasielsk. Shirley recalled the circus coming to Brooklyn. "Oh, that was the most fun. Once a year the circus would come. And with the circus would come—I don't know what we would call it, a carnival? You know, lots of action. Little bumper cars and little Ferris wheels. It was such fun, and it was so close to our house."

The circus in Nasielsk had set up in Leslie's backyard. The Ringling Brothers Circus, Shirley recalled, set up on the grounds that later became Brooklyn College. "It was walking distance, so we were allowed to go, we didn't need anybody to take us. It was fun, because you met all your friends there, you took all these rides. And there was always music and lights. Boy," she said, poking fun at herself for her nostalgia, "those were the good old days."

Morry recalled sneaking away from the watchful eye of his family to eat a slice of ham. Shirley recalled a family joke about eating duck. "My mother once had a dinner party. Even though it was Prohibition, she had elegant dinner parties, none of which I attended, but I probably saw what was going on. And one year she had duck. And everybody who ate the duck got sick. Maybe the bullets were still in the duck. I don't remember, I just know that everybody got ptomaine poisoning. And my mother didn't eat the duck. So she was running up and down the stairs with the bedpans. I think it became a family joke: 'I'll have the duck.'"

If rebellion against his strict upbringing was the theme of Morry's childhood memories, family jokes were the theme for my aunt Shirley. "On Sunday, we'd always go to a movie and eat out. Either we'd go to the Roxie and go to the Brass Rail, or we'd go to Schrafft's," all popular, even legendary places in prewar Brooklyn. "We'd go to the local movies on Flatbush Avenue, and then, you know, on the way home, my father would say, 'Did you do your homework?' And of course none of us had done our homework. Eddie Cantor must have been on the radio from eight to nine on Sunday nights," she said, referring to the most popular radio comedian of the time, singer of the songs "Makin' Whoopee" and "If You Knew Susie." "So we said we'd saved it for after Eddie Cantor." That was the joke. Whenever someone asked, "Did you do your homework?" the answer was, "I'll do it after Eddie Cantor."

As with childhood memories of Nasielsk, it was difficult to date recollections of New York in the 1930s precisely. But occasionally a detail would make it possible. On December 28, 1932, Louis Malina took his daughter and Shirley to the opening of Radio City Music Hall. Shirley was eleven years old. "The Music Hall opened on a Tuesday night," she recalled. "He took us Wednesday. Wednesday was the first daytime performance. They had a whole half hour of opening and closing the curtains. The curtains were so new and such an unusual feat. They pulled them up, and they closed them down, and they pulled them sideways. They had the ushers marching in and marching out. Oh, yeah. There was a tap dance, and there was a ballet." According to the *New York Times*, the opening performance featured "an orchestra of 100, two choirs of 100 each, a ballet corps of 80, and several specialty dance groups," among them Martha Graham. Trumpeters in red satin heralded the arrival of the ushers, and two hundred spotlights illuminated the stage.

But remembering bygone Brooklyn also brought out some of the loneliness of Shirley's age, which Morry and Faiga and Leslie Glodek had expressed, as well. Shirley was happy to talk with me about these memories, but she was only telling me about them, not sharing them. "I'm getting your father and you and my father—I begin to get you mixed up," Shirley sighed after another of our long phone calls. "There are so many things that I want to tell Milt," my father and her brother. "And then I think, I can't tell Milt." Shirley's childhood, too, now exists solely in images and anecdotes that very few people can recall. Like Nasielsk before the war, the world of Brooklyn in the 1930s has also vanished. It is the victim only of time, not violence. Does this change how we feel about the surviving memories and artifacts?

On May 8, 1938, the *New York Times* carried the following notice: "Mr. and Mrs. David Kurtz of 944 East 23d St., Brooklyn, happily announce the bar mitzvah of their son, Milton Herbert, Saturday morning, May 14." Just two months before my grandparents sailed for Europe, my father was bar mitzvahed. I have a photo of him from this day. The image is dark, badly backlit by the temple's high windows. But I see my father clearly in the boyish face. He wears a long tallis around his shoulders and has the leather tefillin wrapped around his forearm. His expression is serious but happy. He seems proud to have achieved this milestone, or perhaps just relieved finally to put it behind him.

"Oh, they had a lovely bar mitzvah," Shirley said, recounting this second event that I could date precisely. "And I remember the gloves my mother wore, they were *so* gorgeous. I don't remember what I wore or what your father wore. But my mother had gloves in soft, soft, soft, light blue, and they were long, so they had buttons up the wrist. But I have no . . . I think it was at the East Midwood Jewish Center. It was in the synagogue. They had a very good caterer."

Shirley's recollection, like the references to people and places that Morry made, enabled me to uncover documentation that helped to spur more memories. In the New York Public Library, I found a commemorative book issued in April 1929, celebrating the dedication of the East Midwood Jewish Center on Ocean Avenue, of which David Kurtz was a founding member. His name does not appear in the volume, but the three Kurtz children, Jerry, Shirley, and Milton, are included in the list of "little builders." I discussed the list with Shirley, and she remembered many of the families, her neighbors. Like the Nasielskers, she recalled them by profession. "The people next door to us were named Lefcourts," she said when she saw their name. "Mr. Lefcourt had a hosiery business, and that was called Valcors. And then one of his sons—he had three sons, I think, and a daughter—started a wine business that was called Chateau Martin. And they advertised on the radio. That was a big deal. Next to the Kasses were the Loingers." I created a mental map of the neighborhood, another lost town, just as I had of Nasielsk.

In June 1938, one month before my grandparents' trip, Shirley graduated from high school. "I remember the graduation, because I think they held it at the Academy of Music in Brooklyn," she said. "And I remember the song," which she proceeded to sing for me, to a tune by Tchaikovsky:

Out of the sleeping hollow,
In the dusk of the dying day.
In the glen where the shadows play.
In the . . .

She could not remember the rest.

After graduation, Shirley left for summer camp, perhaps a few weeks before her parents embarked on the *Nieuw Amsterdam*.

As in David's correspondence, it was sometimes only in casual asides that the texture of an experience or a personality would flash into view. Once I had reconstructed a rough itinerary of my grandparents' 1938 trip, I commented on the beautiful hotels they had patronized. Shirley then remembered the name Jean Berke, the travel agent who had handled the arrangements for all her parents' trips. I was able to locate the offices of the Jean Berke Travel Agency on 518 Fifth Avenue. This triggered another recollection about how the trip had been planned. Liza had devised the itinerary in consultation with Louis Malina, Shirley remembered. "She would talk to Louis. My father and Rosie didn't know where they were going until they got there."

The events that in retrospect appear most significant were not the ones that had been preserved in memory. Shirley could not recall any conversation about her parents' upcoming European tour. "You know, they went away, and we went away," Shirley said, adding that her parents rarely discussed things with the children.

Not even when war broke out in 1939? I wondered.

"I don't remember anything about it. The next thing I remember, of course, was December seventh," the Japanese attack on Pearl Harbor. "But I don't remember discussing the war in Germany or Germany's progress. I remember the newspapers having a map of Europe, and it kept getting smaller and smaller. I do remember that they said all the people were gone. But that had to be years later."

When Shirley and I viewed the film of her parents' 1938 vacation at her summer home in Pittsfield in 2009, the footage contained lost moments of

her childhood, too. She watched with pleasure as her mother smiled ravishingly at the camera and her father pointed to the New York skyline, his tie and suit jacket blowing in the breeze. The very last shots in the film show the crowd on the pier greeting the *Queen Mary*'s arrival.

"Oh, there's Jerry," Shirley said, pointing to the TV screen seven or eight feet away. "Yeah, there's Jerry waving. And there I am."

Shirley, too, recognized herself in my grandfather's film. I would never have noticed her, and this moment, like so many of the scenes in Nasielsk, would have faded into generality. The final image in my grandfather's home movie was not an idle pan over the throng meeting the ship, as I had thought. Instead, it was a long shot of my uncle Jerry, age nineteen, in a gray suit, waving in the lower right of the image, and my aunt Shirley, age seventeen, wearing a white hat, standing three steps to the right.

We examined the image on the TV screen closely, and after a few minutes, we spied my father, age thirteen, in a tweed jacket, in the very bottom of the frame on the left. He had run ahead of his siblings and found a place at the edge of the pier, pushing forward to get to the front of the crowd.

It was September 5, 1938, nine thirty in the morning. Jerry, Shirley, and my father appear on-screen for a little more than a second, about the same length of time as Moszek Tuchendler, also age thirteen, who had leapt into the frame just one month earlier in Nasielsk.

⁕⁕⁕⁕⁕⁕⁕⁕⁕⁕⁕⁕⁕⁕

In 2009, when I first started nagging my family for information about my grandparents, for letters, postcards, photos, and memories, Shirley had mentioned a collection of snapshots from my grandparents' travels, including pictures of their trip to Poland. "They were of a summer camp," Shirley had recalled then. "There were a lot of children. And the assumption was that nobody survived." Shirley said she had donated these photos to the YIVO Institute, which at the time was located on Fifth Avenue, near where Liza lived. "It was probably after my mother died, or after my father died," she said. "If it was after my father died, I don't think I even told my mother." She believed the photos must have belonged to David. "People always say they have a box of snapshots. I don't know if my mother ever had a box of snapshots. She wasn't the kind of person who ever took a picture or cared about a picture."

In the years since Shirley had donated these snapshots, YIVO had moved downtown, where it had become part of a research consortium that formed the Center for Jewish History. I spent years going in and out of those doors, with their metal detectors and security guards, combing the archives for clues about Nasielsk and Berezne. The photographs were not listed in the online catalogue, and they were not to be found in the old card catalogue. I scoured the archive's donation registers from the 1950s, 1960s, 1970s, and 1980s, large, dust-covered ledgers with handwritten entries recording every item received. I ran my finger across the names. Perhaps the photos were lost, or perhaps Shirley misremembered. Perhaps these images were somewhere in storage, uncategorized or mislabeled, buried treasure for someone else to unearth in ten or twenty years. I could find no trace of them.

In November 2012, however, four years after beginning to rummage around in my parents' closet in Florida, looking for my grandfather's film, I came across a photo album I would swear I had never seen before. I

thought I had opened every box and looked at every pile of photos. But here was something new, it seemed, a photo album twelve by eighteen inches, covered in crumbling forest-green leather, with the name "Lena" embossed in the lower right corner. Liza Kurtz apparently cared a great deal about photographs.

The album contained page after page of images from the 1910s, 1920s, 1930s. Pictures of my grandmother and grandfather before they were married; images of Liza's father, my great-grandfather, Chaim Saltzman; baby pictures of Jerry, Shirley, and my father. Some of these photos had annotations on the back in my handwriting. One day in the 1990s, I must have asked Shirley or my father to identify these people. I had no recollection of this at all.

As I leafed further into the album in November 2012, I was stunned to discover travel photos of Europe—Italy, Austria, France, Switzerland—many neatly labeled on the back, this time in my grandmother's hand: "On deck of the Conte di Savoia," "On balcony of Hotel Excelsior overlooking Bay of Naples," "At the ruins of Pompeii." There were forty-two photos from David and Liza's first trip to Europe in 1937, including twelve images of my grandmother in her hometown, Berezne, Poland. Four images fit together to form a panorama of a large group of children at some kind of school or camp, as Shirley had recalled. Fifty-four young children, perhaps ages six to twelve, posing in orderly rows, sitting, kneeling, standing, with several adult supervisors in the back row. One woman, slightly to

the left of the group, wears what looks like a nurse's outfit. Beside her, visible in another photo, a girl in a white smock has a bandage encircling her jaw and the top of her head.

On the following page in Liza's album, I found portraits of my grandmother's Polish family. Liza stands with four women and two children. Two of the women bear an uncanny resemblance to my grandmother. The same women and children stand in another photo with two men, husbands, fathers. Unlike the shots in David's film, these images clearly show the family members my grandparents had traveled so far to visit. Yet the images of Berezne are the only ones from that trip not labeled. The names of her family may have seemed self-evident to Liza. But things that appear self-evident are always among the first to be lost.

The photographs from Berezne in 1937 have the same haunting quality as my grandfather's film of Nasielsk, made one year later. Dozens of people, mostly children, smile for the camera. Except for my grandmother, I cannot identify a single individual. Dana's genealogical research has uncovered the names of a few family members alive in Berezne in 1937. But her list is incomplete, and once again, we have no way to match the names with the faces.

One image in particular captivated my attention. Liza stands in the center of a group, her head inclined toward a woman who must be her aunt or her cousin. Their shoulders touch. My grandmother's arm is draped over one of the children, a boy of about eight. She is pressing him to her

with affection. She has an expression on her face that I had never seen in any photograph of her. In this one image, Liza lacks the determination and willfulness that make her face so attractive and haughty in other photos. Here, her features are attentive but calm. She is not full of assertive pride, but nevertheless she seems utterly proud, her kind smile suffused with love, a woman surrounded by her family.

When I showed this image to Shirley, she suddenly recalled something her mother had said: she had wanted to adopt one of these children. It was a statement difficult to reconcile with the woman Shirley and Bernice had described and the elderly woman I had known. There is no way to discover whether Liza meant her remark seriously. And whatever she may have said, it did not happen. Everyone in this photograph, with the exception of my grandmother, would die five years and one month later, on August 25, 1942. As far as Shirley can recall, Liza never spoke of her family in Poland again.

15

THE STORY OF THE FILM

DAVID KURTZ TRIPS the shutter. The spring-powered motor revolves, and a few feet of film are exposed. A woman emerges from a doorway beneath a sign that says SKLEP SPOŻYWCZY. She looks anxiously down the street. Then David lifts his finger and releases the lever. The camera's motor stops. Next scene. The film leaps forward in time and place.

My grandfather filmed three minutes of the 1,440 minutes in a day. Life continued all around what ended up on film, in all the moments that went unrecorded. But now only these three minutes remain. What is preserved, then, in this artifact? What is the story of this film?

When I dug my grandmother Liza's photo album from the recesses of my parents' closet in Florida in November 2012, I made what will likely be my last discovery about my grandparents' trip. In addition to decades of family photographs and snapshots of their first tour of Europe in 1937, my grandmother's photo album contained thirty-two images from their 1938 vacation, all of them unlabeled, with one exception. As soon as I saw these pictures, I knew exactly where most of them were taken. The sole labeled photograph would tell me when it was taken. From this, four years after I first viewed the film on VHS, I would finally learn the exact date of my grandparents' visit to Nasielsk.

The first image from the 1938 trip shows Liza, Rosie Malina, Essie Diamond, and Louis Malina reclining on deck chairs on board the Holland-America liner *Nieuw Amsterdam*. The photo must have been taken soon after they departed, and a day or two before David documented a similar scene with his home movie camera. In the photo, the travelers are dressed lightly, the women in short-sleeve summer dresses and Louis Malina in a sports jacket. In the film, they wear heavy coats with blankets draped over their legs, bundled up against the midocean chill. Other evidence in the photograph suggests that it was taken the first or second day of their voyage. Liza and Rosie have newspapers in their laps. Peering at the image with a magnifying glass, I could just make out the masthead and layout of the paper Rosie is holding: *The New York Times Magazine*, dated Sunday, July 24, 1938, the day after their departure. The cover of the *Times* magazine section that day, visible in the photo, featured a line drawing of Henry Ford with factories and smokestacks behind him. "Like huge fingers, they point to the skies as the ultimate goal of the machine age," the article rhapsodized. The great manufacturer and noted anti-Semite was celebrating his seventy-fifth birthday. "'Do your own work, don't indulge in controversies,'" Ford is quoted as saying. "'That's the way to get along.'"

In another photo from this trip, the travelers pose for the camera in the driveway of the Carlton Parc Hotel in Geneva, Switzerland. David has his arm slung over Rosie's shoulder in a friendly gesture. In his hand is a Magazine Ciné-Kodak 16mm home movie camera.

Almost half of the 1938 photos in Liza's album show the same place and day. These appear to have been staged tourist photos, the travelers in different groupings, sitting in a horse-drawn buggy in the square of an old town. Eight of the photos are nearly identical, Louis and David sitting together, both wearing expressions that suggest this stop was not their idea.

The women, by contrast, seem to be having a great time. In the five photos of them, they are smiling and relaxed. A young liveried coach driver sits on the bench. An older, more careworn man in a suit stands beside the carriage. He might be the salesman who has lured the tourists to have their picture taken in an old-time open droshke.

My grandmother annotated just one of these group photos. She wrote, "Warsaw, Poland. Aug. 5, 1938."

In January 2012, when we first viewed the film together, Morry Chandler said the footage of Nasielsk could not have been shot on *Shabes*, the Sabbath. August 5, 1938, was a Friday. From my grandfather's postcard, I knew they had been in Brussels the previous Tuesday, August 2, and would change trains in Berlin on Saturday, August 6. To travel from Brussels to Warsaw required a full day or an overnight train ride. The Americans would have arrived in Warsaw on Wednesday, August 3. Early the follow-ing morning, they hired a car to drive them the thirty-five miles north to their destination. My grandfather's three minutes of film show Nasielsk—and so Moszek Tuchendler, Avrum Kubel, his friend Rotstein, "Boortz" the dummy, the stonecutter Chaim Nusen Cwajghaft, "Chezkiah" the itinerant storyteller, Samuel and Faiga Tick, Miriam and Czarna Myrla, and perhaps Chaim Talmud, a Piekarek or a Jedwab boy, the boy Srebro, the boy Wilczynski, a Brzoza or two, and many others whose names we will never learn—on Thursday, August 4, 1938.

Knowing the exact date allows me to place the story of my grandfather's film in historical context, the events of that time that seem important to us today, but through which my grandparents and their friends floated so blithely during the six weeks of their vacation.

I don't know whether David bought a newspaper on this trip, to pass the many hours he would be spending on trains. But if he did, it would almost certainly have been the *New York Herald Tribune*'s Paris Edition, later known as the *International Herald Tribune*, an eight-page digest of the news from its parent newspaper in New York. If David had picked up a copy of this paper on July 31, 1938—the day he and my grandmother and the Malinas visited Volendam, the cute seaside town outside of Amster-dam, where David tested color film in his new camera for the first time—he would have read, "Hitler Decorates Henry Ford on Auto Maker's 75th Birthday." At a lavish banquet the previous day, sixteen hundred guests had witnessed the automaker receiving the Grand Cross of the Order of the German Eagle, a birthday present from Reichschancellor Adolf Hitler.

On August 1, as David, Liza, and their friends made their way to Brussels, the headlines were of the Russo-Japanese war: "200 Russian Soldiers Reported Killed as Japanese Forces Retake Disputed Border Territory in Four-Hour Battle." The following day, when David sent a postcard to Shirley from the Musée Antoine Wiertz in Brussels, another article appeared in the *Herald* about Hitler and Henry Ford: "Hitler Ready to Beat Ford Production." In a newly constructed factory, the largest in the world, German manufacturers were preparing to produce 1.5 million People's Cars, or *Volkswagen*, a year. A small item the same day reported, "Jews Expected to Lose State Jobs in Italy." "Jews will be allowed to remain in the nation, but not in the state, Roberto Farinacci, extremist exponent of anti-Semitic ideas, declared yesterday in the 'Regina Fascista.'"

The coverage of Central Europe was not all political. Page seven of the *Herald Tribune*'s August 2 edition, the travel section, featured articles extolling the charms of Germany for tourists. "Baden-Baden Is Starting Point of Excursions to Black Forest." "Frankfort-am-Main is not only one of the most interesting ancient towns of Germany, but also possesses modern institutions of which any city could be proud." Thousands of Americans were visiting Europe that summer, enjoying a nice glass of *Bier* in Frankfurt, Nuremberg, Berlin, Vienna, and elsewhere. The *Herald*'s "Americans in Europe" column listed dozens of prominent people lodging at Berlin's Hotel Adlon during those hot August weeks.

On August 3, as the five travelers left Brussels and rode the train across Germany to Warsaw, the *Herald Tribune* announced, "Lord Runciman Off for Task in Prague in 'Cheerful' Mood," referring to the British negotiator sent to the Czechoslovakian capital to negotiate a peaceful settlement of the Sudeten crisis on behalf of British prime minister Neville Chamberlain.

On August 4, 1938, the day David Kurtz visited the town in northern Poland where he was born, tension over the ethnic Germans living in the Sudetenland continued to escalate. "British Mediator to Seek Sudeten Crisis Settlement in Patience, Concessions." "'Let me make it clear from the start,'" Lord Runciman declared to the press, "'I have not asked for this job. I have never expressed a desire to take it on. But before I left London both the Sudeten Germans and the Czechoslovak government were in agreement that I would be welcome, and I must thank both for their welcome.'"

Beneath this article, a related item reported an alleged violation of German airspace by three Czechoslovakian planes. The article quoted the German newspaper *Der Angriff*, or "The Attack," edited by Propaganda Minister Josef Goebbels: "'The gentlemen at Prague had better understand that in the face of such provocations our patience can come to an end.'" A brief dispatch on the same page announced, "Hitler Bans Jewish Doctors." "BERLIN, Aug. 3.—All Jewish doctors' permits to practise will expire on September 30, according to a new law published in the official Law Gazette today."

By August 6, 1938, when David, Liza, and the Malinas stopped in Berlin on their way to Switzerland, the news had turned more hopeful. "PRAGUE, Aug. 5.—A significant step toward a satisfactory settlement of Czechoslovakia's dispute with its Sudeten German minority was taken today when Viscount Runciman, on his second day at work as British mediator, postponed direct negotiations between the two sides for at least two weeks."

And on August 7, 1938, when the *Herald Tribune* returned its focus to domestic American news, David might have read this perennial item: "Nation Is Facing Disaster, G.O.P. Group Declares." "CHICAGO, Aug. 6.—Findings of the Republican party's 'summer school,' first undertaking of its kind, were summed up today in an announcement of the Republican Program Committee which said it was convinced the present trends in legislation and governmental administration may plunge the nation into a disaster."

In retrospect, it seems almost incomprehensible that American Jews, visiting their birthplaces in Eastern Europe in 1937 or 1938, could have been oblivious to the death sentence hanging over their relatives. Incomprehensible, even horrifying, that they could sit in a Berlin restaurant and enjoy a refreshment between train connections. *After the German annexation of Austria*, I think, *just months before Kristallnacht*, the "Night of

Broken Glass," when 267 synagogues would be destroyed in Germany, Austria, and the by-then German-occupied Sudetenland. I want my grandparents to have understood the historical moment in which they lived. But historical context is obvious only in retrospect. The moments David and Liza Kurtz lived were not yet historical. For them, it wasn't the 1938 that we know today. It was Monday, August 1. Tuesday, August 2. When my grandparents visited Nasielsk, no one—not even the men who would be responsible for staging it—knew Kristallnacht would happen three months later. Czechoslovakia was in turmoil that summer. Yet British prime minister Neville Chamberlain—whom some clever Frenchmen referred to as "*J'aime* Berlin"—assured the world the conflict would be resolved peacefully. In August 1938, the Polish government viewed its neighbor to the west warily but with confidence. Mutual-defense alliances with France and England buttressed its security. Poland boasted the largest army and the finest cavalry in Europe. They did not know it was an army supremely prepared to fight World War I, not World War II.

Still, some people saw what was happening, what was about to happen. Had David Kurtz been reading the papers at home on August 4, the day he visited Nasielsk, he would have seen this report in the *New York Times*: "Nazi Honor to Ford Stirs Cantor's Ire." "Warning against a spread of anti-Semitism in this country, Eddie Cantor, comedian, bitterly denounced Henry Ford for accepting a decoration from the German government last Saturday." Speaking at New York's Hotel Astor at a luncheon sponsored by Hadassah, the Women's Zionist Organization, the popular radio personality and Kurtz family favorite said, "I question the Americanism of Mr. Ford for accepting a citation from the biggest gangster in the world." He continued, "We can smell the smoke in this country and we've got to start now to save ourselves. Don't think we are safe here, because we are not. And we can't fight Hitler just fifteen minutes a day when he is working twenty-four hours."

G.E.R. Gedye, the British journalist stationed in Vienna, had witnessed the Anschluss of Austria in March 1938, and he witnessed the German occupation of the Sudetenland that October, just two months after my grandparents returned to New York. Gedye saw. He knew. Six months after my grandparents' return, in February 1939, Gedye published an extraordinary book, *Fallen Bastions: The Central European Tragedy*, explaining quite clearly what he knew. "When I say one's Jewish friends spoke to one of their intention to commit suicide with no more emotion than they had formerly talked of making an hour's journey by train, I cannot expect to be believed," he wrote, describing the aftermath of the German annexation of Austria.

> *It is not your fault that you cannot believe me, because it is impossible for you to conceive of the diseased and degenerate mentality which lies behind the pathological Anti-Semitism of the Nazis. Therefore it is impossible for you to imagine what it means for one-sixth of the population of Vienna to be made pariahs over-night, deprived of all civil rights, including the right to retain property large or small, the right to be employed or to give employment, to exercise a profession, to enter restaurants, cafes, bathing beaches, baths or public parks . . . to be liable always to be turned overnight out of house and home, and at any hour of every day and every night to arrest without the pretence of a charge or hope of a definite sentence, however heavy—and with all this to find every country in the world selfishly closing its frontiers to you when, after being plundered of your last farthing, you seek to escape.*

If you did not understand the headlines in July or August 1938, it was not your fault, but rather "your very good fortune," Gedye concludes, bitterly. "I envy you, because you have not known any of these people as I have . . . And so you do not need to feel the horror which I cannot escape as I remember that in all this we acquiesce . . . But yesterday I was asked by an Englishman for the address of a cheap hotel in Vienna where he could spend his holidays—holidays in Austria, amidst all this! Him I did not envy." Perhaps referring to this Englishman, Gedye dedicates his book, "To somebody's summer holiday . . ."

Part of the story of my grandfather's film seems fairly straightforward. David and Liza Kurtz went to Europe because they had become prosperous

Americans and were proud of it. They were enjoying their newfound success. A trip to Europe was what prosperous, cultured people did, and so they went.

Until I found the photo of Liza with her family in Berezne, I had never thought my grandparents felt a close connection to those who remained in Poland. They went to Europe, I believed, not to reconnect with their roots but to prove how far from their roots they had come. When I imagined them projecting the bright color footage of Nasielsk for their children and their friends, I heard them utter the only phrases that had come down to me in the family. *This is that town in Poland where the folks come from. Dirty, primitive, crowded, hot. A button factory.*

Viewing the trip with the hindsight of history, I had wanted my grandparents to be prophets, to have adopted a Polish child or brought a young Jewish emigrant from Nasielsk to safety in the United States. Instead, I learned to accept a more painful, more commonplace truth. My grandparents were of their time. Perhaps they still felt an attachment to the distant towns of their birth. They may even have felt love for the people they visited there. But only in retrospect could David and Liza have known that their attachment, their love, was not enough; only afterward, when it was too late, could they have understood that these people, some of them family, had desperately needed to be saved.

To tell the story of my grandparents' summer vacation, I must acknowledge that they did not save lives. At the same time, however, David and Liza Kurtz did save something of the life they witnessed. David Kurtz's home movie was not particularly important or distinguished in 1938, when he shot it. Only in retrospect did his footage acquire its historical significance. To tell their story, therefore, I must also embrace and honor this great irony: my grandparents, these proud Americans who had come so far from their origins, will be remembered because they captured on film three minutes of the one day they spent as tourists in the town where David was born, in Poland.

||||||||||||||||||||

After years of studying my grandfather's film, I watch it yet again, for what seems like the thousandth time. I still don't know what David Kurtz was thinking, or what he felt when he met these people and experienced these moments. But perhaps now, using the evidence of the film, I can at least tell the story of what happened, restoring the original sequence of his shots, and in this way constructing a tentative narrative of the day he spent in Nasielsk.

Because David's camera used self-contained film magazines, he was able to switch spontaneously between black-and-white and color reels. In the black-and-white reel, the scene jumps from Volendam, Holland, to a street scene in Nasielsk, an indistinct crowd of people accompanying Louis Malina down the sidewalk. In the color reel, the scene jumps from the Grand Place in Brussels to a crowded street in Nasielsk. The camera pans a little to the right, and the front grille of an automobile is briefly visible.

Which scene is first? I believe it is the color scene. David had shot a minute or so of black-and-white film on the ship crossing the Atlantic and a few scenes upon arriving in Holland. But he swapped film magazines when they got to Volendam, in order to capture the colorful natives, arrayed for the tourists in traditional costumes. He then traveled to Brussels, and from there to Warsaw, with the color film magazine still in the camera. On arriving in Nasielsk, the first thing he did was record the scene, catching a momentary glimpse of the car they had hired. Bystanders mill around, and the visitors mill about, too. Word of their arrival has not yet reached the people who would guide them during their visit.

The next scene in both the color and the black-and-white reels shows Louis sitting in a restaurant—perhaps the one owned by Leib Owsianka, perhaps the Bergazyn, Borstein, Kazyński, or Segal place. Both scenes are very dark, and it is difficult to pick out individual faces to determine whether the same people are present in both shots. From the internal evidence of these shots alone, it is impossible to tell which comes first, or even whether they are contiguous.

The third scene in both reels is a street panorama showing the same line of façades. In the black-and-white panorama, children are leaping and waving in front of the camera, Moszek Tuchendler among them. In the background, Liza and Rosie laugh at the commotion. In the color panorama, the street is also crowded with people, but they stand more calmly, observing my grandfather with interest, but not leaping or waving.

There are other important details to notice before I can decide the order of these shots. Both Morry and Zdzisław Suwiński had been certain that the row of buildings seen in the film was located on the north side of the *rynek*, the marketplace. However, on my visit to Nasielsk in May 2012, I was unable to align the visible details in the film with what had remained of the houses on the *rynek*. Examining the film more closely when I returned from Europe, I noticed that the flowers, clearly visible in the interior scene in the restaurant, are also visible from outside, during the panorama. The curtains, too, so pronounced in the interior shots, are visible through the window in the external street scenes. In fact, in the black-and-white panorama, the curtains have blown over the top of the wooden frame and hang suspended from the open window. In the interior shots in the black-and-white reel, I could see the curtains billowing above the window. In the color segment, the curtains are gathered neatly. I also noticed the shadows thrown by the second-story balconies in both the black-and-white and the color panoramas. In the black-and-white, the angle is noticeably sharper than in the color, indicating that the sun was lower. Therefore, it seems probable that the color panorama was shot later, perhaps by as much as an hour.

This is what I believe took place. The travelers arrived in Nasielsk by car from Warsaw on the morning of August 4, 1938. David Kurtz filmed the first moments with the color film still in his camera. While the visitors were waiting to meet the people who would accompany them, David changed film reels for some reason, switching from color to black-and-white. He then filmed the disorderly procession down the street to the restaurant, where the first thing their hosts would want to do is give the Americans something to eat or drink. David filmed a few moments of this gathering, while the crowd of people in the restaurant argued over who would have the honor of escorting the visitors. Louis sat with his hat still on, smoked a cigar, and waited for things around him to settle down.

In the meantime, word spread that Americans had arrived. People started to gather on the street outside. After some time in the restaurant, David stepped outside to see what was happening, and Liza and Rosie came with him. David paced ten or fifteen feet from the buildings, to get some perspective and take a panorama, while the women remained by the doorway just outside the restaurant. Kids from all over Nasielsk had run to the scene, congregating on the street. When David began to film, they erupted in excitement, pushing and shoving in order to get into the frame. While Liza and Rosie laughed in the background, David tried to film the buildings. He wanted to show where he was and what it was like. Instead, he captured who was there. Thirteen-year-old Moszek Tuchendler seized his opportunity. While David panned left, he made his way through the crowd. When David panned back to the right, there he was, in front, just a step or two from my grandfather, an exultant smile on his round, childish face.

With the black-and-white reel still in his camera, David then documented a few brief encounters along the way to the synagogue. Louis walks past a wooden fence accompanied by a beautiful woman in an elegant patterned dress, wearing what may be a pearl necklace. Behind her is a man in a cloth cap who had been sitting with Louis in the restaurant. The shot lasts about two and a half seconds. The next shot shows Louis and Essie standing in front of a brick wall with an open window above their heads. A cluster of rooftops is visible behind them. Several well-dressed women now accompany the Americans, in addition to the ubiquitous children. For a few frames, the church spire becomes visible in the background.

The following scenes show the people of Nasielsk entering and then exiting the synagogue. The Americans had arrived, had tea and a snack, met the people who were expecting them, and had walked through town toward the synagogue. Now the formal visit began. Perhaps there was a special service. Perhaps the guests had donated money and were being shown what their contributions had made possible. I don't know how long they were in the synagogue, or what transpired while they were there. But they sat beneath the murals painted by Fishl Perelmuter, facing the altar decorated with a beautiful representation of Abraham and his two wives, flanked by twelve images symbolizing the tribes of Israel, including the Leviathan, with his tail in his mouth, Joseph and his brothers, Jonah and the whale, a deer and a lion and a biblical phrase enjoining the worshippers to follow God. Whatever happened, it was a major event, since the procession exiting the synagogue includes at least seventy people, including Avrum Kubel, most likely Simcha Rotstein, Samuel Tick, several of the well-dressed women, and the man in the cloth cap who accompanied Louis in an earlier scene. Czarna and Miriam Myrla may have been in the service, as well, because they are standing in front of the synagogue, watching David Kurtz film the scene. Leslie Glodek's nephews might be waving from the steps, competing with Jankiel Piekarek or Leibl Jedwab for my grandfather's attention.

When the event at the synagogue concluded, I believe, the visitors returned to the restaurant for refreshment. After the meal, David once again swapped the magazines in his camera, reinserting the color reel and stuffing the black-and-white reel into his pocket or into a pouch in the camera case. It would remain there until August 7 or 8, when David ran across a street in Lucerne, Switzerland, to film his wife and friends standing in the entrance of the Grand Hotel National, capturing also the hotel doorman, the buttons on his uniform glinting in the sunlight. David then filmed in the restaurant, this time with the color magazine. Louis enjoys an after-lunch cigar. The people of Nasielsk have gotten used to the fact that visitors are in town. Seven or eight spectators, including Samuel Tick and Faiga Milchberg, stand guard outside at the window, ready to report when the Americans are on the move again. David films the scene, catching a young girl bouncing by the window, while outside, the man behind Samuel Tick playfully grabs his friend's hat and waves it in the air above his head.

Once more, David exits the restaurant to document where he is. He takes another panorama of the street he had filmed earlier in the day, this time using color film. Different people are out now, and they are more relaxed about the presence of these strangers. David must have spoken to them, organized them to stand for a group portrait. He films the same panorama from approximately the same location, but he lingers now on the faces in front of him. They look into his camera silently. Even the children, though visibly excited to be captured on film, do not shout. Instead, they scoot sideways, trying to stay in the frame as the lens sweeps to the right. The boy Srebro is among them, as are two other boys who appear in Faiga Tick's class photo, but whose names I do not know. Avrum Kubel stands with his friend Rotstein in the background. Samuel Tick stands with his hands on his hips and speaks something to his future wife, who joins him a few seconds after the filming begins. Chaim Nusen Cwajghaft, the *matzevah kritzer*, stands in a doorway, one hand inserted in his coat. "Boortz," the laborer who could remember the names of all the boys and the names of their fathers and grandfathers, stands on the left side of the crowd. Behind him, a woman emerges from the doorway of a grocery store, beneath a sign that probably bears the store owner's name. The shadow on the balcony above her head cuts at perhaps a fifty-degree angle. It is around eleven in the morning.

David's second panorama lasts forty seconds. There is still a lot of movement, as the children fidget and the adults point and speak among themselves. But not all the movement is focused on David Kurtz's camera. In the background, a few people stroll down the sidewalk, unaware of the activity around them. A worker speaks to someone as he passes. An old woman wearing a red kerchief comes down the steps onto the street.

When he has completed his panorama, David does not walk away. Instead, he steps forward. He films a few individuals in small groups. Chaim Nusen Cwajghaft standing in a doorway with the itinerant storyteller known as Chezkiah, and a young town bully, who shoves a girl with blond braids.

The following forty seconds of film show brief street scenes, most of them in front of the same buildings. Several people recur in these shots, the girl with the blond braids, a workman with an open-collar work shirt. It is later in the day. Life has returned to normal, and David films whoever happens to be on the street, including those kids who are following him around. Essie walks across the *rynek*. Louis stands by a brick wall, beneath the open window, again talking with a bearded man, accompanied by well-dressed women. Next to Essie is an adolescent girl in a green dress, who reminded Leslie Glodek of his niece. A group of girls, one holding a young child, stands in front of a doorway, very likely outside a home where Louis and the others are visiting. The afternoon is taken up with meetings. The Americans make the rounds of important people, or of the people important to them.

The next shot shows the interior of a home. A woman with her back to us fixes her hair. It may be the home of the Kubel family, the *maydlekh*, the girls, and their brother Avrum, whom they treated like a diamond, discussing arrangements for the emigration of their sister, Sura, with their cousins from America. Or it may be a different family, another story that I know nothing about.

Finally, the Americans exit a house, perhaps the same house, but probably not. None of the Kubel sisters is visible, if they were there at all. The visitors descend the steps. Liza emerges first, her arm held by one of the well-dressed women who previously accompanied the travelers on the street. Rosie appears next, followed by Louis, who escorts a rabbi or elder. They might have discussed aid for the poor people in town. The old man might have given the Americans his blessing. All I know is what I see. Essie stands in the doorway and waves at my grandfather as children push rudely past to get outside. A young housewife shakes a pointed finger at the crowd, clearing the way for her guests to leave, undisturbed by the local kids.

The Americans climb back into their hired car and return to their hotel. The following day, they have their picture taken in an open carriage in the old city of Warsaw.

·········||||||||||||||·········

Some people in Nasielsk knew of the impending visit. They had taken particular care in dressing for the occasion and had perhaps arranged a special service at the synagogue. I was unable to learn the names of these people, who are prominent in the film and yet were not recognized by the Nasielskers I met. Memory and documentation overlap obliquely, if at all. In at least some of the shots, David must have meant to capture individual people and particular events. But the identities of the people important to him or to Louis and Essie have not been preserved, even though the film was made, in a sense, to preserve them.

But the camera saw more than he did. Regardless of who David intended to film, the camera captured all the others who were standing around. Even when David packed the frame, arranging a scene with selected people, the film registered background details that he probably never noticed: flowers in the restaurant window; a woman beneath a grocery store sign; a mezuzah in the doorframe of the young housewife's

home. Instead of preserving David's memories, which are completely unknown to me, his film preserved these accidental details. These are what I
inherited from him with this film, and in lieu of his memories, these are
what I attempted to understand.

During my visit to Nasielsk, Zdzisław Suwiński had introduced me to
the librarian of the Nasielsk municipal library, Stanisław Tyc. Stanisław
had recently completed his doctoral dissertation, which analyzed the economic role Nasielsk had played in northern Poland between the eighteenth and the early twentieth centuries. An appendix in his book listed
the names and addresses of the business owners that he had been able to
identify. He gave me a copy of this list, and later, when I ran my finger
down the columns, I found many familiar names: Srul Skalka, "Sales of
Yard Goods and Readymade Garments"; Jankiel Szulim Glodek, "Grocery
Store"; Lejzor Gutman, "Sales of Meat"; Hendla Milchenberg, "Grocery
Store"; Szajndel Kubel, "Sales of Kitchen Utensils."

Leib Owsianka was also on the list, "Cafeteria and Accommodation,"
located on Ulica Warszawska 6. If David Kurtz's film shows the Owsianka
restaurant, both from inside and from outside, and the Owsianka restaurant was on Warsaw Street number 6, I reasoned, then the film must show
Warsaw Street, and not the north side of the *rynek*. When I visited Nasielsk,
I had accepted the identification provided by Morry and Zdzisław, and I
had not paid much attention to Warsaw Street. But now, it seemed as if this
must have been where David was standing when he slipped away from the
table and accidentally captured Morry and his friends on the street outside.

Grace Pahl lived next door to the Owsiankas. When I spoke with her, I
asked whether there had been a grocery store down the street from where
she lived.

"Wait a minute," she said, thinking. "Leib Owsianka? *Es iz gevayn* a
grocery store? Yeah! And you know what their name was? Wait—you have
to give me a few minutes. In the house where we lived upstairs, there was
a grocery store. They were downstairs from us. Because I could go down
from the steps, from my house and go in straight to their store. But for the
life of me, I couldn't remember their name. Would you believe it? And we
lived all my life there."

I showed Grace an enlargement of the grocery store sign from the film, digitally enhanced to bring out the obscure letters at the bottom, which probably stated the name of the owner. But she was not able to read it, and she could not remember the name.

On Stanisław Tyc's list of businesses, however, there were numerous candidates. Srul Wajnberg had a grocery on Warszawska 4. Chaskiel Borensztejn had a grocery and tobacco store on Warszawska 7. Jankiel Bergazyn had a restaurant with liquor on Warszawska 8. Czeslaw Glogowski had a grocery and tobacco shop on Warszawska 10. And Jankiel Glodek's grocery was at Warszawska 16. When I checked with Leslie Glodek, he confirmed his family's address on the list, Warsaw Street 16, although he said that earlier the house had been number 18. House numbers may have been discontinuous, and stores may have come and gone. Just from the list of businesses, it was impossible to say who was next door to whom. But at least the list offered concrete options.

Armed with this new theory of where David Kurtz had been standing when he tripped the shutter of his movie camera, I returned to Nasielsk in June 2013, in order to stand on Warsaw Street and again compare the images in the film with the doors, windows, drainpipes, balconies, and rooflines that still existed.

A year after my first visit, Zdzisław Suwiński and I once more stepped out of his home to explore the town of Nasielsk. But this time, I knew the house at the edge of his driveway had belonged to Wilczynski the blacksmith. I knew that Sana Milchberg and his family had lived across the street, and that the new hotel-casino a few steps closer to town occupied the building that had once been the Piekarek flour mill. We walked down Warsaw Street toward the center of town. A few blocks closer to our goal, we passed the former site of the Filar button works, now occupied by an apartment building. In back of the apartment, I found the brick remnants of the ruined factory. People had attached laundry lines to the crumbling structure. A little patio set was nestled in a corner, a romantic picnic spot amid the ancient, overgrown walls.

Instead of turning right toward the *rynek*, Zdzisław and I kept going in the direction of the triangle where the electrical transformer had once been. We turned onto the little bend in Warsaw Street, where it intersects with Kilińskiskiego, just south of the *rynek*. Farther down to the left, on a street called Szkolna, or School Street, stood the public elementary school, the only building in Nasielsk bombed during the German invasion.

A few steps farther and we faced what had once been Leslie Glodek's house. A single-story building with a wooden door and two small windows occupied one side of the site. Sliding metal gates prevented access to the grounds behind the house. Where Morry had learned to ride a bicycle, and where Grace's sister had torn her skirt, now there were parking garages. On the other side of the lot was a new building, home to a pizzeria and an investment brokerage called Your Money.

The transformer tower was still there, now painted brick red, though the paint was peeling off the walls. A boy sat in front of the tower selling strawberries where the Germans had once parked their vehicles. Across the street, the Harvest Cinema stood where the Nasielsk theater had once been, above the firehouse. What had been the Machnikowska pharmacy was now a hair salon called Chameleon, and Grace Pahl's home and Horowitz's bookstore were now the site of a bakery. Behind the house, where Irving Novetsky had lived, a wall with built-in sheds separated the lot from the grounds where the Perlmutter flour mill had operated. The flour mill was still there, a ruin, like the button factory, although it still had its roof. The windows were mostly broken, and the walls were overgrown with vines. A nearby construction company apparently used the grounds to park equipment, and there were piles of sand almost as high as the two-story buildings. The Owsianka restaurant was still a restaurant, or had become a restaurant again, selling deli meats and sandwiches.

I stood on the triangle across the street from the façades for almost an hour, flipping my depth perception between the photographs in my hand and the buildings across the street. Warsaw Street is Nasielsk's main street, its downtown shopping street. The upper stories of these houses had remained more or less untouched, but the ground floors, which are most clearly visible in my grandfather's film, had been entirely renovated. Not a single doorway, window, or drainpipe had been left in place. As hard as I tried, it was impossible to reconcile the past and the present. Too much had changed. Farther down the block, there were many unrenovated buildings. Across the triangle and to the left, a small street parallel to Warsaw Street, which was called the Russisher Gas, and where Nasielsk's Jewish residents would promenade, where girls would secretly meet their boyfriends at night, where ice cream shops and refreshment stands were once in abundance, had remained almost entirely intact, though now quite run-down. But the few buildings on Warsaw Street in front of which I thought my grandfather had stood were gone.

I had hoped finally to learn the exact location of the film, not only to satisfy my curiosity but also to help identify the woman standing in the doorway beneath the grocery store sign. That sign remained the final outstanding piece of evidence, key to the mystery, both of the film's location and the grocery store owner.

When I returned home, I reported my failure to Lindsay Zarwell at the United States Holocaust Memorial Museum. She offered to take the restored film back to the laboratory at Colorlab. Perhaps with their equipment, she suggested, we could obtain a clearer print of the grocery store sign and finally decipher the name.

Two months later, on August 14, 2013, Lindsay wrote back to me. Russ Suniewick and Tommy Aschenbach had examined the frames under a microscope. They were unable to decipher the letters. The image, they said, was "unintelligible as photographed." The camera had been moving too quickly for the film to register the information. The name at the bottom of the grocery store sign marked the edge of the physical medium, the limit of what it could see.

<hr />

Three minutes of film impose a harsh limit on the visible traces of Jewish Nasielsk. Just these faces, these buildings, these moments. The physical properties of film itself set another limit, two lines of text legible on a sign, but not three. The destruction of the town and the time that has passed enforce further ruthless limits on what we can now learn from my grandfather's film. And yet this single artifact, this slender fact, offered a unique opening onto the life of this town. Researching my grandfather's film led me to a handful of people who still remembered what Jewish Nasielsk had been like. Their memories surpassed the film's boundaries, though memory, too, imposes harsh boundaries of its own. Still, despite all these limitations, new information, new connections continued to emerge.

In December 2012, one year after Marcy Rosen had recognized her grandfather in my grandfather's home movie, the Holocaust Museum released a short video about the film and our meeting to its list of subscribers. A few days later, I received word from Lindsay Zarwell that a woman named Sophia from Montreal had seen the video and was asking about her relatives from Nasielsk, the Perelmuter family. Her mother, Dyna Perelmuter, had had a brother named Fishl, who died during the war, she said.

I contacted her immediately. Fishl Perelmuter? I asked. The photographer?

Yes, Sophia said, he had been a photographer. But he did not live in Nasielsk. Her family was from Bodzanów, about thirty-five miles west of Nasielsk.

I asked Morry, and of course he straightened it out. There were two Fishls, he said. "Fishl from Bodzanów used to come to visit Fishl from Nasielsk. I remember seeing him. If I was at that time maybe ten, eleven, he was already maybe eighteen, twenty." Fishl from Bodzanów was the nephew of Fishl the photographer and artist from Nasielsk. This meant that Dyna Perelmuter, the mother of Sophia in Montreal, was Fishl the Lame's niece.

Morry remembered the patriarch of the family, Mendel Perelmuter, who belonged to the same generation as Morry's grandfather, Srul Skalka. Mendel Perelmuter, he said, was another Orthodox, pious Jew. "As kids, we were all afraid of Mendel Perelmuter. He was very strict. We would run around in the hallway and throw rocks, and he had a cane and would threaten us." Mendel had at least four children: Fishl the photographer; Chaim David, who owned a machine repair shop in Nasielsk; Josef, who moved to Bodzanów and was the father of Sophia's mother, Dyna, and of the other Fishl; and a daughter, Sura.

Sura Perelmuter had married Avrum Landau, who owned a knitting factory in Warsaw. Sura Perelmuter Landau—sister of Fishl the photographer;

Morry's mother's dearest friend—was Sophia in Montreal's great-aunt. It was to Sura Perelmuter Landau and her family that Morry brought a sack of food in the week following the surrender of Warsaw in September 1939; it was Sura's apartment whose broken, empty windows Morry saw from the streetcar, when he rode around and around the ghetto in April 1943, the truth of his family's fate sinking in.

Sura Perelmuter Landau appears in a photograph that Sophia's mother had saved. She is a slightly plump, round-faced woman standing next to her son, Felix. Seated in front of them is her husband, Avrum Landau, and Sura's father, Mendel Perelmuter, his cane clamped firmly between his knees. In the back row, next to Felix, are Chaya and Fishl Perelmuter of Nasielsk, the photographer and his wife.

The photo must have been taken in 1929 or 1930, Morry said, because soon afterward, when he was six or seven, both Mendel Perelmuter and Chaya Perelmuter, Fishl's wife, died.

"She was always sickly," Morry said of Chaya, "and one day, a little bus came into the backyard of ours, and they carried her out, and I never saw her again."

Morry also recalled when Mendel Perelmuter died. "I just remembered Avrum Landau coming in to conduct services for the shiva," he said on the phone in February 2013, after I had sent him the photo I received from Sophia. "I see him like I look at him now. A little, nicely trimmed beard. He was an elegant man."

But seeing Sura Landau in the photograph affected him most. "That picture—I couldn't stop looking at it!" he said. "Because I see my mother talking to Sura. I had such a feeling of closeness for them. You know? This is— Ah. Really—so I want to tell Sophia how important that was for me. It's sort of—a little bit of a healing process."

A month later, after Morry had spoken on the phone with Sophia, he said to me, "I knew them well. And I never, ever thought of talking to somebody that was related to them."

That same month, in March 2013, I received a small package in the mail from a family in Warsaw. The previous December, a Polish television news program had aired a brief segment about this survivor from Nasielsk who had seen himself as a boy in an American's home movie. A few weeks later, I received a message on Facebook. "Hello, sorry to bother you," it began. "My great grandmother took care and helped Moritz Chendler here in Poland during the 2nd war. That's why we have got few photos of him and probably his family. Thank you for help and Merry Christmas." Soon afterward, I received scans of seven photographs, accompanied by a note that recounted a story passed down for three generations in the family of Helena Jagodzińska, the woman who had employed Morry from the fall of 1941 until the summer of 1942, and whose nephew, Stanisław

Pachnik, had stolen the birth certificate that was the basis of Morry's survival.

"I must have given her several pictures," Morry said when I sent him the digital scans of the photos. "Because those pictures I carried with me from the ghetto, and I felt it was not safe for me to carry it. So the night when I left, I left everything that might be compromising for me, I left it with her. I said, 'If I ever come back . . .' She said, 'I'll give it back to you.'"

Morry had remained in touch with Stanisław Pachnik until his death in 2009. "He was a very fine soul," Morry recalled. "He was really a saintly person." He had planned to visit Helena in May 1986, but the trip was canceled because of the accident at the Chernobyl nuclear power plant. The following year, Helena died. But here was another form of preservation, stories passed down through the generations, simplified, perhaps distorted in the process, but saved and now suddenly confirmed, reconnected.

In April 2013, I flew to Florida once more and handed Morry the original photographs that Helena Jagodzińska's family had saved all these years and had sent to me to give back to him, belatedly fulfilling Helena's promise.

During that same visit to Florida, Morry invited me for a festive brunch with Keva Richman and Jerry Goldsmith, who is Faith Ohlstein's brother and the son of Sura Kubel. Two men born in Nasielsk, and the son and a grandson of Nasielskers, joined by Dorris Chandler, Evelyn and Steve Rosen, and Jerry's wife, Nikki. We ate bagels and lox and whitefish and capers, cakes and cookies, and drank coffee, orange juice, and quite a bit of champagne. For several hours, we sat around the table talking about the paths that had led us to be there together, about the connections that made us feel like family.

Jerry Goldsmith had brought the letters and photographs that Sura Kubel's sisters in Nasielsk had sent to her in Brooklyn after her emigration. The letters began soon after Sura's departure in November 1938 and they ended in the spring of 1942, when the German authorities prepared for the destruction of the Warsaw Ghetto. Most of the letters were in Yiddish, which Jerry had never had translated. But one card in Polish had an attached translation, typewritten on the stationery of the International Red Cross. Dated September 17, 1940, it stated, "Our entire family is alive and well. We all live in Warsaw, on Muranowska 1/41 Epelbaum. Please try to secure emigration permit for us."

Elia Epelbaum or Applebaum was Morry's cousin, the chief clothing designer for the Skalka store. Elia had married the daughter of Chaim Fine, the Radzyner Rebbe. The Fine family also had another daughter, who had married and lived in Warsaw. It was through them that Elia Applebaum, his family, and Morry's parents, grandparents, aunts, and uncles had found apartments in Warsaw after the deportation from Nasielsk in December 1939. Looking at the card, we realized that Sura Kubel's sisters, along with their brother Avrum and the eldest sister's husband, Josef Lederman, had also lived in the Applebaums' apartment in the Warsaw Ghetto. Jerry's aunts and uncles had most likely been with Morry's family when all of them were deported to Treblinka sometime after July 22, 1942.

The letters the Kubel family had sent to Sura gave wrenching insight into this time. Sitting at the table, Morry translated some of them for Jerry. The prewar letters, written in beautiful, almost calligraphic Hebrew script, were the kind of chatty letters sisters write to each other. "Dear Sura, why do you write so little? I was hoping for a longer letter," one sister scolds on December 21, 1938. "Shandele had a problem with the landlord. Thank God they made peace. Everything is all right, but it didn't go that easily and Uncle Mendel had to come twice." The sisters mention other families: Blaszke, Pludwinski, Diamant. There was even a reference to Keva's family, the Rychermans, noting the preparations for their departure for America in August 1939.

The letters from a year later are quite different. They are no longer in Hebrew characters; the sisters write Yiddish and Polish in Roman script, to allow the German censors to read. Morry translated another letter with an illegible date, probably from late 1940 or early 1941. "We have it good here," Sura's youngest sister, Leiba, writes. "That's for the censors," Morry commented. He continued reading out loud. "Cousin Jalires grew big." Morry suspected a code that had come into use among the Jews of the Warsaw Ghetto when writing to relatives in the United States. "Jalires," he thought, stood for Germans. *The Germans have grown big.* "They won't let *Lekhem* come visit us." *Lekhem*, Morry explained, is the Hebrew word for bread.

"Same thing my grandmother wrote," Keva said. His grandparents, Szmuel Usher Schwartzberg and his wife, were also in the Warsaw Ghetto at the time, also writing desperate coded letters to their family in America.

Morry continued reading. "We are waiting for Ezra's brother." He stopped again and explained. "You know, *ezra* in Hebrew means 'help.' So this is . . ."

Morry didn't finish his sentence. "Yeah," he said after a moment, and he sighed. The letter was a cry for help.

We sat at the table in silence until Keva asked, "Do you have any idea how many times I've thought about why was I so lucky?"

We were all indescribably lucky. Keva's family had left Poland in the last week before the war. Jerry's mother had escaped in November 1938, with Louis Malina's assistance. Morry had survived the war in Poland, less than one hundred miles from Nasielsk and just thirty miles from Treblinka. And David Kurtz's parents had left Nasielsk in the 1880s to seek a better life in America.

Our brunch that day felt like the culmination of the journey that had begun four years earlier, when I had discovered David Kurtz's film, a journey that took a dramatic, unexpected turn two and a half years later, when I first spoke on the phone with Morry Chandler. Each of us at the table that day had contributed to the others' family histories. But it was my grandfather's film that had led to this symbolic reunion, bringing together the remnants of families and these previously isolated fragments of Nasielsk's Jewish history.

Among the final fragments was a photo preserved in an album that Jerry Goldsmith and his sister, Faith Ohlstein, had inherited from their mother, Sura Kubel. The photo shows a group of thirty-eight men and children, clustered around a table. "This was all from the Agudas," Morry said as soon as he saw it, recognizing members of the religious political party. The image was a slightly different version of a photo he already had, taken in the workshop behind his family's store. On the wall, fashion drawings show the styles of the day in men's suits, coats, and leisure wear. Elia Applebaum, the designer, sits behind Morry's brother, Avrum, and next to Moishe Rotstein, who had helped Morry and Avrum escape to Białystok in 1939. Moishe's brother, Simcha, stands on the left, next to Jerry's uncle Avrum Kubel, both of whom Morry had identified in my grandfather's film.

The version of this photo in Sura Kubel's album must have been taken a few moments before or after the one that Morry had been given years ago by another survivor. In Morry's copy, there is a man standing on the far right of the photo, his face cut off by the edge of the picture. His features are blurry and indistinct. But Morry felt certain the man was his father, Szaja Tuchendler. It was the only picture of his father that Morry had.

In Sura's version, however, Morry's father is clearly visible. He has a full beard and is wearing a high, brimless black hat that today we call a cantor's hat or *chazzan's kepel*. His face is full, and he seems to be in the middle of calling to someone on the opposite side of the photograph. Morry's older brother, Avrum, is also plainly visible in Sura's version of the photo. And among the children clustered in the right foreground, Morry identified his cousins Selig and Brucha, children of his uncle Jankiel Skalka. Standing between them, Morry recognized his younger brother, David. David Tuchendler is about eight years old in the photo and appears a little startled by the photographer. But he strongly resembles Morry and their brother Avrum, with the same brow and mouth that Marcy had recognized as enduring family traits. The picture in Sura Kubel's album is the only surviving photograph of him. This was the first time Morry had seen his younger brother's face since escaping from the Warsaw Ghetto.

One other person appears only in Sura Kubel's version of this photograph, taken in the back of Srul Skalka's store. Moszek Tuchendler sits in the center of the group, his hands on his knees, wearing the black double-breasted jacket and short-brimmed cap of a student at the *szkoła rzemieślnicza*, the trade school in Warsaw where he was studying that spring. He is almost a year older than in David Kurtz's film, and his face is not quite as round. He looks at the camera directly, seemingly unaware of the others around him, and probably ignoring whatever his father is saying.

This photograph is the closest thing Morry has to a family portrait. On the back, someone had written the date, April 15, 1939. We had gathered at Morry's home for brunch on April 14, one day shy of seventy-four years later.

|||||||||||||||||||||

Call it chance, or luck, fate, a miracle, *bashert*. Everything had to have occurred when and how it did for this particular story to unfold.

My grandfather had to have brought a movie camera on his trip to Europe in 1938. The film he shot had to land in our cabinet in Roslyn. It had to survive the dismantling of our household; it had to endure the humidity of Florida for more than sixteen years, moldering in a cardboard box, inside an aluminum can.

I found the film within the final months of its viability. I donated it to the United States Holocaust Memorial Museum in Washington, D.C., and not to another repository, where it might have been equally well cared for but not made accessible to the general public. Leslie Swift at the Holocaust Museum had to commit the resources necessary to preserve it. The film had to become viewable at the Holocaust Museum's website. There had to be websites. There had to be Google.

Maurice Chandler had to survive the war. The chances against this were so great, every other coincidence is meaningless by comparison. Yet he did survive. And in a feat of memory surpassing anything he demonstrated for me, twenty-one-year-old Moszek Tuchendler, alone in Warsaw in 1945, remembered an address he had once seen printed on a luggage tag while he snooped among the belongings of a distant relative who had visited his family in Nasielsk before the war. "I photographed that label in my mind and I remembered it verbatim and I copied it and I wrote a letter," Morry recounted in 1993. "Nashville, Tennessee, with all the *n*'s and the *s*'s and the *e*'s and everything." For ten years, from 1935 to 1945, Morry retained the image in his mind of this luggage tag. After the war, with no family and no prospects for the future, he wrote to this distant relative in Nashville. In those ten years, however, the man had died. The letter sat at the post office, undeliverable. But the postman knew the family, and one day he mentioned the letter to the man's nephew. The nephew had never heard of this young Polish survivor. He did not know how they were related. But he decided to help, setting in motion the process that would eventually bring Moszek Tuchendler to the United States.

Morry had to begin a new life in America. He had to meet and marry his wife, have children and grandchildren who grew up to care about his history and the history of his lost family. He had to revisit Nasielsk in the summer of 2011. His daughter, Evelyn, had to shoot video of the visit, give this video to her daughter, Marcy Rosen, who gave it to her assistant, Jeff Widen, who was fascinated by Marcy's grandfather's story. Jeff had to be curious enough to search for additional information about the town. He had to be skillful enough to find it. Perhaps as astonishing as any other coincidence, Marcy had to recognize her grandfather in the fleeting image on-screen, despite never having seen a photo of him as a boy. She had to recognize her grandfather seventy-three years younger than she knew him.

Maurice Chandler, at age eighty-seven, was in good health. He carried the tragedy of his family and the memory of his own survival with dignity and clarity. He was willing to share his memories with me, to sit for hours and hours, to let his recollection expand into this destroyed town, into his most personal and painful loss.

He recognized Kubel, Rotstein, Cwajghaft; he remembered Piekarek,

Jagoda, Brzoza; he was friends with Leslie Glodek, Grace Pahl, and Keva Richman. From these connections others grew, until I was in touch with ten Nasielskers, the eight survivors and two immigrants, and the list of people identified in my grandfather's film increased to twenty and beyond. Then it turned out that Morry's family had been close to the historian Zdzisław Suwiński's family; that Louis Malina had known the Kubel family; that Keva Richman was related to Mikhail Koprak. And perhaps the eeriest coincidence: Maurice Chandler's grandfather, Skalka, was known as Kurtz. When Morry walked around Nasielsk, people identified him as "Kurtz's grandson," which also describes me. It is probably meaningless. It is just one of those things.

If my grandparents had been in Nasielsk the next day or the day before; if my grandfather had tripped the shutter even one second sooner or later, then different people would have been in the film, different expressions and different details. It would have been a different film. It all could have happened ever so slightly differently, and so perhaps never have happened at all.

In retrospect, it seems so obvious: *Of course we met!* Tuchendler, Skalka, Kubel, Rycherman, Eisenberg, Glodek, Koprak, Yagoda, Skornik, Milchberg, Tick, Lubieniecki, Wlosko, Suwiński, Tomasiński, Jagodzińska, Malina, Kurtz, and Diamond—Di-*AH*-mant. We shake hands. Yet if this were the novel I had intended to write, these coincidences and connections would have felt contrived.

In September 2012, I spent a week in San Francisco visiting my aunt Shirley and my sister, Dana. One night at Dana's apartment, eating pizza from our favorite place up the street, we sorted through Dana's archive of genealogy documents: David Kurtz's bankbook from 1909; David and Liza's marriage certificate from 1912, almost exactly one hundred years earlier; memoranda of the David Kurtz Company. Among the many official documents were copious notes that Dana had gathered during her years of research. One sheet of yellow legal paper, dated June 24, 1998, said the following: "Maurice Chandler (Maury) 72y. Knows Diamond home. 6 weeks after invasion all into shul—magnificent, like a fortress, frescoes. Became a stable. Perlmutter. 3 days in shul then onto train. Maury, parents, grand-parents to Warsaw Ghetto. Escaped, posed as Catholic."

In 1998, thirteen years before Marcy Rosen recognized her grand-father in our grandfather's film, Dana had attended a Jewish genealogy conference in Los Angeles. There she had met a woman hired by Maurice Chandler to search for his family. The two had shared notes, but as with so many contacts in the genealogy world, since there were no apparent fam-ily connections, the conversation went no further. The film was still stew-ing in its can in the closet. It wasn't yet part of the story.

||||||||||||||||||||

Nasielsk was not an important town, unless you lived there. It was just a town. But of all the Polish towns destroyed in the Holocaust, Nasielsk is among the very few that exist in moving pictures, among just a handful preserved in color.

In June 2013, my grandfather's tourist film of Nasielsk became part of the new Jewish Pavilion at the Auschwitz Museum and Memorial in Po-land, located on the site of the former concentration camp. The film runs on a loop in the permanent exhibit documenting prewar Jewish life. A million people a year visit this memorial, which has come to symbolize the Holocaust as a whole. There, for these visitors, the people in my grand-father's film represent the millions of others in thousands of small Jewish towns across Eastern Europe of whom no record remains.

For the survivors from Nasielsk, however, for Morry, Susan, Leslie, Mikhail, Andrzej, Faiga, and Grace, the film represents something else entirely.

"You people have restored some pictures," Morry said to Jerry, Keva, and me as we sat around his table in Florida in April 2013. "We brought them back, sort of, to whatever you call it—some life; memory. But they're gone forever."

He sat in silence. A few moments later he said, "I'm at a certain age al-ready. And after all these years, I never stopped missing my mother. Never. It never goes away."

*   *   *

"I feel like screaming almost," Faiga Tick had said when I visited her in December 2012 at her home in Toronto. "Why didn't everybody run away? My mother told me to go. 'What will they do to me?' she said. And that was the last I saw her. I had such a beautiful two brothers. They cannot be nicer. And perfect, perfect people. And nothing—nothing is left of them. I used to cry nights. And almost—be mad, why I live. I shouldn't live, too. And I live so long! You know? Nobody lives that long."

Faiga stood up and rested her hand on the edge of the dining room table. She bobbed up and down on her toes.

"All those things happened to me," she said. "And I always wanted to remember. I talk a lot and told those stories probably many times. But I didn't write down anything. I thought my memory will last forever after."

My grandfather's film preserves the few moments of Nasielsk's life that survive. We must be grateful for this precious record, which adds nuance to the broad strokes of history, preserving the identities of individuals and a few slender facts about their lives.

For the people who still remember Nasielsk as a living town, however, these three minutes of film reach beyond the frame to the world of their childhoods, their friends and their families. For them, the film, so important to posterity, is just a film. It passes down a fragmentary glimpse into this world. But the reality, the life and loss of their community, is inexpressible. For the survivors, Nasielsk is preserved only in mourning, in the immediacy of their grief.

"There is a word in Hebrew that the rabbis use when someone important to the community dies," Morry Chandler told his family, Keva Richman, Jerry Goldsmith, and me as we sat around his table in Florida. "*Khaval al d'ovdim veloy mishtak' khim,*" he recited. Then he translated, "*Woe unto us for the people we have lost, never to be found.* That's what our loss is. Never to be found."

EPILOGUE

IN NOVEMBER 2012, in Florida for Thanksgiving at my mother's, I visited Saul Gershkowitz again at his home in Delray Beach. Three years had passed since I'd shown him David Kurtz's film. Saul was more tentative in his movements, but he and his wife, Irma, still lived on their own. On the earlier visit, I'd mistakenly believed my grandfather's film documented Berezne, Liza's birthplace, where Saul had grown up. It had been a disappointing interview, though an important one. Now I brought Saul the Kutz family film from the archives of Beit Hatfutsot in Tel Aviv.

"This has got to be outside of Berezne," he said as the film played. "The countryside. Yeah. My father, before he died, he was working in a place like this."

An American family visited Polish relatives. Children crowded the scene. They climbed onto a horse-drawn cart for a ride in the country. The cameraman showed buildings with thatched roofs and the tall wooden tripods used to bring up water from a well. He filmed the synagogue.

"That's the shul," Saul said. "I remember, yeah. Well—I was thirteen years old. But that's the inside of the shul."

This is the shul in Berezne?

"Oh, yeah. Well . . . that's for the Torahs," Saul said, indicating the carved wooden doors. "This is a little familiar to me."

I let the film play in slow motion.

"He looked like the rabbi right there, you know?" A long-faced man in a black coat and hat with a flowing white beard read aloud at a lectern. "Gedaltsche," Saul said, naming the rabbi who had officiated at his bar mitzvah, seventy-three years earlier. "Yeah, I think so."

Later that night, after a family dinner, Dana and I sat in front of the computer, working together as we had since I'd first uncovered David Kurtz's home movie. Dana found the Berezne *Yizkor* book, which is available online. On page 27, there was a photograph of Berezne's famous rabbi, Gedaltsche or Gedalia. It was the man in the film.

NOTES

1. ARTIFACTS

4 "Rains Delay Sailing of Nieuw Amsterdam": *New York Times*, July 24, 1938, p. 25. "Ocean Travelers," *New York Times*, July 23, 1938, p. 14. "E.C. Rick to Sail on European Tour," *Washington Post*, July 10, 1938, p. S5. See also: "Chicagoans Go on Cruise with Swedish Prince," *Chicago Daily Tribune*, July 24, 1938, p. E6.

10 In the film's final six seconds: The film can be viewed online: http://efilms.ushmm .org/film_player?movieID=11&movieSig=EF-NS_011_OeFM&movieSpeed=16.

10 "Hapless Jews were set to work . . .": "Spring Cleaning," *Time*, March 28, 1938. www .time.com/time/magazine/article/0,9171,759369,00.html.

10 "From my window . . .": G.E.R. Gedye, *Fallen Bastions: The Central European Tragedy* (London: Victor Gollansz, 1939), p. 307.

19 There were 1,993 passengers aboard the *Queen Mary*: "Three Liners Bring 2,576 from Europe," *New York Times*, September 5, 1938, p. 29.

19 Among them were the movie star: "Ocean Travelers," *New York Times*, September 5, 1938, p. 12. "Raymond Massey Here," *New York Times*, September 6, 1938, p. 17.

19 "Asked what he thought about the threats . . .": "British Diplomat Here," *New York Times*, September 6, 1938, p. 12.

19 The *Chicago Daily Tribune* reported: "Pound Slumps as British Pour Gold into U.S.," *Chicago Daily Tribune*, September 7, 1938, p. 27.

19 "a flight of capital . . .": "War Fears Induce Near-Record Flow of Gold to U.S.," *Christian Science Monitor*, September 6, 1938, p. 16.

20 In September 1939, Berezne: *The Encyclopedia of Jewish Life Before and During the Holocaust*, edited by Shmuel Spector and Geoffrey Wigoder (New York: NYU Press, 2001), p. 115.

2. PRESERVATION

24 "So he would come each summer . . .": Daniel Mendelsohn, *The Lost: A Search for Six of Six Million* (New York: HarperCollins, 2006), p. 14.

27 Unlike the Ephrussi family: Edmund de Waal, *The Hare with Amber Eyes: A Hidden Inheritance* (New York: Farrar, Straus and Giroux, 2010).

29 "expressive of the conservatism . . .": "Establishing New Club House Centre in Upper Fifth Avenue District," *New York Times*, January 17, 1915, p. XX3.

31 "Thousands of people today . . .": *Vogue*, vol. 89, no. 3 (February 1, 1937), p. 95.

34 "One . . . Two . . . Three . . .": *New York Times*, January 26, 1936, p. SM21. Display ad. 95.

3. INHERITANCE

43 The book I purchased, *The Yellow Star*: Gerhard Schoenberner, *The Yellow Star: The Persecution of the Jews in Europe, 1933–1945*, trans. by Susan Sweet (New York: Bantam Books, 1969). Recently reissued by Fordham University Press (New York, 2004). See also Dan Porat, *The Boy: A Holocaust Story* (New York: Hill and Wang, 2010).

45 "What fueled my curiosity . . .": Theo Richmond, *Konin: A Quest* (New York: Pantheon Books, 1995), p. xx.

45 "a way of keeping them alive": Richmond, *Konin*, p. xxi.

4. PEOPLE AND FACES

49 In September 1941, German military command: The United States Holocaust Memorial Museum's *Encyclopedia of Camps and Ghettos 1933–1945*, volume II: *Ghettos in German-Occupied Eastern Europe*, Geoffrey P. Megargee, general editor, Martin Dean, Volume Editor (Bloomington, IN: Indiana University Press, 2012), Part B, p. 1333. Hereafter *ECG*.

49 S.S.-Obersturmbannführer Günther Karl Pütz: A photo of Pütz is available in one of the many online forums devoted to the war and run by amateur historians: http://forum.axishistory.com/viewtopic.php?f=38&t=82335&hilit=putz.

49 "[The Germans] ordered all inhabitants to leave . . .": Tzilla Kitron and Sonja Schabtay, *Wanderungen: Erinnerungen an das Überleben in den Jahren 1942–1945*, translated from the Hebrew into German by Nurith Yaron (Hanau: Salisberg-Verlag, 1994), p. 9. My translation from German.

49 "He took me so he can send me back . . .": Gershkowitz, Saul. Interview 13219. Visual History Archive. USC Shoah Foundation. 2009. Web. 5 May 2009. http://lib guides.usc.edu/vha.

51 "The Jewish population of Rovno . . .": Dmitry [Nikolaevich] Medvedev, *Stout Hearts: This Happened Near Rovno*, translated by David Skvirsky (Moscow: Foreign Languages Publishing House, 1948), pp. 43–44.

56 Nasielsk's entire Jewish population: *The Encyclopedia of Jewish Life Before and During the Holocaust*, ed. Spector and Wigoder, p. 876. Available online: www.jew

ishvirtuallibrary.org/jsource/judaica/ejud_0002_0014_0_14549.html. See also *Encyclopedia Judaica*, second edition, volume 14, edited by Fred Skolnik (New York: Thompson Gale, 2007), p. 787. The *Encyclopedia Judaica* entry expresses uncertainty over the date of the deportation, suggesting an earlier *Aktion* in September or October. I have found no evidence of this.

60 "Susan Weiss remembered . . .": *ECG*, volume II, part A, pp. 648–649.

61 "In order for me to survive . . .": Weiss, Susan. Interview 48207. Visual History Archive. USC Shoah Foundation. 2010. Web. 9 December 2010. http://libguides.usc.edu/vha.

61 At the New York Public Library: *Nashelsk—A Name A City A People Eternal!,* edited by Benjamin M. Bendat and Abe Korn (privately printed, dated March 12, 1953).

62 Searching online, I discovered: www.nasielsk.pl/en/index.php?option=com_content&view=article&id=598&Itemid=104.

63 Aleksander Kurtz, I learned: Stefan Kieniewicz, "Aleksander Kurtz," *Polska Słownik Biograficzny* (Warsaw: Polish Academy of Sciences, 1935–present), volume 16, pp. 283–285. Google translation, edited.

64 "We are all busy rushing our little flags . . .": A. A. Davidson, "Bolsheviki in Panic Abandon Their Guns," *New York Times*, August 20, 1920, p. 2.

64 "1939–1945: the city and municipality of Nasielsk are . . .": www.nasielsk.pl/en/index.php?option=com_content&view=article&id=598&Itemid=104.

64 "Another Blood Ritual Accusation Exploded": *Jewish Telegraphic Agency*, June 13, 1923: http://archive.jta.org/article/1923/06/13/2755270/another-ritual-blood-accusation-exploded.

64 "Poles Beat Jews": *Washington Post*, June 18, 1937, p. 2.

65 "Its constructor was Simche Weiss . . .": Tomasz Kawski, "Nasielsk." http://www.sztetl.org.pl/en/article/nasielsk/5,history/?action=view&page=1. Kawski is quoting from *Encyklopedyi Powszechnej* from 1865, volume 18, p. 227. See also *Mitteilungen zur jüdischen Volkskunde*, Volumes 6–7, Herausgegeben von M. Grunwald, Heft XI (Hamburg, 1903), p. 12.

65 This famous wooden synagogue: See Janusz Szczepański, *Dzieje Społeczności Żydowskiej Powiatów Pułtusk i Maków Mazowiecki* (Warszawa: Pułtuskie Towarzystwo Społeczno-Kulturalne Towarzystwo Miłośników Makowa Mazowieckiego, 1993), pp. 165–179.

65 A drawing and a scale model: Maria and Kazimierz Piechotka, *Heaven's Gates: Wooden Synagogues in the Territories of the Former Polish-Lithuanian Commonwealth* (Warsaw: Krupski I S-Ka, N.D.). For Moshe Verbin's wooden models, see http://www.zchor.org/verbin/verbin.htm.

65 "In the period between 1830 and . . .": Szczepański, *Dzieje Społeczności Żydowskiej*, p. 168.

65 "The biggest share in the expenses . . .": Szczepański, *Dzieje Społeczności Żydowskiej*, p. 170.

65 The film called out: For home movies as a source of historical information, see *Mining the Home Movie: Excavations in Histories and Memories*, edited by Karen L.

Ishizuka and Patricia R. Zimmerman (Berkeley: University of California Press, 2008). For "microhistory," see Nicolas Mariot and Claire Zalc, *Face à la persécution, 991 Juifs dans la guerre* (Paris: Jacob, 2010), and Michael Loebenstein and Siegfried Mattl, "Missratene Figuren: Der 'Anschluss' 1938 im 'ephemeren' Film," *Zeitgeschichte*, volume 35, no. 1 (2008), pp. 35–46.

65 In the archives of the YIVO Institute in New York: For the history of the American Jewish Joint Distribution Committee, see Yehuda Bauer, *My Brother's Keeper: A History of the American Joint Distribution Committee 1929–1939* (Philadelphia: The Jewish Publication Society of America, 1974).

66 "The Jewish population numbers . . .": "Social Institutions in Nashelsk Affiliated with American Joint Distribution Committee" [undated], YIVO, RG 335.7, Box 8, Folder 284, "Nasielsk."

66 "The Kassa writes to us . . .": Letter to Dr. Bernhard Kahn, Paris, from I. Giterman, dated March 11, 1938, YIVO, RG 335.7, Box 8, File 284, "Nasielsk." The author of the memo uses the German spelling, *Landsleut*. I prefer the Yiddish, *landslayt*.

66 "Last year the sum of . . .": *Jewish Daily Forward*, July 7, 1938, YIVO, RG 335.7, Box 8, Folder 284, "Nasielsk."

67 These sums are the equivalent: Historical value conversions from www.measuring worth.com/uscompare/relativevalue.php.

67 "is subsidized by a wealthy Landsmann . . .": "Report on a visit to Nasielsk on August 7th, 1938, by Mr. D. Towbin," received October 18, 1938, YIVO, RG 335.7, Box 8, File 284, "Nasielsk." Original in American Jewish Joint Distribution Committee Archives, NY_AR3344_14_01053. Hereafter, JDC.

67 On October 14, 1938: Memorandum by I. Giterman, dated October 14, 1938, YIVO, RG 335.7, Box 8, Folder 284, "Nasielsk."

68 The final two documents I found at YIVO: YIVO, RG 335.7, Box 30, Folder 751, "Landsmanshaft-Nasielsk."

68 In the photo archives of the United States Holocaust Memorial Museum: The Holocaust Museum's catalogue data for Faiga Tick: http://digitalassets.ushmm.org /photoarchives/detail.aspx?id=1146886&search=Faiga+Tick&index=6.

69 Digging into the databases hosted by JewishGen.org: http://data.jewishgen.org/jri -pl/1929/1929top819.htm. Registration required.

69 "a nice little community, mostly Jews": Rubin, Gloria. Interview 15693. Visual History Archive. USC Shoah Foundation. 2010. Web. 21 March 2010. http://libguides .usc.edu/vha.

69 Czarna Ida Zimmer's maiden name: Zimmer, Czarna Ida. Interview 2445. Visual History Archive. USC Shoah Foundation. 2010. Web. 21 March 2010. http://lib guides.usc.edu/vha. The other Nasielsk interviews are Cohen, Saul, Interview 3164; Pietruszka, Joseph, Interview 2076; Weiss, Susan, Interview 48207.

70 In this way, a year and a half: At the end of December 2010, I presented my research at YIVO in conjunction with the exhibit *16mm Postcards: Home Movies of American Jewish Visitors to 1930s Poland*, cocurated by YIVO and the Yeshiva University Museum. www.cjh.org/16mmPostcards/.

5. A SEA OF GHOSTS

76 He comes up with a page at the Museum of Family History: www.museumoffamily history.com/pfh.nasielsk_perlmutter.htm.

76 He finds a photo of the German Wehrmacht: www.1939.pl/galerie/miejsca/.

6. IT'S GOOD TO BE BACK

97 "With great difficulties, and after experiencing attacks . . .": Sarah Achicam-Fine, "With My Father the Rabbi Chaim Fine in Russia," *Sefer Radzyn* (*Radzyn Memorial Book*), Editorial Board: Y. Avi-Ara, B. Borshtein, M. Gotesdiener, L. Vinderboim, Y. Lust, A. Lazar, A. Danilak (Toronto), M. Lichtenshtein (New York) (Tel Aviv, 1957), p. 284. Translation edited by Yitzchak Zigelman. Available online through the Yizkor Book Project: www.jewishgen.org/yizkor/radzyn/rad281.html.

98 Morry's family belonged to: Glenn Davis Dynner, "Vurke Hasidic Dynasty," *The YIVO Encyclopedia of Jews in Eastern Europe*, November 2010, 19 January 2014: www.yivoencyclopedia.org/article.aspx/Vurke_Hasidic_Dynasty.

102 After Morry mentioned the name: Statue of Liberty–Ellis Island Foundation, Inc. David Schmerlak: www.ellisisland.org/search/matchMore.asp?LNM=SCHMERLAK &PLNM=SCHMERLAK&kind=exact&offset=0&dwpdone=1.

103 Szmerlak's yeshiva in Nasielsk: The school is mentioned in numerous documents held in the American Joint Distribution Committee Archives. "List of Educational Establishments for Children Associated with the 'Chojrew' School Organization in Warsaw" (NY_AR3344_Poland_08_00544), p. 3. The "Cheder Jasoda Hatora" is number 135 of 208 schools on the list. The school also appears in "Report on Jewish Schools in Poland" from 1935 (NY_AR3344_Poland_08_00018), p. 36. This document lists a monthly income of 958 zloty against monthly expenses of 1,780 zloty, resulting in a monthly deficit of 814 zloty, about $154. In 1939, a report on repairs conducted on school facilities between January 1936 and January 1939 shows 67,087 zloty ($12,679) spent on the school in Nasielsk, repairs which incurred a deficit of 10,605 zloty ($2,004). "Statement of Costs of Buildings, Repairs & Equipment Carried Out in Schools from January 1st 1936 till January 1st 1939," (NY_AR3344_Poland_08_00145), p. 16.

7. LISTS

118 "NASIELSKI COMMITTEE IN WARSAW . . .": YIVO, RG 335.7, Box 30, Folder 751, "Nasielsk." Original in JDC Archive: NY_AR45-54_00166_00768.

120 One of the photos donated by Faiga Tick: United States Holocaust Memorial Museum. Photograph number 62933. http://digitalassets.ushmm.org/photoarchives /detail.aspx?id=1146885&search=faiga+tick&index=4.

122 Yad Vashem, the primary Holocaust memorial: Yad Vashem, Central Database of Shoah Victims' Names. http://db.yadvashem.org/names/search.html?language=en.

122 A complementary database at the United States Holocaust Memorial Museum:

Holocaust Survivor and Victims Database. http://www.ushmm.org/remember/the
-holocaust-survivors-and-victims-resource-center/holocaust-survivors-and-vic
tims-database.

123 "Chaim Cwajgaft": Yad Vashem, Testimony ID: 550144. Sara Cwajghaft, Testimony
ID: 8799024. Moti Cwajghaft, Testimony ID: 8799025.

123 "Chaim Cwajghaft (or Tzvighaft)": Yad Vashem, Testimony ID: 1408869. Abrahm
(Avraham Isser) Cwajghaft, Testimony ID: 779273. Mrs. Cwajghaft, Testimony ID:
1517743.

123 A photo that I would later find: Ghetto Fighters' House Museum Archives, "Members of the Local Branch of the He-Chaluts Movement in Nasielsk," catalogue
number 4712. http://iis.infocenters.co.il/gfh/multimedia/GFH/0000053843/00000
53843_1_web.jpg.

123 "Jehoszua Tuchhendler": Yad Vashem, Testimony ID: 670677.

124 In January, when we sat together in Florida: Among the documents included in the
Nasielsk file of the JDC's Landsmanshaftn Department in the YIVO archives are
the minutes of the 1939 convention. Item 10 names the new directors of the Joint's
kassa for 1939. Among them is Jehoshua Tuchendler, Morry's father. YIVO, RG
335.7, Box 30, Folder 751, "Nasielsk."

125 "Avraham Kubel": Yad Vashem, Testimony ID: 8734659. Elazar Kubel, Testimony
ID: 8734660. Chana Kubel, Testimony ID: 3901395.

125 "Moshe Cyrlak": Yad Vashem, Testimony ID: 660976.

125 "Zylbersztajn, Mair, Zelig": Yad Vashem, Testimony ID: 583925.

126 In the Ellis Island database: Lejba Zylbersztajn. http://www.ellisisland.org/search
/passRecord.asp?MID=19580913370897439968&LNM=ZYLBERSZTEJN&PLNM
=ZYLBERSZTEJN&last_kind=0&TOWN=null&SHIP=null&RF=6&pID=60003
2030150.

128 Faiwel Lejbowicz: Yad Vashem, Testimony ID: 3988644. David Lejbowicz, Testimony ID: 3988654. Szlomo Lejbowicz, Testimony ID: 3988655. Schulem Lejbowicz, Testimony ID: 3988657. Szoszke Lejbowicz, Testimony ID: 3988656. Szeindla
Waligura Lejbowicz, Testimony ID: 3988643.

128 Chaim Huberman: Yad Vashem, Testimony ID: 327708. Fajge Kubel Huberman,
Yad Vashem, Testimony ID: 1619011.

128 Hersz Jagoda: Warszawa Ghetto Death Card Index at the Jewish Historical Institute, Warsaw, card number 16677. List accessed at JewishGen.org: http://data.jew
ishgen.org/wconnect/wc.dll?jg~jgsys~jripllat2.

129 Aron Figa: Yad Vashem, Testimony ID: 668349. Mrs. Figa, Yad Vashem, Testimony
ID: 1603317.

129 Fishel Pairlmuter: Yad Vashem, Testimony ID: 905664. "Fisl Perlmuter." Yad
Vashem, Testimony ID: 907168. Bila Pairlmuter, Yad Vashem, Testimony ID:
8934308. Liba Perelmuter, Yad Vashem, Testimony ID: 1013377. Zeda Pairlmuter,
Yad Vashem, Testimony ID: 8934306.

130 Surprisingly, in the Ellis Island database: www.ellisisland.org/search/shipManifest
.asp?MID=19580913370897439968&LNM=PERLMUTTER&PLNM=PERLMUT

TER&last_kind=0&RF=525&pID=100056050415&lookup=100056050415&show=
%5C%5C192%2E168%2E100%2E11%5Cimages%5CT715%2D3045%5CT715
%2D30450208%2ETIF&origFN=%5C%5C192%2E168%2E100%2E11%5CIM
AGES%5CT715%2D3045%5CT715%2D30450207%2ETIF.

131 In the Pułtusk *Yizkor* or memorial book: Pultusk Sefer Zicaron, edited by "Irgun
Yitzei Pultusk" in Israel (Tel-Aviv: Irgun yots'e Pułṭusḳ be-Yiśra'el, 1971), p. 61.
http://yizkor.nypl.org/index.php?id=2548.

132 "The Button-Manufacturing Industry in Poland": *Gazeta Handlowa*, number 64
(March 18, 1930), p. 4. http://ebuw.uw.edu.pl/dlibra/plain-content?id=12866. Google
translation, edited.

133 "80 years old, funeral organized by . . .": Polish Center for Holocaust Research,
Warsaw Ghetto Database. www.getto.pl/index.php?mod=view_record&rid=0212199
6215657000175&tid=osoby. See also Regina Domańska, *Pawiak: Więzienie Gestapo, Kronika 1939–1944* (Warszawa: Ksiażka I Wiedza, 1978).

136 Chaja, born in 1913: Chaya Kubel, Yad Vashem, Testimony ID: 2034046. Mindl
Kubel, Yad Vashem, Testimony ID: 1624879. Abrahm Kubel, Yad Vashem, Testi-
mony ID: 512372. Lieba Kubel, Yad Vashem, Testimony ID: 449292 and Testimony
ID: 449295. Rachel Kubel, Yad Vashem, Testimony ID: 1615237.

140 According to a notice in the *New York Times*: "Business Notes," *New York Times*,
October 29, 1924, p. 34.

140 "Included in the long list of rentals . . .": "Apartment Leasing Holds Active Level:
Louis Malina Leases Duplex of 12 Rooms and Terrace in Central Park West," *New
York Times*, August 11, 1937, p. 37.

142 "My family was from Nasielsk . . .": Gail Simone, Aaron Lopresti, Matt Ryan, *Wonder Woman*, no. 34 (DC Comics, September 2009). T. O. Morrow first appeared in
DC Comics' *The Flash*, vol. 1, no. 143 (March 1964).

143 The American artist Frank Stella: See Mark Godfrey, *Abstraction and the Holocaust* (New Haven: Yale University Press, 2007), p. 92.

8. NOW WE'RE ONTO SOMETHING

146 In his magisterial history of Poland: Norman Davies, *God's Playground: A History
of Poland, Volume II: 1795 to the Present*, revised 2nd edition (New York: Columbia
University Press, 2005), p. 206.

9. DARKNESS AND RAIN

171 "Four Americans—I was one . . .": "Tribune Writer Tells of Seeing Poles' Breakup,"
Chicago Daily Tribune, October 5, 1939, p. 1.

172 "It was a night that I will never forget . . .": Chandler, Maurice. Interview October 3,
1993. The Voice/Vision Holocaust Survivor Oral History Archive, University of
Michigan–Dearborn. http://holocaust.umd.umich.edu/chandler. Used with permission.

174 Pułtusk had been occupied: See Andreas Schulz, "Regierungsbezirk Zichenau," in Wolf Gruner and Jörg Osterloh, eds., *Das 'Grossdeutsche Reich' und die Juden. Nationalsozialistische Verfolgung in den 'angegliederten Gebieten'* (Frankfurt am Main: Campus Verlag, 2010), pp. 262–263. Klaus-Peter Friedrich gives the date of the occupation of Pułtusk as September 7 in *Die Verfolgung und Ermordung der europäischen Juden durch das nationalsozialistische Deutschland 1933–1945*, Bearbeitet von Klaus-Peter Friedrich (München: R. Oldenbourg Verlag, 2011), Bd. 4: Polen: September 1939–Juli 1941, p. 130, footnote 4. See also Janusz Szczepański, *Dzieje Społeczności Żydowskiej*, p. 176. Szczepanski cites two expulsions, on September 11 and 22, 1939. Martin Gilbert gives the date of the main expulsion of Pułtusk's eight thousand Jews as September 28. Martin Gilbert, *The Holocaust: A History of the Jews of Europe During the Second World War* (New York: Holt, Rinehart and Winston, 1985), p. 93.

177 "As our caravan headed north . . .": Julien Bryan, *Siege* (New York: Doubleday, Doran & Co., Inc., 1940). The book was reissued in 1959 as *Warsaw: 1939 Siege* (Warsaw: Polonia Publishing House, distributed by the International Film Foundation, New York, 1959), and most recently as *The Colors of War: The Siege of Warsaw in Julien Bryan's Color Photographs* (Berlin: Deutscher Kunstverlag, 2012). See also the United States Holocaust Memorial Museum's collection of films and documents by Julien Bryan: www.ushmm.org/research/collections/highlights /bryan/.

178 As a prominent Jewish merchant in Nasielsk: In 1946, the Central Historical Commission of the Central Committee of the Liberated Jews in the American Zone circulated questionnaires among survivors, seeking detailed information about events in the survivors' hometowns during the German occupation. One anonymous questionnaire regarding Nasielsk contains the following: "On the 14–15 [of September] 1939 the German military marched in and took over all Jewish shops, led out all Jewish people from Filar's button factory, and [looted] the large shop of David Skalka." David Skalka, Morry's uncle, was a tailor. It is likely the survivor is confusing David with his father, Srul Skalka, Morry's grandfather, who owned the large clothing store on the *rynek*. United States Holocaust Memorial Museum, RG-68.099M.0002.00000581. Translation from the Yiddish by Natan Gadoth.

10. *DAS VATERLAND DEINES GROSSVATERS*

188 She has published widely: See in particular *Źródła do badań nad zagładą Żydów na okupowanych ziemiach polskich. Przewodnik archiwalno-bibliograficzny* [Sources for the Study of the Extermination of the Jews in the Occupied Polish Territories. Archival Guide and Bibliography] (Warsaw: Centrum Badań nad Zagładą Żydów oraz Wydawnitwo 'Cyklady,' 2007), and Tadeusz Markiel and Alina Skibińska, "Jakie to ma znaczenie, czy zrobili to z chciwości?" *Zagłada domu Trynczerów* ["What does it matter whether they did it out of greed?" *Fall of the House of Trynczerów*] (Warsaw: Stowarzyszenie Centrum Badań nad Zagładą Żydów, 2011).

190 *The Poles were worse than the Germans:* On the difficulty of determining the extent of Polish assistance to Germans in identifying Jews, see Jan Grabowski, *Hunt for the Jews: Betrayal and Murder in German-Occupied Poland* (Bloomington: Indiana University Press, 2013), p. 51. See also Yisrael Gutman and Szmul Krakowski, *Unequal Victims: Poles and Jews During World War Two* (New York: Holocaust Library, 1986).

190 I knew these conversations from having lived in Austria: "75 Years After Anschluss: Austrian President Says Nazi Past Cannot Be Forgotten," *Haaretz*, March 12, 2013. http://www.haaretz.com/jewish-world/jewish-world-news/75-years-after-anschluss-austrian-president-says-nazi-past-cannot-be-forgotten-1.508952.

191 In my offer to talk to students: In May 2014, however, under the auspices of the Forum for Dialogue Among Nations, students viewed my grandfather's film and participated in an hour-long video conference with Morry Chandler about the former Jewish community of Nasielsk. www.dialog.org.pl/en/.

200 In 1941, the German archaeologist Otto Kleemann: Mariusz Blonski, "Lotnicze zdjecie Nasielska z okresu II wojny swiatowej [World War II Aerial Photo of Nasielsk]," in *Rocznik Mazowiecki* XVIII (2006), pp. 204–207. See also *Geographical Dictionary of Polish Kingdom and Lithuania*, volume 6 (Warsaw 1885), p. 925.

203 "He is mostly recognized for his literary achievements . . .": "Jarosław Iwaszkiewicz," *Wikipedia* entry: http://en.wikipedia.org/wiki/Jarosław_Iwaszkiewicz, retrieved August 9, 2013.

203 October 30, 1939: "Himmler orders . . .": Hershel Edelheit and Abraham J. Edelheit, *A World in Turmoil: An Integrated Chronology of the Holocaust and World War II* (New York: Greenwood Press, 1991), pp. 171–173.

203 "By the end of 1939 some 7,000 . . .": Szczepański, *Dzieje Społeczności Żydowskiej*, p. 177.

204 "Once gathered in the market . . .": Michał Grynberg, *Żydzi w Rejencji Ciechanowskiej (1939–1942)* [Jews in Ciechanów (1939–1942)] (Warsaw: Państwowe Wydawnictwo Naukowe, 1984), p. 93. Google translation, edited.

204 "*On December 3, 1939 at 7:30 in the morning . . .*": Ringelblum Archive, ARG I 933 (Ring. I/873). *Archiwum Ringelbluma Konspiracyjne Archiwum Getta Warszawy, Inwentarz Archiwum Ringelbluma* (Warsaw: Żydowski Instytut Historyczny im. Emanuela Ringelbluma; Wydawnictwo DiG, 2011), volume 8, pp. 155–157. Hereafter *Archiwum Ringelbluma*. Translation by Iza Wojciechowska.

207 Another testimony in the Ringelblum archive: Ringelblum Archive, ARG I 995 (Ring. I/907). *Archiwum Ringelbluma*, volume 8, p. 179.

208 "In order to mistreat, scare, and terrify them . . .": Tomasinski, Tadeusz. Interview 7 April 2006. Warsaw Rising Museum, Oral History Archive. http://ahm.1944.pl/Tadeusz_Tomasinski/?q=Tomasinski.

208 Another source in the documents Zdzisław gave me: Stanislaw Pazyry, *Szkice z Dziejow Nasielska I dawnej Ziemi Zakroczymskiej* [Sketches from the History of the Territory Nasielsk and Former Zakroczym] (Warsaw: Książka i Wiedza, 1970), p. 69.

208 "Shortly before Christmas 1939 . . .": Wolfgang Curilla, *Der Judenmord in Polen und die deutsche Ordnungspolizei 1939–1945* (Paderborn, München, Wien, Zürich: Ferdinand Schöningh, 2011), p. 230. My translation. Curilla cites his source as "Notiz für Vertrag Oberost beim ObdH in Spala am 15.2.1940 vom 6.2.1940, in BA-MA RH 53-23/23, Bl. 27." The incident is also mentioned in Raul Hilberg, *The Destruction of the European Jews*, revised and definitive edition (New York: Holmes & Meier, 1985), volume I, pp. 190–191. Hilberg's topic is not the atrocity, but the presentation given by Blaskowitz to his superiors.

209 "Red moor" is a typographical error: Blaskowitz's report is also cited in Gerhard Schoenberner (Hg.), *Wir haben es gesehen. Augenzeugenberichte über Terror und Judenverfolgung im Dritten Reich* (Hamburg: Rütten & Loening Verlag, 1962), p. 88. Schoenberner corrects the word to "*Meer*," but does not indicate whether the correction is his or comes from his source at the Centre de Documentation Juive Contemporaine, Paris. Schoenberner's citation is "Notizen des Oberbefehlshabers Ost, Generaloberst Johannes Blaskowitz, für den Vortrag beim Oberbefehlshaber des Heeres am 15.2.1940 in Spala; NO-3011, CDJC CXXVI-15." (Gerhard Schoenberner is also the author of *The Yellow Star*, which I purchased as a child at my Hebrew school book sale.) Blaskowitz's report, without the reference to Nasielsk, was among the documents published by the Nuremburg International Military Tribunal, NO-3011. It is also included in Hans-Adolf Jacobsen, *1939–1945: Der Zweite Weltkrieg in Chronik und Dokumenten*, fifth edition (Darmstadt: Wehr und Wissen Verlagsgesellschaft, 1961), pp. 606–609. The document I viewed is in the Archivum Akt Nowych [Archive of Modern Records], Warsaw: Akt nr. 1335, Niemieckie władze okupacyjne, sygn. 214/V-7. This document states "*rotes Moor.*"

211 The little forest follows the boundaries of the cemetery: The website Virtual Shtetl, associated with the Museum of the History of Polish Jews, has made a video of the Nasielsk cemetery: www.youtube.com/watch?v=0WtTCNDIuo8.

212 "In a place where there is no person . . .": William Berkson, *Pirke Avot: Timeless Wisdom for Modern Life* (Philadelphia: The Jewish Publication Society, 2010), p. 70.

214 He has been researching it for many years: Zdzisław Suwiński, *"Anlage": nieznana historia lotniska w Chreynnie* (Oświecim: F.H.U. Napóleon V, 2014).

11: A DIFFERENT STYLE OF TORTURE

220 The apartment was at Kupiecka 8: Barbara Engelking-Boni and Jacek Leociak, *The Warsaw Ghetto: A Guide to the Perished City* (New Haven: Yale University Press, 2009), p. 126.

224 Timothy Snyder, in his essential book: Timothy Snyder, *Bloodlands: Europe Between Hitler and Stalin* (New York: Basic Books, 2010), p. 141. See also notes 54ff.

225 The historian Norman Davies: Norman Davies, *God's Playground: A History of Poland, Volume II: 1795 to the Present*, p. 334. The mortality rate among Polish deportees is a hotly contested issue.

225 Of the approximately 2,900 Jewish Nasielskers: Jan Grabowski estimates that 250,000 Jews (or approximately 10 percent of Poland's prewar Jewish population) sought to evade the German authorities by hiding among the Polish population. Of these, Grabowski estimates that fewer than 50,000 survived. Grabowski, *Hunt for the Jews*, pp. 2 and 172.

225 The list was received in New York: JDC Archives, NY_AR3344_Poland_18_0053.

226 He also appears on another list: JDC Archives, NY_AR33-44_00053_00792 (May 6, 1941, and March 12, 1941). Moszek Rotstein (List 2, March 5, 1941); Josek Gurfinkiel (February 4, 1941, and List 2, March 5, 1941). For Jewish refugees in Japan, see Martin Gilbert, *The Holocaust*, p. 118, and Saul Friedländer, *Nazi Germany and the Jews 1939–1945: The Years of Extermination* (New York: HarperPerennial, 2007), pp. 193–194.

227 "On December 31, 1939, there was a meeting . . .": "List of Jewish Refugees from Nasielsk in Lukow, 31.12/1939." Yad Vashem, document ID: 9258618, RG M.54, file number JM/10010. Original in the collection of Jewish Historical Institute, Warsaw. Translation by Maurice Chandler and Iza Wojciechowska.

228 "On October 15 our comrade . . .": Ringelblum Archive, ARG I 984 (Ring. I/794), *Archiwum Ringelbluma*, volume 6, p. 159.

228 On May 20, 1941, just as the Warsaw Ghetto's population peaked: Saul Friedländer, *Nazi Germany and the Jews 1939–1945: The Years of Extermination*, p. 105. Yisrael Gutman puts the peak population in March 1941. Yisrael Gutman, *The Jews of Warsaw, 1939–1943: Ghetto, Underground, Revolt* (Bloomington: Indiana University Press, 1982), p. 63. According to Gutman, the mortality rate for the month of May 1941 was 3,821.

229 Later, I found records to show that Mottl Brzoza: Institute of National Remembrance, Warsaw. Index of Victims of Soviet Repression, "Motel Brzozar": www .indeks.karta.org.pl/en/szczegoly.jsp?id=60672. Source reference: Wykaz spraw prowadzonych przez organa NKWD Zachodniej Ukrainy i Białorusi (wybór z Księgi Rejestracji Spraw Archiwalno-Śledczych NKWD ZSRR), kopia Ministerstwo Sprawiedliwości RP i Ośrodek KARTA - tom, strona, pozycja (numer nadany w OK), Signature: ZUB- -/399/91/10.

229 These "transit" lines had a police escort: Engelking-Boni and Leociak, *The Warsaw Ghetto*, p. 112.

230 "On the other side of the barbed wire . . .": Mary Berg, *The Diary of Mary Berg: Growing Up in the Warsaw Ghetto* (Oxford: Oneworld Publications, 2007), translated by Norbert Guterman and Sylvia Glass (1945), p. 50.

231 These bands of extorters were known: See Jan Tomasz Gross and Irena Grudzinska Gross, *Golden Harvest: Events at the Periphery of the Holocaust* (New York: Oxford University Press, 2012), pp. 94–96. See also Jan Grabowski, *Hunt for the Jews*, p. 84. Grabowski uses the Polish spelling, *smalcowniks*.

232 Avruml Jedwab, Shimon Kaminski, and Shiye Brzoza: Avraham Jedwab, Yad Vashem, Testimony ID: 8649870. Shiye Bzhoza, Yad Vashem, Testimony ID: 1141739. Szymszon Kaminski, Yad Vashem, Testimony ID: 438987. Shiye Brzoza's

birth year in the testimony is 1931, and therefore almost certainly incorrect. Shimshon (Szymszon) Kaminski, born 1922, was the son of Janina Kaminski, a grocery store owner who also had a small vinegar factory in his basement in Nasielsk.

232 Morry recalled sending parcels: For information about mail service in the ghetto, especially food packages, see Gutman, *The Jews of Warsaw*, p. 112.

233 A report by the Kałuszyn *Judenrat*: *ECG*, volume II, part A, pp. 383–384.

234 "Kałuszyn's Jewish Police was charged . . .": *ECG*, volume II, part A, p. 383.

235 "It was staffed by Jewish doctors . . .": Shraga Feivel Bielawski, *The Last Jew from Wegrow: The Memoirs of a Survivor of the Step-by-Step Genocide in Poland*, edited and rewritten by Louis W. Liebovich (New York: Praeger, 1991), p. 21.

235 "Suspicions about the camp . . .": *ECG*, volume II, part A, p. 463.

237 "They went from house to house . . .": *ECG*, volume II, part A, pp. 463–464.

239 "Unlike so many of the Nazi killing units . . .": Christopher R. Browning, *Ordinary Men: Reserve Police Battalion 101 and the Final Solution in Poland* (New York: HarperPerennial, 1992), p. xvii.

239 According to Christopher Browning, by the end of these two operations: Browning, *Ordinary Men*, p. 142.

240 "To receive more Jews from elsewhere . . .": Browning, *Ordinary Men*, pp. 90–91.

240 "Hiwi" stands for *Hilfswilligen*: Browning, *Ordinary Men*, p. 52.

240 "During the Aktion, members of Reserve Police Battalion 101 . . .": *ECG*, volume II, part A, p. 685.

240 "Some of the policemen arrived . . .": Browning, *Ordinary Men*, p. 91.

240 "This," Daniel Goldhagen comments: Daniel Goldhagen, *Hitler's Willing Executioners* (New York: Knopf, 1996), p. 242.

241 "When the convoy carrying Wohlauf . . .": Browning, *Ordinary Men*, pp. 93–94.

242 In his memoir, "Eighteen Days in Treblinka": Abraham Krzepicki, "Eighteen Days in Treblinka," quoted in Alexander Donat, ed., *The Death Camp Treblinka: A Documentary* (New York: Schocken Books, 1979), p. 88. Jankiel Wiernik, deported to Treblinka on August 23, 1942, from Warsaw, wrote of August 26: "Late in the afternoon another train arrived from Miedzyrzec (Mezrich), but 80 percent of its human cargo consisted of corpses." Jankiel Wiernik, "One Year in Treblinka," in Donat, p. 152. See also Martin Gilbert, *The Holocaust*, p. 431. For descriptions of the operations at Treblinka, see Yitzhak Arad, *Belzec, Sobibor, Treblinka: The Operation Reinhard Death Camps* (Bloomington: Indiana University Press, 1987), pp. 81–88.

242 Those among the eleven thousand Jews deported: Martin Gilbert, *The Holocaust*, p. 425. See also Raul Hilberg, *The Destruction of the European Jews*, volume III, p. 878.

242 "an almost unimaginable ferocity . . .": Browning, *Ordinary Men*, pp. 94–95.

242 According to the *Encyclopedia of Camps and Ghettos*, the number of Jews: *ECG*, volume II, part B, p. 1223. See also Tzilla Kitron and Sonja Schabtay, *Wanderungen: Erinnerungen an das Überleben in den Jahren 1942–1945*.

243 The German authorities had given him assurances: *ECG*, volume II, part A, p. 679.

243 "After ordering the Jews assembled . . .": *ECG*, volume II, part A, p. 680.

244 "The men of Second Company . . .": Browning, *Ordinary Men*, pp. 107–109.

244 But on November 7, 1942: Browning, *Ordinary Men*, p. 111.

245 The German policemen from Hamburg: Browning, *Ordinary Men*, p. 123. See also Jan Grabowski, *Hunt for the Jews*.

246 The ghetto at Wołomin (aka Sosnówa): *ECG*, volume II, part A, p. 468.

249 "The Czyżewo ghetto resembled . . .": *ECG*, volume II, part A, p. 878.

250 "In the fall of 1942, the ghetto residents learned . . .": *ECG*, volume II, part A, p. 878.

250 The Czyżew *Yizkor* book, however: *Czyżew Yizkor Book*: "The Death of the Jewish Population in Czyzewo," by Shimon Kanc, translated by Gloria Berkenstat Freund, p. 855. www.jewishgen.org/yizkor/Czyzew/czy0855.html. *Sefer Zikaron Czyzewo*, edited by Szymon Kanc (Tel Aviv, 1961).

250 They were killed in Auschwitz-Birkenau: *ECG*, volume II, part A, p. 878.

250 "A mass execution of fifty-five Polish . . .": "Death of 55 Poles in Day Reported," *New York Times*, November 1, 1942, p. 6.

251 "It says, 'We tell God . . .'": From Psalm 20:8–10, part of the daily morning liturgy. "They—the chariots, and they—the horses/but we—the name of the Lord our God invoke." Robert Alter, *The Book of Psalms* (New York: W. W. Norton & Company, 2007), p. 67.

255 In the Kałuszyn *Yizkor* book: Dr. Yosef Kermish, "Martyrdom, Resistance and Destruction of the Jewish Community in Kałuszyn," translated by Gooter Goldberg. Kałuszyn *Yizkor* Book, p. 315ff. www.jewishgen.org/yizkor/kaluszyn/kal314.html. The firm of Wolfer & Goebel Bau, GmbH, of Stuttgart, still exists. www.wolfer-goebel .de/Impressum.html.

12. SOMETHING GOES FROM THE PICTURE

263 "Following the artillery action . . .": "The Texts of the Day's Communiques on the Fighting in Various War Zones," *New York Times*, January 18, 1945, p. 2.

263 "When the armies retreated . . .": Felix Rostkowski, Memoirs. Unpublished, courtesy of Zdzisław Suwiński. Translation by Iza Wojciechowska.

272 "We are splinters of a bygone whole . . .": Translation by Iza Wojciechowska.

272 "TO AVOID MISTAKES . . .": JDC Archives, NY_AR45-54_00166_00785.

273 In fact, Leon Finkelstein was one of the seventy survivors: Central Commission for Investigation of German Crimes in Poland, *German Crimes in Poland* (New York: Howard Fertig, 1982), p. 95.

274 In February 1943, in preparation for the abandonment: For the escape from Treblinka, see Yitzhak Arad, *Belzec, Sobibor, Treblinka*, pp. 270–298. Arad gives the number of victims as 750,000 and the number of survivors as 70 (p. 363). See also Donat, *The Death Camp Treblinka*, p. 286. Donat writes that over a million Jews were killed at Treblinka, perhaps as many as 1,300,000, and gives the number of survivors as 60 (p. 14 and p. 284). The Central Commission for the Investigation of

German Crimes in Poland gives two figures for the number of Jews murdered: 731,600 (p. 104) and 760,000 (p. 161).

280 Anat Aderet is the granddaughter of Ita Melman: Anat Aderet's family history and her drawing of her grandmother's block is available at Virtual Shtetl. www.sztetl .org.pl/pl/article/nasielsk/16,relacje-wspomnienia/14247,anat-aderet-about-her -grandmother-ita-meirsdorf-nee-melman-born-in-nasielsk-in-1918-the-life-of -her-family-in-pultusk-their-escape-to-the-soviet-union-and-immigration-to-is rael-/.

287 "Pre-war Nashelsk used to come on a visit to relatives . . .": United Nashelsker Relief Society, 1956. YIVO, RG 976.

287 At the Ghetto Fighters' House Museum: Ghetto Fighters' House Photo Archive, "A door of the synagogue in Nasielsk, with carved decorations," catalogue number 29436, http://infocenters.co.il/gfh/multimedia/GFH/0000082612/0000082612_1_ web.jpg. "The synagogue in Nasielsk," catalogue number 29435, http://infocenters .co.il/gfh/multimedia/GFH/0000082611/0000082611_1_web.jpg.

287 The people in this photo are identified in the catalogue: Ghetto Fighers' House Archive, www.infocenters.co.il/gfh/notebook_ext.asp?item=52613&site=gfh&lang =ENG&menu=1.

13. A TOWN OF MEMORIES

295 Boyes Sheinbaum or Szejnbaum, the droshke driver: Boyes Szejnbaum: www.mu seumoffamilyhistory.com/lee-hww-coachman-nasielsk-szejnbaum.htm.

295 "Before, Moyshe Hokhman transported merchandise . . .": YIVO, RG 1343. (Menahem Kipnis) Collection PO, catalogue number 2611, frame 27921.

301 Andrzej was born Avraham Moishe in Zakroczym: Abraham Andrzej Lubieniecki has also given oral history testimony, held at the Holocaust Memorial Center, Zekelman Family Campus, Farmington Hills, Michigan, May 28, 2000. www .holocaustcenter.org/page.aspx?pid=645.

315 Of the three, I found Shoah testimony: Manya Goldwasser, Yad Vashem, Testimony ID: 697774.

316 In a database of Victims of Soviet Oppression: Institute of National Remembrance, Warsaw. Faiga Tyk. www.indeks.karta.org.pl/en/szczegoly.jsp?id=218948. Samuel Tyk. www.indeks.karta.org.pl/en/szczegoly.jsp?id=218947. Ruchul (Rachela) Tyk. www.indeks.karta.org.pl/en/szczegoly.jsp?id=218946. Leslie Glodek is not listed in the database.

319 Czarna Myrla did not survive the war: Czarna Myrla, Yad Vashem, Testimony ID: 783188.

320 Miriam Myrla's first husband and young son: Josef Skurnik, Yad Vashem, Testimony ID: 679092. Khaim Skurnik, Yad Vashem, Testimony ID: 8853438.

325 Mordekhai Vilchinski, the man on the Joint's Vilna list: Abraham Vilchinski, Yad Vashem, Testimony ID: 320484. Leja Vilchinski, Yad Vashem, Testimony ID: 336013 and Testimony ID: 893345. Yitzkhak Vilchinski, Yad Vashem, Testimony ID: 8697468.

332 The German *Aktion* that destroyed the Jablonna Ghetto: *ECG*, volume II, part A, pp. 253–254.

337 What he saw, or thought he may have seen: The situation resembles the plot of Ian McEwan's 2003 novel *Atonement*, in which a young girl witnesses an encounter between her older sister and a man and interprets it according to her childish understanding, in a false and disastrous way.

14. FAMILY HISTORY

349 "an orchestra of 100, two choirs of 100 each . . .": "Radio City Premier Is a Notable Event," *New York Times*, December 28, 1932, p. 1.

349 "Mr. and Mrs. David Kurtz of 944 East 23d St., Brooklyn . . .": "Confirmations," *New York Times*, May 8, 1938, p. 53.

354 Four images fit together to form a panorama of a large group of children: In the archives of the Joint Distribution Committee in New York, I learned that the organization supported an orphanage in Berezne. It is possible the children in this photo belonged to the orphanage. "Annual Financial Report for the Year 1926," supplement 1g, p. 37. JDC Archives, NY_AR2132_03725.

15. THE STORY OF THE FILM

358 "Like huge fingers, they point . . .": S. J. Woolf, "Henry Ford, at 75, States His Faith Simply," *New York Times*, July 24, 1938, p. 91.

360 "Hitler Decorates Henry Ford on Auto Maker's 75th Birthday": *New York Herald Tribune*, European Edition, July 31, 1938, p. 1.

361 "200 Russian Soldiers Reported Killed as Japanese Forces Retake Disputed Border Territory in Four-Hour Battle": *New York Herald Tribune*, European Edition, August 1, 1938, p. 1.

361 "Hitler Ready to Beat Ford Production": *New York Herald Tribune*, European Edition, August 2, 1938, p. 1.

361 "Jews Expected to Lose State Jobs in Italy": *New York Herald Tribune*, European Edition, August 2, 1938, p. 3.

361 "Baden-Baden Is Starting Point . . .": *New York Herald Tribune*, European Edition, August 2, 1938, p. 7.

361 "Lord Runciman Off for Task in Prague in 'Cheerful' Mood": *New York Herald Tribune*, European Edition, August 3, 1938, p. 1.

361 "'Let me make it clear from the start'": "Lord Runciman Reaches Prague; Parleys Delayed," *New York Herald Tribune*, European Edition, August 4, 1938, p. 3.

362 "'The gentlemen at Prague had better understand . . .'": "Berlin Assails Prague," *New York Herald Tribune*, European Edition, August 4, 1938, p. 3.

362 "Hitler Bans Jewish Doctors": *New York Herald Tribune*, European Edition, August 4, 1938, p. 3.

362 "PRAGUE, Aug. 5.—A significant step . . .": "Runciman Puts Czech Dispute 'On

Ice' 2 Weeks, Halts Talks to Seek Solution of Problems," *New York Herald Tribune*, European Edition, August 6, 1938, p. 1.

362 "Nation Is Facing Disaster, G.O.P. Group Declares": *New York Herald Tribune*, European Edition, August 7, 1938, p. 1.

363 Yet British prime minister Neville Chamberlain: Dieter Wagner and Gerhard Tomkowitz, *Ein Volk, Ein Reich, Ein Führer: The Nazi Annexation of Austria 1938*, translated by Geoffrey Strahan (London: Longman Group Limited, 1971), p. 48.

363 "Nazi Honor to Ford Stirs Cantor's Ire": *New York Times*, August 4, 1938, p. 13.

364 "When I say one's Jewish friends . . .": G.E.R. Gedye, *Fallen Bastions*, pp. 305–307.

373 An appendix in his book: Stanisław Tyc, *Nasielsk Jako Ośrodek Życia Gospodarczego na Północnym Mazowszu w Latach 1795–1939* (Pułtusk: Akademia Humanistyczna im. Aleksandra Gieysztora, 2011), appendix.

377 In December 2012, one year after Marcy Rosen: This video is available online: www .youtube.com/watch?feature=player_embedded&v=V9PzAlbvA08.

381 "Cousin Jalires grew big": Yisrael Gutman mentions the use of these code words. Gutman, *The Jews of Warsaw*, p. 111.

388 *"Woe unto us for the people we have lost . . ."*: From the Babylonian Talmud Sanhedrin 111a.

EPILOGUE

390 On page 27: G. Bejgiel, *Mayn Shtetele Berezne* (Tel Aviv, 1954), p. 27 (image 31). http://yizkor.nypl.org/index.php?id=1124.

AUTHOR'S NOTE

All interviews cited in this book were recorded. Some quotations have been edited to remove interjections, false starts, and repetition. For the sake of coherence, comments about the same subject or person, recorded at different times, have occasionally been placed together as a single statement. A very few misstatements have been corrected, and certain inconsistencies of tense common to spoken language, but jarring in print, have been rationalized. Punctuation and a few transcription errors in Maurice Chandler's 1993 oral history, collected by the Voice/Vision Holocaust Survivor Oral History Archive at the University of Michigan–Dearborn, have been corrected for clarity. Changes to quoted material have been approved by the speaker whenever possible.

Where the language spoken was not English, I have quoted or paraphrased translations commissioned for this book. Zdzisław Suwiński's narration of the deportation from Nasielsk in Chapter 10 was spoken in Polish and German and simultaneously translated and paraphrased by Alina Skibińska. In this instance, I have omitted quotation marks. The transliteration of Yiddish words conforms to the YIVO standard, with slight modifications to reflect the regional accents of the speakers. Yiddish words that have come into English—"chutzpah," "shul," "cheder," etc.—are spelled according to their anglicized form, regardless of context.

Proper names often appear in multiple forms, depending on source, language, time, and place. So Zylbersztajn may also be Zylbersztejn, Zylbestein, and Silverstein. When a name appears in a document, I have retained the original spelling, adding an English alternative for clarity if the context was insufficient. Polish place names are referred to according to the 1938 political map of Europe unless an English equivalent is more common, e.g., Warsaw.

In 1938, Nasielsk had approximately 7,000 residents. To those who grew up there, it was a city. Today it would be a small town or a village. Except when used by others, I have avoided calling it a "shtetl," which has come to be a term of nostalgic endearment, conjuring images from *Fiddler on the Roof*. When my grandparents visited, Nasielsk was a modern town, with electricity, telephones, industrial machinery, and automobiles.

All mistakes in transcription, translation, proper and place names, family relationships, or historical accuracy—and there are many, I'm sure—are mine alone.

ACKNOWLEDGMENTS

I owe profound gratitude to those who shared their stories with me. Maurice and Dorris Chandler welcomed me like family long before DNA testing revealed that we are, in fact, family. This book would be inconceivable without Morry Chandler's friendship, intelligence, patience, humor, and wisdom. To Dorris Chandler, Evelyn and Steve Rosen, Marcy Rosen and David Eisenberg, Jason and Esther Lee Rosen, Emily Rosen, Paul and Chika Chandler, Debra Chandler, Gerald and Page Chandler, and their families, I can only express again how fortunate I feel to know you. It seems—as we have often remarked—like magic.

Leslie and Celia Glodek graciously invited me into their home and conveyed far more than it seems possible two days could contain. I'm grateful to Graham and Maria Glodek and, with special warmth, to Jennifer Benn, and I will always remember the kindness and exuberance of Jonathan Benn. Saul and Irma Gershkowitz were generous with their time and memories, which first set me on the right path. Susan Weiss, Rachel Laks, Mikhail Koprak, Ida Aisner, Andrzej Lubieniecki, Grace Pahl, Helene Pahl, Lila Pahl, Irving and Doris Novetsky, Laurie Novetsky, Faiga Tick, Heather Tick, and Malca and David Reiss all accepted me, a stranger, into their lives and taught me the meaning of *landslayt*. It barely hints at my admiration and gratitude to say that this story could never have been written without them. In July 2013, Faiga Tick passed away at the age of ninety-six. Among her photographs was a lovely portrait of Leslie Glodek's sister, Gittla. Irv Novetsky passed away in April 2014. He was ninety-seven.

For sharing memories, documents, and treasured photographs, I'm indebted to Keva and Beverly Richman, Arlene Schneider, Faith Ohlstein, Jerry and Nikki Goldsmith, Felicia Langwiser, Carla Sadik Blumenthal, Jonathan Sadik,

Sophia Wolkowicz, David Malina, Jane Malina Levinson, Ronnie Diamond, Michael Valihora, Connie Newman, Michael Loboda, Gary Pietruszka, Marvin Pietruszka, Jack Pietruszka, Justin and Alicia Denman, and Sue Blackwell. For help with Nasielsk genealogy, a thank-you to Erika Herzog and Eli Rabinowitz. My surprise that Martyna Dudkiewicz found me on Facebook is surpassed only by my gratitude to her and to her parents, Jacek and Monika Dudkiewicz, for sharing the delight of their beautiful family and artifacts from their family's history.

None of this would have happened without Jeff and Denise Widen. I would still be utterly *farblundzhet* without the friendship and assistance of Arie and Shifra Yagoda, Natan and Sara Gadoth, Iris Rubenstien, Anat Aderet, Chani Levene-Nachshon and Yechezkel Nachshon Szlang, and Yaniv Goldberg. Alina Skibińska, whose scholarship is an inspiration, provided invaluable support in Warsaw and greatly enriched my first visit to Nasielsk. She also introduced me (virtually) to Jakub Petelewicz and Monika Kozuń at the Forum for Dialogue Among Nations, setting in motion an extraordinary workshop for high school students in Nasielsk in the spring of 2014. Zdzisław and Anne Suwiński's home became the bridge between past and present. Their friendship is one of the great rewards of this project.

Leslie Swift and Lindsay Zarwell at the Steven Spielberg Film and Video Archive of the United States Holocaust Memorial Museum have become dear friends. Their excitement, encouragement, and professional expertise infuse every page of this story. For help in archival matters, I particularly wish to thank Vincent Slatt at the Holocaust Museum's Research Library and Teresa Pollin and Kyra Schuster in the Photo Archives. Elissa Schein, Dana Sherman Marine, and Josh Blinder also contributed their considerable talents. Patricia Heberer Rice, historian at the Jack, Joseph and Morton Mandel Center for Advanced Holocaust Studies, and Alexandr Kruglov, Senior Scholar-in-Residence, generously corrected errors and suggested improvements in the manuscript.

Over several years I have benefited greatly from the guidance of Eleanor Yadin and Amanda Siegel at the Dorot Jewish Division of the New York Public Library; the librarians and archivists at the Center for Jewish History in New York, in particular at the YIVO Institute for Jewish Research; and Misha Mitsel at the American Jewish Joint Distribution Committee. For invaluable research assistance, my gratitude to Roberta Newman; Efrat Komisar at Yad Vashem (Jerusalem); Zvika Oren, Director of the Photo Archive at the Ghetto Fighters' House Museum (Western Galilee, Israel); Gila Cohen and Rifka Aderet at Beit Hatfutsot, The Museum of the Jewish People (Tel Aviv); the archivists at the Central Archive of the History of the Jewish People (Jerusalem); Daria Borkowska at Archiwum Akt Nowych (Warsaw); Aleksandra Dybkowska at the Jewish Genealogy and Family Heritage Center of the Emanuel Ringelblum Jewish Historical Institute (Warsaw); Stanisław Tyc at the Nasielsk Library; Barbara Kirschenblatt-Gimblett and Tamara Sztyma-Knasiecka at the Museum of the History of Polish Jews (Warsaw); Krzysztof Bielawski at Virtual Shtetl (Warsaw); Jennifer Young, Director of Education at the Max Weinreich Center at YIVO; and Hasia Diner, Director of the Goldstein-Goren Center for American Jewish History at New York University, who fostered many of these connections.

For permission to quote from archival materials, I gratefully acknowledge Agnieszka Reszka, Head of Archives, and Ryszard Burek, Director, the Jewish Historical Institute, Warsaw; Jamie L. Wraight, Curator and Historian, The Voice/Vision Holocaust Survivor Oral History Archive, The University of Michigan–Dearborn; Misha Mitsel, Senior Archivist, the American Jewish Joint Distribution Committee; the United States Holocaust Memorial Museum; Yad Vashem; Beit Lohamei Haghetaot (Ghetto Fighters' House Museum); and Georgiana Gomez, Access Supervisor, USC Shoah Foundation and the Institute for Visual History and Education. Thank you to the Holland-America Line for help in tracking my grandfather's postcard. My apologies to any individuals or institutions I have inadvertently neglected to recognize by name.

For their expert translations and transliterations from Yiddish, *a groysen dank* to Eddy Portnoy at the YIVO Max Weinreich Center for Advanced Jewish Study and to Amelia Glaser, Director of the Russian and Soviet Studies Program at the University of California, San Diego. For her graceful translations from the Polish, my deep appreciation to Iza Wojciechowska. For help in identifying biblical phrases, thank you to Professor Burton L. Visotzky of the Jewish Theological Seminary. For their magnificent restoration of David Kurtz's home movie, and for advice and guidance in all matters concerning film and film preservation, I'm grateful to Russ Suniewick, AJ Rohner, Tommy Aschenbach, Dean Plionis, Julia Nicoll, and the staff at Colorlab Corp.

Michael Loebenstein first demonstrated to me what could be done with a fragment of old film. Peter Mendelsund first encouraged me to drop everything else and follow suit. This book would not have been written without them. For thoughtful contributions as the story developed, for camaraderie, and for their friendship, both new and spanning decades, my heartfelt thanks to David Albert, Susan Bernofsky, Randy Briggs and Elaine McCarthy, Stephanie Cain, Jay Cantor, Teju Cole, Nick Davis and Jane Mendelsohn, Alan Emtage, Ellen Rosner Feig, Rhonda Garelick, DW Gibson and Writers Omi at Ledig House, Janice Gitterman and Stephen Kirschner, Allison Gold, Rick Hilles and Nancy Reisman, Toby Hobish, Linda Karshan, Suzanne Jill Levine, Franziska Liepe, John Lowell, Jim McCarthy, Daniel Mendelsohn, Jessica Mihaly and Craig Baker, Carl Pritzkat and Tony Travostino, Michael Rhodes, Christine Richter-Nilssen, Ellen Rosenbaum, Julia Ruszkiewicz, Celene Ryan, Kit Schulte, Dani Shapiro, Barbara Sofer, and the late Michael Shugrue. For their volunteer field research, I'm deeply obliged to my friends Joshua-Michele Ross and Yvette Molina, B.C.C. (Bob) van der Zwaan, and Xiaoyan Zhang, and to Carolyn Jackson and Michael Haviken for giving me the space to write.

Ileene Smith, my marvelous and meticulous editor at Farrar, Straus and Giroux, had no idea when we began working together that her family, too, was part of the story. Her passionate attention to the manuscript made this a better book than I could have ever written alone. No doubt our grandfathers (-in-law) are having a good laugh together somewhere. John Knight steered the manuscript (and me) through production masterfully and displayed exceptional insight, judgment, and tact at every stage of the process. I'm grateful to everyone at FSG, in particular to the production staff and to Adrienne Ottenberg for their artistry, and to Jeff Seroy, Brian Gittis, and the publicity department for their support and untiring professionalism. Malaga Baldi, my extraordinary literary agent, first received Marcy Rosen's e-mail. Her commitment to this project never waivered, and her enthusiasm has accompanied me every step of the way. A big thank-you to Betsy Lerner, who generously offered timely and invaluable advice.

Finally, in this story about family, my sister Dana has been more than coauthor and confidant. Our collaboration has been this project's greatest gift, one shared with, and sustained by, Shirley Kurtz Mandel, Bernice Schechter, Dede and Milton Kurtz, Cynthia Mandel Kurtz, David Kurtz (the younger), Rob Mackenzie, and the memory of our brother Roger (on whose fifty-fifth birthday I first spoke with Morry). For my part, I could never have persevered without the love of Alys George.

It is my great privilege to thank you all.

ILLUSTRATION CREDITS

110 Kubel and Rotstein on the street. (United States Holocaust Memorial Museum, Collections, Gift of Glenn Kurtz, in memory of David and Liza Kurtz)

111 Restaurant with curtains. (United States Holocaust Memorial Museum, Collections, Gift of Glenn Kurtz, in memory of David and Liza Kurtz)

112 Girl with braids. (United States Holocaust Memorial Museum, Collections, Gift of Glenn Kurtz, in memory of David and Liza Kurtz)

113 Yitzhak "Boortz." (United States Holocaust Memorial Museum, Collections, Gift of Glenn Kurtz, in memory of David and Liza Kurtz)

115 Chaim Nusen Cwajghaft and "Chezkiah." (United States Holocaust Memorial Museum, Collections, Gift of Glenn Kurtz, in memory of David and Liza Kurtz)

121 Faiga Tick, class portrait. (United States Holocaust Memorial Museum, Collections, Gift of Heather Tick, in memory of Faiga Tick)

127 "Committee for the Needy." (Courtesy of Keva Richman and Arlene Schneider)

135 Kubel family. (Courtesy of Faith Ohlstein and Gerald Goldsmith)

137 Woman fixing her hair. (United States Holocaust Memorial Museum, Collections, Gift of Glenn Kurtz, in memory of David and Liza Kurtz)

161 Four boys. (Courtesy of Leslie Glodek and family)

218 Four young men, 1943. (Courtesy of Maurice Chandler and family)

237 Zdzisław Pływacz, birth certificate. (Courtesy of Maurice Chandler and family)

253 *Kennkarte.* (Courtesy of Maurice Chandler and family)

271 Morry's letter to Leslie, November 1945. (Courtesy of Leslie Glodek and family)

288 Synagogue doors. (Beit Lohamei Hagetaot, Ghetto Fighters' House Museum, Israel)

288 Synagogue, unfinished. (Beit Lohamei Hagetaot, Ghetto Fighters' House Museum, Israel)

294 Irving Novetsky. (Courtesy of Irving Novetsky and Gerald Goldsmith)

302 Abraham Andrzej Lubieniecki. (Courtesy of Abraham Andrzej Lubieniecki and family)

315 Faiga Milchberg Tick and three friends. (United States Holocaust Memorial Museum, Collections, Gift of Heather Tick, in memory of Faiga Tick)

318 Szmuel Tyk exits the synagogue. (United States Holocaust Memorial Museum, Collections, Gift of Glenn Kurtz, in memory of David and Liza Kurtz)

319 Samuel and Faiga at the window. (United States Holocaust Memorial Museum, Collections, Gift of Glenn Kurtz, in memory of David and Liza Kurtz)

320 Czarna and Miriam Myrla. (United States Holocaust Memorial Museum, Collections, Gift of Glenn Kurtz, in memory of David and Liza Kurtz)

328 Grace Pahl (Gittla Gutman) and family. (Courtesy of Grace Pahl and family)

352 Crowd greeting the *Queen Mary.* (United States Holocaust Memorial Museum, Collections, Gift of Glenn Kurtz, in memory of David and Liza Kurtz)

354–355 Children in Berezne. (Courtesy of the author)

356 Liza Kurtz and family in Berezne. (Courtesy of the author)

359 Louis and David in Warsaw. (Courtesy of the author)

359 Liza and friends in Warsaw, front. (Courtesy of the author)

A NOTE ABOUT THE AUTHOR

Glenn Kurtz is the author of *Practicing: A Musician's Return to Music* and the host of Conversations on Practice, a series of public conversations about writing held at McNally Jackson Books in New York City.